01 JUL 9 1

Early Black American Playwrights and Dramatic Writers

Early Black American Playwrights and Dramatic Writers

A Biographical Directory and Catalog of Plays, Films, and Broadcasting Scripts

BERNARD L. PETERSON, JR.

GREENWOOD PRESS

NEW YORK
WESTPORT, CONNECTICUT
LONDON

Library of Congress Cataloging-in-Publication Data

Peterson, Bernard L.
    Early Black American playwrights and dramatic writers : a
biographical directory and catalog of plays, films, and broadcasting
scripts / Bernard L. Peterson, Jr.
        p.   cm.
    Includes bibliographical references.
    ISBN 0-313-26621-2 (lib. bdg. : alk. paper)
    1. Afro-American dramatists—Biography—Dictionaries. 2. American
drama—Afro-American authors—Bio-bibliography.   3. Afro-Americans
in literature—Bibliography.   I. Title.
PS153.N5P44   1990
812.009′896073—dc20   90-2961

British Library Cataloguing in Publication Data is available.

Library of Congress Catalog Card Number: 90-2961
ISBN: 0-313-26621-2

First published in 1990

Greenwood Press, 88 Post Road West, Westport, CT 06881
An imprint of Greenwood Publishing Group, Inc.

Printed in the United States of America

The paper used in this book complies with the
Permanent Paper Standard issued by the National
Information Standards Organization (Z39.48-1984).

10 9 8 7 6 5 4 3 2 1

To my two sisters, LENA McPHATTER and LORRAINE COCKRELL, for their continued support of my writing endeavors, and to the memory of my beloved parents, ROSETTA and BERNARD L. PETERSON, SR.;

To DR. JIMMY R. JENKINS, Chancellor of Elizabeth City State University, for the honors that he has conferred upon me in recognition of my services to the University, and especially for his efforts in my behalf to secure foundation support for the completion of this project; *and*

To my former English teachers at Atlanta University, Professor Emeritus LUCY C. GRIGSBY and President Emeritus THOMAS D. JARRETT, for their inspiration and encouragement, and for instilling in me a lifelong love of literature and scholarship.

CONTENTS

ACKNOWLEDGMENTS

Appreciation is hereby expressed to all playwrights who personally furnished information concerning themselves and their plays, and to the following individuals and organizations for their assistance in completing this Directory.

To Errol Hill, author, playwright, and former Willard Professor of Drama at Dartmouth College—for his enthusiastic support of this project, and for valuable information that he furnished from his Caribbean Collection concerning the Black Caribs of St. Vincent Island, in connection with the entry for Mr. Brown, resident playwright of the African Company; and to Walter N. Ridley, President Emeritus of Elizabeth City State University—for providing pertinent information concerning the life and career of playwright Randolph Edmonds, and for his efforts to secure foundation support for this project.

To Mrs. Ruth Caston Mueller Hill of New York City, widow of playwright Abram Hill—for furnishing pertinent information concerning the life and plays of her late husband, and for making available to me many of his published and unpublished scripts; and to Mrs. Leonard C. Archer, widow of playwright Leonard Courtney Archer, for furnishing biographical information concerning her late husband and a list of his dramatic works.

To the following playwrights who furnished information on themselves and their plays: James W. Butcher, Jr., Alice Childress, Owen Dodson (deceased), Shirley Graham DuBois (deceased), Randolph Edmonds (deceased), Frederick Lights, May Miller, Loften Mitchell, Thomas D. Pawley III, and Willis Richardson (deceased).

Thanks also go to the curators, librarians, and personnel—past and present—of the following libraries and repositories, for providing pertinent information and materials used throughout this study: The Library of Congress and the National Archives, Washington, DC; the Research Center for the Federal Theatre Project, George Mason University, Fairfax, VA; the Moorland-Spingarn Center of the Howard University Libraries, Washington, DC; the Schomburg Center for Research in Black Culture and the Performing Arts Research Center of the New York Public Library, New York City; the James Weldon Johnson Memorial Collection of the Beineck Library of Yale University; and other libraries and repositories specifically named in the Information Sources at the end of the study.

To the following individual curators, librarians, and library personnel: Hobson Thompson, Jr., Head Librarian of the Legler Branch of the Chicago Public Library—for his encouragement in the writing of this book, and for his generosity in making available to me all the research facilities of the Chicago Public Libraries; to James V. Hatch, playwright, editor, and Curator of the Hatch-Billops Collection, New York City—for his many valuable published writings in connection with black theatre, and for loaning me a list of scripts and other artifacts in his archives; and to James B. Law, retired reference librarian of Elizabeth City State University and Johnson C. Smith University—for his efforts in locating pertinent reference materials needed for this book, and particularly for furnishing important information concerning the novels of filmmaker Oscar Micheaux.

To Claude Green, Administrative Librarian of the G. R. Little Library, Elizabeth City State University: to his secretary Freida Burke; and to the following members of the library staff—Jutta Choudhury, Patricia Hines, Odessa Williams, Rebecca Ware, Jackie King, Reginald Riddick, Michael Williams, Cornelius Goodwin, Burnella Griffin, Brenda Sawyer, Kathy Turner, James Blount, David Bibb, and Handsel Ingram—for location, acquisition, and loan of books, periodicals, and research materials needed by this researcher; for making available all the facilities and services of the library, even during off-duty hours, and for their gracious cooperation and assistance in all phases of the research and writing of this book, from its inception to completion.

To Carol C. Jones, Director of the University Honors Program, Elizabeth City State University, Elizabeth City, NC, and to her secretary Edna Bonds; to Anne M. Henderson, Chairperson, Department of Language, Literature and Communication, and to her secretary Robin Beamon; and to the following faculty members of the Department of Language, Literature and Communication—Robert E. Thorne, Carlton R. and Venus E. Deonanan, Samuel C. Moore, Glenda Davis, Hazel G. Spellman, Shawn Smith, and Stephen S. March—for their encouragement, support, editorial assistance, proofing of manuscript, use of secretarial and photocopying facilities, typing, collating, transportation, use of office facilities, and other services in connection with the completion of this book.

To Augustus Sutton of Washington, DC, for research assistance on this and other projects over a period of 15 years; to Russell A. Gray of Richmond, VA, and Anne Law of Charlotte, NC, for typing services during the early stages of this work; to Casper McDaniel of Elizabeth City, my trusted clerical assistant and all-around helper, for his invaluable services during the past five years; and to Gladys Banks of Elizabeth City State University for photocopying services.

To William D. Butts of Newport News, VA, and Elizabeth City State University; Harold D. Coppedge of Raleigh, NC; and my sister, Lena McPhatter of New York City, for keeping me informed of many dramatic events that came to their attention through the media and the mails, in connection with black drama and theatre.

To my editor and mentor at Greenwood Press, Marilyn Brownstein, whom I consider a true collaborator in this project, for her helpful suggestions in guiding me through the completion of this second book (while we were also working on a third!), and for her usual understanding, patience, diplomacy, and encouragement.

And, finally, to the following persons for a variety of services that helped to make my life easier while completing this book: William T. Skinner, Robert D. Williams, Carlotta Jordan, Benjamin Hardy, Adolphus McDaniel, Vida Redd, Emanuel Williams, Herman H. Barrow, Jr., and Lawrence E. Gatling.

PREFACE

There is perhaps no bigger gap in the history of the American theatre than that represented by the omission or inadequacy of information in most standard reference books on the majority of serious or legitimate black American playwrights prior to 1950, whose works were produced in hundreds of theatres, community auditoriums, churches, schools, and halls throughout the United States and abroad from the antebellum period to World War II.

How many theatrical history books, for example, include information on the contributions of Willis Richardson and Randolph Edmonds, both of whom are among the most prolific American playwrights, black or white, writing and having their plays produced during the 1920s? Richardson, also a pioneer anthologist and the first black playwright to have a serious play produced on Broadway, wrote more than 40 individual plays and provided the first black-authored plays to a number of early drama groups during the twenties and thirties. Edmonds, often called "The Dean of Black Academic Theatre," published three collections of his plays and wrote at least 50 individual plays between 1922 and 1956. He also established several black collegiate drama associations in the Southeast, which presented annual drama festivals and encouraged the writing and production of plays by college students and faculty.

Although slightly more than a dozen black playwrights had their plays produced on or off Broadway during the period from 1925 to 1945, only two of them are occasionally mentioned in standard theatrical reference books: Langston Hughes (*Mulatto*, 1935) and Richard Wright's dramatization of his 1940 novel (*Native Son*, 1941) in collaboration with Paul Green. Less well known Broadway and off-Broadway playwrights prior to World War II include Garland Anderson (*Appearances*, 1925), Frank Wilson (*Meek Mose*, 1928), Wallace Thurman (*Harlem*, 1929), Augustus Smith (*Louisiana*, 1933), Hall Johnson (*Run Little Chillun*, 1933), Dennis Donoghue (*Legal Murder*, 1934), Hughes Allison (*The Trial of Dr. Beck*, 1937), George Norford (*Joy Exceeding Glory*, 1939), Theodore Ward

(*Big White Fog*, 1938, and *Our Lan'*, 1947), and Abram Hill (*On Striver's Row*, 1946).

Other significant early black playwrights whose works have been all but doomed to oblivion by major references on the American theatre include Victor Séjour, William Wells Brown, Joseph S. Cotter, Sr., Georgia Douglas Johnson, Arna Bontemps, Owen Dodson, Shirley Graham DuBois, Arthur Clifton Lamb, Thomas Pawley, May Miller, and Jean Toomer.

Early black filmmakers, screenwriters, and radio scriptwriters have fared even less well than playwrights in historical accounts devoted to these types of writers. Oscar Micheaux, for example, wrote, produced, and directed more than 40 feature films between 1918 and 1948, but accounts of his accomplishments are rarely recorded in American film histories. Other early screenwriters include Spencer Williams, Langston Hughes, Clarence Muse, Richard Wright, and Carlton Moss. Hughes, Wright, and Moss also wrote radio scripts, as did Bontemps, Dodson, Shirley Graham DuBois, and Roi Ottley.

Early Black American Playwrights and Dramatic Writers is a comprehensive reference work that seeks to bridge the significant gap in the history of early American drama by providing a convenient source of information on approximately 218 pioneer black American playwrights, screenwriters, and other originators of dramatic works written and/or produced in the United States and in Europe during the nineteenth century and the first half of the twentieth century. Of these 218 playwrights, 136 are included in the main Directory, and 82 are included in two of the three appendixes at the back of this book.

Although the main Directory and Appendix A are devoted primarily to the nonmusical stage, screen, and broadcasting, the musical works of those writers who have also written legitimate plays are naturally included among their lists of dramatic works. However, to satisfy the expectations of many users of this Directory, 38 additional musical librettists (or writers of books for musical stage works) with brief descriptions of their musical shows, are included in Appendix B.

For readers interested in more information on musical stage works, the writer is in the final stages of preparing an *Encyclopedia of the Black American Musical Stage*, scheduled for publication in 1991/92, which will include among its more than 1,000 entries, biographical data on librettists, lyricists, composers, performers, producers, choreographers, directors, and other contributors to the black American musical stage; descriptions, casts, and production data on hundreds of musical shows; and information on important theatres, companies, genres, terminologies, and other topics pertinent to an understanding of black participation in the American musical theatre.

Early Black American Playwrights and Dramatic Writers is a companion volume to the writer's *Contemporary Black American Playwrights and Their Plays: A Biographical Directory and Dramatic Index*, also published by Greenwood Press, in 1988, as well as to the forthcoming musical stage encyclopedia described above. Together these three volumes represent the ongoing research and collection of black theatre materials by the writer over a period of almost 25 years. This research was begun in the libraries of North Carolina and was expanded to include the major research collections and archives on the East Coast of the United States, including the Research Center for the Federal Theatre Project, located at George Mason University in Fairfax, Virginia; the various repositories of the federal government, such as the National Archives and the Library of Congress in Washington, DC; the Moorland-Spingarn Research Center at Howard University, also in Washington; the Schomburg Center for Research in Black Culture of the New York Public Library; the Theatre Collection of the New York Public Library at Lincoln Center; the Hatch-Billops Collection in New York City; and the James Weldon Johnson Memorial Collection at Yale University. These and other archives that contain published and unpublished plays and other resources are listed under Information Sources at the back of this Directory. Also, information about relevant materials in these collections is noted within the appropriate playwright entries.

Among the research materials that the writer has examined extensively in preparation of this and the two companion volumes are published and unpublished playscripts, librettos, programs, advertisements, periodicals, newspapers, clipping files, scrapbooks, letters, bibliographies, dissertations, histories, catalogs of libraries and publishing companies, and other types of printed matter, as well as recordings, videotapes, and films. These materials have often been supplemented by questionnaires, letters, telephone calls, mailgrams, and personal interviews.

It is the firm belief of this researcher that *Early Black American Playwrights and Dramatic Writers,* as well as its two companion volumes, will be of inestimable value to librarians, teachers, students, and all others in need of information on black-authored and black-oriented plays, films, and dramatic works in other media, including radio scripts. These three volumes provide a concise library of essential information that almost covers black theatre in America. Moreover, the information sources provided in the bibliographies of each volume will lead the serious researcher to other more detailed and more specialized studies in the specific areas of his or her interest.

This research should be most useful to individuals and institutions engaged in black studies, black literature, and especially black drama. It will be of obvious value to other playwrights and dramatists in all media, as well as to producers, directors, actors, and theatrical organizations. It will be essential to serious black theatre researchers who might otherwise have to travel to distant repositories and libraries in several cities to locate the information contained in this volume and its two companions. It is hoped that this book will also be useful to graduate and undergraduate students, college and university professors, librarians, theatre critics, and authors of scholarly papers, articles, and books.

Because of the limited number of early black American writers for the stage, screen, and broadcasting, it was decided to establish only four firm criteria for inclusion in this Directory:

1. All writers must be black, or partly black.

2. All must be American citizens or long-term residents of the United States (even if such residency is intermittent). For purposes of inclusion, all expatriot writers will be classified as American citizens.

3. All must have written at least one play prior to 1950.

4. There must have been available to the writer enough information on either the playwright or his/her plays to construct a respectable entry. This criterion has been waived in the case of (a) published playwrights and (b) playwrights whose plays are available or accessible in major libraries or repositories.

Every effort has been made to provide some biographical information for the majority of playwrights, ranging in length from a few lines of information to a brief or full biographical sketch of from one-half to two or even three pages.

Depending upon availability of information, a playwright's entry in the Directory begins with a biographical sketch that seeks to include the following information, roughly in the order given:

1. The playwright's name(s), including pseudonyms, nicknames, married names, and/ or titles, etc.

2. Inclusive dates of birth and death, if known or applicable.

3. Major theatrical or literary occupations, followed by other fields of specialization.

4. Place of birth, followed by other places in which the playwright was reared, educated, or where he/she has worked or resided.

5. Family background, if pertinent, including relationships to other playwrights, theatrical personalities, or celebrities.

6. Education, including earned degrees, certificates, or private study.

7. Military or other service.

8. Marital status and children.

9. Highlights of career, with emphasis on literary, artistic, and theatrical activities and achievements, listed in chronological order.

10. Nondramatic writings and publications, and/or artistic or musical productions.

11. Memberships and offices held.

12. Honors and awards, including fellowships, grants, and honorary degrees.

Biographical sketches are immediately followed, where applicable, by one or more of the following types of collective works, analyzed for their individual plays or components, if possible:

1. The author's published or unpublished collections and self-edited anthologies that include one or more of his/her plays. An example of an unpublished collection is a doctoral dissertation that includes one or more plays. [NOTE: Other collections or anthologies not edited or authored by the playwright are not included in this section,

but may be located in the Analytical Title List of Play Anthologies, under Information Sources at the back of this Directory.]

2. Groups of related plays, including programs of two or more plays that are produced under a different title (or only one of the titles) than that of the individual plays, or cycles and series of plays, including trilogies, which are of special significance.

These collective works are followed by an annotated index of the playwright's individual works, presented in chronological order, either in a single list, or within two or more subgroups. Depending upon availability of information, the following format will be used for each type of dramatic work listed within a playwright's entry:

1. Title of play, musical, or dramatic work. If the title is in a foreign language, or in dialect, the standard English equivalent is given in quotation marks within parentheses. (If the original title is in quotation marks, then the equivalent is given in parentheses without quotations.) If the work has been produced under, or known by, another title (or other titles) than its present one, these other titles are also given (and labeled as original title, alternate title, etc.).

2. Genre, length, and earliest date of composition, copyright, production, or publication—given within parentheses after the title(s).

3. Subtitle—sometimes given under genre and length, when applicable—but in most instances given separately, following 2 above.

4. Coauthors or collaborators, including their specific contributions, if known (especially for musicals), and identification of those collaborators *known* to be black. If the collaborator is another early playwright listed in the Directory, his/her name is put in all capitals (e.g., LANGSTON HUGHES). (See also the section on Symbols for identification of *contemporary playwrights* and *musical librettists*.)

5. Title and author of original work on which each dramatic work is based, if adapted or dramatized (including date, if known).

6. Circumstances that led to the writing of the work, if commissioned or written under the aegis or tutelage of some individual or group.

7. Synopsis of plot or description, and/or themes and subjects.

8. Significance of the dramatic work, if applicable, and/or awards received by the play, the playwright, or other contributors. [NOTE: The position of this information may vary considerably within an entry, in order to place awards as close to other related information as possible. Note also that there is *deliberate* redundancy in listing awards within the play entries which have also been listed in the author's biographical sketch.]

9. Production history, including identification of black producers, all known directors, and best-known actors featured in the cast. (Because of space limitations, important actors are named mainly in professional productions.)

10. Location of published or unpublished scripts (or films, recordings, etc., if applicable), if available from publishers or agents, or deposited in established collections or archives.

11. Sources of important commentary or criticism (including reviews), if these may lead to more detailed information on the play than is included in the entry.

An author's complete entry is followed by a list of his/her other pertinent writings, if any, to include published articles and books on the theatre, autobiographical writings, etc. The entry ends with a supplementary list of further references if any, which may be consulted for more information by the interested reader. These may also include books, articles, tapes, and other types of recordings, as well as scrapbooks, folders, and papers of the playwright that are located in special repositories.

Whenever possible, primary sources have been used for both the playwright's biographical sketch and descriptions of plays. However, for most unestablished playwrights, and where primary sources are unavailable, secondary sources have been heavily relied on.

This Preface is immediately followed by a list of abbreviations and a list of symbols used in this volume. As a supplement to the Biographical Directory, there are several additional features. The first is an introductory essay by the writer, presenting a survey or panoramic overview of the important black American playwrights of each major historical, theatrical, or literary period from before the Civil War to the end of World War II, as well as the major social, political, or literary influences that stimulated the activities of these playwrights.

Following the Biographical Directory are three appendixes. Appendix A provides a list of other black American playwrights and their plays. Appendix B, as previously stated, provides a list of additional librettists and brief descriptions of their shows. Appendix C provides a chronology of plays and other dramatic works by the writers in this volume, classified by genre, so that they can be seen in their historical relationships.

These three appendixes are followed by an extensive bibliography of information sources on early black American playwrights and plays, which includes a list of libraries and repositories with strong collections in black theatre and drama; a title index of play anthologies that contain one or more plays by black American playwrights; an author list of reference books and critical studies pertinent to black theatre; a list of dissertations and theses, most available from University Microfilms International; and a list of periodicals, including journals, magazines, and newspapers, which were regularly consulted for reviews and articles on the writers included in this volume.

The Directory concludes with three indexes: a title index of all plays by black American playwrights listed or referred to throughout this book; an index of early black American theatre organizations and producing groups that produced one or more of the plays in this directory; and a general subject index. [NOTE: Names of playwrights included in the main directory are not indexed unless they are also referred to in other entries or in other sections of the book.]

ABBREVIATIONS

Two types of abbreviations appear with regularity throughout this directory: (1) Bibliographical Abbreviations and (2) General Abbreviations.

BIBLIOGRAPHICAL ABBREVIATIONS

Most Frequently Cited References and Sources

The following abbreviations are used for the most frequently cited books, periodicals, and library collections. These abbreviations may or may not be followed by the author's last name and the date of publication in parentheses. Full publication information is included in the Information Sources at the back of the Directory.

AfrAmWW   *Afro-American Women Writers, 1746—1933,* by Ann Allen Shockley. Boston, 1988.

AmLitNA   *American Literature by Negro Authors,* ed. by Herman Dreer. New York, 1950.

AnthANT   *Anthology of the American Negro in the Theatre,* ed. by Lindsay Patterson. New York, 1927.

BesPls   *The Best Plays of 1894–99/1949–50.* (The Burns Mantle Theatre Yearbooks.) New York, years as indicated.

BioDAfMus   *Biographical Dictionary of Afro-American and African Musicians,* by Eileen Southern. Westport, CT, 1982.

BlkDr   *Black Drama: The Story of the American Negro in the Theatre,* by Loften Mitchell. New York, 1967.

BlkDrAm   *Black Drama in America: An Anthology,* ed. by Darwin T. Turner. Greenwich, CT, 1971.

BlKMagic   *Black Magic: A Pictorial History of the Negro in American Entertainment,* ed. by Langston Hughes and Milton Meltzer. Englewood Cliffs, NJ, 1967.

BlkManh   *Black Manhattan,* by James Weldon Johnson. New York, 1930.

BlkPlots   *Black Plots and Black Characters,* by Robert L. Southgate. Syracuse, NY, 1979.

BlksB&W   *Blacks in Black and White: A Source Book on Black Films,* by Henry T. Sampson. Metuchen, NJ, 1977.

BlksBF   *Blacks in Blackface: A Source Book on Early Black Musical Shows,* by Henry T. Sampson. Metuchen, NJ, 1980.

BlkThUSA   *Black Theater, U.S.A.,* ed. by James V. Hatch and Ted Shine, consultant. New York, 1974.

CLAJ   *College Language Association Journal;* also *CLA Journal*

DAB   *Dictionary of American Biography*

DANB   *Dictionary of American Negro Biography,* ed. by Rayford W. Logan and Michael R. Winston. New York, 1982.

DBlkTh   *Dictionary of the Black Theatre: Broadway, Off-Broadway, and Selected Harlem Theatres,* by Allen Woll. Westport, CT, 1983.

DirAmSchol   *Directory of American Scholars,* 5th ed. (1969), 2 vols.

DirBlksPA   *Directory of Blacks in the Performing Arts,* by Edward Mapp. Metuchen, NJ, 1978.

ETJ   *Educational Theatre Journal*

FTP/GMU   Federal Theatre Project Collection, Research Center for the Federal Theatre Project, George Mason University, Fairfax, VA.

HarlRenD   *The Harlem Renaissance: A Historical Dictionary for the Era,* by Bruce Kellner. Westport, CT, 1984.

Hatch-Billops   Hatch-Billops Collection, New York.

JWJ/YUL   James Weldon Johnson Memorial Collection, Yale University, New Haven, CT

LC   Library of Congress, Washington, DC

ListNegPls   *A List of Negro Plays.* WPA Federal Theatre Project. Washington, DC, 1938.

Moorland-   The Moorland-Spingarn Collection, Howard University, Washington,
  Spingarn   DC

MusBlkAms	*The Music of Black Americans,* by Eileen Southern. New York, 1971; rev. 1983.
NegAmTh	*The Negro in the American Theatre,* by Edith J.R. Isaacs. New York, 1947.
Neg&Dr	*The Negro and the Drama,* by Frederick W. Bond. Washington, DC, 1940.
NegCarav	*The Negro Caravan,* ed. by Sterling A. Brown et al. New York, 1941.
NegGen	*The Negro Genius,* by Benjamin Brawley. New York, 1937.
NegHist13	*Negro History in Thirteen Plays,* ed. by Willis Richardson and May Miller. Washington, DC, 1935.
NegMus&M	*Negro Musicians and Their Music,* by Maud Cuney-Hare. Washington, DC, 1936.
NegPlaywrs	*Negro Playwrights in the American Theatre,* by Doris Abramson. New York, 1969.
NewNegRen	*The New Negro Renaissance,* ed. by Arthur P. Davis and Michael W. Peplow. New York, 1975.
NYT	*New York Times*
Plays&Pags	*Plays and Pageants from the Life of the Negro,* by Willis Richardson. Washington, DC, 1930.
PlaysNegL	*Plays of Negro Life: A Source-Book of Native American Drama,* ed. by Alain Locke and Montgomery Gregory. New York, 1927.
ReadingsNA	*Readings from Negro Authors for Schools and Colleges,* ed. by Otelia Cromwell et al. New York, 1931.
Schomburg	The Schomburg Collection, Schomburg Center for Research in Black Culture, New York Public Library
TC/NYPL	Theatre Collection (also Billy Rose Theatre Collection), Performing Arts Research Center, New York Public Library
TomsCoons	*Toms, Coons, Mulattoes, Mammies, and Bucks,* by Donald Bogle. New York, 1973.
VoicesBTh	*Voices of the Black Theatre,* by Loften Mitchell. Clifton, NJ, 1975.
WWCA	*Who's Who in Colored America*

Other Bibliographical Abbreviations

The following abbreviations will frequently be used for other references and sources not listed above:

Afro-Am.	Afro-American
Am(s).	America, American(s)
&	and
Anth.	Anthology
ASCAP	American Society of Composers, Authors and Publishers
Auth(s).	Author(s)
Bibliog.	Bibliography, Bibliographical
Biog.	Biography, Biographical
Bk.	Book
Blk(s).	Black(s)
Bull.	Bulletin
Col.	Colored
Cong.	Congress
Dict.	Dictionary
Dig.	Digest
diss.	disseration
Encyc.	Encyclopedia
Eve.	Evening
FTP	Federal Theatre Project
Harl.	Harlem
Hist.	History
J.	Journal
Lib.	Library
Lit.	Literature
Mag.	Magazine
Morn.	Morning
Mus.	Music
Musn(s).	Musician(s)
N.	News
Neg(s).	Negro(es)
NY or N.Y.	New York

NYPL	New York Public Library
Pag(s).	Pageant(s)
Perfg.	Performing
Pitts.	Pittsburgh
Pl(s).	Play(s)
Playwr(s).	Playwright(s)
Pub., Pub.'s	Publisher, Publisher's
Q., qtr.	Quarterly, quarter
Renais.	Renaissance
Rev.	Review
rev.	revised
Sat.	Saturday
Schol(s).	Scholar(s)
SF	San Francisco
Sun.	Sunday
T.	Times
TC	Theatre Collection
Th.	Theatre
Wh.	White
Wom.	Women
Wr(s).	Writer(s)
WW	Who's Who
Yrbk, YrBk	Yearbook, Year Book

GENERAL ABBREVIATIONS

No attempt is made to list all the general abbreviations used in this Directory.
Most can be found in a standard American collegiate or unabridged dictionary.
Only the most frequently used abbreviations are listed below:

A. & I.	Agricultural and Industrial
A. & M.	Agricultural and Mechanical
A. & T.	Agricultural and Technical

AEA	Actors Equity Association
AETA	American Educational Theatre Association
AFL-CIO	American Federation of Labor and Congress of Industrial Organizations
A.M.E.	African Methodist Episcopal
ANT	American National Theatre and Academy
Bway	Broadway
CCNY	City College of New York
CLA	College Language Association
Conf.	Conference
dir.	directed
doc.	documentary
FTP	Federal Theatre Project
Inst.	Institute
instr.	instructor
Lib.	Library
NAACP	National Association for the Advancement of Colored People
NADSA	National Association of Dramatic and Speech Arts
NAG	Negro Actors Guild
N.E.A.	National Education Association
NYPL	New York Public Library
NYU	New York University
orig.	original
prod.	produced
prodn.	production
pseud.	pseudonym
SADSA	Southern Association of Dramatic and Speech Arts
TOBA	Theatre Owners Booking Association
UCLA	University of California at Los Angeles
unpub.	unpublished

WPA	Works Projects Administration
YMCA	Young Men's Christian Association
YUL	Yale University Library
YWCA	Young Women's Christian Association

Symbols

1. Symbols used with names of persons, including writers and their collaborators:
   a. A degree sign before a person's name (°Paul Green) indicates that the person is known to be white, or non-black. (This symbol is omitted from the names of such world-famous writers as Shakespeare and Aristophanes whose racial identity is well known.)
   b. A person or collaborator is assumed to be black if no symbol is used with his or her name. This is especially true in the case of coauthors, directors, and performers.
   c. A name in all capitals within an entry (ARNA BONTEMPS) indicates that the person or collaborator is an early black American playwright or dramatic writer whose separate entry is also included in the Directory.
   d. A name in all capitals preceded by a dagger or obelisk (†FLOURNOY E. MILLER) indicates that the person is an early musical librettist whose entry is included in Appendix B.
   e. A name in roman type preceded by a dagger or obelisk (†James Weldon Johnson) indicates that the person is a significant early black American librettist, lyricist, composer, or other originator of musical shows written before 1950, who is not included in this Directory; these writers will be included in my forthcoming *Encyclopedia of the Black American Musical Stage,* now in progress.
   f. A name in roman type preceded by an asterisk (*Lorraine Hansberry) indicates that the person or collaborator is a significant contemporary black American writer for the stage, screen, or broadcasting who is not included in this Directory. Information on these writers is contained

in my earlier volume, *Contemporary Black American Playwrights and Their Plays* (Westport, CT: Greenwood Press, 1988).

2. Symbols used in titles of plays, screenplays, radio scripts, and other dramatic works:

   a. **Boldface roman type** is used within an entry to indicate the titles of plays and stage works written by the subject of an entry. It is also used in Information Sources to indicate titles of plays by black playwrights included in anthologies and collections cited.

   b. **"Boldface roman type"** within quotation marks is used to indicate the titles of radio scripts and other works for broadcasting.

   c. *Boldface italic type* is used within an entry to indicate the names of film works, including screenplays and scenarios.

   d. **"BOLDFACE CAPITALS"** within quotation marks are used to indicate overall production titles (also called blanket titles) covering a group of at least two related plays by the subject writer.

   e. *ITALICIZED CAPITALS* are used to indicate published collections of plays by the subject writer.

   f. "ROMAN CAPITALS" within quotation marks are used to indicate unpublished collections of plays by the subject writer.

   g. *Italic type* is used to indicate most titles of plays, films, and published works, other than the titles of radio scripts, songs, and very short segments or sketches within a single dramatic work.

   h. "Titles in Quotation Marks" indicate subtitles of plays, English translations of foreign titles or titles in dialect, and titles of radio scripts, songs, and very short segments or sketches within a single play or dramatic work.

   i. Double virgules (//) are used to separate current titles from original or earlier titles of the same work, and vice versa.

3. Symbols used in dating plays and dramatic works:

   a. Single virgules (/) are ordinarily used to show the length of a play's run, such as 1898/99 or 1903/5.

   b. Dashes (–) are ordinarily used to separate consecutive years of a single dramatic season, such as 1883–84, when the specific date within the season is unknown.

INTRODUCTION: The Origin and Development of the Black American Playwright from the Antebellum Period to World War II

Black playwrights began to emerge in American society before the Civil War, but their development as serious artists was exceedingly slow—much slower, for example, than that of black actors and performers, who seem to have been traditionally more acceptable to white slaveholders in their roles as entertainers.

Both slavery and racial prejudice are certainly among the factors that hindered blacks from utilizing the stage as a medium for the expression of their political, intellectual, and social concerns. The playwright has always needed the formal or informal trappings of the stage to exercise his talents and to develop artistically. This is not true of the actor or entertainer. Even in slavery, blacks were able to amuse themselves and their masters by singing and dancing, playing on crudely constructed musical instruments, and engaging in playful banter and mimicry. It has been documented that slave performers were frequently used to entertain visitors to the plantation, and that the best of these performers were often brought by their masters to neighboring towns, or even hired out to other plantation owners to perform at parties, weddings, and the like. There were no such opportunities for slaves to exercise the art of playwriting.

It is not surprising, therefore, that the earliest playwrights were all educated and cultured free men, all of whom were associated with a temporary or permanent theatre. Before entering into a discussion of the earliest black writers for the stage, it might be well to consider briefly the background from which these dramatists emerged.

As Clinton F. Oliver has observed in the introduction to his pioneer anthology *Contemporary Black Drama* (coedited with Stephanie Sills, 1971), "The black American, as in other aspects of our national life, was in the American theatre long before he was a genuine part of it." Oliver's observation underscores the fact that the Negro as a stage type had been portrayed by white actors and performers for many years before black performers were even permitted to participate in the theatre.

By the time that blacks were able to perform on the stage in this country, certain images and stereotypes had already become crystallized through the dramas and other types of popular entertainment that dominated the American theatre from the Revolutionary War to the Civil War and beyond.

As first presented in American productions by British touring companies before the American Revolution, the black man was portrayed as a noble or heroic character through such tragedies as Shakespeare's *Othello* and Thomas Southern's *Oronooko,* based on Aphra Behn's novel *The History of Oronooko, or The Royal Slave.* It is understandable why these noble or heroic images of blacks were unacceptable to slaveholding audiences. Sterling Brown tells us that *Oronooko,* when revived in America in 1799, was "made more congenial" to slaveholders by the addition of "a song 'The Gay Negro Boy' sung in black-face to banjo strumming." ["Negro in American Theatre," in *Oxford Companion to the Theatre,* 3rd ed. (Hartnoll, 1970), p. 671.]

The prototype for the creation of the American stage Negro by white playwrights was established by English dramatist Isaac Bickerstaff's comic opera *The Padlock* (1769), which introduced the character of Mungo, a lazy, impudent, talkative, crafty, lewd, and habitually intoxicated West Indian slave, who also loved to sing and dance. Mungo helped to sire a century of plays by white American playwrights portraying black characters as comic slaves, buffoons, and shiftless servants. According to a statement attributed to theatre historian George C.D. Odell [*Annals of the New York Stage* (1927/39)], *The Padlock* "stands at the head of every chapter on the subject of Negro minstrelsy." [Quotation included in Fannin S. Belcher's Ph.D. diss., "The Place of the Negro in the Evolution of the American Theatre, 1767 to 1940" (1945), but no citation given.]

An American play in the main line of development of *The Padlock* is James Murdoch's *The Triumph of Love* (1795), which introduced a character called Sambo, whose dialect, ludicrous actions, and name have all come to epitomize the comic Negro servant as a stage type. Other plays in this genre include John Leacock's *The Fall of British Tyranny* (1776), which includes the character of Cudjo, whose mouth is compared to the hatchway of a ship, the sight of which "is enough to breed a famine on board," and his eating habits to Jonah swallowing the whale; and Mrs. Anna Cora Mowatt's *Fashion* (1845), which includes a black servant named Zeke who reflects the social snobbery of his mistress by his gaudy costume, his foppish manner, and his fondness for long words, which he speaks in dialect and mispronounces in every sentence.

It was against this background—slavery, the lack of opportunity for blacks to participate in the American theatre, and the distortion of black images in the early plays of white authorship—that the first black American playwrights began to emerge. These playwrights, in addition to being free men of color, were all expatriots who had left their native countries in search of better opportunities in a free land. They were Mr. Brown (first name unknown), manager of the African Company; Ira Aldridge, the noted Shakespearean actor; and Victor Séjour, a New Orleans–born Creole of color.

Mr. Brown was a West Indian native who had been a ship's steward aboard a Liverpool liner before giving up his life at sea to live in New York City. There he operated a tea garden during the summer months; around 1816 he organized the talented and cultured men and women of the black community into a theatre group called the African Company, which frequently provided the entertainment for his patrons. In 1820 the group eventually acquired a theatre, remodeled from the old African Grove Hospital at Mercer and Bleeker Streets, which they renamed the African Grove Theatre. At its new theatre, the African Company performed musicales, ballets, Shakespearean dramas, and other plays, including at least one original drama by Mr. Brown, who apparently was the company's manager, director, and resident playwright. Brown's play, *King Shotaway*, dramatized an insurrection that had occurred in the West Indies during the author's lifetime, and according to an extant playbill of the production, "was written from experience by Mr. Brown." *King Shotaway* was performed at least twice at the African Grove Theatre in 1823 and has been documented in *Annals of the New York Stage* [Odell, op. cit.] as "the first Negro drama." The part of King Shotaway was played by James Hewlett, who achieved some reputation as a Shakespearean actor. Also in the company was Ira Aldridge, one of the three earliest black American playwrights. The African Grove Theatre flourished for only two or three years (1821–23) at its Bleeker Street location, and during this period was under constant harassment from white hoodlums and the police, who finally closed the establishment, ostensibly for disturbance of the peace and for violation of fire regulations and other city ordinances.

Victor Séjour (1817–74), the second recorded black American playwright, was a New Orleans–born Creole of color who was sent by his parents to Paris at age 17 to further his education and to avoid the racial prejudice that even free blacks experienced in this country. In Paris, Séjour was accepted into the important drama and literary circles, which included such playwrights as Alexandre Dumas and Emile Augier, both of whom befriended him and encouraged him to write for the theatre. When he was 27, Séjour had his first play, *Diégarias,* produced by the Théâtre Français, in Paris (1844); and by age 35 he had become one of the most popular and commercially successful French playwrights of the nineteenth century. *Diégarias* is a revenge play on the theme of anti-Semitism, set in Spain and involving a persecuted Jew who has kept the secret of his ethnic identity even from his daughter. Séjour also dealt with anti-Semitism in a later play, *La Tireuse de Cartes* ("The Lady Who Pulls the Cards," or "The Fortuneteller," 1860), about a Jewish child who is kidnapped and brought up as a Christian, until she is finally located by her mother and informed of her ethnic heritage. In all, Séjour wrote, produced, and published more than 20 plays, including melodramas, comedies, romantic dramas, and historical dramas, such as his masterpiece and most popular play, *Richard III* (1852), which shows the strong influence of Shakespeare, whom Séjour greatly admired. Although Séjour wrote no plays on an American theme or about the mistreatment of blacks, he did write a short story, "Le Mulâtre" ("The Mulatto"), published in Paris in 1835, which dealt with slavery in the French colonial empire. Only one of his plays, *Le Martyre du Coeur* ("The Martyrdom of the Heart," 1858), includes a black character—a trusted servant who is sent from Jamaica, with a large fortune, to carry out his master's death wish that this inheritance be delivered to his estranged daughter. Other noteworthy plays by Séjour include *La Chute de Séjan* ("The Fall of Sejanus," 1844), *Les Noces Vénitiennes* ("Venetian Weddings," 1855), *Le Fils de la Nuit* ("Son of the Night," 1856), and his only one-act play, *Le Paletot Brun* ("The Brown Overcoat," 1858). (Descriptions of these and all other plays are given in Séjour's entry in the main section of this volume.)

Ira Aldridge (1807–67), the preeminent black Shakespearean actor of the nineteenth century, is also credited as the third black American playwright, because of his efforts as an adaptor. Although the facts of Aldridge's early life are obscure, it is certain that he was born in the United States, attended the African Free School in New York City, and performed in at least one production of the African Company. He apparently worked as a callboy at a New York professional theatre. Inspired to become an actor and convinced that he could not achieve success in this country, he made his way to London, presumably as a ship's steward or as a personal attendant to one of the professional English actors who regularly performed in New York. In London, Aldridge developed his talents, possibly under the tutelage of Edmund Kean, and soon gained international acclaim for his portrayals of Othello, Shylock, King Lear, Oronooko, Mungo, and other roles. Because of the difficulty of finding suitable plays for his repertoire, Aldridge adapted two plays: *The Black Doctor* (1847), from *Le Docteur Noir,* a French drama of interracial love and marriage between a mulatto doctor and a beautiful white noblewoman whose life he had saved, and *Titus Andronicus* (1849), from the tragedy of blood by Shakespeare, in which Aldridge changed the principal character, Aaron the Moor, from a black-hearted villain to a more sympathetic character. *The Black Doctor* was published with Aldridge's credit line as adaptor on the cover and is accessible to the modern reader.

Although neither Brown nor Séjour nor Aldridge experienced first hand the evils of slavery, it is apparent that they were all acutely aware of the problem of racial prejudice, which had prevented them from achieving success in the theatre in this country. Brown saw his theatre closed by white hoodlums and the police. Both Séjour and Aldridge had to immigrate to Europe to pursue their theatrical careers; but both were able to achieve fame and recognition at a time when other blacks were still being held in bondage. Had these two men been given the opportunities in this country that they found abroad, our own theatre would undoubtedly have been much richer. So, too, had Brown's African Grove

Theatre been permitted to thrive, the whole course of black theatre history in America might have been vastly changed.

In the meantime, while Séjour and Aldridge were beginning their illustrious careers in Europe, two completely new theatrical genres were developing in America that greatly affected how blacks were being portrayed on the stage. These were the minstrel shows and the antislavery propaganda plays.

Blackface minstrelsy (or more properly, Ethiopian minstrelsy) conventional- ized the comic black stereotypes that had been introduced in the legitimate plays by white playwrights. Minstrelsy began as an all-white, all-male genre around 1843. Mr. Tambo and Mr. Bones, the two endmen or main comedians of the show, could trace their genealogical roots back to Isaac Bickerstaff's Mungo and James Murdoch's Sambo; and Tambo and Bones were themselves the pro- genitors of a century of blackface comedy teams, both Negro and white. The comic black wench, originally played by white men, was also a staple of the minstrel show, thus establishing the first black female stereotypes.

From the 1840s to the 1880s the minstrel show was one of the most popular forms of American entertainment. It was not until after the Civil War that blacks were permitted to perform in these shows, advertising themselves as the "orig- inal" or "genuine" plantation minstrels. However, by this time the minstrel pattern had become so well established that black performers were obliged to continue the tradition begun by the white minstrels—blackening their faces, exaggerating their lips, and perpetuating the comic stereotypes that white au- diences had come to expect. They became what can be described as an imitation of a caricature of the original slave entertainers. Nevertheless, the minstrel show, which gradually evolved into other theatrical forms, paved the way for blacks to enter the theatre for the first time as performers, and many of the stars of vaudeville, musical comedy, and legitimate drama of the next century began their careers in blackface minstrelsy.

While white minstrel shows were flourishing in the South, another popular genre, the antislavery propaganda play, was developing in the North, sponsored by the abolitionist movement. Such plays included dramatizations of Harriet Beecher Stowe's famous novel *Uncle Tom's Cabin* (1851), which has been credited with bringing about the Civil War; J. T. Trowbridge's dramatization of his novel *Neighbor Jackwood*; and Dion Boucicault's *The Octoroon* (1859). These antislavery plays and their antecedent novels gained enormous sympathy in the North for the plight of Negro slaves, but they also were responsible for creating new black stereotypes, such as the Christian slave and the tragic mulatto, and helped to perpetuate the old stereotypes of the minstrel tradition. Of these antislavery plays, the dramatizations of *Uncle Tom's Cabin,* or the "Tom shows," as they came to be called, were the most popular. At one period, four companies were performing the play simultaneously in New York. The stereo- types of Uncle Tom (the contented, or Christian, slave), Aunt Chloe (mammy, the prototype of Aunt Jemima), Eliza and George (the discontented, or tragic, mulattoes), and Topsy (the comic wench or pickaninny) have been immortalized in four film versions, and their counterparts can be found in numerous early Hollywood films, including *Gone with the Wind* (1939), *Stormy Weather* (1943), and *Pinky* (1949). It should be noted that in the "Tom shows," the major black characters were originally played by white actors in blackface, and it was not until 1877 that a black actor, Sam Lucas, was cast in the role of Uncle Tom.

It was out of this tradition of antislavery plays that the first indigenous black American playwright emerged. William Wells Brown (1815–84), the first black American novelist and one of the earliest black historians, was also the first truly native black playwright. Not only was he born a slave, but he wrote extensively about this problem and the condition of blacks in America. When he escaped from bondage, he fled to the North, educated himself, and became an ardent antislavery crusader, lecturer, and author. His writings include a narrative of his life as a fugitive slave, a novel about miscegenation, several books on the history and achievements of the black race, and two antislavery dramas: *Experience; or, How to Give a Northern Man a Backbone* (1856), about a northern white minister who is kidnapped and sold into slavery, where he learns to understand the evils of the institution that he has previously condoned; and *The Escape; or, A Leap for Freedom* (1857), about the thrilling escape of a young married slave couple from the clutches of a lecherous master who wishes to separate them in order to possess the beautiful young wife. Although Brown's plays were never produced, and only one was published, he was quite skilled as a dramatic reader, and read them aloud at numerous antislavery meetings and lyceums. Brown's plays, like those of the three earliest playwrights, did not alter the course of black theatre history in America, but they do mark the beginning of a truly indigenous black American drama, which did not develop or flourish until well into the twentieth century.

Although the minstrel show has been spoken of somewhat disparagingly, it should be noted that within this genre blacks were able to make numerous original contributions, in the form of skits, songs, dances, comedy routines, and specialty acts, which comprised the content of the show. As the minstrel show evolved, they were able to incorporate more and more relevant aspects of black American culture into its content.

Even at the height of the minstrel show's popularity, some efforts at serious drama by blacks can be discerned, although these attempts are somewhat irregular and isolated. In 1871 the Hyers Sisters, a talented operatic duo that included Anna Madah Hyers and Emma Louise Hyers, began to tour the nation for several seasons in a series of concerts that won critical acclaim and established them as the first black women to gain success on the American stage, then dominated by male performers. In 1875 the Hyers Sisters decided to enlarge their repertoire to include dramas, in which they continued to tour extensively until 1883. These musical plays were *Out of Bondage* (1875), about the aftermath of emancipation, adapted by the sisters from a play by Joseph Bradford (white); *Princess Orelia of Madagascar* (1877), about a royal African princess, which apparently was cowritten by the sisters; and *The Underground Railroad,* about the covert operation that helped slaves to escape to the North, written especially for the sisters by Pauline Elizabeth Hopkins (1859–1930), a black playwright and novelist who is also credited with at least one other dramatization.

John Patterson Sampson (1837–?), an A.M.E. churchman, lecturer, and author, wrote *The Disappointed Bride; or Love at First Sight* (1883), which was published by the Hampton School (later Institute, now University) Press. J. Mord Allen (1875–1906), a poet, dramatist, and boilermaker, is credited with having written a number of stage works for a traveling theatre group, 1889–92, although no titles have been located. William Edgar Easton (1861–?), a Massachusetts-born playwright who could trace his family history back to the Revolutionary War, wrote the first of his two plays on Haitian history, *Dessalines* (1893), about the revolutionary general who helped to achieve Haiti's independence and who became the country's first king; the play was produced at the Haitian Pavilion of the Chicago World's Fair in January 1893 and published the same year. Easton's second play, *Christophe* (1911), dealt with the overthrow of Dessalines.

Paul Laurence Dunbar (1892–1906), better known as America's first major black poet, also tried his hand at serious drama. His plays and librettos include *Dream Lovers* (1898), an operatic romance, with music by Samuel Coleridge-Taylor; *Robert Herrick* (1899), based on the life of the English poet, and *Winter Roses* (1899), about a chance reunion between two former lovers, now grown old—two plays written for his friend, the noted actor Richard B. Harrison; and an unfinished musical comedy, *On the Island of Tanawana* (1900). Dunbar also provided lyrics for several other musical shows, in collaboration with Will Marion Cook and Jesse A. Shipp, discussed below.

By the 1890s, the minstrel show was well into its decline, and many young, talented black performers considered this genre too degrading and artistically constraining. America was not yet ready for black participation in serious dramas; so these young theatre artists began to turn their creative talents toward the development of new types of black shows that would help to free them from the minstrel tradition. Many of these early musical shows included blackface comedy and other minstrel elements, but these were more skillfully blended into a new structure that represented a gradual but definite departure from the old minstrel patterns and a step in the direction of musical comedy, which was then in its infancy in America.

Although musical comedy per se is beyond the discussion of this work, this introduction will focus primarily on the librettists or the writers of the books from which these musicals were developed. However, since the musical is by its nature a collective creation, some consideration will also be given to the lyricists, composers, and performers of these early musicals. [NOTE: Only those librettists who also wrote legitimate plays are included in the main Directory.

Appendix B lists 38 additional musical librettists with brief descriptions of their shows.]

The most successful black musicals from the turn of the century to the 1930s were written by only a dozen or so talented young black men who stand out as the leading librettists of the period: Bob Cole and his collaborator William ("Billy") Johnson; Will Marion Cook; Jesse A. Shipp and Alex C. Rogers; Salem Tutt Whitney and J. Homer Tutt; Flournoy E. Miller and Aubrey Lyles; J. Leubrie Hill, Irvin C. Miller, and Eddie Hunter.

Bob Cole (1864–1911), a talented librettist, lyricist, composer, producer, director, and performer, is credited with writing the first black-authored musical comedy, *A Trip to Coontown* (1897), in collaboration with William ("Billy") Johnson (1858–1916). Earlier Cole had contributed a number of sketches to two transitional shows: *Black Patti's Troubadours* (first produced in 1896), which combined elements of the minstrel show, the vaudeville show, and the serious musical comedy; and *The Creole Show* (1899), which substituted a chorus of beautiful girls for the usual all-male minstrel chorus. Although *A Trip to Coontown*, as its title suggests, was only a step away from the minstrel show, it did have a definite story line from beginning to end to connect the various musical numbers, comedy routines, and specialty acts. The plot revolved around the efforts of a flimflam artist to swindle an old man out of his life's savings. In addition to being the first black musical comedy (although the term *musical farce* is more appropriate), *A Trip to Coontown* was also the first musical show to be conceived, produced, directed, and managed entirely by blacks.

Between 1900 and 1904, Bob Cole, in collaboration with J. Rosamond Johnson (1873–1954) and James Weldon Johnson (1871–1934), contributed the music and lyrics to more than a dozen white musicals in New York City. After this period, Cole wrote the librettos for two of the best black musicals of the early 1900s: *The Shoo-Fly Regiment* (1907), with lyrics by James Weldon Johnson and music by J. Rosamond Johnson, which dealt with the heroism of black soldiers in the Spanish-American War; and *The Red Moon* (1909), with music and lyrics by J. Rosamond Johnson and Joe Jordan (1882–1971), which dramatized a love story between a black man and a part-black Indian woman, whose Indian father has abducted her and returned her to his tribe.

Although Will Marion Cook (1865–1944) was primarily a composer and musician, he originated one of the most important musicals of the period, *Clorindy, the Origin of the Cakewalk*, which is credited as the first black musical to play on Broadway, the first to use syncopated ragtime music, and the first to introduce the cakewalk (a plantation dance) to Broadway audiences. Cook also contributed the music to the Williams and Walker musicals, which were among the most successful black shows of the turn of the century.

The Williams and Walker musicals starred Bert Williams (1874–1922) and George Walker (1873–1911), who became the leading black performers of the early musical stage. Their best-known musicals were *The Sons of Ham* (1899),

The Policy Players (1900), *In Dahomey* (1902), *Abyssinia* (1906), and *Bandanna Land* (1908).

Jesse A. Shipp (1869–1934) was the chief librettist and director of the Williams and Walker musicals, and Will Marion Cook was the chief composer. Shipp was one of the earliest, if not the first, black director of a Broadway play, and is credited with helping to destroy the minstrel pattern for blacks in the musicals with which he was associated. *The Sons of Ham* concerned two bums (played by Williams and Walker) who are mistaken for a pair of twin brothers who are heirs to a large fortune. *The Policy Players* (originally entitled *4–7–11*) dealt with the numbers racket. *In Dahomey,* the most successful of the Williams and Walker musicals and the first to introduce native African elements, concerned a fraudulent scheme to colonize some land in that African country as a home for dissatisfied American blacks. *Abyssinia,* also on an African theme, dramatized a trip to Ethiopia by a group of naive black American tourists, who discover the grandeur, majesty, and stern legal justice system of that African kingdom. *Bandanna Land* dramatized a black real estate scam, in which blacks profit from moving into a white neighborhood by creating such a ''scare'' among their neighbors that they are paid double their real estate investment to move out again.

Alex C. Rogers (18–?–1930) collaborated with Shipp on most of the Williams and Walker musicals, coauthoring the book and lyrics of *Abyssinia* and *Bandanna Land,* and providing additional lyrics for *In Dahomey.* Together Rogers and Shipp wrote the book for *Mr. Lode of Koal* (1909), starring Bert Williams alone, about a coal worker who dreams that he is an island king. Rogers also wrote scripts with Henry S. Creamer (1879–1930) for *The Traitor* (1912) and *Old Man's Boy* (1914), the latter play starring the noted actor Charles Gilpin. With J. Leubrie Hill (1888–1974), Rogers wrote *The Darktown Follies* (1911), which by 1913 was one of the most popular shows produced in Harlem and started the vogue of white theatregoers coming uptown to see black shows. Florenz Ziegfeld, after seeing the show, bought the finale for inclusion in his famous *Ziegfeld Follies.*

One of the most prolific and enduring black musical comedy writing and performing teams was that of the Tutt/Whitney Brothers, also known as Whitney and Tutt. Salem Tutt Whitney (1868–1934), the elder, and J. Homer Tutt (dates unknown), either singly or together wrote more than 30 original musical shows, many of which were produced by their Smart Set Company between 1903 and 1923. Earlier, the brothers had traveled in a tent show, *Silas Green from New Orleans,* from 1888 to 1905. All rights to this show, including the book, music, and lyrics by Salem Tutt Whitney, were ''bought'' on credit by one of their partners, Eph Williams, who died without reimbursing them, having already sold the show to another producer. *Silas Green* became the longest-running black musical show in America, reportedly lasting until 1950, or for more than 60 years. Among the numerous shows by Whitney and Tutt are *The Mayor of*

Newton [also *Newtown*](1909), *His Excellency the President* (1913), *George Washington Bullion Abroad* (1915), *My People* (1917), and *Oh Joy!* (1922), which ran for four weeks on Broadway, with Ethel Waters in the cast.

Another pair of musical collaborators, Flournoy E. Miller (1887–1971) and Aubrey Lyles (1884–1932), known as Miller and Lyles, wrote and performed in about 10 musical shows from 1906 to Lyles' death in 1932. Their most successful musicals include *The Oyster Man* (1907), *Shuffle Along* (1921, 1930, 1933, and 1952), and *Runnin' Wild* (1923). *The Oyster Man,* which featured Ernest Hogan as an oyster vendor, was the last show in which he appeared before his death. *Shuffle Along,* the most successful black musical comedy up to the 1920s, featured lyrics and music by Noble Sissle (1889–1975) and Eubie Blake (1883–1933), and revolved around the rivalry between two candidates for mayor of a small southern town. The plot served as a framework for elaborately staged and beautifully costumed musical numbers, spectacular singing and dancing, hilarious comedy routines, and a chorus of beautiful girls. This show launched the careers of Florence Mills and Josephine Baker, who became the leading stars of their time.

Miller and Lyles' *Runnin' Wild* helped to popularize the Charleston, a new black dance sensation that had been introduced to Broadway the preceding year by another successful black show, *Liza* (1921), with book by Irvin C. Miller (dates unknown), brother of Flournoy Miller.

Other important musicals and their librettists are presented in Appendix B.

During the first two decades of the twentieth century, black playwrights began to emerge in increasing numbers, although none were writers for the professional stage. Joseph Seamon Cotter, Sr. (1861–1949), a poet, author, and educator, published his first play, *Caleb, the Degenerate* (1903), which was a dramatization of the work philosophy of Booker T. Washington. Two playwrights celebrated the fiftieth anniversary of the Emancipation Proclamation (1863): Katherine Davis Tillman, with the publication of her play *Fifty Years of Freedom; or, From Cabin to Congress* (1910), on the life of Benjamin Banneker; and W.E.B. DuBois (1868–1963), the eminent sociologist, author, and editor, with the first of his two pageants, *The Star of Ethiopia* (1911), dramatizing the gifts that black people have given to the world. Henry Francis Downing (1846?–1928), a novelist, playwright, and historian who spent a number of years in London and Liberia as a representative of the United States government, published six plays in London in 1913, and three more the following year. One of his plays, *Voodoo* (1914), concerns a woman who is pursued from London to the West Indies by her spurned lover against a background of voodoo and black magic.

During World War I, several other playwrights were published: Olivia Ward Bush, *Memories of Calvary* (1915), an Easter pageant; Alice Dunbar-Nelson (1875–1935), the wife of Paul Laurence Dunbar, *Mine Eyes Have Seen* (1918), a patriotic play about the loyalty of blacks during the war; F. Grant

Gilmore, *The Problem* (1915), a military play; and Powell Willard Gibson, *Jake Among the Indians* (1917), a comedy about the trials of an Indian maiden. One noteworthy playwright to emerge during the war years was Angelina Weld Grimké (1880–1958), a poet and teacher who is credited as the first historically significant black woman playwright. Her play *Rachel,* which dealt with the theme of lynching, was produced by the Drama Committee of the NAACP in New York City in 1917, and advertised as "the first attempt to use the stage for race propaganda in order to enlighten the American people relative to the lamentable condition of ten millions of colored citizens of this free republic"—Program Notes.

Immediately following the war, another significant woman playwright, Mary Burrill, a high school English teacher, published two plays in periodicals in 1919: *Aftermath,* a tragedy of a returning black soldier; and *They That Sit in Darkness,* a nonracial play advocating birth control among the poor.

It was also after the war that Oscar Micheaux (1884–1951), the first major black filmmaker, produced the first of his more than 40 feature films, *The Homesteader* (1919), based on his novel *The Conquest* (1917), a fictionalized account of his life in South Dakota. Micheaux made nearly two films a year between 1919 and 1940.

The decade of the 1920s, which has been called the Harlem Renaissance, or more correctly the Black Renaissance, was a period of unparalleled black theatrical and literary activity, not only in New York City, but also in Washington, DC, Boston, Chicago, and other parts of the nation.

This burst of activity among black playwrights was stimulated by a number of factors, including (a) the impact and aftermath of World War I; (b) the encouragement of literary activity by the NAACP and the National Urban League through their respective publications—*Crisis* and *Opportunity*—and the literary contests sponsored by both magazines between 1925 and 1927; (c) the successful productions of Negro folk and problem plays by such white playwrights as Ridgely Torrence, Eugene O'Neill, Paul Green, and Dorothy and DuBose Heyward, which gained acceptance for the black actor and paved the way for the black playwright to be produced on the New York stage; (d) the enthusiastic reception by Broadway theatregoers of such black musical shows as *Shuffle Along, Liza,* and *Runnin' Wild*; (e) the publication of articles on black drama and theatre, not only in *Crisis* and *Opportunity,* but also in *Carolina Magazine, Theatre Arts, New Republic, Drama,* and *Theatre*; and (f) the publication of plays in several of the above periodicals and in two anthologies edited and compiled by Alain Locke: *The New Negro* (1925) and *Plays of Negro Life* (1927), the latter coedited by Montgomery Gregory.

More than 30 black playwrights began their writing careers in the 1920s, the most significant of whom are Willis Richardson, Randolph Edmonds, Garland Anderson, Frank Wilson, Wallace Thurman, Jean Toomer, Georgia Douglas Johnson, Eulalie Spence, and John Matheus.

Willis Richardson (1889–1977) and Randolph Edmonds (1900–1983) are, perhaps, the most prolific and enduring of the above playwrights, spanning several decades until the 1950s and beyond. Richardson wrote more than 40 plays, nearly half of them completed during the 1920s. His plays, which showed the strong influence of the folk tradition of Ridgely Torrence and Paul Green, were among the first black-authored plays to be produced by a number of early drama groups searching for black plays. He is the first to have a serious play produced on Broadway, *The Chip Woman's Fortune* (1923), a one-act play presented on a bill of three plays by the Ethiopian Folk Theatre from Chicago. *The Chip Woman's Fortune* centers around an old woman who ekes out a living by picking up chips of wood and bits of coal in the street, and who is suspected of having a large sum of money stored away in a secret place. In 1925 Richardson won honorable mention in the *Opportunity* Contest Awards for his play *Fall of the Conjurer* and was twice winner of first prize in the *Crisis* Contest Awards— for *The Broken Banjo* in 1925 and *The Bootblack Lover* in 1926. Other important plays by Richardson include *Compromise* (1925), *The Broken Banjo* (1925), and *Flight of the Natives* (1927). Richardson was also a pioneer anthologist whose two collections, *Plays and Pageants from the Life of the Negro* (1930) and *Negro History in Thirteen Plays* (1935), include the works of several other important playwrights of the 1920s and 1930s.

Randolph Edmonds, called "The Dean of Black Academic Theatre," wrote at least 50 individual plays, many of which were published in his three collections: *Shades and Shadows* (1930), *Six Plays for a Negro Theatre* (1934), and *The Land of Cotton and Other Plays* (1942). In October 1926, Edmonds received honorable mention in the *Crisis* Contest Awards for two of his plays: *Illicit Love*, a Romeo and Juliet–like story of interracial love, involving a black sharecropper and the daughter of a white southern planter; and *Peter Stith*, which he retitled *Old Man Pete*, about an old couple from the South who freeze to death in New York because of the inhospitality of their children, who are ashamed of their parents' country ways. His play *Bleeding Hearts* received honorable mention in the *Opportunity* Contest Awards in June 1927. Edmonds produced his plays at three colleges and universities with which he was associated during his long career: Morgan College (now State University) in Baltimore, where he organized and directed the Morgan College Players, 1926–34; Dillard University in New Orleans, where he directed the Dillard Players Guild, 1935–47; and Florida A. & M. University in Tallahassee, where he served for more than 20 years as chairman of the Department of Speech and Drama and as director of the FAMU Playmakers Guild, 1947–69. Edmonds also established several black collegiate drama associations in the South and Southeast, which presented drama festivals and encouraged the writing and production of plays by college students and faculty. Edmonds' most important plays include *Bad Man* (1932), *Breeders* (1934), *Nat Turner* (1934), and *Earth and Stars* (1946). The latter play, revised in 1961, explored the problems of southern black leadership, and the leading character, a minister, is reminiscent of Dr. Martin Luther King, Jr., and his involvement with the civil rights struggle.

Garland Anderson (1886–1939), Frank Wilson (1886–1956), and Wallace Thurman (1902–1934) were among the four serious black playwrights produced on Broadway during the 1920s. The first, Willis Richardson, has already been discussed. Anderson, a former bellhop and philosopher of constructive thinking, was the second Broadway playwright, but the first to have a serious, full-length play produced there. (Richardson's play had been a one-act.) Anderson's play *Appearances* (1925) is a courtroom drama in which a black bellhop is tried and exonerated for the rape of a white woman. This was reportedly the first Broadway play with an interracial cast in which a black man had a leading part. There were, in fact, two leading roles played by blacks—one by Lionel Monagas, a light-skinned actor generally thought to be white, and the other by Doe Doe Green, thought to be the only Negro in the cast.

Frank Wilson, a stage and film actor, was represented on Broadway by a social drama with music and spirituals, *Meek Mose* (1928), about the loss of confidence in a black leader who is accused by his followers of giving in to white demands, causing them to have to move from their homes to a tract of swampland in order to make room for the building of a factory. The leader is vindicated when oil is discovered on the new site. An earlier play by Wilson, *Sugar Cain* (1920), had won first place in the *Opportunity* Contest Awards of 1926.

Wallace Thurman, a novelist and playwright, saw his play *Harlem,* cowritten with William Jourdan Rapp (white), produced on Broadway in 1929, where it had a long run. This was the first realistic portrait of Harlem to focus on its seamier aspects, including gambling and playing the numbers, rent parties, drinking, racketeering, prostitution, and murder.

Jean Toomer (1894–1967), a mulatto short story writer, essayist, and novelist, published only one book, *Cane* (1923)—a collection of poems, stories, sketches—and an experimental drama, *Kabnis*, which was not produced because of its avant-garde style. *Kabnis*, which has obvious biographical significance, asserts that the black artist can never realize his artistic potential in a racist society. In all, Toomer wrote about five expressionistic dramas, which remain in manuscript in the Jean Toomer Collection of Fisk University in Nashville.

Georgia Douglas Johnson, Eulalie Spence, and John Frederick Matheus were also winners of *Crisis* and *Opportunity* literary prizes. Johnson, a poet, playwright, and leading member of the Washington, D.C., literati, received honorable mention in the *Opportunity* Contest Awards of 1926 for her play *Blue Blood,* about the discovery by a black couple on their wedding night that they are children of the same white father. This was one of the earliest plays anthologized in a non-black anthology, *Fifty More Contemporary One-Act Plays* (1928), edited by Frank Shay and Pierre Loving. Johnson won first prize in the *Opportunity* Contest Awards for her play *Plumes,* in which a black mother tries to decide whether she should spend her meager savings on an operation for her daughter, which may not save her life, or on a grand funeral after her daughter's death. This play was published in both *Opportunity* and *Plays of Negro Life* (Locke and, Gregory 1927). Johnson also wrote a number of black history plays that have been widely produced by school groups.

Eulalie Spence (1894–1981), a high school teacher, drama director, and pioneer playwright, wrote many one-act plays of domestic life, several of which were awarded prizes. These include *The Hunch,* which won second prize, and *The Starter,* which tied for third place in the June 1927 *Opportunity* Contest and was published in *Plays of Negro Life; Foreign Mail,* which won second prize in the October 1926 *Crisis* Contest; and two additional plays, *Hot Stuff* and *Undertow,* which tied for third place in the December 1927 *Crisis* Contest. *Undertow*, published in *Carolina Magazine,* involved a domestic triangle, including the husband, wife, and "other woman," who had borne an illegitimate child by the husband. Most of Spence's plays were produced by the Krigwa Players. Another play, *The Fool's Errand,* won the Samuel French Prize of $200 in the National Little Theatre Tournament of 1927 and was published by French. A screenplay by Spence, *The Whipping,* was sold to Paramount Pictures in 1934 and made into a film under the title *Ready to Love,* starring Ida Lupino and Richard Arlen.

Dr. John Frederick Matheus (1887–1983), a West Virginia State University foreign language professor and playwright, won the *Opportunity* Contest Awards in 1926 for his play *'Cruiter,* published in *Plays of Negro Life,* about tenant farmworkers who are recruited from their miserable lives of poverty in the South by glowing promises of a better life in the North. Another play, *Black Damp* (1929), about coal miners, was published in *Carolina Magazine.* Two of Matheus' plays have been provided with musical scores by black composer Clarence Cameron White: *Ouanga* (1941), a libretto for an opera in three acts about the life of Dessalines, emperor of Haiti; and *Tambour* (1929), a folk comedy in one act about a young Haitian who has a passion for his drum.

Other noteworthy playwrights of the 1920s include G. D. Lipscomb (1898–   ), Eloise Bibb Thompson (1878–1928), Zora Neale Hurston (c. 1891–1960), May Miller (Sullivan) (1899–   ), Myrtle Smith Livingston (1902–1974), Marita O. Bonner (1899–1971), Richard Bruce Nugent (1905–   ), Leslie Pinckney Hill (1890–1960), Nannie Burroughs (1879–1961), and Joseph Seamon Cotter, Jr. (1895–1919).

Oscar Micheaux was the most prolific filmmaker of the 1920s, having produced some 22 low-budget silent feature films during the decade, including *The Brute* (1920), *Deceit* (1921), *The Dungeon* (1922), *The House Behind the Cedars* (1923), *Body and Soul* (1924), *The Spider's Web* (1926), *Thirty Years Later* (1928), and *The Wages of Sin* (1929). Other films were written by Clarence Muse, George P. Johnson, and Spencer Williams.

Although the 1930s are generally characterized by the devastating effects of the Great Depression, including unemployment, homelessness, and poverty, and although blacks suffered from these economic effects to a greater extent than did most whites, one of the ironies of the Depression is that more black playwrights emerged during the 1930s than in any previous decade. Even with the closing of many theatres and the curtailment of expensive productions, four black American playwrights were able to see their plays produced on Broadway and in downtown New York theatres between 1930 and 1936—even before the economic reform programs of Franklin Delano Roosevelt had been put into place. These playwrights were J. Augustus Smith, Hall Johnson, Dennis Donoghue, and Langston Hughes.

J. Augustus Smith (1891–1950), also known as Gus Smith, an actor and director as well as a playwright, was represented on Broadway by *Louisiana,* a folk drama dealing with a popular subject of the period: the conflict between Christianity and pagan or voodoo worship among blacks. The play was produced in 1933 by the Negro Theatre Guild at the 48th Street Theatre for a short run.

Hall Johnson (1888–1970), the famous choir director and founder of the Hall Johnson Choir, was represented also in 1933 by a folk drama on the same theme as Smith's play, *Run, Little Chillun!,* which was produced at the Lyric Theatre for 126 performances.

Dennis Donoghue was the author of *Legal Murder,* a dramatization of the Scottsboro case, involving the accusation, conviction, and sentencing to death of nine black youths for the alleged rape of two white women. The play was produced at the President Theatre in 1934. Two other plays by Donoghue were also produced in New York during the 1930s: *Beale Street* (1934) and *The Black Messiah* (1939), and latter about Father Divine, the black religious cult leader— also a popular subject of plays of this period.

Langston Hughes (1902–1967) was undoubtedly the best-known and most important playwright to arise during the 1930s. His tragedy of miscegenation, *Mulatto,* was produced on Broadway at the Vanderbilt Theatre in 1935, where it established a record of 373 performances—the longest run on Broadway up to that time for a black-authored play. Other plays by Hughes produced during this decade include *Little Ham* (1935), *The Emperor of Haiti* (1935), and *Don't You Want to Be Free* (1937), which was produced by the Harlem Suitcase Theatre for a record run of 1,935 performances, playing mainly on weekends.

The major influence on black playwriting during the Depression was the establishment of the WPA Federal Theatre as a part of the economic recovery program of Roosevelt's New Deal. This project established Negro units in some 23 cities throughout the United States, many of which had resident playwrights who wrote original scripts or adapted classics and other standard plays for production by black groups. The most productive units were New York, Boston, Hartford, Philadelphia, and Newark (in the East); Raleigh, Durham, and Birmingham (in the South); Chicago, Cleveland, and Peoria (in the Midwest); and Seattle and Los Angeles (in the West).

The New York Unit (also called the Negro Theatre Project), headed by white directors John Houseman and Orson Welles, was by far the best known and most active, having produced some 27 works during its five-year life from 1935 to 1939. (Most other units were begun in 1936.) The most popular production of the New York Unit was the Haitian *Macbeth* (1935), adapted by Welles from Shakespeare. In order to satisfy the black community, Houseman and Welles were replaced in 1936 by three black directors, Edward Perry, Carlton Moss, and Harry (F. V.) Edward, the latter two of whom were also playwrights.

Frank Wilson, who had been an active playwright since the 1920s, was the first black playwright to be produced by the New York Unit, when his *Walk Together Children,* a social drama with Negro spirituals, was produced in February 1936. This play revolved around a labor dispute between New York State and southern migrant black workers brought up north to supply cheap labor.

The most popular play produced by the New York Unit was *The Conjur Man Dies,* adapted by playwrights Countee Cullen (1903–1946) and Arna Bontemps (1902–1973) from the novel by Rudolph Fisher (1897–1934) two years after Fisher's death. A mystery-comedy-drama, this play deals with superstition and the occult among Harlem blacks and was produced at the Lafayette Theatre in March and April 1936.

J. Augustus Smith, who earlier in 1933 saw one of his plays produced on Broadway, also had two plays produced by the New York Unit: *Turpentine,* a social drama exposing conditions in southern labor camps, produced in June 1936; and *Just Ten Days,* a melodrama about a family economic crisis during the Depression, produced by the unit's mobile theatre, which toured the streets of New York, presenting it to thousands of black children during late August and early September 1937.

The short-lived Negro Youth Theatre, a subdivision of the New York Negro Theatre Project, produced only one play before its demise—*Sweet Land,* a social drama by Conrad Seiler presented in 1937, about the plight of black sharecroppers, who, as returning World War I veterans, try to unionize black farmworkers in order to improve their economic condition in the South.

The Chicago Negro Unit of the Federal Theatre Project (FTP) rivaled the New York Unit in the originality, variety, and popularity of its offerings, the most successful of which was *The Swing Mikado.* Adapted from the Gilbert and Sullivan operetta, it reached Broadway for a short run and spawned a number of imitators, including *The Hot Mikado* (1939), produced on Broadway starring Bill Robinson. Shirley Graham DuBois (1906–1977), a playwright and composer, was supervisor of this unit, although none of her plays was produced by the FTP. The most important black-authored play to arise from the Chicago Unit was *Big White Fog* by Theodore Ward (1902–1983), whose drama of black unemployment and poverty during the Depression opened at Chicago's Great Northern Theatre in April 1938.

The Negro Unit in Seattle, Washington, had as its resident playwright Theodore Browne (1910?–1979), who wrote four plays staged by this unit. *Lysistrata,* an Afro-American adaptation of the comedy by Aristophanes, was produced in 1936. *Natural Man,* a dramatization of the John Henry myth; *Go Down Moses,* a drama about Harriet Tubman and the Underground Railroad; and *Swing, Gates, Swing,* a musical revue, were produced in 1937.

The Los Angeles Unit produced two outstanding plays by black playwrights: *John Henry,* another version about the legendary railroad worker by Frank B. Wells, produced in 1936; and *Run, Little Chillun!,* a revival of Hall Johnson's folk drama in 1938/39, which earlier had been produced on Broadway (1933).

Plays of black authorship produced by other Negro units include *Swing Song* (1938) by Ralf Coleman, produced by the Boston Unit; *Trilogy in Black* (c. 1936) by Ward Courtney, produced by the Hartford Unit (formerly the Charles Gilpin Players—not to be confused with the famous Cleveland group); *Heaven Bound* (1936) by Laura Edwards, produced by the Raleigh (North Carolina) Unit; and *Prelude in Swing* (1939), a musical documentary by Carlton Moss, produced by the Philadelphia Unit. One of the most successful FTP productions of a black-authored play was *The Trial of Dr. Beck,* a courtroom melodrama about color prejudices among middle-class blacks by Hughes Allison, produced by the New Jersey Unit in 1937. This production was transferred to Broadway, where it had a run of four weeks.

During the 1930s, the works of some 20 black American playwrights were made accessible to amateur theatrical groups and to Negro units of FTP through publication in several anthologies. Willis Richardson, in collaboration with May Miller, published two anthologies (although Miller was not credited as coeditor of the first): *Plays and Pageants from the Life of the Negro* (1930) includes three plays by Richardson, two by Miller, and one each by Inez Burke, Maud Cuney-Hare, Thelma Duncan, John Matheus, Dorothy Guinn, Frances Gunner, and Edward McCoo. *Negro History in Thirteen Plays* (1935) includes five plays by Richardson, four by Miller, two by Georgia Douglas Johnson, and one each by Helen Webb Harris and Randolph Edmonds. Another important anthology was *Readings from Negro Authors* (1931), edited by Otelia Cromwell et al. (The contents of these three anthologies are given in the Information Sources.)

A number of black playwrights emerged from universities and colleges, either as graduate students of playwriting or as members of English and drama faculties of various black colleges. Among these were Randolph Edmonds (previously cited), Arthur Clifton Lamb, Thomas D. Pawley, and Owen Dodson.

Arthur Clifton Lamb (1909–   ) had his first plays produced at Grinnell College during the 1930s, where his *Shades of Cottonlips* (1931) won the Henry Steiner Memorial Prize in playwriting in 1933, and his *Two Gifts,* a Christmas play, was published in *Grinnell Plays* (1935). Lamb taught for more than 25 years at Morgan State College in Baltimore, where many of his more recent plays were produced.

Thomas D. Pawley (1917–   ) studied playwriting at the University of Iowa, where he received both the master's and Ph.D. degrees. His master's thesis plays include *Jedgement Day* (1938), about the harrowing experiences of an errant husband; *Smokey* (1938), about a mild-mannered black farmhand turned murderer; and *Freedom in My Soul* (1939). Pawley served for many years as head of the Department of Speech and Theatre at Lincoln University in Jefferson City, Missouri, where most of his plays were produced.

Owen Dodson received the B.F.A. in playwriting and directing from Yale University School of Drama in 1939, where his two best-known plays, *Divine Comedy* (1938) and *Garden of Time* (1939), were both written and first produced. The first play dealt with the Father Divine story, the second with the Jason-Medea tragedy of interracial love.

Other playwrights emerging from or associated with universities include Shirley Graham DuBois (Oberlin, Yale, and Atlanta University), James W. Butcher (Howard), Frederick W. Bond (West Virginia State), George A. Towns (Fort Valley State), Ira DeA. Reid (Atlanta University), and Haleemon Shaik Felton (Xavier and Dillard).

Finally, a growing number of black theatre organizations and community theatres also helped to stimulate playwriting activities during this decade. In New York City the following new community theatres emerged: the Negro People's Theatre, organized by Dick Campbell and Rose McClendon in 1935; the Harlem Suitcase Theatre, founded by Langston Hughes around 1936; the Rose McClendon Players, a metamorphosis of the Harlem People's Theatre after the death of Rose McClendon, founded by Dick Campbell and Muriel Rahn; and the American Negro Theatre, organized by playwright-director Abram Hill in 1939. Other groups that produced the work of black playwrights during the 1930s were the Harlem Experimental Theatre and the Negro Theatre Guild in New York; the Gilpin Players of Cleveland, Ohio; the Unity Players of the Bronx, New York; and the Negro Community Theatre of Richmond, Virginia.

Oscar Micheaux continued to be the chief film screenwriter of the 1940s, having written and produced about 18 films, including *A Daughter of the Congo* (1930), an African adventure-melodrama adapted from Henry Francis Downing's novels (Downing was also a playwright), *Temptation* (1936), a seduction melodrama in the manner of Cecil B. DeMille, and *Underworld* (1936), a typical Hollywood gangster melodrama. Langston Hughes and Clarence Muse coscripted the screenplay for *Way Down South* (1939), a stereotypical plantation melodrama starring Muse and Bobby Breen. Other screenwriters of the 1930s were Donald Heywood, Eulalie Spence, and Spencer Williams. Carlton Moss wrote several radio scripts, including a soap opera series entitled *Careless Love*.

During the 1940s, playwriting activities were substantially reduced because of World War II. Scheduled productions of plays by a number of community theatre groups were cancelled after Pearl Harbor, and many playwrights served in the armed forces.

Owen Dodson, who served in the navy from 1942 to 1943, wrote a number of morale-building plays on naval, military, and civilian heroism while stationed at Camp Robert Smalls at the Great Lakes Naval Training Station in Illinois. These were produced under the title *Heroes on Parade*. After the war, he wrote scripts for the *New World A-Coming* radio series, based on the book of the same title by Roi Ottley, who also contributed scripts.

Among the professionally produced playwrights of the 1940s was Richard Wright, whose stage adaptation of his novel *Native Son,* in collaboration with white playwright Paul Green, produced by Orson Welles and John Houseman, was one of the major dramatic offerings on Broadway in 1941. It was taken on tour after its Broadway run, and a second New York production also reached Broadway in 1942/43. Starring in the role of Bigger Thomas was Canada Lee, one of the outstanding black actors of that time.

The most enduring playwright of the decade was Langston Hughes, who saw a number of his plays produced between 1940 and 1950, including *Tropics After Dark* and *Cavalcade of the Negro Theatre* (1940), at the American Negro Exposition in Chicago; *The Sun Do Move* (1942), by the Hayloft Theatre in Chicago; *That Eagle* (a patriotic play with music, 1942), at the Stage Door Canteen in New York; *Street Scene* (1947), a folk opera with libretto by Elmer Rice, lyrics by Hughes, and music by Kurt Weill, which was produced on Broadway at the Adelphi Theatre; and *Troubled Island* (an opera, 1949), with libretto by Hughes and musical score by William Grant Still, which was produced by the New York City Opera Company at City Center in New York.

Arna Bontemps and Countee Cullen saw their musical play, *St. Louis Woman,* produced on Broadway at the Martin Beck Theatre in 1946, where it ran for 115 performances.

Abram Hill (1911–1986), founder of the American Negro Theatre and its resident playwright, had three of his plays produced during the 1940s, including *On Striver's Row,* a comedy of social striving among middle-class Harlemites, produced by the Rose McClendon Players, 1940, and revived the same year by the American Negro Theatre (ANT); *Anna Lucasta,* adapted by Hill for an all-black cast from the play by Philip Yordan, produced in Harlem by ANT, and transferred to Broadway, where it played for 957 performances (a second company toured the United States, and a third went on tour in England); and *The Power of Darkness,* adapted by Hill from Leo Tolstoy's novel, produced by ANT, 1948.

Theodore Ward, whose first full-length play, *Big White Fog,* was first produced in 1938 by the Negro Unit of the Chicago Federal Theatre, saw his play again produced in New York City by the Negro Playwrights Company, a group that he helped to found, in 1940. His *Our Lan',* one of the most successful black plays of the 1940s, was produced on Broadway under the auspices of the Theatre Guild in 1947, where it also won the Theatre Guild Award.

Spencer Williams was the dominant screenwriter of the 1940s, having written and produced at least six films during the decade, including *Son of Ingagi* (1940), *The Blood of Jesus* (1941), *Go Down Death* (1944), *Marching On* and *Of One Blood* (1945), and *Juke Joint* (1947). Carlton Moss contributed the best documentary film on the participation of black servicemen in World War II, for which he received an award from the Schomburg Collection. Oscar Micheaux, the most prolific screenwriter and film producer of the 1920s, ended his lengthy film career with only one film, his last, *The Betrayal* (1948). Langston Hughes was the most prolific radio scriptwriter of the 1940s, having written a number of scripts for the war effort. Other radio scripts were written by Owen Dodson, Richard Wright, Arna Bontemps, Roi Ottley, and Arthur Clifton Lamb.

This essay has shown the origin and development of the black American playwright from the pre–Civil War period to the end of World War II. The best summary of this chronicle is given in Appendix C, which classifies by genre the plays and other dramatic works written and/or produced during each decade from the 1820s to 1950.

Mr. Brown of the African Grove Theatre was the only black playwright to emerge prior to 1840. The three decades from 1840 to 1870 were dominated by three writers, Victor Séjour, Ira Aldridge, and William Wells Brown—Brown being the only one whose works were indigenous to the United States.

From the 1870s to the turn of the century, a number of musical shows were written and produced through the collaborative efforts of several theatre artists. However, the few serious plays of this period were, for the most part, only closet dramas, privately printed but not produced.

During the first two decades of the twentieth century, musicals continued to be the major form of dramatic writing, except for the privately published plays of Henry Francis Downing and a few others, a single effort in pageantry by W.E.B. DuBois, and the propaganda plays of Angelina Grimké, Alice Dunbar-Nelson, and Mary Burrill. Oscar Micheaux was the sole filmwriter/producer to emerge prior to the 1920s.

During the Black or so-called Harlem Renaissance of the 1920s, more than 30 new black playwrights appeared on the scene, several of whom saw their works produced on Broadway or published in periodicals or anthologies; many were recipients of contest awards that were designed to stimulate playwriting and other literary activities. A number of important musicals were also cowritten by black writers during this period. Oscar Micheaux was the preeminent film-maker/scriptwriter, producing more than 20 films during this decade.

In spite of the debilitating effects of the Depression on the American economy during the 1930s, more black playwrights emerged during the 1930s than during any previous decade, mainly due to the increasing number of community and college theatre groups, the publication of several new anthologies, and the activities of the WPA Federal Theatre, which encouraged playwriting by members of its Negro Units, located in many major cities throughout the United States, from New York to Seattle, Washington.

Although a few playwrights had their works produced professionally early in the 1940s, including Richard Wright, whose *Native Son* reached Broadway in 1941, this decade saw a temporary decline in playwriting during World War II. Several playwrights were drafted into the armed forces, where many wrote scripts for the Special Services Division; other civilians devoted their writing energies to the war effort. More radio scripts emerged during this decade than previously, and one of the best films was a documentary about the role of black servicemen during the war. Nevertheless, by the mid–1940s, playwriting activities were on the increase. The American Negro Theatre, which flourished during the 1940s, reached Broadway in 1944 with its production of *Anna Lucasta,* adapted by Abram Hill in collaboration with white director Henry Wagstaff Gribble. This production boosted a number of black performers to stardom in other plays and films. Other playwrights to reach Broadway during the 1940s were Arna Bontemps and Countee Cullen (with *St. Louis Woman,* in 1946) and Theodore Ward (with *Big White Fog,* in 1947).

Although no significant playwriting awards were won by black writers prior to 1950, these pioneer playwrights nevertheless paved the way for the Golden Age of black theatre that was to follow in the fifties, sixties, seventies, and eighties, which produced such outstanding playwrights as Lorraine Hansberry (New York Drama Critics Award), Alice Childress (Obie Award), LeRoi Jones (Amiri Baraka) (Obie Award), Ed Bullins (New York Drama Critics Circle and Obie Awards), Ntozake Shange (Outer Critics' Circle Award), and three black Pulitzer Prize-winning playwrights: Charles Gordone, Charles Fuller, and August Wilson (Tony Awards).

This book is a tribute to those early black American playwrights, from Mr. Brown of the African Company of the 1820s, to Abram Hill of the American Negro Theatre of the 1940s—and such other outstanding playwrights and dramatic writers along the way as William Wells Brown, Joseph Seamon Cotter, Sr., Garland Anderson, Angelina Grimké, Alice Dunbar-Nelson, Marita Bonner, Oscar Micheaux, Jean Toomer, John Matheus, Willis Richardson, Randolph Edmonds, Langston Hughes, Owen Dodson, May Miller, Theodore Browne, Richard Wright, and Thomas Pawley (to name only a few)—for their courageous efforts to present truthful dramatizations of the lives and concerns of black people on the American stage, while also attempting to correct the distorted images and stereotypes that have too long been perpetuated by writers who lacked a true knowledge of the black experience. Although many of the plays of these playwrights remain unproduced and unpublished, and countless others have been lost, those that still survive stand as a monumental record of black artistry, culture, history, and achievement, which remains for present and future generations to discover, appreciate, and enjoy. It is my hope that this book will aid in that process.

A BIOGRAPHICAL
DIRECTORY

A

ALDRIDGE, IRA (FREDERICK) (1807–1967), Preeminent black Shakespearean actor of the nineteenth century, known as the African Roscius. Also
credited with being the third recorded black American playwright because of his
work as an adaptor of plays with strong black leading roles for inclusion in his
repertoire. Aldridge was born and reared in the United States, reputedly the son
of a Senegalese prince—a legendary heritage that he himself helped to propagate.
Educated at the African Free School in New York and later at Glasgow University
in Scotland. Gained an interest and experience in the theatre through participation
as a minor actor in the productions of the African Grove Theatre, the first resident
black theatre in the United States, which was founded by cultured West Indians
and situated near the site of present-day Broadway. There Aldridge may have
been greatly inspired by the performances of James Hewlett, the star of the
African Company, who later achieved some measure of fame for his Shakespearean roles. Also, in the nearby Park Theatre, which provided segregated
seating for blacks, and where Aldridge reputedly worked as a callboy, he was
able to see professional productions of both popular and classical plays, performed by some of the leading actors of the American and English stage. Convinced that he could not achieve success as an actor in the United State, he made
Europe his permanent home. There he developed his talents, reportedly under
the tutelage of the English actor Edmund Kean—a fact that is in dispute. It is
certain that Aldridge received the commendation of Kean and that Aldridge
performed in at least two productions with Edmund's son, Charles Kean. In any
event, Aldridge soon attained international acclaim for his portrayals of Shakespeare's Othello and King Lear, Mungo in *The Padlock,* Rollo in *Pizarro,* Ginger
Blue in *The Virginia Mammy,* Gambia in *The Slave,* Alboan in *Oronooko,* and
leading roles in his own adaptations of the two plays cited below. Among the
numerous honors received by Aldridge were the Prussian Gold Medal Award
for Arts and Science from King Frederick; the Medal of Ferdinand from Franz

Joseph of Austria (for *Othello*); the Golden Cross of Leopold from the Czar of Russia; the Golden Order of Service from the Royal House of Saxony; the Maltese Cross from Berne, Switzerland; and a chair named in his honor at the Shakespeare Memorial Theatre at Stratford-on-Avon. He was the first black American actor to achieve international fame; the first to be honored by the Republic of Haiti for his outstanding achievements, which brought honor to his race. He was twice married: first to an English woman whose first name was Margaret, who died in 1864; and second to Amanda Pauline von Brandt, a gifted Swedish singer who bore him three talented children—two daughters and a son. The boy, who bore his father's name, was a promising piano student when he died at age 23; one daughter, Luranah, became a dramatic contralto in London; the second daughter, Amanda Ira, became a composer and music teacher of some renown. Aldridge became a British citizen at age 56 and died in Poland at age 60.

Stage Works:

The Black Doctor (drama, 4 acts, 1847). Adapt. by Aldridge from *Le Docteur Noir* (1846) by French dramatists °Auguste Anicet-Bourgeois and °Pinel Dumanoir. A romantic tragedy of interracial love and marriage, involving a mulatto doctor and a beautiful white noblewoman whose life he had saved. As the plot develops, "there follows the inevitable family conflict, imprisonment, insanity, and a predictable denouement."—*BlkThUSA* (Hatch, 1974), p. 3. Historically important as the second recorded play in English by a black American playwright, although an adaptation (see credit line below). First prod. on the English stage, in Aldridge's adaptn., in Bath and Dublin, 1847, with Aldridge in the title role. Pub. in Dick's Standard Plays, London, 1870, with the credit line "by Ira Aldridge" on the cover; by DeWitt Pub. House, 1880s; and in *BlkThUSA*, which includes critical commentary. OTHER COMMENTARY: See Marshall & Stock, cited below.

Titus Andronicus (adaptn., full length, 1849). By Aldridge in collaboration with °C. A. Somerset. From the play by William Shakespeare. Alterations consisted mainly in turning Aaron the Moor into the central character, the omission of horror scenes, while retaining the "poetic gems," and the interpolation of great scenes from other plays. First perf. of record, with Aldridge in the title role, in Paisley, Scotland, Nov. 1849. Also presented in Belfast, Ireland, May 13, 1850; and in Edinburgh, Scotland, July 24, 1850. COMMENTARY: See Marshall & Stock.

FURTHER REFERENCE: *Blk. World* 4–1972. *DANB*. *Ira Aldridge* (Marshall & Stock).

ALEXANDER, LEWIS M. (1900–1945), Actor, poet, essayist, theatre director and pioneer playwright of the 1920s. Born and educated in Washington, DC, where he attended Dunbar High School and Howard Univ. Also studied at the Univ. of Pennsylvania. Appeared on Broadway in 1923 in the Ethiopian Art Players' production of *Salome* and *The Comedy of Errors*. Was a member of the Playwriters' Circle and the Ira Aldridge Players, and directed several black theatre groups in Washington, including the St. Vincent de Paul Players, the Ira Aldridge Players of Grover Cleveland School, and the Randall Community Center Players. His poetry has appeared in *Crisis, Carolina Magazine,* and in several anthologies of black writers, including those of Locke, Byars, and Davis & Peplow, cited among references below.

Stage Work:
Pierrot at Sea (harlequinade, 1 act, 1929). Prod. by the Krigwa Players, Washington, DC, Fall 1929.

Other Pertinent Writing:
"Plays of Negro Life: A Survey," *Carolina Mag.*, April 1929, pp. 45–47.
FURTHER REFERENCE: *Blk. and Wh.* (J. C. Byars, Jr., Crane, Washington, DC, 1927). *Caroling Dusk* (Cullen). Hicklin diss. *New Neg.* (Locke). *NewNegRen* (Davis & Peplow). *ReadingsNA* (Cromwell et al.)

ALLISON, HUGHES (deceased), Short story writer and Federal Theatre playwright of the 1930s, associated with the Newark, NJ, Negro Unit and the National Service Bureau. A native of Newark, he was the grandson of a Reconstruction period judge; his mother had been a concert pianist. He was educated at Upsala College in East Orange, NJ, where he majored in English and history before joining the Federal Theatre Project (FTP). He was married to Elitea Anderson, who survived him. His short stories were published in *Challenge* (Feb. 1938) and *Ellery Queen Magazine*. Hallie Flanagan, director of FTP, called him "one of the best Negro playwrights in America."—Ross, Ph.D. diss. (1972), p. 150. Alain Locke wrote that "the talent of Hughes Allison, more mature in dramatic technique than any Negro playwright to date, warrants hopeful watching and encouragement."—*Opportunity,* Feb. 1938, p. 39.

Stage Works:
The Trial of Dr. Beck (courtroom melodrama, 3 acts, 1937). A mulatto doctor is on trial in a white court for the murder of his dark-skinned wife, whom he did not love. Although he is subsequently acquitted, the trial affords an opportunity for extensive analysis of black middle-class color complexes and of the paradoxes and ironies of race prejudice. Significant as one of the earliest plays (approximately the ninth) by a black American playwright to be produced on Broadway. Opened in Union City and Newark, NJ, where it was prod. by the New Jersey Negro Unit of FTP. Transferred to the Maxine Elliot Theatre on Broadway, Aug. 9, 1937, where it ran for four weeks; dir. by Louis M. Simon. With Kenneth Renwick in the title role and William Bendix, the noted film star, also in the cast, which featured Tessie Green, Jane Ferrell, Clifford Dempsey, and Frank Harrington. Also prod. by the Harlem Unit of the WPA Federal Theatre Project. Unpub. script in Hatch-Billops and in FTP/GMU. COMMENTARY: *NegPlaywrs* (Abramson, 1969), pp. 63–64. *NYT* 8–10–1937.

Panyared (c. 1938). The first play in a projected trilogy; it resulted from the author's "extended research as a member of the National Service Bureau."—*Free, Adult, Uncensored: The Living History of the Federal Theatre Project* (O'Connor & Brown, 1978), p. 22. About an African prince who was sold into slavery. The trilogy "would have followed the progress of the young prince, his son, and grandson, up through the Civil War and Reconstruction periods."—Ibid. Unprod. because of the closing of the Federal Theatre in 1939. Unpub. script and a separately written *Foreword to Panyared* in Hatch-Billops and FTP/GMU.

It's Midnight over Newark (living newspaper doc., 3 acts, 1941). Dramatizes the plight of Newark, NJ's black physicians during the period when they were denied the

opportunity to practice in the city's hospitals. Prod. at the Mosque Theatre, Newark, May 1941. Unpub. script in Hatch-Billops.
FURTHER REFERENCE: Taped interview of Mrs. Hughes Allison in Hatch-Billops.

ANDERSON, ALFRED. See Appendix B.

ANDERSON, GARLAND (1886–1939), Former bellhop, philosopher of constructive thinking, and pioneer playwright. Achieved national fame as "The San Francisco Bellhop Playwright." [See publicity photo in *AnthANT* (Patterson), p. 85, or *BlkMagic* (Hughes & Meltzer), p. 220.] Credited with being the first black American to have a serious, full-length play produced on Broadway. Born in Wichita, KS, where he completed only four years of formal schooling before his family moved to California. Worked as a bellhop in a San Francisco hotel, where he impressed the guests with his optimistic philosophy of life; namely, that the subconscious mind can accomplish all things through faith. After seeing a production of Channing Pollock's moralistic drama *The Fool,* Anderson decided to write a play that would carry his message of optimism to a wider audience. With no training in playwriting or stage technique, he completed his first play, **Appearances** (1924), in only three weeks. Failing to find a producer, he personally raised $15,000 toward the production, and in spite of numerous obstacles his play opened on Broadway in 1925. The story of his achievement in the face of overwhelming racial, financial, and educational limitations was widely publicized and considered a better drama and more convincing proof of the efficacy of his constructive philosophy than was the play itself, which enjoyed only a modest run. Following his triumph in America, his play was produced in London, where he met his wife, Doris, a white Englishwoman who wrote her memoirs of her life with Garland, *Nigger Lover* (1938). Anderson is credited with having written three other plays, but only one other title has been located. He spent the last period of his life lecturing on constructive thinking and wrote a book on his beliefs entitled *Uncommon Sense* (1933).

Stage Works:
Appearances // Orig. title: **Don't Judge by Appearances** // copyrighted as **Judge Not According to Appearances** (drama, 3 acts, prologue, and epilogue, 1924). Concerns the trial of a morally upright black bellhop named Carl (played by the fair-skinned black Venezuelan actor Lionel Monagas, who was generally thought at the time to be white), who is falsely charged with attempted rape of a white woman. One of Carl's friends is a stereotypical comic black character named Rufus, who is also implicated in the crime as an accessory. (Rufus was played by Doe Doe Green, a dark-skinned actor, and was widely reported in the press as the only black actor in the cast with a leading role.) Although both men are exonerated, they are acquitted not by virtue of their innocence, but by the revelation that the woman who accuses them is a person of disreputable character—actually "a light-skinned Negress" passing for white! Public reading held at the Waldorf-Astoria Hotel, New York, April 1925, with the noted actor Richard B. Harrison as reader. Prod. by Lester W. Wagar, premiering in Scranton, PA, Sept. 28, 1925, prior to opening on Bway at the Frolic Theatre, Oct. 13, 1925, where it played

for 23 perfs.; dir. by °John Hayden. Other cast members (all white) included Frank Hatch (as Judge Thornton), Louis Frohoff (Judge Robinson), Mildred Hall (Elsie), Robert Toms (Fred Kellard), Joseph Sweeney (Jack Wilson), Daisy Atherton (Mrs. Thompson), Edward Keane (Frank Thompson), and Evelyn Mason (Ella). Toured the United States, playing in San Francisco, Los Angeles, Chicago, and other mid-western cities. Prod. for the second time in New York by C. Mischell Picard, with a revised script (making the prosecuting attorney, and not the woman accuser, the villain), opening at the Hudson Theatre, April 1, 1929, for 24 perfs.; staged by °Lee Miller. With a new cast, except for Doe Doe Green, who appeared in his orig. role. Prod. in London at the Royalty Theatre, opening in March 1930. Pub. in *BlkThUSA* (Hatch, 1974), which also includes commentary. Film reproduction of orig. script in TC/NYPL. REVIEWS AND OTHER COM-MENTARY: *BesPls 1925–26; 1928–29. Messenger* 6–1924. *NY Age* 11–7–1925. *NYT* 4–7–1925; 6–21–1925; 8–22–1925; 9–12–1925; 10–15–1925; 11–2–1925; 3–3–1930. *NY World* 10–30–1925. *SF News* 9–11–1925. *Vancouver Sun* 7–4–1925. *Wall St. J.* 10–27–1925. Copies of reviews in Anderson scrapbook, cited below.

Extortion (drama, full length, 1929). Nonracial play, sold to David Belasco in 1929, but apparently never prod. COMMENTARY: *NY Eve. J.* 10–7–1929.

Other Pertinent Writings:
From Newsboy and Bellhop to Playwright. San Francisco, privately printed, c. 1929.
"My Experience in Writing and Having 'Appearances' Produced," *Everyman* (London), May 1928, 19 pp.; copy in Moorland-Spingarn. Reprinted as "How I Became a Playwright," *AnthANT* (Patterson, 1967), pp. 85–86.
FURTHER REFERENCE: *AnthANT* (Patterson). *BlkMagic* (Hughes & Meltzer). Garland Anderson Scrapbook, TC/NYPL. Monroe diss. Hicklin diss. *NegGen* (Brawley). *NegPlaywrs* (Abramson). *Nigger Lover* (D. Anderson).

ANDREWS, REGINA M. (Regina Anderson; Mrs. William T. Andrews; Ursala Trelling, pseud.) (1901–   ), Public librarian, black theatre organizer, and outstanding figure of the Harlem Renaissance. Born Regina M. Anderson in Chicago. Educated at Wilberforce University, the University of Chicago, CCNY, and Columbia University library school. Apparently she first worked as a public librarian in Chicago before coming to New York City during the early 1920s as a staff member of the 135th Street Branch of the New York Public Library (NYPL). It was in this branch that the Schomburg Collection was established. Also, it was in the basement of this library that W.E.B. DuBOIS had earlier established the Krigwa Little Negro Theatre in 1926, and where the then Miss Anderson helped to organize a few years later the Harlem Experimental Theatre (Exp. Th.)—with Harold Jackman, Jessie Fauset, Dorothy Williams, Gladys Reid, Benjamin Locke, and Inez Wilson—and served as its executive director. Several of her plays (of which only two titles have been located) were produced by this group and directed by Jackman. Anderson, who has been described as a woman of great beauty, shared an apartment with Ethel Ray Nance and Luella Tucker at 580 St. Nicholas Ave., which became a salon for artists and intellectuals of the period. Later married to New York assemblyman William T. Andrews, Regina became head librarian of the 115th St. Branch of NYPL and was the first woman of any race to head a public library branch in New

York City. She retired from NYPL in 1947. Author of *Intergroup Relations in the United States: A Compilation of Source Materials and Service Organizations* (1959). Recipient of numerous civic awards; she was one of 10 outstanding black women honored at the New York World's Fair of 1939.

Stage Works:

Climbing Jacob's Ladder (drama, 1 act, 1931). Written as Ursala Trelling. Described by the author as "the story of a lynching [that] took place while people were in church praying."—*VoicesBT* (Mitchell, 1975). She goes on to state: "This was one of my first plays. . . . When I was a child and first heard of lynchings, they were incomprehensible. It's understandable that in my twenties I would have to write about lynching. And I did, in the year 1931."—Ibid., p. 78. She then submitted the play to her mentor, W.E.B. DuBois, for criticism and, at his suggestion, rewrote it. It was eventually produced by the Harlem Exp. Th., at the 135th St. Library Branch, New York, 1931; dir. by Harold Jackman. DuBois, who was invited to see the production, wrote to her afterward: "Your play was thrilling. I enjoyed it immensely, and it gripped the audience. Congratulations."—Ibid., p. 79.

Underground (drama, 1 act, 1932). Written as Ursala Trelling. Historical play of slave escape through the famed Underground Railroad. Prod. as a joint venture of the Dramatic Committee of the NYPL Staff Assn. and the Harlem Exp. Th. Presented at the New School for Social Research, New York, opening April 4, 1932, for 2 perfs., and at St. Philips Parish House, Harlem, April 7, 1932, for 2 add. perfs.; dir. by Harold Jackman.

FURTHER REFERENCE: *AfrAmWW* (Shockley). *HarlRenD* (Kellner). Taped interview of Regina Andrews in Hatch-Billops. *VoicesBTh* (Mitchell).

ARCHER, LEONARD C. (Courtney) (1911–1974), University professor, drama director, and black theatre historian. Born in Atlanta, GA. Educated at Morehouse Academy (secondary school) and Morehouse College (B.A. 1934), where his father, Dr. Samuel Howard Archer, was president; the University of Toronto/Ontario (M.A. 1940); and Ohio State University (Ph.D., with a major in theatre and a minor in radio and dramatic literature, 1956). Married to Alice Durham, who in 1983 was a sociology teacher at Tennessee State University. Taught English and dramatics in Georgia, Mississippi, and Arkansas before accepting the chairmanship of the Speech and Drama Dept. at Central State College (now University), Wilberforce, OH. After earning his doctorate, he joined the faculty of Tennessee State University/Nashville in 1956, as professor of dramatic literature. Author of *From Confucius to Dante* (1960) and *Black Images in the American Theatre* (1973), the latter based on his Ph.D. dissertation, "The National Association for the Advancement of Colored People and the American Theatre" (1950). Member of AETA, CLA, SADSA, NADSA (vice pres., 1946), and A.M.E. Church. Recipient of Dr. Christian Award for radio scriptwriting, 1943; Governor's Award for contribution to the success of the Ohio Sesquicentennial historical drama, "The Seventeenth Star"; Mayor's Award for work with Nashville Committee on Metropolitan Zoning Ordinance; and numerous other civic, athletic, and dramatic awards.

Stage and Broadcast Works:
Frederick Douglass: A Testament of Freedom (black history docudrama, with traditional music; called by the author "A Cantata" [subtitle], 1950). A tribute to the famed abolitionist and race leader, whom the author calls "the Moses [of the black people], raised up by God, to deliver a modern Israel from bondage."—Pub. script, p. 138. Characters include Anna Douglass, William Lloyd Garrison, and John Brown. Written and prod. "in observance of the twenty-fifth annual celebration of Negro History Week," at the State College of Education (now Central State University), Wilberforce, OH, 1950. Pub. in *Neg. Hist. Bull.*, March 1950, pp. 134–39.

Crosswise (children's play, 1 act, 1950). Prod. by Wilberforce College of Education (now Wilberforce University) at the Fourth Annual Conf. of SADSA, held at Kentucky State College/Frankfort, April 27–28, 1950.

Heralds of the Cross (docudrama, full length, 1956). Written and prod. for the Wilberforce University Centennial Celebration, c. 1956.

Other Pertinent Writings:
"Negro Life as a Folk Basis in Contemporary American Drama," Master of Arts thesis, Univ. of Toronto, 1940.

"The National Association for the Advancement of Colored People and the American Theatre: A Study of Relationships and Influences," Ph.D. diss., 2 vols., Ohio State Univ., 1956. Copies available from Univ. Microfilms, Ann Arbor, MI.

Black Images in the American Theatre. Pageant-Poseidon Ltd., New York, 1973.

ASHBY, WILLIAM M. (Mobile) (1889–?), Urban League executive, finance corporation manager, theatre organizer, and pioneer playwright. A graduate of Lincoln University in Pennsylvania and Yale University. Exec. secy. of the Newark, NJ, branch of the National Urban League; later exec. secy. of the Springfield, IL, branch. Organized the Bank St. Players in Newark, late 1920s, which was reportedly the first black little theatre group in the state.—*NY Age,* May 7, 1927. In addition to three plays, he wrote a novel, *The Redder Blood* (1915), and numerous articles on social problems, published mainly in *Opportunity* (the official organ of the National Urban League) between 1927 and 1947.

Stage Works:
Helen Harmon (1927). Prod. by the Bank St. Players, at the Robert Treat School, Newark, April 29, 1927.

The Road to Damascus (biblical drama, 7 episodes, 1935). About Paul the Apostle. Pub. by Christopher Pub. House, Boston, 1935; copy in Moorland-Spingarn.

Booker T. Washington // Orig. title: **Let Me Die in the South** (biographical drama, 3 acts, 1939). About the founder of Tuskegee Institute and famed race leader, who advocated industrial education as the way to economic and racial progress for blacks in the South. The play begins in the decade following the founding of Tuskegee and covers the remainder of Washington's career. Characters portrayed include Washington's wife Margaret, T. Thomas Fortune, William H. Baldwin, John D. Rockefeller, Theodore Roosevelt, Andrew Carnegie, and numerous others. Prod. by the Rose McClendon Players at the Harlem Branch Lib., New York, March 27–April 13, 1940; dir. by *Dick Campbell. Professional actor Dooley Wilson starred in the role of Washington, with Add Bates and P. Jay Sidney also in the cast.

AUSTIN, ELSIE, Attorney, public official, and lecturer. The first black woman graduate of the University of Cincinnati Law College. Served with the United States Information Agency (USIA) in Nairobi, Kenya. Also served as an assistant state attorney general.

Stage Work:

Blood Doesn't Tell (thesis play, 1 act, 1945). "About Blood Plasma and Blood Donors" [subtitle]. Propaganda in support of the efforts of Dr. Charles Drew, who established the first blood bank during World War II, dispelling the popular notion that the blood of black people would contaminate white blood if mixed in transfusions. Pub. by the Woman's Press, New York, 1945.

FURTHER REFERENCE: *Ebony* 8–1947.

B

BATES, H. JACK, Playwright associated with the Boston Negro Unit of the WPA Federal Theatre Project during the mid–1930s.

Stage Works:
(All mid–1930s)
Cinda. Prod. by the WPA Federal Theatre, at the Bijou Theatre, Boston, c. 1935. Unpub. script reportedly in FTP/GMU, but has not been located.
Dear Morpheus (fantasy, 9 scenes). Deals with love and marriage from the time of Adam and Eve to the present day. Unpub. script in Hatch-Billops.
Streets of Gold. Unpub. script reportedly in FTP/GMU, but has not been located.
OTHER PLAYS: **Black Acres. The Legend of Jo Emma. The Lost Disciple. Yules**.

BAXTER, (Rev.) DANIEL MINORT (1872–1938), African Methodist Episcopal (A.M.E.) minister, church author, and playwright. Author of *Back to Methodism* (1926).

Stage Work:
Richard Allen: From a Slave to the First Bishop of African Methodist Episcopal Church, 1716–1816 (church history play, 4 acts, 1934). About the founder of the A.M.E. Church, the oldest black religious denomination in the United States. Pub. by A.M.E. Book Concern, Philadelphia, 1934; copy in Moorland-Spingarn.

BLACK, JEAN BELCHER. See Appendix A.

BOND, FREDERICK W. (Weldon) (deceased), Pioneer black historian, for many years professor of speech and drama at West Virginia State College (now University), Institute, WV. Received his Ph.D. from New York University in 1938. His dissertation, ''The Direct and Indirect Contributions Which the American Negro Has Made to the Drama and to the Legitimate Stage, with the

Underlying Conditions Responsible,'' was one of the pioneer studies in the field, and was published as *The Negro and the Drama* (1940).

Stage Work:

Family Affair (drama, 1 act, 1939). Described by the author as ''the story of a family that has become victimized by the Depression. Unable to find employment, Henry, the chief character, is reduced to humiliating distress. The situation is all the more desperate [because] the family has to eat and sleep in the same room [and] the relatives make their visits frequent and long.''—*Neg&Dr* (Bond, 1940), p. 189. Apparently prod. at West Virginia State Coll., Institute, WV, 1939. Unpub. script in Moorland-Spingarn.

Other Pertinent Writings:

See biographical sketch.

BONNER, MARITA O. (Odette) (Mrs. Marita Bonner Occomy) (1899–1971), Author, homemaker, and mother; pioneer playwright of the 1920s; a product of the literary activities of *Crisis* and *Opportunity* magazines. Born in Brookline, MA. Received the A.B. from Radcliffe in 1922, where she majored in English and studied writing under Charles Townsend Copeland (a distinction accorded only 16 students per academic year). Taught English at Bluefield Colored Institute, Bluefield, VA, 1922–24; and Armstrong High School, Washington, DC, 1925–30. Winner of a *Crisis* Award in 1925 for her essay ''On Being Young—a Woman—and Colored,'' pub. in *Crisis,* Dec. 1925, p. 63. [Note that the title anticipates by more than 45 years °Robert Nemiroff's portrait of *Lorraine Hansberry, *To Be Young, Gifted and Black* (1971).] Received honorable mention in the *Opportunity* Awards, 1925, for her short story ''The Hands,'' pub. in *Opportunity,* Aug. 1925, pp. 235–37. Awarded first prize in the *Crisis* Contest Awards of 1927 for four of her works, including a short story (''Drab Rambles''), an essay (''The Young Blood Hungers''), and two plays (**The Purple Flower** and **Exit, an Illusion**). Married to William Occomy, an accountant, in 1930, and resigned her teaching post the same year. During this period, she gave birth to three children and worked as a secretary for a Washington, DC, settlement house for blacks. From 1927 to 1935, she was actively involved with the Washington, DC, branch of the Krigwa Players, which also included playwright WILLIS RICHARDSON. She was also a member of a literary salon, ''The Saturday Nighters,'' which met at the home of playwright GEORGIA DOUGLAS JOHNSON. More interested in writing fiction than plays, Bonner published 14 of her short stories in *Crisis* and *Opportunity* magazines and by 1939 was ''well-known to readers of Negro publications for the excellent fiction she [had] written during the past ten years.''—*Crisis,* Dec. 1939, p. 358. Moved to Chicago during the 1940s, where she resumed her teaching career at Phillips High School, 1944–49, and Doolittle School, 1950–63. Died in 1971 from the effects of a fire in her Chicago apartment.

Collection:

FRYE STREET AND ENVIRONS: The Collected Works of Marita Bonner. Ed. with an intro. by Joyce Flynn and Joyce Stricklin. Beacon Press, Boston, 1987. Includes the author's stage works.

Stage Works:

Exit, an Illusion (fantasy, 1 act, 1927). Experimental dream play dealing with the psychological effects of color complexes among blacks, also utilizing expressionistic stage techniques. Buddy, a dark-skinned black man, is extremely jealous of his fair-skinned girlfriend Dot, although he refuses to admit that he loves her. When Dot announces that she is preparing for a date with Exit Man, Buddy becomes enraged, believing that Exit Man is white. When Exit arrives, Buddy shoots at him, putting out the light instead of killing him. Striking a match to see in the dark, Buddy discovers Dot's lifeless body, and now realizes that the mysterious visitor named Exit is in reality Death. Won first prize (jointly with the author's **Purple Flower**) in the *Crisis* Contest Awards of 1927. Pub. in *Crisis,* Oct. 1923, pp. 339–40; and in the author's *FRYE STREET AND ENVIRONS*. COMMENTARY: Austin diss.

The Pot Maker (melodrama, 1 act, 1927). A jealous husband engineers the "accidental" drowning of his wife's lover. Pub. in *Opportunity,* Feb. 1927, pp. 43–46, and in *Wines in the Wilderness* (Brown-Guillory, 1990).

The Purple Flower (fantasy, 1 act, 1927). Allegorical treatment of black-white relations in the United States, in which blacks are depicted as wormlike creatures living in the valley, trying to climb the Hill of Somewhere to reach the purple flower of Life-at-Its-Finest; and whites as the "sundry devils" living on the side of the hill, using every artful trick to keep the "worms" from getting to the top. Won first place (jointly with the author's **Exit, an Illusion**) in the *Crisis* Contest Awards of 1927. Pub. in *Crisis,* Jan. 1928, pp. 9–11, 28; in *BlkThUSA* (Hatch, 1974), which also includes commentary; and in the author's *FRYE STREET AND ENVIRONS*. OTHER COMMENTARY: Austin diss. *BlkPlots* (Southgate).

FURTHER REFERENCE: Austin diss. *HarlRenD* (Kellner).

BONTEMPS, ARNA (Wendell) (1902–1973), Poet, playwright, biographer, historian, novelist, author of short stories and children's fiction, essayist, editor, and librarian. One of the important literary figures arising from the Harlem Renaissance. Born in Alexandria, VA; reared in Los Angeles. Married to Alberta Johnson, 1926; the father of five children. Educated at San Fernando (CA) Academy (1917–20); Pacific Union College, Angwin, CA (A.B. 1923); the University of Chicago (A.M. in Lib. Science, 1943). Rosenwald Fellow, 1938–39, 1942–43; Guggenheim Fellow, 1949–50, 1954. Taught for several years at a number of private schools, including the Harlem Academy in New York City, 1924–31: Oakland Jr. College, Huntsville, AL, 1932–35; the Shiloh Academy, Chicago, 1935–38. For many years, 1943–65, head librarian, and later public relations director and writer-in-residence, at Fisk University in Nashville, TN. Following a brief period as professor at the University of Illinois, 1966–69, and as curator of the James Weldon Johnson Memorial Collection at Yale University (JWJ/YUL), 1969–71, he returned to Fisk as librarian emeritus and writer-in-residence, where he remained until his death in 1973. A prolific writer since the 1920s, he has contributed more than 30 individual written and coauthored volumes to American literature, as well as innumerable shorter writings that have been widely published in periodicals and anthologies. Among his most significant works are *God Sends Sunday* (novel, 1931); *Black Thunder* (novel, 1936); *Father*

search of New York City directories of 1820–21 and discovered an entry for one James Brown, black, who resided at 56 Mercer Street. This is the same vicinity where our [Mister] Brown is credited with having established the African Grove Theatre—at the corner of Mercer and Bleeker Streets—in 1821. After Brown's retirement as a ship's steward, he established a summer tea garden on Thomas Street in 1816/17, which was enlivened by musical and dramatic entertainment provided by talented members of the black community, who formed the nucleus of what later became known as the African Company. Brown's tea garden and his African Company became so successful that he moved his establishment to the site of the old African Grove Hospital at Mercer and Bleeker Streets, converting the second story of the building into the African Grove Theatre—presumably using the first story for the tea garden, which could now operate in both summer and winter months. The African Grove Theatre flourished from 1820 to 1823, offering performances of Shakespeare and other classical and popular plays, programs of classical music and opera, and ballet. This theatre, which operated near the site of the famous Park Theatre (the oldest legitimate theatre in New York City), was extremely popular with black audiences and seated approximately 300 patrons, including whites, who were allowed to sit in a special section. During the three-year period of the theatre's operation, it was under constant harassment by a few white hoodlums who attended the performances only to make fun, and from the police, who once arrested the entire cast of a production of *Richard III* and ordered them never to do Shakespeare again! The theatre was finally closed by police in 1823, ostensibly for violation of several city ordinances, including disturbance of the peace. *Samuel A. Hay, professor of theatre arts at Morgan State University, has theorized that the African Company was an economic threat to the nearby Park Theatre, which had a segregated seating gallery for black patrons, and conjectures that Brown's theatre was closed because it attracted black customers away from the Park Theatre, thereby greatly reducing its profits.—"Final Report, National Conf. on Black American Protest Drama and Theatre, Morgan State Univ., Baltimore, 1985," p. 2. In any event, both Brown and the African Grove Theatre seem to have disappeared from the public record after 1823, although there seems to be some evidence that the theatre moved for a short time to another site. In honor of this playwright, an annual Mister Brown Award was established in 1985 by the National Conf. on African American Theatre, held each year since 1985 at Morgan State University under the direction of Samuel Hay (cited above). The first recipients of the Mister Brown Award, presented in 1985, were RANDOLPH EDMONDS, to whom it was awarded posthumously, and ARTHUR CLIFTON LAMB. The Mister Brown Award is presented for excellence and other pioneering achievements in African American Theatre.

Stage Works:
Tom and Jerry; or, Life in London (adaptn., full length [9–10 scenes], c. 1823). "Got up under the Direction of Mr. Brown."—Extant playbill in TC/NYPL. According to the *Annals of the N.Y. Stage* (Odell, vol. 3, p. 70), the orig. play had first been

presented at the Park Theatre on March 3, 1823, where it might have been seen by Brown. Scenes and performers listed for this adaptn. were as follows: Scene 1, "Life in the Country," with Mr. Williams (Corinthian Tom) and Mr. Jackson (Jerry Hawthorn); Scene 2, "Life on Foot," with Mr. Bates ([Bob] Logic) and Mr. Jackson (Tommy Green); Scene 3, "Life on Horse Back," with Mr. Matthews (the Honorable Dick Trifle) and Mr. Bates (Gullem); Scene 4, "Life in Fancy," with Mr. Dusenberry (Cap), Mr. Jackson (Primefit), Miss Peterson (Miss Tartar), and Miss Johnson (Jane); Scene 5, "Life in the Dark," with Mr. Smith (Watchman) and Mr. Johnson (Dusty Bob); Scene 6, "Life in Rags," with Mr. Wilson (Crib) and Mr. Jackson (African Sal); Scene 7, "Life in Bond Street," with Miss Davis ([K]ate) and Miss Foot (Sue); Scene 8, "Life in Wapping," with Miss Johnson and Mr. Davis (*sic*); and an additional scene, not in the orig. prodn., "Life . . . in Charleston, On the Slave Market," with Mr. Smith (Auctioneer) and Members of the Company (Slaves). *Carlton Molette has characterized "On the Slave Market" as "an afterpiece, . . . apparently a farce lampooning the institution of slavery."—*Players,* April-May 1970, pp. 162–63. Brown's adaptn. of *Tom and Jerry* was presented by the African Company, at the African Grove Theatre, Saturday evening, June 7, 1823; and scheduled to be presented again "on Monday evening next," with a promised additional scene, "Life in Fulton Street."—Extant playbill, op. cit. No extant script.

King Shotaway // Also known as **The Drama of King Shotaway** (historical drama, full length, 1823). Significant as the first orig. play by a black American playwright. "Founded on facts, taken from the Insurrection of the Caravs [Caribs] on the Island of St. Vincent. Written from experience by Mr. Brown."—Extant playbill, quoted in *Annals of the N.Y. Stage,* op. cit., pp. 79–81. About the insurrection of the Black Caribs of St. Vincent's Island in the West Indies, led by their paramount chief Joseph Chatoyer (called in this play *King Shotaway*) and his brother Duvallé, or DuVallet (here called Prince Duvalls), to avoid being driven off their island by British military forces in order to make room for English settlers to peacefully establish large, profitable sugar plantations there. [HISTORICAL NOTE: The Black Caribs, descendants of fugitive slaves from other West Indian islands, had intermixed with the predominantly Indian population known as Yellow Caribs, and eventually overpowered them as their population increased. When the island was intermittently settled by the French in the early 1700s, the Black Caribs assimilated French culture, language, names, and manners in order to avoid being mistaken for the slaves that the French brought with them to St. Vincent. By 1770 the British government assumed possession of the island and was determined to settle the land by eventually conquering and enslaving the Black Caribs. Led by Chief Chatoyer and his brother, the Caribs fiercely resisted encroachment upon their land by brutal guerrilla warfare, which resulted in a peace treaty between the Crown and the Caribs that lasted some 20 years. Encouraged by the French (who had been ousted by the British), the Caribs revolted against the British in 1795, as the boundaries of their original territory began to be greatly reduced and redefined in order that the planters could have access to the best sugar lands. By this time, however, the British had greatly strengthened their military forces and were able to resist the guerrilla tactics of the Caribs with greater effectiveness. Chatoyer, who had come to believe the legends concerning his own invincibility, made the fatal mistake of challenging a trained English officer to a duel by swords, in which the Carib chief, greatly at a disadvantage, was killed. His followers, now without a leader, were forced to flee to other islands in the Caribbean or to Central and South America to avoid being decimated or enslaved by the British.—Based on *The Rise and Fall of the Black Caribs of St. Vincent* (Kirby & Martin, 1972).] The play was prod. by the African Company, at the African Grove Theatre in 1823, the exact date of the first perf. not recorded. Presented for the second time, as a benefit to Brown, on June 20–21, for 2 perfs., with the following cast: James Hewlett (King Shotaway [Chatoyer], paramount chief of the Black Caribs), Mr. Bates (Prince Duvalls [DuVallé], the king's brother and principal advisor), Miss Hicks (Queen Margaretta, one of the king's many wives), Miss Lavatt (Queen Caroline, another of the king's wives), Mr. Benedict (General Hunter, a British army officer), and Mr. Matthews (Colonel Garden, another British army officer). No extant script.

BROWN, MANUEL W., Washington, DC, public school teacher, who in 1940 taught at the Anthony Bowen School. Studied radio in education at New York University.

Stage and Broadcast Work:

George Washington Carver, the Wizard of Tuskegee (radio-style public school docudrama, with musical sequences, 3 short acts [6 scenes], 1940). About Tuskegee Institute's famed agricultural chemist, who developed 200 products from the peanut and 100 products from the sweet potato. Focuses on Carver's slave origin; his kidnapping as a baby by night riders; his eventual return to his master, who traded a horse for him, raised him, and named him after himself (Carver) and President George Washington; his being welcomed to the faculty of Tuskegee by President Booker T. Washington; and his eventual contributions. Musical sequences consisted of spirituals and classical master-pieces. Prod. before the student body of the Anthony Bowen School, Washington, DC, 1940; dir. by the author. Pub. in *Neg. Hist. Bull.*, May 1948, pp. 117–20.

BROWN, WILLIAM WELLS (1815–1884), Historian, novelist, abolitionist, lecturer, practical physician, and playwright. Born a slave on a plantation near Lexington, KY. His master moved to the vicinity of St. Louis, MO, where Brown grew to manhood under three different owners, until he was able to escape from bondage while traveling with his last owner to Cincinnati. Took his middle name and surname from a Quaker friend and benefactor, William Wells. First settled in Cleveland, where he worked hard, educated himself, and married his first wife, Elizabeth Schooner, in 1834, by whom he had three daughters. Moved his family first to Buffalo, then to Farmington, NY, a small town near Rochester. During this period, he worked on Lake Erie steamships, in which capacity he was able to assist the Underground Railroad in conducting escaped slaves to freedom in Canada. Actively participated in temperance society and antislavery society meetings in New York, thereby obtaining valuable ex-perience in public speaking. Later moved to Boston, where he became a lecturer for both the Massachusetts and the American Anti-Slavery Societies. In 1847 he completed the first of his many books, *Narrative of William Wells Brown, a Fugitive Slave, Written by Himself,* which was published both in America and Great Britain. Traveled abroad in 1849 as a representative of the American Peace Society to the International Peace Congress in Paris, and as an antislavery cru-sader and lecturer in England, where he sought to win British support for this cause. Although he had planned to return to the United States sooner, he was forced to remain in England for several years because of the passage of the harsh U.S. Fugitive Slave Act of 1860, under which he could have been arrested and returned to slavery because he had never been legally freed. While his friends in England worked to purchase his freedom, Brown wrote and published several books and pamphlets and undertook the private study of practical medicine. By 1854 he was able to return to the United States as a free man, after which he became a "dermapathic and practical physician" while continuing his writing and lecturing activities. His first wife having died while he was abroad, Brown married Annie Elizabeth Gray in 1860 and had two children by her, both of whom died in early childhood. Earlier, in 1856, he completed the first of his two antislavery plays, **Experience; or, How to Give a Northern Man a Backbone;** and the following year he completed and published **The Escape; or, A Leap for Freedom**. Neither of these plays was produced, but Brown gave many public readings of them during his many lectures at antislavery meetings and lyceum programs. Although he was technically the third black American playwright of record, Brown was the first to be born in slavery, the first to write a full-length drama on the problems of American slavery, and the first to have a play published in the United States. He is also credited with being the first black American novelist and one of the earliest black historians and writers of travel books. His novel, *Clotel; or, The President's Daughter* (London, 1853), was published in three modified versions in the United States before the original version (referring by its title to the alleged mulatto daughter of President Thomas Jefferson by his slave mistress) was eventually published in 1969. In this country, it was first serialized as *Miralda; or, The Beautiful Quadroon: A Romance of American Slavery, Founded on Fact* (1860–61); then published in book form as *Clotelle: A Tale of the Southern States* (1864); and later as *Clotelle; or, The Colored Heroine: A Tale of the Southern States* (1867). His travel book, *Three Years in Europe; or, Places I Have Seen and People I Have Met* (London, 1852), was published in America as *The American Fugitive in Europe: Sketches of Places and People Abroad* (1855). His histories include *The Black Man: His Antecedents, His Genius and His Achievements* (1853), *The Negro in the American Rebellion: His Heroism and His Fidelity* (1867), and *The Rising Son; or, The Antecedents and Achievements of the Colored Race* (1874). Brown died in his home in Chelsea, MA, near Boston, at the age of 69, from a tumor of the bladder. He was survived by his second wife and two children of his first marriage.

Collection:
WORKS OF WILLIAM WELLS BROWN. Kraus Reprint, New York, 1970. Contains: **The Escape; or, A Leap for Freedom** (1857).

Stage Works:
Experience; or, How to Give a Northern Man a Backbone // Orig. title: **Doughface** (antislavery drama, full length, 1856). A northern white minister, who previously had been defending slavery in his sermons (a type referred to in the slang of the period as a "doughface"), is himself kidnapped and sold into slavery, where he learns through "experience" to abhor the institution and to repent his previous condonement of it. When

he is finally released and returned to the North, the minister gains a "backbone" and begins to work actively for the cause of abolition. Historically important as the first recorded play by a black American playwright to treat American slavery as a theme. Read publicly for the first time, under the orig. title of *Doughface,* in Brinley Hall, Worcester, MA, April 9, 1856. Presented only in the form of dramatic readings given by the author at numerous antislavery meetings and lyceum programs in Massachusetts, Vermont, Ohio, New York, Philadelphia, Connecticut, and Rhode Island, from the spring of 1856 to the spring of 1857. No extant script. COMMENTARY: See Farrison and Abramson, cited below.

The Escape; or, A Leap for Freedom // Also referred to as **Life at the South** (antislavery drama, 5 acts, 1857). Melodrama, mixed with minstrel elements and satire, of slave life on a Mississippi plantation. Focuses on the tragic plight of a recently married slave couple, whose master wishes to separate them in order to enjoy the sexual favors of the beautiful young wife. The black editors of *NegCarav* (Brown et al., 1941, p. 497) found structural faults in the play's use of an abolitionist as *deus ex machina* to aid the lovers in their escape, the simplicity of the triangular plot, the use of stock language, the insertion of comic scenes "among the lugubrious and elegant passages," and the author's reliance upon "the prevailing minstrel tradition when he attempted comedy." Doris Abramson, noted white critic and authority on black playwrights (*NegPlaywrs,* 1969, pp. 9–10), felt that *The Escape* is about as well written as most white-authored melodramas of the period and that there is something admirable in the author's own statement published in his preface: "The play, no doubt, abounds in defects, but as I was born in slavery, and never had a day's schooling in my life, I owe no apologies for errors." *The Escape* is historically significant as the first black American play to be published in the United States and the first extant play by a black playwright to dramatize the problems of American slavery. Although the work was never staged during the author's lifetime, he gave numerous readings of it at antislavery meetings and lyceum programs. The first recorded reading was held on Wednesday, Feb. 4, 1857, in the Town Hall of Salem, MA. Pub. by R. F. Walcutt, Boston, 1858 (copy in the Boston Atheneum Lib.); by Samuel French, 1858 (copy reportedly in TC/NYPL); by Prologue Press, New York, 1969; by Rhistoric [sic] Publns., Philadelphia, 1969; in *WORKS OF WILLIAM WELLS BROWN* (1970); and in *BlkThUSA* (Hatch, 1974), which includes commentary. COMMENTARY: See Farrison and Abramson, cited below.

FURTHER REFERENCE: *CLAJ* 12–1958 (Edward Farrison, "Brown's First Drama," pp. 104–110). *DANB. ETJ* 10–1968 (Doris Abramson, "William Wells Brown, First American Negro Playwright," pp. 371–75). *NegPlaywrs* (Abramson). *William Wells Brown* (Farrison).

BROWNE, THEODORE (R.) (1910?–1979), Pioneer playwright, actor, author, and teacher. Born in Suffolk, VA. Educated in the public schools of New York City; at the City College of New York (A.B. 1941); and at Northeastern University in Boston (M.Ed.). Gained theatrical experience with the Civic Repertory Theatre in Seattle, WA, during the early 1930s; when the Federal Theatre began its operation in Seattle in 1936, he became assistant director of the Negro Unit, where he also acted, directed, and was its resident playwright. During this period, four of his plays were produced by the unit: **Natural Man,** an adaptation of **Lysistrata, Go Down Moses,** and **Swing, Gates, Swing.** After the demise of the Federal Theatre, Browne was the recipient of a Rockefeller/Dramatist's Guild Fellowship in Playwriting, the first black American to be so honored. He was a pioneer member of the American Negro Theatre and one of the founders of the Negro Playwrights Company, both in New York. He is the author of a suspense novel, *The Band Will Not Play Dixie* (Exposition, 1955). After World War II, he resided, taught, and lectured in Roxbury, MA, and was associated with the New England Repertory Theatre. He died in Boston, MA, at age 68.

Stage Works:

Lysistrata (adaptn., full length, 1936). Afro-American version of the comedy by Aristophanes, about how the women of ancient Greece (in this version Ethiopia) withheld sex from their mates in order to bring peace among their warring nations. Prod. by the Negro Unit of the WPA Theatre in Seattle, this prodn. was halted after only 1 perf., ostensibly because it was too risqué for Seattle audiences. According to Ronald Patrick Ross, however, "In reality, the production . . . was closed because Browne had changed the setting of the play from classical Greece to the troubled Ethiopian scene. The Roosevelt administration . . . was extremely cautious about any government reference to hostilities there."—Ph.D. diss. (1972), p. 182. Unpub. script in the National Archives, Washington, DC, and possibly in WPA/FTP.

Natural Man // Orig. title: **This Ole Hammer** (folk drama with music, 8 episodes, 1936). Based on the legend of John Henry, one of the best-known black folk heroes, whose prodigious physical strength as a "steel driving man," with his famous hammer, is tested in a contest with a modern steam drill. According to Doris Abramson, "Although he loses his battle against machinery, . . . John Henry has become a symbol of indomitable human pride and an expression of the Negro's will to survive impossible odds."— *NegPlaywrs* (1969), p. 103. Throughout Brown's version, he comments on the injustices that blacks have suffered, and John Henry is portrayed as a militant black man whose mental belligerence matches his physical strength. Although he dies, his death is a glorious one because he has proven his manhood, not only against a machine, but also against American social injustice and oppression. First prod. as "a full-length Negro opera" by the Negro Unit of the Federal Theatre in Seattle, WA, Jan. 28–Feb. 28, 1937. Again prod. as a folk drama with music by the American Negro Theatre, at the 135th St. Library Theatre, May 7, 1941; dir. by Benjamin Zemach. With Stanley Greene as John Henry. Also in the cast were ALVIN CHILDRESS, James Jackson, Ruby Wallace (*Ruby Dee), Kenneth Mannigault, Claude Sloane, Frederick O'Neal, and *Alice Childress. Excerpt pub. in *Blk. Scenes* (Childress, 1971). Full script in *BlkThUSA* (Hatch, 1974). Federal Theatre Project script in the National Archives, Washington, DC, and possibly in FTP/GMU. ANT scripts in Schomburg and TC/NYPL. REVIEWS AND COMMENTARY: *List of Neg. Plays* (WPA/FTP). *NegPlaywrs* (Abramson). *NYT* 5–8–1941. Pitts diss. *PM* 5–8–1941. Ross diss.

A Black Woman Called Moses // Orig. title: **Go Down Moses** (drama, 2 acts, 1937). About Harriet Tubman and the Underground Railroad. Written for, and first prod. under its orig. title by, the Negro Unit of the WPA Federal Theatre, Seattle, c. 1937. Unpub. scripts in FTP/GMU and Hatch-Billops.

Swing, Gates, Swing (musical revue, full length, 1937). Prod. by the Negro Unit of the WPA Federal Theatre, Seattle, 1937.

The Gravy Train (drama, 3 acts, 1940). "About a sensitive young man, trying to work, go to school, and keep his wandering wife happy.''—*BlkThUSA* (Hatch, 1974), p. 875. Unpub. script, dated 1940, in Schomburg.

The Seven Cities of Gold (historical fantasy, 2 acts plus epilogue, pre–1974). Dramatizes the legend of Esteban (Stephen) Dorantes, a Moor who accompanied the Spanish conquistadors in their exploration of the Southwest.

Steppin' High // Also called **Minstrel** (musical extravaganza, 5 acts, pre–1974). Book by Browne. Dramatizes the life of a black entertainer from his early days as a "tent show" performer on the minstrel circuit in the South to his rise on the Broadway stage. Presumably based on the life of early black musical star Bert Williams.

The Day of the Midnight Ride of Paul Revere (historical play, 2 acts, 1975).

FURTHER REFERENCE: *NegPlaywrs* (Abramson). Pitts diss. Ross diss. Theodore Browne Folder in Schomburg.

BRUCE, RICHARD. See NUGENT, RICHARD BRUCE.

BUNDY, FLORENCE, and CLARA LEDERER, Student playwrights associated with the Gilpin Players, Cleveland, OH, during the 1930s.

Stage Work:
Osceola (historical drama, 3 acts, 1928). About the famous half-black Seminole Indian of Florida, who led a band of Indians and fugitive slaves in a revolt against U.S. government forces in 1834 to prevent the government from removing the tribe to the West and returning the slaves to bondage. The fugitive slaves had settled among the Seminoles and intermarried with them. Osceola's army was defeated, and he was taken prisoner and confined in a military fort until his death in 1838. Written especially for the Gilpin Players and sched. for prodn. at the Karamu Theatre, Cleveland, April 18, 1928. No record of the actual prodn. No extant script.

BURKE, INEZ M., Former Washington, DC, elementary school teacher. The author of a number of plays and pageants for children (only one of which has been located), which were presented by her pupils during the 1920s.

Stage Work:
Two Races (children's black history play, 1 act, 1920s). While playing with a young white boy on their way to school, a young black boy becomes attracted to a history book that the white boy accidentally drops. Curious to know what the book is all about, the black child is told that it is "a volume giving the achievements of the great men of all races except the Negro, who apparently had done nothing worth recording."—Carter G. Woodson, intro. to pub. script, cited below. This information causes the black youth to become angry with his friend. Just at that moment, the Spirit of Negro Progress appears and presents "a panorama of great men of African blood who had done much for the benefit of mankind."—Ibid. The black boy becomes inspired to achieve something great, and the two boys become friends once again. Presented by fifth grade pupils in Washington, DC, public schools, in celebration of Negro History Week during the 1920s. Pub. in *Plays&Pags* (Richardson, 1930), which includes commentary by Woodson.

BURRILL, MARY (Maimie P. Burrill) (1879–1946), Washington, DC, high school English teacher and one of the earliest black women playwrights. Taught mainly at Dunbar High School, 1905–44, where she greatly encouraged her students' interests in drama and poetry. One of her outstanding pupils was playwright WILLIS RICHARDSON, the first black American dramatist to have a serious play produced on Broadway. Burrill is said to have been an active member of the NAACP and the Birth Control League, and her two plays reflect her support of these causes. She was also active as a public reader and served as narrator for the Howard University choir's production of *The Other Wise Man.*

Stage Works:

Aftermath (tragedy, 1 act, 1919). About a black soldier who returns from World War I to find that his father has been lynched by a white mob. Apparently written in response to the NAACP's editorials calling attention to the mistreatment of returning black soldiers who fought bravely for their country abroad. Prod. by the Krigwa Players, in association with the Workers Drama League of Manhattan, at the National Little Theatre Tournament, staged at the Frolic Theatre, New York, May 8, 1928. Pub. in *Liberator,* April 1919, pp. 10–14.

They That Sit in Darkness (folk tragedy, 1 act, 1919). Birth control propaganda play in the black speech idiom, addressed to women "that sit in darkness, having year after year, children that [they] are physically too weak to bring into the world—children that [they] are unable not only to educate but even to clothe and feed."—Pub. script. In this play, a young woman is forced to abandon her plans to attend college after her mother dies from complications after giving birth to her seventh child—a tragedy that might have been prevented had she been given the necessary birth control information. Pub. in *Birth Control Rev.,* Sept. 1919; and in *BlkThUSA* (Hatch, 1974), which also includes commentary. REVIEWS AND COMMENTARY: *BesPls 1927–28. BlkPlots* (Southgate). *Blk. World* 4–1976. *Their Place on Stage* (Brown-Guillory).

BURRIS, ANDREW M., Pioneer New York City playwright, who is cited by black drama historian *Loften Mitchell as one of the cultural and civic leaders of the Harlem community during Mitchell's youth in the 1930s. Said Mitchell concerning Burris and two other outstanding Harlem personalities: "Andrew Burris, and later Zell Ingram and Glenn Carrington—leaders of boys' clubs to which I belonged—were no drawling characters. They and other dedicated Negroes were in the streets, building clubs, organizing meetings and bringing celebrated Negro figures to speak to us."—*BlkDr* (Mitchell, 1967), p. 2. Mitchell also credits Burris with helping him to get a scholarship to Talladega College.—Ibid., p. 4. It is certain that Burris was associated with the Harlem Branch of the New York Public Library, where his play, cited below, was first produced.

Stage Work:

You Must Be Bo'n Again (drama, 3 acts, 1930). Although little is known of Burris' play, it apparently involved a clash of ideologies between a group of conservative blacks and one individual dissident who expresses a more nationalistic point of view. According to James V. Hatch, these conservative blacks, "outraged by Clem Coleman's 'nationalism' toward their established institutions, contrive to make him accept their standards."—*Blk. Playwrs., 1823–1977* (Hatch & Abdullah, 1977). First prod. by the Harlem Experimental Theatre, New York, early 1930s, prior to its prodn. by the Gilpin Players at Karamu House, Cleveland, Feb. 25–March 1, 1931, with an extra perf. given for the Interracial Committee of the Women's International League for Peace and Freedom, March 14, 1931; dir. by Rowena Jelliffe. Apparently also prod. by black units of the Federal Theatre Project. Unpub. script in FTP/GMU.

BURROUGHS, CHARLES, Actor, playwright, and theatrical director, who toured the United States giving recitations and dramatic readings prior to the 1920s. In 1914 he directed *The Star of Ethiopia*, a pageant by W.E.B. DuBOIS. With the Allied Arts Theatre in Boston, he performed the title role in the 1924 production of MAUD CUNEY-HARE's historical romance, *Antar of Araby*. He was artistic director of the Krigwa Players Little Negro Theatre, an organization that grew out of the *Crisis* drama awards, organized in 1926 by DuBois and established in the basement of the Harlem Branch of the New York Public Library.

Stage Work:
Black Man: A Fantasy (pageant-masque, full length presumed, 1925). A dramatic prophecy of the development of drama, art, music, and literature among blacks in America. Written to launch the little theatre movement of the NAACP, conceived and developed by W.E.B. DuBois and the *Crisis* playwriting competition, held annually from 1925 to 1927. The contest was initially known as the *Crisis* Contest Awards, from which was derived the acronym Krigwa [Cri-C-Awa] by which the competition was also called. Prod. by the Krigwa Players Little Negro Theatre in New York City, 1925; dir. by the author.

BURROUGHS, NANNIE H. (1879–1961), Virginia-born educator and church-woman; author of two popular fund-raising church plays. One of the outstanding black women in America. Cofounder and first president of the National Training School for Women and Girls, later called the Nannie H. Burroughs School, in Washington, DC. Active member of the NAACP and secretary of the Women's Auxiliary of the National Baptist Convention.

Stage Works:
The Slabtown District Convention (church comedy mainly for women, 1 long act [full length], 1920s). One of the most popular fund-raising plays of its time, satirizing many of the stereotypes of the early black Baptist church conventions—in this case, that of a women's auxiliary. Among the events hilariously depicted are the boisterousness and tardiness of the arriving members; the frantic call for order by the ample sergeant-at-arms; the complaints and dissatisfactions expressed by many of the disgruntled delegates; the welcome-yet-not-so-welcome address by the president; the meager financial reports of the delegates; the treasurer's brief report, complaining about the inadequacy of funds and offering to resign; the various humorous speeches on the local activities of the member churches; the endless choir selections; the annual sermon by the pompous hosting pastor; and the anxious move to adjourn on the part of all. Prod. by numerous black church, club, and school groups since the 1920s. Privately printed by Nannie H. Burroughs Publications, Nannie H. Burroughs School, Washington, DC. In 1972 the play was in its twenty-first printing; copy in Moorland-Spingarn.
Where Is My Wandering Boy Tonight? (Mother's Day play, 1 act, 1920s). Program material for church, club, and school groups, apparently more sentimental and moralistic

in tone than **The Slabtown District Convention** above. Presumably prod. by a number of amateur groups during the 1920s. Privately printed, Washington, DC, 1920s; copy in Moorland-Spingarn.
FURTHER REFERENCE: *DANB*.

BUSEY, DeREATH IRENE (DeReath Irene Byrd; DeReath Byrd Busey), Student playwright and short story writer at Howard University in Washington, DC, during the 1920s. Among the earliest "neophyte playwrights whose plays were presented by their fellow students" under the tutelage of Montgomery Gregory, who "encouraged Howard University students to write plays dealing with racial situations and to produce them."—Hicklin, Ph.D. diss., 1965, p. 134. The short story on which her play was based was published in *Crisis* magazine.

Stage Work:
The Yellow Tree (drama, 1 act, 1922). Adapt. from her short story by the same title, pub. in *Crisis,* Oct. 1922, pp. 253–56. Apparently written at the suggestion of Montgomery Gregory. About a superstitious yet socially ambitious mother, striving to improve her status in the black community. She "grows to feel that the glory of her ambition [will] come through her daughter," on whom she "center[s] all of her love and energies."—Ibid., p. 255. Throughout her life, she has believed in signs and predictions, and when the leaves on one of the trees in her front yard turn yellow, she accepts the local superstition that this signifies that death will come to her family before the year is out. When her daughter comes down with an attack of "the grippe" (influenza), and the townspeople are certain that the prediction will be fulfilled, the mother frantically saws down the "yellow tree" in the middle of the night in an effort "to thwart the threatening evil."—Ibid., p. 256. The next morning her dead body is discovered underneath the fallen tree, and the townspeople wonder why the tree took the wrong one. Prod. by the Howard Univ. Players, Washington, DC, 1922. Pub. only as a short story, cited above.

BUSH, (Mrs.) OLIVIA WARD (later Mrs. Olivia Ward Bush-Banks) (1869–1944), Poet, playwright, drama instructor, and coach. Born in Long Island, NY, of mixed black and Indian parents of the Montauk tribe of Long Island. Her father moved his family to Providence, RI, where, after the early death of her mother and her father's remarriage, Bush lived with her mother's sister who raised her. She was educated at Providence High School, with the intention of becoming a nurse. Married Frank Bush in 1889; they had two daughters, before the marriage was dissolved by divorce around the turn of the century. She turned her efforts to poetry and drama, and published a book of twelve *Original Poems* in 1899, and a larger collection, *Driftwood,* in 1914. Married Anthony Banks in the 1920s, and the couple moved to Chicago where she was drama instructor in the public schools and founded the Bush-Banks School of Expression for private instruction in dramatic arts. Returned to New York some 15 years later, making her home between New Rochelle and New York City during the 1930s. Wrote a cultural arts column for the *Westchester Record-Courier,* and was employed under the WPA program as a drama coach for the Abyssinia (Church)

Community Center, where Adam Clayton Powell, Sr., was pastor. Also wrote short stories and an unfinished autobiography, *The Lure of the Distance*.

Stage Works:
Memories of Calvary (Easter religious pageant, 2 scenes [16 pp.], 1915). Includes 15 poems by the author intended to be used between the two scenes of the pageant. Pub. by the A.M.E. Book Concern, Philadelphia, 1915.

Indian Trails (drama, 3 acts, not dated). Based on her ancestral Indian tribe, the Montauks of Long Island, NY. An unsuccessful effort was purportedly made by Maggie Walker, the famous black banker, to have it produced.

OTHER PLAYS (not dated, unprod., unpub.): **Shadows** (dramatic monologue using dance and poetry to extol the African culture). **A Shantytown Scandal** (1 act, dramatizing an incident of viciousness and gossip among a group of black women).
FURTHER REFERENCE: Guillaume diss.

BUTCHER, JAMES W., JR. (**"Beanie" Butcher**), Washington, DC, drama professor, play director, and pioneer playwright; for many years on the faculty of Howard University. Born in Washington, DC. Educated at Howard (3 years); the University of Illinois (A.B. 1932); and the University of Iowa (M.A. 1941). Formerly married to Margaret Just Butcher, an author and Howard University professor. Joined the faculty of Howard in 1937 as instructor of English and director of the Howard Players. For several summers also taught and directed in the Atlanta University Summer Theatre, 1940s and 1950s. An accomplished actor, he has performed with the Morningside Players of Columbia University, the University Players of the University of Iowa, and the Atlanta University Players. He directed the Negro Repertory Theatre of Washington, and during World War II was appointed a drama coach to develop amateur theatricals among the troops stationed at Ft. Huachuca, AZ.

Stage Works:
The Seer (farce, 1 act, c. 1937). Satirical treatment of superstitions among an older generation of blacks. A black charlatan (who capitalizes on these superstitions to accomplish his own selfish purposes) is taught a lesson by a young black man who poses as a ghost. First prod. at the Univ. of Iowa and Howard Univ., Washington, DC, during the late 1930s. Also prod. by the Dillard Univ. Players, at the Fourth Annual Conf. of SADSA, held at Talladega Coll., AL, April 28, 1939. Pub. in *NegCarav* (Brown et al., 1941).

Milk and Honey (farce, 1 act, late 1930s). Prod. at Howard Univ., late 1930s.

C

CAMP, HARRY. See Appendix A.

CAMPBELL, DICK. See Appendix A.

CARTER, JEAN (Emma Loyal Lexa). See Appendix A.

CHILDRESS, ALICE. See Appendix A.

CHILDRESS, ALVIN (1908–1986), Veteran actor of stage, films, and television, best known for his role as Amos in the "Amos 'n Andy" TV series. Elected to the Black Filmmakers Hall of Fame, 1974. Born in Meridian, MS. Received the B.A. in sociology from Rust College. Married to the former Alice Herndon; marriage dissolved. [*Alice Childress, now married to Nathan Woodard, has established herself as an important contemporary author and playwright. See *Contemporary Black American Playwrights and Their Plays* (Peterson, 1988), pp. 106–8.] Alvin Childress' professional career began in New York with the Lafayette Players during the 1930s, when he appeared in a number of stage productions and independently made films. He also wrote and acted for the Harlem Unit of the WPA Federal Theatre and for the American Negro Theatre (ANT). Stage appearances include *Savage Rhythm* (1931), *Brown Sugar* (1934), *Sweet Land* (1935), *The Case of Philip Lawrence* (1937), *Haiti* (1938), *Natural Man* (1941), *Anna Lucasta* (1944), *On Striver's Row* (1946), and *Amen Corner* (Los Angeles, 1968). Films include *Harlem Is Heaven* (1932), *Dixie Love* (1934), *Anna Lucasta* (1959), *The Day of the Locust* (1975), and *The Bingo Long Traveling All-Stars and Motor Kings* (1976). TV shows, in addition to "Amos 'n Andy," include appearances on "Playhouse 90," "Juvenile Court," "Night Court," "Sanford and Son," "Good Times" (1974), and "The Jeffersons" (1975—as Mother Jefferson's boyfriend). Following the demise of the "Amos 'n Andy'' show, and while appearing in bit parts on other television shows, Childress began working in 1961 for the Los Angeles County Dept. of Personnel as an unemployment interviewer, until his retirement in 1973. He died in Los Angeles at age 78, from complications of diabetes, pneumonia, and Parkinson's disease.

Stage Work:
Hell's Alley (drama, 1938). Coauthored with his wife, Alice Herndon (Alice Childress). Concerns a notorious alley in which the main character, a professional swindler, victimizes unsuspecting ''suckers'' who pass through. Prod. by the Lafayette Players, New York, 1938. With Hayes Pryer, Alice Herndon [Childress], Tom Mosely, Laura Brown, Billy Sheppard, and A. B. Comathiere.
FURTHER REFERENCE: *BlksB&W* (Sampson). *Blk. Stars* 7–1975. *DirBlksPA* (Mapp). *Ebony* 5–1951; 7–1973. *Jet* 5–5–1986. *Neg&Dr* (Bond). *NY Amst.N.* 7–9–1986.

COGMAN, GEORGE. See Appendix A.

COLE, BOB. See Appendix B.

COLEMAN, RALF (MeShack) (1898–), Actor, stage manager, theatrical director, playwright, and pioneer in the little theatre movement in New England during the 1920s and 1930s. Born in Newark, NJ. Studied theatre at Harvard University under H.W.L. Dana; at Provincetown Wharf Theatre, MA; and at Boston Experimental Theatre. Acted with and directed the Allied Arts Players, Boston, 1927; the Boston Players, 1930–33; and the Beacon Hill Little Theatre, 1930s. Made his professional debut with the New York production of Paul Green's *Roll, Sweet Chariot* (1933–34), playing the romantic lead. Directed the Negro Unit of the WPA Federal Theatre of Massachusetts, 1935–39. Produced and directed plays for the USO circuit during World War II, and for the NAACP and Negro College Fund in Boston. Served as stage manager for *Anna Lucasta* on Broadway, in Chicago, and on tour, 1945–49. Member of Actors Equity Assn., Negro Actors Guild, and the Saturday Evening Quill Club (a Boston writers' group).

Stage Works:
The Girl from Back Home // Also known as **The Girl from Bam** (''Alabama'') (drama, 1 act, 1929). ''Mistress of a Harlem racketeer makes her escape from vicious circumstances in which she is living.''—*Dict. Catalog of the Moorland Collection.* Pub. in *Sat. Eve. Quill* (Cambridge, MA), April 1929; copies in Moorland-Spingarn and Schomburg.
Paradox (1 act, 1930). Prod. at The Barn, Boston, 1930. Pub. in *Sat. Eve. Quill,* April 1930; copies in Moorland-Spingarn and Schomburg.
Swing Song (protest drama, 1 act, 1937). Melodrama set in the Deep South, centering around the town's discovery that a white woman has been made pregnant by her black lover, and his pursuit by a lynch mob. Prod. by the Federal Theatre of Boston, c. 1938. Unpub. script in Hatch-Billops.

FURTHER REFERENCE: *Blk. Playwrs., 1823–1977* (Hatch & Abdullah). Hicklin diss. Taped interview in Hatch-Billops. *WWCA.*

COLEMAN, WARREN. See Appendix A.

COLES, EROSTINE. See Appendix A.

COOK, (Dr.) MERCER (W. Mercer) (1903–   ), Composer, educator, author, and diplomat. For many years professor and head of the Department of Romance Languages at Howard University. Born in Washington, DC, the son of noted musical comedy composer †WILL MARION COOK and concert singer–actress Abbie Mitchell. Educated at Amherst, the University of Paris, and Brown University, from which he received both the A.B. and Ph.D. degrees. Taught languages at Atlanta University and the University of Haiti before going to Howard. He has held a number of foreign posts, including Director of African Affairs at the Congress of Cultural Freedom in Paris, U.S. Envoy to Senegal and Gambia, and Ambassador to the Republic of Niger. For his contributions on behalf of the French-speaking Negro people, he was decorated by the Haitian government. A member of ASCAP, he has written several popular songs, including "Stop the Sun, Stop the Moon," "Is I in Love? I Is," and "How Can I Hi-de-Hi When I Feel So Low-de-Low?" His writings include *Five French Negro Authors* (1939) and *The Militant Black Writer in Africa and the United States* (with Stephen E. Henderson, 1969), as well as numerous articles in *Crisis, Opportunity, Journal of Negro History,* the *French Review, Free World,* the *Romantic Review, Books Abroad,* and other periodicals and journals.

Stage Works:
St. Louis 'Ooman (folk opera, also called a music drama, full length, 1929). Libretto by Mercer Cook; musical score by Will Marion Cook (his father). About blacks living on the Mississippi River during the Gay Nineties. Apparently unprod.

Famous Women in Haitian History (sketch, 1 act, 1944). English translation by Cook of *Les Aieules* by Jean Fernand Brierre (Haitian poet-playwright). Dramatizes the contributions of Sanite Belair, Suzanne Simon (Mme. Toussaint L'Ouverture), Mme. Pageot, Marie Jeanne, and Defilee to Haitian history. Pub. in *Neg. Hist. Bull.,* Nov. 1944, pp. 36, 38–39. Also pub., together with the orig. French text, by Henri Deschamps, Port-au-Prince, Haiti, 1950.

Other Pertinent Writings:
"*Imitation of Life* [the orig. film] in Paris," *Crisis,* June 1935, pp. 182, 188.

" 'De Lawd' and Jazz: An Incident in the Life of Richard B. Harrison [star of *The Green Pastures*]," *Crisis,* April 1940, pp. 112, 114.

Five French Negro Authors. Associated Pubs., Washington, DC, 1943. (Includes a biography of Alexandre Dumas père.)

"Will Marion Cook: He Helped Them All," *Crisis,* Oct. 1944, pp. 322, 328.

"Jean F. Brierre, Poet and Hero," *Neg. Hist. Bull.,* March 1946, pp. 125–27, 141–42.

FURTHER REFERENCE: *ASCAP Biog. Dict. of Composers, Authors, and Pubs.* (Ewen). *Music of Blk. Ams.* (Southern). *Neg. Hist. Bull.* 6–1946. *WWCA 1950.*

COOK, S. N. See Appendix A.

COOK, WILL A. See Appendix B.

COOK, WILL MARION. See Appendix B.

COOPER, ANNA JULIA. See Appendix A.

COTTER, JOSEPH SEAMON, JR. (1895–1919), Poet-playwright. The talented son of JOSEPH SEAMON COTTER, SR. Born and reared in Louisville, KY, where his father was a teacher at Central High School, which Cotter, Jr., also attended. Studied for two years at Fisk University in Nashville, TN, before being obliged to abandon his college education at age 17 after contracting tuberculosis. In the remaining seven years of his life, which were spent "on a bed of pain," he wrote *The Band of Gideon* (a collection of poems, 1919), *Out of the Shadows* (an unfinished sequence of sonnets and lyrics, 1920), and **On the Fields of France** (1920), the play cited below. He reportedly completed a collection of one-act plays, to be entitled "The White Folks' Nigger" [according to *Crisis*, Jan. 1920, p. 126; and *Caroling Dusk* (Cullen, 1920), p. 100], which was apparently never published. He died at the age of 24.

Stage Work:
On the Fields of France (protest play, 1 short act, 1920). Concerns two American army officers, one black, one white, both mortally wounded, who die hand in hand on a battlefield in northern France, wondering why they could not have lived in peace and friendship in America. Pub. in *Crisis*, June 1920, p. 77.

COTTER, JOSEPH SEAMON, SR. (1861–1949), Poet, author, and educator, historically significant as one of the earliest published black American playwrights. Born in Bardstown, KY, located in Nelson County. Self-educated, except for three years of early schooling and 10 months of night school at age 22. Worked as a manual laborer until he was 24. Taught in several private and public schools in Kentucky, 1885–93. Founder and principal of Samuel-Taylor School, 1911–mid-1930s. Father of poet-playwright JOSEPH SEAMON COTTER, JR., one of two children, both of whom died of tuberculosis. Author of *A Rhyming* (poetry, 1895), *Links of Friendship* (poetry, 1909), *A White Song and a Black* (poetry, 1909), *Negro Tales* (1912), *Collected Poems* (1938), *Sequel to the "Pied Piper of Hamelin" and Other Poems* (1939), and *Negroes and Others at Work and Play* (selected writings, 1947).

Collection:
NEGROES AND OTHERS AT WORK AND PLAY [NEGROES AND OTHERS]. Paebar Co., New York, 1947. Contains: **The Chastisement** and **Caesar Driftwood**.

Stage Works:
Caleb, the Degenerate (thesis play, 4 acts, 1903). Subtitled "A Study of the Types, Customs, and Needs of the American Negro." A dramatization of the educational philosophy of Booker T. Washington, who extolled the value of industrial education over liberal arts education as a means of achieving race progress. Considered "more of a tract than a play." Historically significant as one of the earliest plays by a black American playwright to be published in the United States. Read at public meetings, but apparently never staged. Pub. by Bradley & Gilbert Co., Louisville, KY, 1903, which includes a "Preface" by the author; xerographic reprints available from Univ. Microfilms International, Ann Arbor, MI. Also pub. by Henry Harrison, New York, 1940; and in *BlkThUSA* (Hatch, 1974), which also includes critical commentary. OTHER COMMENTARY: *BlkPlots* (Southgate). *NegPlaywrs* (Abramson).

Caesar Driftwood (comedy, 1 act, early 1900s). On the eve of a family wedding, a rumor is circulating that a rival suitor named Caesar Driftwood will disrupt the marriage and possibly assassinate the groom. The rumor, it is finally learned, has been planted by the bride herself as a joke on her more serious-minded sister. The play's stilted dialogue, outmoded structure, and style all indicate that it was probably written around the turn of the century. Pub. in the author's *NEGROES AND OTHERS*.

The Chastisement (thesis play, 1 act, early 1900s). Moralistic skit in short staccato dialogue, presumably written around the turn of the century. A stern Victorian father, who refuses to pay his servants promptly (although he freely gives his daughter money to buy a party dress), and who attempts to flog his nearly grown-up son for smoking cigarettes and keeping late hours (though the father does both), is taught a lesson by his family—that he is setting a bad example for them and the servants by not practicing what he preaches. Pub. in *NEGROES AND OTHERS*.
FURTHER REFERENCE: *CLAJ* 3–1975 (Ann Allen Shockley, "Biographical Sketch of a Black Louisville Bard," pp. 338–39). *DANB*. *NegPlayrs* (Abramson). Papers of Joseph S. Cotter, Sr. (1920–43), including plays, in the Louisville Free Pub. Lib., Western Branch, Louisville, KY. *WWCA 1941–44* (also earlier eds.).

COURTNEY, WARD, Hartford, CT, playwright associated with the local Charles Gilpin Players, and later the Negro Unit of the Federal Theatre Project in Hartford. The Charles Gilpin Players, not to be confused with the Gilpin Players of Cleveland, OH, had been an important part of Hartford cultural life for more than 15 years, when it was reorganized as a Negro Unit of WPA/FTP.

Stage Works:
Stars and Bars ("living newspaper," full length, c. 1936). Focused on the abuses in housing, medicine, employment, and use of public facilities in Hartford, CT, the author's home city. Prod. by the Negro Unit of the WPA Federal Theatre in Hartford, CT, c. 1936.

Trilogy in Black ("a modern tragedy on the Greek pattern," full length, c. 1937). Utilized themes from Greek tragedy to explore problems of blacks after World War I. Prod. by the Hartford Negro Unit of the WPA Federal Theatre, c. 1937.

CREAMER, HENRY. See Appendix B.

CULLEN, COUNTEE (Porter) (1903–1946), Leading black American poet and one of the outstanding figures of the Harlem Renaissance; also a novelist, author of children's books, and playwright. Born Countee Porter in Baltimore,

MD, he was adopted by the Rev. Frederick Cullen, pastor of Salem Methodist Church in New York City. Educated in the New York public schools and at DeWitt Clinton High School, New York University (A.B 1925, Phi Beta Kappa), and Harvard University (A.M. 1926). Married Yolande DuBois, daughter of W.E.B. DuBOIS, in 1928; marriage dissolved, 1929. Began writing poetry while a student at NYU, where he won the Witter Bynner Award, and published his first volume of poetry, *Color* (1925), which established his reputation as a poet when it won the Harmon Foundation's gold medal for literature in 1927. Also in 1927, he published his second and third poetry volumes, *Copper Sun* and *The Ballad of the Brown Girl,* and edited an anthology of Negro American poetry, *Caroling Dusk.* In 1928, on a two-year Guggenheim Fellowship for study and creative writing, he went to Paris, where he wrote *The Black Christ,* published in 1929. On his return, he began teaching in the public schools of Harlem, where he remained until his death in 1946. During brief intervals he also served as asst. editor of *Opportunity* and *Crisis* magazines. Other published works include *One Way to Heaven* (novel, 1932), *The Medea and Some Poems* (drama and poetry, 1935), *The Lost Zoo* (children's poetry, 1940), *My Nine Lives and How I Lost Them (by Christopher Cat)* (children's prose, 1942), and *On These I Stand* (collection of his best poems, 1947). The Countee Cullen Memorial Collection was established by Harold Jackman at Atlanta University (now Clark Atlanta University) in 1947.

Collection:
THE MEDEA AND SOME POEMS. Harper & Row, New York, 1935. Contains: **The Medea** (1935).

Stage Works:
St. Louis Woman (musical play, 3 acts, 1933). Book by ARNA BONTEMPS and Cullen. Adapt. from Bontemps' novel *God Sends Sunday* (1931). The play is set in a saloon in St. Louis during the 1890s, when black jockeys were in their heyday, and focuses on the triangular romantic involvement of one of the jockeys with the saloon keeper and a prostitute. First prod. by the Gilpin Players at Karamu House, Cleveland, Nov. 22–26, 1933, for 5 perfs.; revived June 5–10, 1935, for 5 perfs. Prod. on Bway at the Martin Beck Theatre, March 30–July 6, 1946, for 115 perfs.; with music by Harold Arlen and lyrics by Johnny Mercer. Featuring Ruby Hill in the leading role and Pearl Bailey in her Bway debut. Orig. cast recording by Capitol (1946), reissued in 1967. Pub. in *Blk. Th.* (Patterson, 1971). Unpub. script in Schomburg. A revision of the orig. script, made by LANGSTON HUGHES in 1935, is located in JWJ/YUL.

The Medea // Orig. title: **By-Word for Evil** (prologue, 2 acts, and epilogue, 1935). Modern adaptn. of the tragedy of Euripides, written as a starring vehicle for the noted actress ROSE McCLENDON. Originally intended for prodn. by the Hedgerow Theatre, Moylan-Rose Valley, PA, in 1935, but plans were abandoned after McClendon's untimely death. Premiere prodn., under its orig. title, was eventually held at Atlanta Univ. in March 1940, dir. by OWEN DODSON. Prod. by the Fisk Univ. Stagecrafters, Nashville, TN, 1944–45. Prod. in an adaptn. by Dodson, entitled *Medea in Africa,* by the Howard Players and the Howard Univ. Drama Dept., Washington, DC, April 25–May 3, 1963, and on tour of a number of colleges in New England, including Dartmouth, the Univ.

of New Hampshire, Bowdoin, Middlebury, and Williams, dir. by Dodson. Pub. without prologue and epilogue in the author's *MEDEA AND SOME POEMS*, cited above. Unpub. script of the orig. prodn., containing the prologue and epilogue, as well as orig. longhand manuscripts of the prologue and epilogue, are located in JWJ/YUL.

One Way to Heaven (adaptn., full length, 1936). Based on Cullen's novel by the same title. Explores the importance of the church in the Harlem community, through the story of a devout woman who is married to a nonbeliever. Prod. by the Hedgerow Theatre, Moylan-Rose Valley, PA, Sept. 28, 1936; dir. by Jasper Deeter. Featuring Robert Watson and Goldie Ervin. Prod. by the American Negro Theatre, at the 135th St. Library Theatre in Harlem, opening Nov. 18, 1943, for 37 perfs. Also presented at the (Harlem?) YMCA and the Hempstead (NY?) USO. Unpub. script in JWJ/YUL.

(The) Conjur Man Dies (farcical mystery, 3 acts [15 scenes], 1936). Dramatization by Arna Bontemps and Cullen of the novel *The Conjur Man Dies: A Mystery Tale of Dark Harlem* by RUDOLPH FISHER, who is usually credited erroneously as the adaptor. A black physician, investigating the murder of an African "conjure man" in Harlem, discovers that the corpse is not that of the supposed victim, but his assistant. When the real conjure man reappears, he is indeed murdered. Although primarily a mystery-drama with comic elements, the play also deals with the themes of voodoo and sorcery, as well as the problem of superstitions, among Harlem blacks. Considered the most popular Federal Theatre play among Harlem audiences, it was seen by more than 20,000 theatregoers, according to Hallie Flanagan, director of the federal program.—*Arena* (Flanagan, 1940), p. 62. First prod., two years after Fisher's death, by the Negro Unit of the Federal Theatre Project, at the Lafayette Theatre, New York, March 11–April 4, 1936, for 24 perfs.; dir. by J. AUGUSTUS SMITH and Joe Losey, with music perfd. by the WPA Orchestra, dir. by Joe Jordan. Went on tour with a traveling unit of the WPA players as part of the New York City Recreation Department's outdoor recreation program. Prod. in Cleveland, first by the Cleveland Federal Theatre, 1936, then by the Gilpin Players at the Karamu Theatre, Feb. 2–7, 1938. Unpub. scripts in Schomburg and TC/ NYPL.

The Third Fourth of July (symbolic drama, 1 act, 1946). Coauthored with Owen Dodson. Utilizes movement, poetry, and music to portray how the death of a son during World War II united two families, one black, one white, who had not communicated before. Commissioned by the Drama Division of the New School for Social Research, New York. Pub. in *Th. Arts*, Aug. 1946, pp. 488–93.

Free and Easy ("Blues opera" [subtitle], full length, 1959). Adapt. by Harold Arlen from **St. Louis Woman** [above], a musical play by Arna Bontemps and Cullen. "The entire structure was extended to make the work more of an opera than a popular musical production."—*Complete Bk. of Musical Th.*, rev. ed. (Ewen, 1959), pp. 460–61. Arlen added several songs that he had previously written for other prodns., such as "That Old Black Magic" and "Blues in the Night," and made extensive revisions of the orig. play, hoping to make it more successful. Opened in Amsterdam, the Netherlands, Dec. 1959, with presentations in Brussels and Paris, with the intention of being brought to Bway, but closed early in 1960 after only a brief run. Pub. only in the musical play version, *St. Louis Woman,* cited above.

FURTHER REFERENCE: *Bio-Bibliog. of Countee P. Cullen* (Perry). *Countee Cullen and the Neg. Renais.* (Ferguson). Countee Cullen/Harold Jackman Collection in Clark Atlanta Univ. Research Center. Countee Cullen Papers in Fisk Univ. Lib. and Media Center. *DANB. Harl. Renais. Remembered* (Bontemps). *NYT* 9–29–1936.

CUNEY-HARE, MAUD (also Maud Cuney Hare) (1874–1936), Boston pianist, lecturer, musicologist, author, composer, and pioneer playwright of the 1920s. Born in Galveston, TX. Educated at Howard University and the New England Conservatory of Music. Married to William P. Hare. Director of music at the Deaf, Dumb and Blind Institute of Texas, and at Prairie View State College. Established the Musical Art Studio, Boston. Concert pianist who appeared in recitals in the New England area. One of the leading figures in the Negro Little Theatre Movement in Boston, where she was prominently associated with the Allied Arts Theatre Group. Author of poetry, nonfiction, and scholarly works on black music history. Books include *Norris Wright Cuney: A Tribune of the Black People* (biography, 1913); *The Message of the Trees: An Anthology of Leaves and Branches* (poetry, 1918); *Six Creole Folk Songs: With Original Creole and Translated English Text* (1921); and *Negro Musicians and Their Music* (1936), which is a classic in its field. Also edited a music column in *Crisis* for many years.

Stage Work:

Antar of Araby (historical romance in poetic prose, with an overture and incidental music; prologue and 4 short acts, 1926). Overture ("Antar") by Clarence Cameron White; incidental music (from "Four Moorish Pictures") by Montague Ring (pseud. of Amanda Ira Aldridge, daughter of IRA ALDRIDGE). Adaptn. of Cuney-Hare's article entitled "Antar, Negro Poet of Arabia," pub. in two parts in *Crisis* (June 1924, pp. 66–67; and July 1924, pp. 117–19). About the legendary exploits of Antar Bin Shaddad, a black Arabian poet, storyteller, and warrior of humble birth who became one of the most celebrated heroes of Arabic literature. Focuses on Antar's great love for Abla, an Arabian maiden of noble heritage, and the physical conflicts in his life from which he emerges victoriously, thus enabling him to win the hand of his beloved. First prod. by the Allied Arts Center, Boston, 1926. With CHARLES BURROUGHS in the title role, William Richardson as the Court Singer, and Bernice Hughes Martin in the role of Abla. Again prod. by the same group in 1928. Pub. in *Plays&Pags* (Richardson, 1930) and in *Neg. Q.*, Spring 1942. "Four Moorish Pictures" (music by Montague Ring) pub. by Ascherber, Hopwood and Crew, London. All music, including overture, was available from Carl Fischer, New York, in 1930.

Other Pertinent Writing:

Negro Musicians and Their Music. Associated Pubs., Washington, DC, 1936; reprinted by Da Capo Press, 1974. Includes "Native African Musicians and Opera," pp. 30–31; "Negro Minstrelsy" and "Negro Minstrel Troops," pp. 37–45; and "Musical Comedy," pp. 157–77.

FURTHER REFERENCE: *Afro-Am. Encyc. Crisis* 3–1926; 8–1928. *DANB*. Hicklin diss. Maud Cuney-Hare Papers (1900–1936) in Clark Atlanta Univ. Lib. *Profiles of Neg. Womanhood* (Dannett).

D

DAVIS, OSSIE. See Appendix A.

DIXON, PHELON. See Appendix A.

DODSON, OWEN (Vincent) (1914–1983), Prolific poet, playwright, and writer of fiction and essays, recognized as one of the most influential drama teachers and directors in the academic theatre. He is credited with encouraging, developing, and/or training such outstanding talents as Earle Hyman, Gordon Heath, *Richard Wesley, *Ted Shine, *Frederick Lights, *Louis Peterson, *Vantile Whitfield, *Mike Malone, and *Glenda Dickerson, and has worked with numerous other theatrical personalities such as *James Baldwin, FRANK SILVERA, LANGSTON HUGHES, *Ossie Davis, and *Charles Sebree. Born in Brooklyn, NY. Educated in the New York public schools; at Bates College (B.A. 1936, Phi Beta Kappa), from which he also received an honorary Doctor of Letters in 1967; and at Yale University School of Drama (B.F.A. in directing and playwriting, 1939), under a General Education Board Fellowship. At Yale, he also wrote two of his best-known plays, **Divine Comedy** (1938) and **Garden of Time** (1939). After graduating from Yale, he taught and directed plays at a number of schools, including Atlanta University, 1939–42; Hampton Institute, 1943–44; and Howard University, 1949–70. Enlisted in the U.S. Navy, 1942–43, with the rank of seaman first class. While stationed at Camp Robert Smalls, at the Great Lakes, IL, Training Station, he wrote, produced, and directed about 16 short plays on naval, military, and civilian heroism, which were broadcast to members of the regiment and produced by other naval and military drama groups throughout the allied world. His books include *Powerful Long Ladder* (poetry, 1946), *Boy at the Window* (novel, 1951; republished as *When Trees Were Green,* 1974), *The Confession Stone* (poetry, 1970), *Come Home Early, Child* (novel, 1977, originally entitled *The Bent House*), and *The Harlem Book* *of the Dead* (poetry, with Camille Billops and James Van Der Zee, c. 1981). Other works include poems, short stories, and articles in numerous periodicals and anthologies; and numerous individual theatrical works, including plays, operas, and radio scripts. He directed the premiere production of James Baldwin's *The Amen Corner* in 1935, almost a decade before it was produced on Broadway. One of the founders of the Negro Playwrights Company in 1940. Winner of the Maxwell Verse Play Contest, 1940, for his **Garden of Time** (1939); and first prize of $100 in a playwriting contest sponsored by Tuskegee Institute, 1941, for his **Gargoyles in Florida**. Recipient of a Rosenwald Fellowship, 1944–45; a Guggenheim Fellowship, 1953–55; and a Rockefeller Grant, 1969–70. Recipient of an AUDELCO (Audience Development Co.) Outstanding Pioneer Award, 1975, for his contributions to the development and growth of black theatre. In 1974 Dodson was accorded the significant honor of having a theatrical retrospective created and produced as a tribute to him by two of his students, Glenda Dickerson and Mike Malone. The work, entitled *Owen's Song,* was described by the presenters as "a collage, weaving together lines from [Dodson's] works, including *Divine Comedy, Powerful Long Ladder,* his many poems, and his full length play *Bayou Legend.*"—Prog. notes. The play was produced by the DC Black Repertory Company, at the Last Colony Theatre in Washington, DC, opening Oct. 24, 1974, for six weeks, and also performed at other locations in Washington and New York City. Dodson died in New York City at the age of 69.

Stage, Screen, and Broadcast Works:
PRIOR TO 1950
[Untitled Play] (1 act, 1932). Concerns the dilemma of a black playwright who is torn between his artistic ideals and his wish to become involved in the civil rights struggle. Written at Bates Coll., 1932. Unpub. script in Hatch-Billops.

Jane (adapt., 2 scenes, c. 1936). Incomplete dramatization of a story by Somerset Maugham. Coauthored with William Swallow. Written at Bates Coll. around 1936. Unpub. script in Hatch-Billops.

Including Laughter (poetic play, 3 acts, 1936). Dramatizes how interracial friendships among college students are affected by racial violence. Begun at Bates Coll.; completed at Yale Univ., 1936. Unpub. script in Hatch-Billops.

The Shining Town (drama, 1 act, 1937). Set in a subway during the Depression, this play deals with a white woman's attempt to bargain for a black domestic worker's services as her maid. Unpub. script in Hatch-Billops.

Divine Comedy (verse drama with music, 2 acts, 1938). Concerns the life and career of the famous black cult leader, Father Divine. First prod. at Yale Univ. Theatre, New Haven, Feb. 16–18, 1938. Prod. at the Atlanta Univ. Summer Theatre, Atlanta, July 1938. Prod. at the Hampton Inst. Summer Theatre Workshop, Hampton, VA, July 23, 1942. Prod. at Jackson State Coll., Jackson, MS, Oct. 23, 1952. Excerpt in *NegCarav* (Brown et al., 1941); and in its Italian ed., *La Caravella*. Sched. for publication by Harper & Row, 1973. In *BlkThUSA* (Hatch, 1974). Script in JWJ/YUL.

Garden of Time // Former title: **With This Darkness** (drama, 4 acts [6 scenes], 1939). The interracial story of Jason and Medea, first in its ancient Greek setting, then in a modern black-white analogy, set first in Athens, GA, then in Haiti. Winner of the Maxwell Anderson Verse Play Contest at Stanford Univ., 1940. First prod., under its orig. title, at the Yale Univ. Theatre, New Haven, May 17–19, 1939, with music by SHIRLEY GRAHAM DuBOIS. Prod. by the American Negro Theatre at the 135th St. Library Theatre, opening March 7, 1945; dir. by the author. With Sadie Brown (Medea) and William Greaves (Jason). Several predominantly black colleges throughout the South have produced this work. Unpub. scripts are located in JWJ/YUL, Moorland-Spingarn, and Hatch-Billops.

The Amistad (historical drama, 5 scenes, 1939). Based on the famous insurrection aboard a slave ship, led by Cinque, an African slave. Commissioned by Talladega Coll., AL, through one of its trustees on the faculty of Yale. Presumably prod. at Talladega's Founders' Day Centennial Celebration and the dedication of its new library, 1939. Unpub. scripts in JWJ/YUL, Hatch-Billops, and the Amistad Research Center at Dillard Univ., New Orleans, LA.

Doomsday Tale (drama, 1941/42). About the burning of an all-black town in the U.S. South on a Good Friday. Sched. for prodn. by the Karamu Theatre, Cleveland, during the 1941–42 season, but cancelled because of Pearl Harbor. Unpub. scripts in JWJ/YUL and Hatch-Billops.

Someday We're Gonna Tear Them Pillars Down (a short poetic piece for speech choir, 1942). Pub. in *Neg. Q.*, Summer 1942; also reprinted in the author's *Powerful Long Ladder* (1946).

Heroes on Parade (series of about 16 short morale-building plays on naval, military, and civilian heroism, 1942/43). Written, prod., and dir. by the author while stationed at Camp Robert Smalls, at the Great Lakes Naval Training Station, IL. Presented in a series of weekly programs by and for members of his regiment. Some were also prod. by other naval and military drama groups all over the allied world. Only six of these 16 titles have been located: **Everybody Join Hands** (choric play, 1 act), a tribute to the fight for freedom by the Chinese people during the war, dedicated to Pearl Buck; with choreography by Charles Sebree (whose play, *Mrs. Patterson,* was prod. on Bway in 1954) and music by Herman Hill. Also prod. at Spelman Coll., May 1, 1943, dir. by Baldwin Burroughs; with Louis Peterson (author of *Take a Giant Step*) in the role of narrator, and Bernard L. Peterson, Jr. (this writer), as a member of the chorus. Pub. in *Th. Arts,* Sept. 1943, and in *Cavalcade* (Davis & Redding, 1971). OTHER PLAYS IN THIS SERIES INCLUDE: **The Ballad of Dorrie Miller** (a poem-play, written in tribute to Russian guerrilla fighters who demonstrated great valor in their defense against the Germans in World War II); **Climbing to the Soil** (a dramatization of the life of George Washington Carver); **Don't Give Up the Ship** (about the heroism of Commodore Matthew Perry); **Lord Nelson: Naval Hero** (a tribute to the British admiral who achieved a naval victory over the French and Spanish fleets in the Battle of Cape Trafalgar, 1805); **Robert Smalls** (a tribute to the black naval captain who served in the Civil War). Unpub. scripts are located in JWJ/YUL and Hatch-Billops.

The Midwest Mobilizes (radio doc., half hour, 1943). About the midwestern black community's participation in World War II. Prod. on station WBBM, Chicago, in May 1943. Unpub. script in Hatch-Billops.

New World A-Coming (pageant, 7 scenes, 1944). Apparently based on the book *New World A'Coming* (1943) by ROI OTTLEY. Dramatizes the struggle of black people for freedom throughout the world. Prod. at Madison Square Garden, New York, 1943. Unpub. script in Hatch-Billops.

"New World A'Coming" (radio drama for this series, half hour, 1945). Adapt. from *They Knew Lincoln,* about four blacks who met President Abraham Lincoln. Prod. with members of the American Negro Theatre on station WMCA, New York, in Feb. 1945. Unpub. script in Hatch-Billops. [See next entry; see also ROI OTTLEY.]

St. Louis Woman (radio script, half hour, c. 1945). Adaptn. of the play by Countee Cullen and Arna Bontemps, apparently for prodn. on the **"New World A'Coming"** radio series, prod. on station WMCA, New York, around 1945.

They Seek a City // Alternate titles: **Migration, Journey to Paradise,** and **Where You From?** (drafts of a screenplay, 1945). Various versions of Dodson's screen treatment of black migration from the rural South to the urban North, apparently based on *They Seek a City* (later revised as *Anyplace But Here*) by ARNA BONTEMPS and Jack Conroy (1945).

The Third Fourth of July (symbolic drama, 1 act, 1946). Coauthored with COUNTEE CULLEN. Commissioned by the Drama Div. of the New School for Social Research, New York. Utilized movement and music to tell the story of how the wartime death of a son united two families, one black, the other white, who had not previously communicated with each other. Pub. in *Th. Arts,* Aug. 1946.

Bayou Legend (fantasy, 2 acts, 1948). Poetic adaptn. of Henrik Ibsen's story of Peer Gynt, set in a Louisiana bayou, and drawing upon folklore and legend to create a drama relevant to American blacks. First prod. by Howard Univ., Washington, DC, May 1948. Prod. jointly by the theatre workshops of Hunter Coll. and CCNY, in the Hunter Coll. Playhouse, NY, May 13–21, 1950. Prod. as a puppet play at the Southeastern Theatre Conf., Atlanta, March 1952. Again prod. by the Howard Univ. Players, at Spaulding Hall, May 1, 1957; dir. by *Shauneille Perry. Pub. in *Topic No. 5,* Special Issue on "The Negro in the American Arts," Washington Press and Publications Service, U.S. Information Agency, c. 1965; copy in Schomburg. Also in *BlkDrAm* (Turner, 1971) and *BlkThUSA* (Hatch, 1974).

SINCE 1950

(For descriptions of these works, see my earlier volume, *Contemporary Black American Playwrights and Their Plays,* Greenwood Press, Westport, CT, 1988.)

Constellation of Women (pageant, 1950). **A Christmas Miracle** // Orig. title: **A Southern Star** (opera, 1 act: libretto, 1958). Musical score by Mark Fax. **Medea in Africa** (adaptn., full length, 1959). Apparently based on Countee Cullen's *The Medea* (1935) and Dodson's **Garden of Time** (1939). **Till Victory Is Won** (opera: libretto, 1965). Musical score by Mark Fax. **The Confession Stone** (song cycle, full length, 1968). **The Dream Awake** (radio drama and filmscript [also adaptable to the stage], 1969). **Owen's Song** (theatrical collage, 2 acts, 1974). Conceived, directed, and choreographed by Glenda Dickerson and Mike Malone. Based on Dodson's plays and poems. **The Morning Duke Ellington Praised the Lord and Seven Little Black Davids Tap-Danced Unto** (ceremonial entertainment, with blues, jazz, and dance, full length, 1976). Music by Roscoe Gill. **The Story of Soul** (musical, combining dance, music, and poetry, 1978). Coauthor, with Gary Keys. Prod. by the Howard Univ. Ensemble, Jan., Feb., and March, at the State Theatre in St. Gallens, Switzerland, 1979. **Justice Blindfolded** (three plays, in progress late 1970s).

Other Pertinent Writings:

"Countee Cullen (1903–1946)," *Phylon,* 1st qtr. 1946, pp. 19–21.

"The World Seemed Wide and Open," *Th. Arts,* March 1950, p. 55.

"Playwrights in Dark Glasses," *Neg. Digest*, April 1968, pp. 30–36.
FURTHER REFERENCE: *Crisis* 11–1979 (Bernard L. Peterson, Jr., "The Legendary Owen Dodson of Howard University: His Contributions to the American Theatre," pp. 373–78). Hicklin diss. Taped interview in Hatch-Billops.

DONOGHUE, DENNIS, Representative playwright of the 1930s, historically significant as one of the first 10 black playwrights to have a play produced on Broadway, **Legal Murder** (1934). Although five of his plays were produced in New York between 1929 and 1939, no biographical information has been located. FREDERICK W. BOND (*Neg&Dr*, 1940, p. 114) described Donoghue as "an inexperienced dramatist," who is "to be commended on his sincerity of purpose." According to Bond, Donoghue demonstrated in his plays an irritation "with some of the practices and customs of American life," and expressed effectively "his disgust and anger with social oppression."

Stage Works:
Malinda (musical melodrama, full length, 1929). Book by Donoghue. Music and lyrics by Ronald Loving and Earl B. Westfield. About a Florida schoolteacher, aspiring to become a singer, who goes to New York City's Harlem, where she falls into the clutches of a professional swindler. She is ultimately rescued by her suitor, a handsome young detective. Prod. in New York, Dec. 1929. [See also next entry.]

Ham's Daughter (musical drama, full length, 1932). A reworking of his earlier musical **Malinda** (1929), described above, with a view to Bway prodn. The plot line, similar to the above show, concerns an inexperienced young southern black woman who is lured from her comfortable home to New York by a professional swindler, on the pretense of helping her to realize her dream of becoming a professional singer. There she is deserted by him and has a number of disillusioning experiences before finally being rescued by her devoted sweetheart, who has come to New York looking for her. Prod. by the author at the Lafayette Theatre, New York, 1932, for a brief run, but was unsuccessful in its attempt to reach Bway. Cast included Mary Watkins (Eliza, the young woman), ALVIN CHILDRESS (Slick Harris, the swindler), and Lorenzo Tucker (Ned Daniels, Eliza's sweetheart).

Legal Murder (melodrama, 3 acts, 1934). Donoghue's best-known play. One of a number of dramatizations of the infamous Scottsboro case, in which nine black youths were accused, convicted, and sentenced to death for the alleged rape of two white girls. The black youths, in this version, are depicted as members of a neighborhood singing group who decide to go north to Chicago in search of jobs as radio singers. Having no funds, they hop a railroad freight car, which is also occupied by two white girls and two white men, who resent their presence in the car. When one of the men pulls a gun and orders the blacks to get off the train, the boys beat up the men, leaving the girls unharmed. In the next town, the boys are arrested and charged with rape. The rest of the play is concerned with the trial of one of the youths who is defended by a Jewish New York attorney, in which both the youth and his lawyer are "made sport of by both a biased court and a biased populace."—*BesPls 1933–34*, p. 498. Significant as one of the earliest protest plays by a black playwright to be presented on Bway, at the President Theatre, opening Feb. 15, 1934, for 7 perfs.; prod. by J. A. Allen Productions. Cast included Baby Kid as Rastus Johnson, Zeb Jones as Sam Jackson, and Richard Freye as Paul Claver.

Beale Street (play of black life, full length, 1934). Apparently focused on the seamier side of black life in Memphis, TN, where the blues is supposed to have originated. According to Fannin Belcher (Ph.D. diss., 1945, p. 259), this play "created a furor among the Negro members of the audience," apparently because of the coarseness of the scenes, characters, and languages depicted. Donoghue "justified the play," according to Belcher (ibid.), "on the grounds that it was the type which apparently appealed to audiences and producers alike since it had been accepted while more meritorious scripts he had written were gathering dust." Prod. at the Mecca Temple, New York, Dec. 30, 1934.

The Black Messiah // Former title: **The Demi-God** (comedy, full length, 1939). Coauthored with James H. Dunmore. Based on the life of the famous black religious cult leader, Father Divine. Prod. by the Cooperative Players at the Transport Theatre, New York, June 1939. In the cast of this prodn. was drama historian and contemporary playwright *Loften Mitchell, who reported (*BlkDr*, 1967, p. 4) that the play was produced "at the Nora Bayes Theatre" in 1939, and was responsible for ending his career as an actor. According to Mitchell (ibid.), the critics considered many of the performances "amateurish" and included his among that number. Again prod. in Harlem in 1946, dir. by coauthor James H. Dunmore.

FURTHER REFERENCE: *BesPls 1938–39*. *Blk. Dr.* (Brasmer & Consolo). *Blk. Playwrs., 1823–1977* (Hatch & Abdullah). *BlksB&W* (Sampson). *NYT* 12–4–1929; 2–16–1934.

DORSEY, ROBERT. See Appendix A.

DOWNING, HENRY F. (Francis) (1846/47–1928), Novelist, playwright, historian, and public figure, who spent several years in London and Liberia. The author of more than a dozen plays, as well as several books on Liberia. According to the Neale Publishing Company, a New York firm that published his first novel, *The American Cavalryman* (1917):

Mr. Downing perhaps has had a more varied career than any other living Negro from the Civil War to the war between the United States and Germany [World War I]. He was the first colored man to represent the United States in a city of a white government [i.e., Angola, then a colony of Portugal] by appointment of President Cleveland. He introduced [Samuel] Coleridge-Taylor [the distinguished black English composer] to the London public. He persuaded Liberia to open its doors to foreign capital. Merely to recount his activities in public life of the last fifty years would take a volume. But his highest renown has been as a man of letters. [Publisher's advt. in *Crisis,* May 1917, p. 46]

Born in New York's lower Manhattan district, Henry Downing was the descendant of a family of free blacks who maintained an oyster business and an eating establishment there. His uncle was George Thomas Downing, the well-known politician and businessman whose biographical sketch is included in *Men of Mark* (Simmons, 1887), a record of early black achievement in the United States. Nothing of Henry Downing's education is known. He served two terms in the Union Navy, 1864–65 and 1872–75. Between these terms he visited Liberia, where his cousin Hilary Johnson was a public official who was later to become president of Liberia (1884–92). There Downing remained for about three years, working as a private secretary to the Secretary of State. Following his second term in the navy, he returned to New York, where he worked at a number of insignificant jobs, including letter carrier, messenger, clerk, and waiter. In 1876 he married for the first time at age 30, and three years later was the father of two children, a boy and a girl. Influenced by his famous uncle, George Downing, Henry entered politics as an active supporter of the Democratic Party and was rewarded by President Cleveland with an appointment as consul to Luanda (or Loanda), Angola, a colony of Portugal in West Africa, where he served slightly more than a year, from 1887 to 1888. Unable to obtain a government appointment to Liberia, which he ardently desired, Downing resigned from consular service and returned to politics in New York, continuing to support the causes of Liberia in the United States. In 1894, following the dissolution of his first marriage, he married a white Irish woman from Boston, and the following year they immigrated to London, where Downing became a commercial agent for Liberia, working vigorously to open its doors to Western trade and advocating migration by black Americans to help develop that country. Remaining in London for some 22 years, he turned his talents to writing more than a dozen plays, several of which were published between 1913 and 1914. He returned to New York in 1917, living on a government pension, where he completed and published three books about Liberia: *The American Cavalryman* (a Liberian romance, 1917), *Liberia and Her People* (1925), and *A Short History of Liberia, 1816–1908*). He died from nephritis and arteriosclerosis in Harlem Hospital at the age of 82, survived by his two wives and one daughter.

Stage Works:
EARLIEST WORKS: **The Exiles**. **Melic Ric**. **The Pulcherian War Loan**. **The Sinews of War**. **The Statue and the Wasp**. **Which Should She Have Saved?** (All unpub. plays, pre–1913.)

The Arabian Lioness; or, The Sacred Jar ("An Eastern tale in four acts" [subtitle], 85 pp., 1913). Pub. by F. Griffiths, London, 1913; copy in Schomburg.

Human Nature; or, The Traduced Wife ("An original English domestic drama, in four acts" [subtitle], 75 pp., 1913). Melodrama of a wife who forgives her husband, who has disgraced her by his scandalous behavior. Pub. by F. Griffiths, London, 1913; copy in Schomburg.

Lord Eldred's Other Daughter ("An original comedy in four acts" [subtitle], 83 pp., 1913). Pub. by F. Griffiths, London, 1913; copy in TC/NYPL.

Placing Paul's Play (1913). Coauthored with Mrs. H. F. Downing. Pub. by F. Griffiths, London, 1913.

The Shuttlecock; or, Israel in Russia ("An original drama in four acts" [subtitle], 96 pp., 1913). Pub. by F. Griffiths, London, 1913; copy in TC/NYPL.

Voodoo (melodrama, 4 acts, 1914). Against a background of voodoo and black magic, a woman is pursued by her spurned lover from London to the West Indies. Pub. by F. Griffiths, London, 1914; copy in TC/NYPL.

Incentives ("A drama in four acts" [subtitle], 98 pp., c.1914). About a potential scandal that could ruin the lives of several innocent people if a secret is told. Unpub. script in Schomburg.

A New Coon in Town ("A farcical comedy made in England," 80 pp., c.1914). Unpub. script in Schomburg.

The Racial Tangle (1920). Accepted for prodn. by the Quality Amusement Corp., a stock company of the Lafayette Players, New York, 1920. Made into a silent film entitled *Thirty Years Later* (7 reels, 1928), prod. by OSCAR MICHEAUX, which told the story of the mulatto son of a white father and black mother, who is brought up believing that he is white. He falls in love with and proposes to a black girl who refuses to marry him on racial grounds. The romantic entanglement is eventually straightened out when the young man's true racial identity is revealed.
FURTHER REFERENCE: *DANB*.

DREER, HERMAN (1889–?), Educator, literary historian, minister, author, and editor. Born in Washington, DC. Educated at Bowdoin College (A.B. 1910), Virginia Theological Seminary (A.M. 1912), the University of Chicago (1930–31, A.M. 1942), and Douglas University in St. Louis, MO (D.D. 1938). Also studied at the University of Illinois (1912–14) and Columbia University (1919). Professor of Latin and Science, Virginia Theological Seminary, Lynchburg, VA, 1910–14. Taught English and directed plays at Sumner High School, St. Louis, 1914–26. Professor of English, Stowe Teachers College, 1926–30; asst. principal, 1930–45; professor of social science, 1945–50s. Author of *Out of the Night* (1916), *American Literature by Negro Authors* (anthology, 1950), and *The Tie that Binds* (novel, 1958). Editor-in-chief of *The Oracle,* journal of the Omega Psi Phi fraternity; director of its achievement project, 1934–36; and author of *The History of Omega Psi Phi Fraternity, 1911–1939* (c.1941). Elected to Phi Beta Kappa.

Stage Works:
Sunrise (drama, 4 acts, 1931). Unpub. script in Moorland-Spingarn.

The Man of God (religious drama, 1 act, 1936). Pub. in *The Oracle* (Omega Psi Phi Fraternity), vol. 15, Sept. 1936, p. 15; copy in Moorland-Spingarn.

OTHER STAGE WORKS (all unpub. 1-act historical and religious plays, pre–1941): **Christmas Gifts. Christmas Morning. Jacob and Esau. A Leap in the Dark. The Prodigal Son. Samuel. Tell Mother I'll Be There**.

Other Pertinent Writing:
American Lit. by Neg. Authors. Ed. by Dreer. Macmillan, New York, 1950.
FURTHER REFERENCE: *WWCA 1950*.

DuBOIS, SHIRLEY GRAHAM (Shirley Graham; Mrs. W.E.B. DuBOIS) (1906–1977), Biographical historian, composer, and playwright. Born in Indianapolis, IN. Educated at the Sorbonne in Paris (advanced musical composition, 1926–29); Oberlin College (B.A. 1934, M.A. 1935); and Yale University School of Drama (Julius Rosenwald Fellow, 1936–40). Most of her plays were written and produced during the decade from 1932 to 1942, while a student at Oberlin and Yale. Music teacher at Morgan State College (now University), Baltimore, 1929–31; head, Fine Arts Dept., Tennessee State College (now University), 1935–36. Director of the Negro Unit, Chicago Federal Theatre, 1936–38, where she was actively involved in producing, directing, designing, and writing music for the shows for this unit, including *Little Black Sambo* (1937) and *The Swing Mikado* (1938). Served as USO director, YMCA director, and NAACP field secretary, 1940–44. Recipient of a Guggenheim Fellowship for historical research, 1945–47. Author of a number of biographies of famous persons of color, including George Washington Carver, Paul Robeson, Phillis Wheatley, Jean Baptiste Point de Sable, Pocahantas, Booker T. Washington, and Gamel Abdel Nasser. Received the Julian Massner Award of $6,500 for her historical novel, *There Was Once a Slave* (1947), and the Ainsfeld-Wolf Prize for *Your Most Humble Servant* (1949), the biography of Benjamin Banneker. Organizing director, Ghana Television, 1964–66; founder and first president of *Freedomways* magazine, 1960–63; English editor, Afro-Asian Bureau, Peking, China, 1968. Recipient of an honorary L.H.D. from the University of Massachusetts, 1973. Her most recent books include a memoir of her famous husband, *W.E.B. DuBois: His Day Is Marching On*; and *Zulu Heart*, a novel laid in South Africa. Died in Peking at the age of 70.

Stage and Broadcast Works:

Tom-Tom (opera; also called a music drama, 3 acts, 1932). Concerns the odyssey of the black man from the jungles of Africa to America and his eventual arrival in New York's Harlem. The music utilizes African themes, rhythms, and instruments, featuring tom-toms, with the style of the recitative based on the chants of the old-time Negro preachers. Prod. in abridged concert from over NBC Radio, June 26, 1932. Prod. in its first stage perf. by the Cleveland Summer Opera Co., at Cleveland Stadium, June 30, 1932; dir. by Ernest Lert. With Jules Bledsoe in the leading role. Prog. notes in Moorland-Spingarn.

Dust to Earth // Orig. title: **Coal Dust** (drama, 3 acts [originally 28 scenes], 1938). Tragedy of black labor in the West Virginia coal mines, in which a father, who owns the mine, dies while trying to rescue his son. First prod. under its orig. title by the Gilpin Players at Karamu Theatre, Cleveland, for two weeks, April 26–May 7, 1938. Revised and retitled while the author was at Yale, and prod. by the Yale Univ. Theatre, New Haven, Jan. 1941. Again prod. under its present title by the Gilpin Players at Karamu Theatre, Cleveland, 1941.

I Gotta Home (1940). Prod. by the Gilpin Players, Cleveland, and presented at several locations in Ohio, including Oberlin Coll., Feb. 17, 1940, as a benefit for the Phillis Wheatley Community Center; at Case Western Reserve Univ., Feb. 21, 1940; at the Goodyear Theatre, Akron, March 23, 1940, as a benefit for the Assn. for Colored Community Work.

It's Morning (tragedy, 1 act, 1940). About a black mother who kills her own daughter to keep her from being sold into slavery. Prod. at the Yale Univ. School of Drama, New Haven, 1940; dir. by Otto Preminger, who was on the faculty at that time. Pub. in *Wines in the Wilderness* (Brown-Guillory, 1990).

Track Thirteen (radio comedy, 1 act, 1940). About the superstitions of black train porters who consider it bad luck if their train is scheduled to leave on track thirteen. Prod. by students at Yale Univ. School of Drama, over WICC Radio, New Haven, c. 1940. Sched. for prodn. by the Karamu Theatre, Cleveland, Dec. 1941, but prodn. cancelled because of Pearl Harbor. Pub. in *Yale Radio Plays* (Welch, 1940).

Elijah's Ravens (comedy, 3 acts, 1941). Title based on the Bible (1 Kings xvi: 4, 6), wherein God commands the ravens to feed the prophet Elijah by the brook of Cherith: "And I [God] have commanded the ravens to feed thee there. . . . And the ravens brought him bread and flesh in the morning, and bread and flesh in the evening; and he drank of the brook." About a preacher who believes that God will provide for him, as he did for Elijah, by means of an inheritance at his sister's death. Prod. by the Gilpin Players, Cleveland, 1941. Prod. by the Florida A. & M. State Coll. (now Univ.) Players, Tallahassee, 1940s; dir. by RANDOLPH EDMONDS. Also prod. by Atlanta Univ. Summer Theatre, 1941.

FURTHER REFERENCE: *Crisis* 5–1977 (Bernard L. Peterson, Jr., "Shirley Graham DuBois: Composer and Playwright," pp. 177–79). *Current Biog. 1946*. Hicklin diss. Silver diss. *WW in Am. 1972–73. WWCA 1950*.

DuBOIS, W.E.B. (William Edward Burghardt DuBois) (1868–1963), Distinguished American scholar, author, critic, editor, founder of organizations and periodicals, civil rights advocate, noted authority on black American and African culture, and pioneer pageant writer, who has been credited with being the inspiration for many of the developments in black American drama and theatre that occurred during the Black Renaissance. (Not to be confused, as he often was, with William DuBois, a white playwright and author of *Haiti*, a Federal Theatre play of black life.) Born in Great Barrington, MA, of mixed ethnic heritage, including Negro, French, Huguenot, and Dutch (" . . . but thank God! no 'Anglo-Saxon' "). Educated at Fisk University (B.A. 1888), Harvard University (B.A. cum laude, 1890; M.A. 1891; Ph.D. 1896), and the University of Berlin (graduate study, 1892–94). Twice married: first, in 1896, to Nina Gomer, who died in 1950; second, in 1951, to SHIRLEY GRAHAM [DuBOIS], an author, composer, and playwright, who died in 1977. Father of two children (both deceased) by his first marriage. Taught at Wilberforce University (professor of Greek and Latin, 1894–96); the University of Pennsylvania/Philadelphia (asst. instructor in sociology, 1896–97); Atlanta University (professor and chairman of dept. of sociology 1934–44). Cofounder and general secretary of the Niagara Movement, 1905–9, a movement in defense of rights for blacks, so named because its first meeting was held at Niagara Falls, NY. This movement was one of the most important precursors of the National Association for the Advancement of Colored People (NAACP), of which he was also one of the founding members. Associated with the NAACP in New York City from 1910 to about 1934 as director of publicity and research and editor of *Crisis*. During this period, DuBois wrote a number of pageants to educate black people themselves, as well as whites, about black history and culture, the rich emotional nature of blacks, and their numerous contributions to America and the world. Through articles and editorials in *Crisis*, he launched the NAACP's little theatre movement, which resulted in the formation of a number of little theatre groups throughout the East; initiated the *Crisis* Contest Awards, also called Krigwa [after Cri-C-Awa], 1925–27, to encourage the writing of plays and other literary forms; established the Krigwa Players Little Negro Theatre as a producing organization in New York City, Washington, DC, and other cities to produce the prizewinning plays of the *Crisis* Contest; and was responsible for helping to establish the NAACP Drama Committee in Washington, DC. Among the publications he founded and edited are *Moon* (1905–6), *Horizon* (1908–10), *Brownies' Book* (the NAACP's children's magazine, 1920–21), *Phylon Quarterly* (Atlanta University's review of race and culture, 1940–41), *Encyclopedia of the Negro* (editor-in-chief, 1933–45) and *Encyclopedia Africana* (head, preliminary planning, 1961–?). Author of numerous books, a few of which include: fiction: *Quest of the Silver Fleece* (novel, 1911), *Dark Princess, a Romance* (1928), *The Black Flame* (trilogy, 1957–61); nonfiction: *The Suppression of the African Slave Trade to the United States of America, 1638–1870* (published Ph.D. diss., Harvard Historical Series, 1896), *Atlanta University Studies* (ed., 1897–1911), *The Philadelphia Negro* (1899), *The Souls of Black Folk* (1903), *Darkwater: Voices from Within the Veil* (autobiog., 1920), *The Gift of Black Folk* (essays, 1924), *Dusk of Dawn: An Essay Toward the Autobiography of a Race Concept* (1940), *ABC of Color: Selections from over a Half-Century of the Writings of W.E.B. DuBois* (1963), *The Autobiography of W.E.B. DuBois: A Soliloquy on Viewing My Life from the Last Decade of Its First Century* (1968). Organizer, Pan-African Congress, 1919; vice chairman, Council of African Affairs, 1949; member of Communist Party, 1961. Recipient of numerous awards, including honorary doctor's degrees from Fisk University, Howard University, Atlanta University, Wilberforce University, Morgan State College, the University of Berlin, and Charles University in Prague; elected a Fellow of American Association for Advancement of Science; the first black man elected to the National Institute of Arts and Letters, 1943; made a Knight Commander of the Liberian Humane Order of African Redemption by the Liberian government; appointed Minister Plenipotentiary and Envoy Extraordinary by President Calvin Coolidge; recipient of the Spingarn Medal from NAACP, 1932; Lenin International Peace Prize, 1958. Immigrated to Ghana in 1960, where he became a Ghanian citizen in 1964, the year of his death at age 95 in Accra, Ghana, where he is buried.

Stage Works:

The Star of Ethiopia // Former titles: **The People of Peoples and Their Gifts to Men**; **The Jewel of Ethiopia** (pageant of black history, prelude and 6 episodes, 1911). Dramatizes the six gifts the black man has given the world: the Gift of Iron, the Gift of the Nile, the Gift of Faith, the Gift of Humiliation [*sic*], the Gift of Struggle Toward Freedom, and the Gift of Freedom for the Workers. This pageant is historically significant as the first successful venture in pageantry by a black writer and as one of the sparks that ignited the Black or so-called Harlem Renaissance. According to David Levering Lewis, professor of history at Howard Univ., DuBois wrote this pageant to ''get people interested in the development of Negro drama and to teach, on the one hand, the colored people themselves the meaning of their history and their rich emotional life through a new theatre, and, on the other, to reveal the Negro to the white world as a human, feeling thing.''—Paper read at the National Conf. on Black American Protest Drama and Theatre, Morgan State Univ., Baltimore, April 18–19, 1985. Conceived in 1911. Prod. with 350 actors at the National Emancipation Exposition, New York City, Oct. 25, 28, and 30,

1913; prod. and dir. by CHARLES BURROUGHS, assisted by Dora Cole Norman, Marie Stuart Jackson, and Augustus G. Dill. A total audience of 30,000 was reported to have witnessed this production. The pageant was presented in the New York City Armory, before the Exposition's Temple of Beauty, which served as its background. The *New York Times* (Oct. 23, 1913, p. 5) described the scene as follows:

The interior of the Armory has been artistically decorated [with an] Egyptian Art Temple constructed in the center of the Armory floor. . . . In it are shown the paintings, sculpture and other works of art executed by colored people. In the center stands an eight foot group of statuary, "Humanity Freeing the Slaves," the work of Miss Meta Warrick, a young colored woman from Philadelphia who studied three years under Rodin.

Prod. in Philadelphia, PA, at the General Conf. of the A.M.E. Church, May 16, 18, and 20, 1914. Prod. by the Horizon Guild in Washington, DC, in the open air, with 1,200 participants, in 1916. Prod. in Los Angeles, CA, 1925. Scenario pub. in *Crisis*, Nov. 1913, pp. 338–41. REVIEWS AND COMMENTARY: Author's commentary pub. in *Crisis* 10–1913; 12–1913; 12–1915; 8–1916. Excerpts from reviews in *Atlanta J.*, *Chicago Herald*, *New Haven* (CT) *Register*, and *Ohio State J.* pub. in *Crisis* 12–1915. Other commentary in Archer diss.

George Washington and the Black Folk ("A Pageant for the Bicentenary, 1732–1932" [subtitle], 5 scenes, 1932). The black Witch of Endor (who is veiled, with her gray robes flowing down to the floor) reads from the Book of Fate in her hand, recounting to George Washington (who symbolizes America) the accomplishments and deeds of great black men and women throughout history who speak in their own words and enact scenes from their roles in American history. Among the leading black speakers are Crispus Attucks, Phillis Wheatley, Benjamin Banneker, Richard Allen, and Prince Hall. Apparently based in part on W. W. Mazyck's *George Washington and the Negro* and Carter G. Woodson's *The Negro in Our History*. Pub. in *Crisis*, April 1932, pp. 121–24.

Other Pertinent Writings:
"Colored Folk in Theatres," *Crisis*, May 1912, p. 20.
"A Pageant," *Crisis*, Sept. 1915, pp. 230–31.
"The Star of Ethiopia," *Crisis*, Dec. 1915, pp. 90–94.
"The Drama Among Black Folk," *Crisis*, Aug. 1916, pp. 169–173.
"Another Pageant," *Crisis*, Aug. 1916, p. 196.
"The Negro Theatre," *Crisis*, Feb. 1918, unsigned.
"We Shuffle Along," *Crisis*, Sept. 1922, p. 143.
"Negro Theatre," *Crisis*, April 1923, p. 25.
"Can the Negro Serve the Drama?" *Theatre*, July 1923, p. 68.
"Ethiopian Art Theatre," *Crisis*, July 1923, pp. 103–4.
"Krigwa," *Crisis*, June 1925.
"Pageant of the Angels," *Crisis*, Sept. 1925, p. 217.
"Krigwa, 1926," *Crisis*, Nov. 1925.
"Krigwa, 1926," *Crisis*, Jan. 1926, p. 115.
"Krigwa," *Crisis*, June 1926, p. 59.
"Krigwa Players Little Negro Theatre," *Crisis*, July 1926, pp. 134–36.
"Krigwa, *Crisis* Prizes in Literature and Art, 1926," *Crisis*, Dec. 1926, pp. 7–71.
"Krigwa, 1927," *Crisis*, Jan. 1927, p. 128.

"Krigwa," *Crisis*, Nov. 1927, p. 312.
FURTHER REFERENCE: Archer diss. *Blk. Am. Writers* (Rush). *Contemp. Auths.*

DUDLEY, S. H. See Appendix B.

DUNBAR, PAUL LAURENCE (1872–1906), Major black American poet, best known for his poems in dialect; novelist, short story writer, playwright, and musical comedy lyricist. Born in Dayton, OH, the son of ex-slaves. Graduated from Central High School in Dayton in 1891, as the only black member of his class, where he had been class poet, president of the literary society, and editor of the school newspaper. After high school, he abandoned plans to attend college for lack of money, and took a job working as an elevator operator. During this period, he wrote poetry, some of which was published in various newspapers. His first volume of verse, *Oak and Ivy* (1893), was privately printed with the help of a loan from a white friend. In the spring of 1893, he went to Chicago, where the World's Fair was opening, in search of a good job. There, through the efforts of Frederick Douglass, who was commissioner in charge of the Haitian exhibit, he obtained a position as a clerical assistant, his salary being partly paid by Douglass. In Chicago he also met the noted actor Richard B. Harrison, who became a close personal friend for whom he wrote some stage works. With the help of other white friends, he privately printed his second collection of verse, *Majors and Minors* (1896), which included poems in both standard English (which he regarded as his "majors") and dialect (his "minors"). Critical opinion immediately reversed this classification. The book was reviewed in *Harper's Weekly* by William Dean Howells, who praised the dialect poems and all but dismissed the others. On the basis of this review, Dunbar went on a successful reading tour, which culminated in the publication by Dodd, Mead and Company of his third volume of poems, *Lyrics of Lowly Life* (1896), with the famous introduction by William Dean Howells that assured the book's success and established Dunbar securely as the most important black poet of his time. In 1898 he married Alice Ruth Moore [ALICE MOORE DUNBAR-NELSON], a poet and schoolteacher, from whom he separated in 1902. The couple lived in Washington, DC, where they fully participated in Washington society. Dunbar's later writings include novels, short story collections, several more volumes of poetry, plays, and musical comedy lyrics. His four novels are *The Uncalled* (1898), *The Love of Landry* (1900), *The Fanatics* (1901), and *The Sport of the Gods* (1902); only the latter is concerned primarily with black characters. His collections of short stories include *Folks from Dixie* (1898), *The Strength of Gideon* (1900), *In Old Plantation Days* (1903), and *The Heart of Happy Hollow* (1904). Among his later volumes of poetry are *Lyrics of the Hearthside* (1899), *Lyrics of Love and Laughter* (1903), and *Lyrics of Sunshine and Shadow* (1905). In 1899 Dunbar became seriously ill with pneumonia, from which he developed chronic lung trouble—complicated by addiction to alcohol—which gradually led to his early death from tuberculosis at age 34.

Stage Works:

PLAYS

The Stolen Calf (drama, 1 act, c. 1891). No description has been located, although there is reportedly a plot narration by Randolph Tams.—*Paul Laurence Dunbar and His Song* (Cunningham, 1948), pp. 273–74. First prod. by the Philodramian Club of Central High School, Dayton, OH, during the 1890s; presumably dir. and acted in by the author while he was a student, around 1891.

Uncle Eph's Christmas (vaudeville sketch, 1 act, 1899). Music by †WILL MARION COOK. One of several sketches written for vaudeville star †Ernest Hogan. Dialect play with interpolated songs, depicting a Christmas celebration in the cabin of Uncle Eph, Aunt Chloe, and their children, in which Uncle Eph becomes intoxicated in the presence of their neighbors and guests, among which are the village gossip and Parson Jones. Ends with the cakewalk, a very popular dance finale of the period. First prod. in Boston Music Hall during Christmas week, Dec. 1899.

Robert Herrick // Also cited as **Herrick** (comedy of manners, 3 acts, c. 1899). Dunbar's only full-length play, written in a style imitative of Richard Brinsley Sheridan or Oscar Wilde. Described by Benjamin Brawley (*Paul Laurence Dunbar: Poet of His People,* 1935, p. 85) as "a light, airy drama . . . based on the life of the English poet. . . . " The first of two plays written for his friend, the noted actor and dramatic reader Richard B. Harrison, c. 1899. Unpub. script in the Dunbar Collection, Ohio Historical Society, Columbus, OH.

Winter Roses (drama, 1 act, 1899). According to Brawley (ibid.), this play "used the theme of an old man who was urged by his son to see his sweetheart, the daughter of a widow, and who, going to call on the maiden, found that her mother was his first love years before." The second of two plays written for Richard B. Harrison, c. 1899.

The Quibbler's Wife (unfinished melodrama, 5 pp., c. 1900). Based on the author's story "The Gambler's Wife," printed in the Dayton *Tatler,* Dec. 13, 20, and 27, 1890. Described by Brawley (ibid.) as "a melodrama in which the neglected heroine, Madge, seeks to escape from a tedious marriage to her gambler husband by eloping with a lover." Unpub. script in the Dunbar Collection; issues of the *Tatler* in which Dunbar's story appeared are presumably in the archives of the Ohio Historical Society.

MUSICALS

[NOTE: Librettos are listed first, followed by OTHER MUSICALS to which Dunbar contributed. Musicals marked with a plus sign (+) are briefly annotated in Appendix B. Coauthors marked with an obelisk (†) are also listed in Appendix B.]

Dream Lovers ("operatic romance," 1 act, 1898). Libretto by Dunbar. Music by Samuel Coleridge-Taylor. Serving as a background for six musical numbers, the loosely constructed plot, according to THOMAS PAWLEY (*Black World,* April 1975, p. 73), revolves around the love of "Torado, a mulatto prince from Madagascar, baritone" for "Katherine, a quadroon lady, soprano." No record of prodn. Pub. by Boosey & Co., London, 1898.

On the Island of Tanawana (unfinished musical comedy, fragment of 1 act and a few additional pages, c. 1900). Libretto by Dunbar. Described by Pawley (ibid.) as follows: "A millionaire soap manufacturer is crowned king of a mythical island only to discover his daughter has eloped with a native prince."

OTHER MUSICALS: **+Clorindy, the Origin of the Cakewalk** (ragtime musical show, also called an operetta, full length, 1898/1901). Lyrics by Dunbar, who also wrote a libretto that was never used. Concept, orig. sketch, and music by Will Marion Cook. Prod. at the Casino Roof Garden, New York, summer of 1898, running the entire summer; with Ernest Hogan, Belle Davis, and Abbie Mitchell. Continued to be performed on the road from 1898 to 1901. **+Jes Lak White Folks** (musical, full length, 1900). Additional lyrics by Dunbar. Book and lyrics mainly by Will Marion Cook. Prod. at the New York Winter Garden, June 26, 1900; with Abbie Mitchell and Irving Jones. **+In Dahomey** (musical farce, 3 acts, 1902/5). Lyrics by Dunbar and †JESSE A. SHIPP. Book by Shipp. Music by Will Marion Cook and others. Opened on the road in 1902, reaching Bway at the New York Theatre, Feb. 18, 1903, for 53 perfs. Taken to London the same year, running for seven months at the Shaftsbury Theatre, for 150 perfs. Became a London hit after a command perf. at Buckingham Palace in honor of the ninth birthday of the Prince of Wales. After touring the English provinces for about five months, returned to the United States, touring for 40 weeks before closing in 1905. **Mr. Bluebeard** (white-oriented musical extravaganza, 3 acts, 1903). Based on the Drury Lane pantomime of the same title, brought over from London and adapted for the American stage. Included one interpolated song, ''W'en de Colo'ed Ban' Comes Ma'chin Down de Street,'' with words by Dunbar, music by †BOB COLE and †J. ROSAMOND JOHNSON. Prod. at the Knickerbocker Theatre, New York, opening Jan. 21, 1903, for 134 perfs.; with an all-white cast.

FURTHER REFERENCE: *Blk. World* 4–1975 (Thomas D. Pawley, ''Dunbar as Playwright,'' pp. 70–79). *DANB. Paul Laurence Dunbar and His Song* (Cunningham). *Paul Laurence Dunbar: Poet of His People* (Brawley). Paul Laurence Dunbar Papers (1872–1906) in the Dunbar Collection, Ohio Historical Society, Columbus, OH. Other resources in Schomburg and Moorland-Spingarn.

DUNBAR-NELSON, ALICE MOORE (formerly Mrs. Paul Laurence Dunbar) (1875–1935), Teacher, lecturer, author, editor, and playwright, described by Ann Allen Shockley (*AfrAmWW*, 1988, p. 262) as ''a precursor of the Harlem Renaissance, as well as a participant in it.'' Born in New Orleans, LA, the daughter of a member of the merchant marine and a seamstress. Educated at Straight College (now Dillard University), New Orleans, graduating in 1892; the University of Pennsylvania; Cornell University; and the School of Industrial Arts in Philadelphia. Married three times: first, in 1898, to PAUL LAURENCE DUNBAR, who died in 1906; second, in 1910, to Arthur Callis, a teacher; and third, in 1916, to Robert John Nelson, a newspaper publisher. Taught school in New Orleans and Brooklyn, NY, prior to her marriage to Dunbar. Headed the English Dept. of Howard High School in Wilmington, DE, 1902–20. One of the founders of, and a teacher in, the Industrial School for Colored Girls in Delaware, 1924–28. Assoc. editor of the *African Methodist Review* for a while, and editor of the *Wilmington Advocate* for three years. Contributed short stories and essays to a number of periodicals and newspapers, including the *Washington Eagle, Journal of Negro History, Negro History Bulletin, Crisis,* and *Opportunity.* Editor of *Masterpieces of Negro Eloquence* (1914) and *The Dunbar Speaker and Entertainer* (1920), cited below. Author of *Violets and Other Tales* (essays, poems, sketches, and stories, 1895); *The Goodness of St. Rocque and Other Stories* (14 stories, 1899); two unpublished novels: *This Lofty Oak* and *Confessions of a Lazy Woman*; and a posthumously published diary, *Give Us Each Day* (ed. by Gloria T. Hull, 1984). [Hull also edited her collected *Works,* cited below.] A member of numerous clubs, including the Women's International League for Peace and Freedom, the National Federation of Colored Women's Clubs, the NAACP, and Delta Sigma Theta sorority. She died of a heart ailment in a Philadelphia hospital at age 60.

Collections:
THE DUNBAR SPEAKER AND ENTERTAINER, Containing the Best Prose and Poetic Selections by and About the Negro Race. Ed. by Dunbar-Nelson. J. L. Nicholas & Co., Naperville, IL, 1920. Contains: **Mine Eyes Have Seen** (1918).

AN ALICE DUNBAR-NELSON READER. Ed. by Ruby Ora Williams. Univ. Press of America, Washington, DC, 1979. Contents not analyzed.

THE WORKS OF ALICE DUNBAR-NELSON. 3 vols. Ed. by Gloria T. Hull. Oxford Univ. Press, New York, 1988. Contents not analyzed.

Stage Works:
The Author's Evening at Home (sketch, 1900). Pub. in *The Smart Set,* Sept. 1900, pp. 105–6.

An Hawaiian Idyll (operetta, 3 acts, 1916). Music arranged by Etta A. Reach. High school operetta, set in Hawaii. Prod. as a Christmas entertainment by Howard High School, Wilmington, DE, Dec. 1916, with costumes designed by Agatha F. Jones and an orchestra of native Hawaiian instruments; dir. by Conwell Benton.

Mine Eyes Have Seen (melodrama, 1 act, 1918). Patriotic play, taking its title from "The Battle Hymn of the Republic," written during World War I, and dramatizing the loyalty of blacks to their country in spite of the terrible racial injustices that they have faced. A young man who receives a military draft notice feels that he should claim an exemption from service as the sole support of his crippled brother and older sister, neither of whom is able to work. They are the last remaining members of a prosperous middle-class family forced to flee north after their house was burned down in the South and their father murdered. Their mother is now dead from grief and exposure. Why, the young man asks, should he serve a country that has done nothing for him? But he is exhorted by his family and their white friends (all members of various ethnic minorities) to answer the call of his country—not only out of patriotism and loyalty, but for the love of humanity, which needs him, and for the honor of his race, which has served in every war from 1776 to the present. Prod. by the author at Howard High School, Wilmington, DE, prior to its publication in *Crisis,* April 1919, pp. 271–75. Also pub. in *THE DUNBAR SPEAKER AND ENTERTAINER; BlkThUSA* (Hatch, 1974); and presumably in *AN ALICE DUNBAR-NELSON READER* and *THE WORKS OF ALICE DUNBAR-NELSON.*
FURTHER REFERENCE: *AfroAmWW* (Shockley). *NegGen* (Brawley). *Neg. Hist. Bull.* 4–1968. *Profiles of Neg. Womanhood* (1964). *Their Place on Stage* (Brown-Guillory).

DUNCAN, THELMA MYRTLE (1902–   ), Pioneer playwright of the 1920s and 1930s; a product of the activity in drama at Howard University under professors Alain Locke and Montgomery Gregory. Studied playwriting under Gregory; at least two of her plays were written in his class. Was among the first playwrights whose works were produced at Howard and later anthologized by Locke and Gregory in their classic anthology, *Plays of Negro Life* (1927).

Stage Works:

The Death Dance (''An African Play'' [subtitle] with music and dancing, 1 act, 1923). Musical score by Victor Kerney. Drama of love and death, set in an African village, using drums and dance for theatrical effect. During a ''trial by ordeal,'' a powerful and respected medicine man is exposed as a murderer, robber, and cheat when he attempts to use his medicines to influence the outcome of the ''trial.'' Written in Montgomery Gregory's class at Howard and first prod. by the Howard Players, Washington, DC, opening April 7, 1923. Pub. in *PlaysNegL* (Locke & Gregory, 1927).

The Scarlet Shawl (1 act, 1920s).

Sacrifice (drama, 1 act, 1930). Concerns the sacrifices that a widowed mother and a good friend make in order that a seemingly undeserving student (who has stolen the questions for a final exam) can graduate from college. Pub. in *Plays&Pags* (Richardson, 1930).

Black Magic (comedy, 1 act, 1931). A satire of black folk superstitions, in which a husband, thinking that his wife has deserted him, engages the services of a fake voodoo man. Pub. in *Yrbk. of Short Plays* (1931).

FURTHER REFERENCE: Hicklin diss.

E

EASTON, SIDNEY (1891–?), Early vaudeville performer, film actor, songwriter, screenwriter, and playwright. Born in the South, where he began his theatrical career working in minstrel shows, tent shows, and carnivals. Came to New York in the early 1900s, where he met and came under the influence of the popular musical comedy stars Bert Williams and George Walker. With their aid, he developed his comedic skills and later branched out on his own, traveling around the country on the vaudeville circuits. During the 1930s, he appeared in several Hollywood films. He composed a few popular songs, including "Go Back Where You Stayed Last Night," in collaboration with Ethel Waters, who sang it in her one-woman show, *At Home with Ethel Waters* (1953).

Stage and Screen Works:

Lifeboat 13 (screenplay, full length, late 1930s). Allegedly, this script was illegally used by Twentieth Century-Fox as a basis of its 1944 film *Lifeboat,* which was credited to John Steinbeck and directed by Alfred Hitchcock, starring Canada Lee, Tallulah Bankhead, William Bendix, John Hodiak, and Henry Hull. According to *Loften Mitchell (*BlkDr,* 1967, p. 160), Easton asked actor Leigh Whipper to use his influence to present his screenplay to Fox, which Whipper did, but nothing was ever heard of it. Years later, Easton saw the Hitchcock film and realized that his script had actually been used. He immediately filed a suit for damages and eventually received an out-of-court settlement.

Miss Trudie Fair (drama, full length, c. 1953). A period-play about a kind-hearted, churchgoing Harlem woman, a former theatre worker, who now operates a boardinghouse for theatrical people. Among the types who populate her home are small-time actors, producers, agents, and two-bit hustlers, many of whom are frequently behind in their rent but still allowed to stay. Miss Trudie falls under the spell of one of the hustlers, who marries her and tries to take control of her establishment, completely destroying the harmony and tranquility that had previously existed within Miss Trudie's menage. However, everything eventually comes out all right in the end. Loften Mitchell (ibid., p. 159) states that this was "the last professional show to be seen in Harlem during the 1950s." Prod. by the New Playwrights Co., around 1953, under the management of Stanley

Green. Opened first in White Plains, NY, moving next to St. Albans in Queens, and finally to the Harlem Showcase at 290 Lenox Ave., where it was a tremendous success. Cast included Juanita Bethea and Ted Butler in the principal roles; with Mary and Freddie Simpson, Frank Cottrell, Howard Augusta, Service Bell, Javott Sutton, and Grace Kemp. *Harold Cruse was stage manager and Loften Mitchell was assoc. producer and dir. of public relations.
FURTHER REFERENCE: *BlkDr* (Mitchell).

EASTON, WILLIAM EDGAR (1861–?), Pioneer playwright who wrote two plays of Haitian history. Born in New Bedford, MA, where his family can be traced back to the Revolutionary War. His great-grandfather was a captain of Indian Scouts, and his grand uncle, James Easton, was reportedly the engineer who designed the fortification for Bunker Hill, then known as Breed's Hill. Dissatisfied with the comic portrayals of blacks on the stage during his time, he decided to write more serious plays of a time and place when blacks had a noble history and great military heroes. As he wrote in his introduction to **Dessalines** (1893): "Indeed we have had excellent caricaturists of the Negro, in his only recognized school of legitimate drama, i.e., buffoonery. But the author of this work hopes to see a happier era inaugurated by the constant production of legitimate drama written exclusively for Negro players."—Pub. script. In 1911 Easton was living in Los Angeles, CA, where his second play, **Christophe,** was published and the following year produced. In 1915 he was appointed subcustodian of the California state capitol building at Sacramento.

Stage Works:

Dessalines (historical drama in verse, 4 acts, 1893). Subtitled "A Dramatic Tale: A Single Chapter from Haiti's History." Melodramatic treatment of the life of Jean Jacques Dessalines (1758–1806), the Haitian revolutionary general who roused his countrymen to revolt against the French and their allies to achieve Haiti's independence. As a result of his leadership in this successful revolt, Dessalines rose to become emperor of Haiti, reigning for two years, from 1804 to his assassination in 1806. Fannin Belcher praised the play as "a colorful melodrama far superior to any play written by a Negro thus far [1945]," and considered its "major flaws" to be "a confusion of scenes and fondness for declamatory speeches."—Belcher, Ph.D. diss. (1945), p. 327n2. Prod. by a black company organized in Chicago by Henrietta Vinton Davis, and presented at the Haitian Pavilion of the Chicago World's Fair, Jan. 1893. Pub. by J. W. Burson Co., Galveston, TX, 1893; copies in Moorland-Spingarn, Schomburg, Hatch-Billops, and TC/NYPL.

  Christophe ("A Tragedy in Prose of Imperial Haiti" [subtitle], 4 acts, 1911). About Henri Christophe (1767–1820), the Haitian revolutionary general who became king of Haiti (1811–20) after the assassination of Dessalines (above). A melodrama, set in imperial Haiti, dramatizing through a series of tragic episodes the circumstances that led to Christophe's overthrow and death. Prod. at the Gamut Auditorium, Los Angeles, 1912. Pub. by Grafton Pub. Co., Los Angeles, 1911; copies in Moorland-Spingarn and Schomburg.
FURTHER REFERENCE: *CLAJ* 9–1975.

EDMONDS, RANDOLPH (S[heppard] Randolph Edmonds) (1900–1983), Prolific pioneer playwright, drama teacher, director, and organizer of drama associations and festivals among predominantly black colleges in the Southeast.

Well known as "The Dean of Black Academic Theatre." Born in Lawrenceville, VA, the son of sharecroppers and the grandson of ex-slaves. Attended St.
Paul's Normal and Industrial School (now St. Paul's College) in Lawrenceville,
graduating as valedictorian (high school) in 1921 and winning both the English
and history prizes. Received further education at Oberlin College (B.A. in English, 1926), where he began playwriting and also organized the Dunbar Forum,
a cultural organization for black students that produced several of his early plays;
Columbia University (A.M. in English and drama, 1934); Yale University School
of Drama (on a General Education Board Fellowship, 1934–35); Dublin University and the London School of Speech Training and Dramatic Arts, while
making an observational study of amateur drama organizations in England, Ireland, Scotland, and Wales (on a Rosenwald Fellowship, 1937–38). Served in
the U.S. Army, 1943–44, as a captain in the Special Services Div., stationed
at Ft. Huachuca, AZ, where he was assigned to develop a program of soldier
shows for black troops. First married in 1931 to *Irene Colbert [Edmonds], a
pioneer playwright and director in the children's theatre at Dillard University
and Florida A. & M. University; she died in 1968. They were parents of two
children: *Henriette Edmonds, a drama director, playwright, and former chairman of the Drama Dept. of Howard University, and S. Randolph Edmonds, Jr.,
a successful pediatrician. His second marriage was to Ara Manson Turner, a
Lawrenceville, VA, widow and businesswoman. After graduating from Oberlin,
Edmonds took a position as instructor of English and drama (moving up to
professor and chairman of the dept.) at Morgan College (now State University),
Baltimore, where he organized and directed the Morgan College Players, 1926–
34. Joined the faculty of Dillard University, New Orleans, where he directed
the Dillard Players' Guild, 1935–47. Finally moved to Florida A. & M. University, Tallahassee, where he served for more than 20 years as chairman of the
Dept. of Speech and Drama and directed the Florida A. & M. [FAMU] Playmakers Guild, 1947–69, when he retired and returned to Lawrenceville. Founder
of the Negro Intercollegiate Drama Association (NIDA), 1930; the Southern
Association of Dramatic and Speech Arts (SADSA), 1936, which later became
the National Association of Dramatic and Speech Arts (NADSA); and helped to
organize the high school speech and drama groups of Louisiana and Florida into
statewide associations. Author of three published collections of plays, more than
50 individual plays, and numerous articles on drama and the theatre. Memberships included American Theatre Association, National Theatre Conference,
Southeastern Theatre Conference, American National Theatre and Academy,
Florida Speech Association, Association for the Study of Negro Life and History,
and American Association of University Professors. In addition to the fellowships
named above, honors and awards include a Carnegie Foundation Grant-in-Aid,
1948, to write a "history of the Negro in the Western world theatre"; an honorary
Doctor of Letters from Bethune-Cookman College, 1959; appointment to Fellow
by the American Educational Theatre Association, 1968; election to the Board
of Trustees of St. Paul's College, 1972; and a Special Citation from the American

Theatre Association, 1972, "for his contributions to the Association and the theatre." Presented posthumously with the Mister Brown Award (named after the playwright [Mister] BROWN, manager of the African Grove Theatre), "for Excellence in Theatre," by the National Conference on Black American Drama and Theatre, Morgan State University, Baltimore, 1985. Other prizes and awards are cited below.

Collections:

SHADES AND SHADOWS. Meador Pub. Co., Boston, 1930. Xerographic reprints available from Univ. Microfilms International, Ann Arbor, MI. Contains: **The Devil's Price** (1930), **Hewers of Wood** (1930), **Shades and Shadows** (1930), **Everyman's Land** (1930), **The Tribal Chief** (1930), and **The Phantom Treasure** (1930).

SIX PLAYS FOR A NEGRO THEATRE. [*SIX PLAYS*] Walter Baker, Boston, 1934. Xerographic reprints available from Univ. Microfilms International, Ann Arbor, MI. Contains: **Bad Man** (1932), **Old Man Pete** (1934), **Nat Turner** (1934), **Breeders** (1934), **Bleeding Hearts** (1927), and **The New Window** (1934).

THE LAND OF COTTON AND OTHER PLAYS [LAND OF COTTON]. Associated Pubs., Washington, DC, 1942. Xerographic reprints available from Univ. Microfilms International, Ann Arbor, MI. Contains: **The Land of Cotton** (1938), **Gangsters over Harlem** (1939), **Yellow Death** (1935), **Silas Brown** (1927), and **The High Court of Historia** (1939).

Stage Works before 1950:

(All directed by the author.)

Job Hunting (folk play, short 1 act, 1922). Sitting on a park bench, two lazy, un-employed black men complain about the difficulty of finding a job, but have no serious intention of looking for work. Received honorable mention in the *Opportunity* Contest Awards, 1922. Prod.

Christmas Gift (1 act, 1922). A wealthy old woman outwits two con artists who gain entry to her home on the pretense of soliciting a Christmas donation for a local hero.

A Merchant in Dixie (drama, 1 act, 1923). A white merchant in the Deep South proves his friendship to a black NAACP worker whom he has known since childhood, and with whom he fought on the battlefields of France during World War I.

Doom (folk play, 1 act, 1924). An aunt who has prophesied that her nephew will come to no good end if he does not follow the work philosophy of Booker T. Washington sees her prophecy fulfilled when her nephew becomes a bootlegger and is shot by the sheriff. No extant script.

The [Black] Highwayman (tragedy, 1 act, 1925). Dramatization of Alfred Noyes' poem "The Highwayman." A romantic young black bootlegger is entrapped by the sheriff of a small southern town, who uses the bootlegger's sweetheart as bait to lure him into the trap. Prod.

Illicit Love (folk tragedy, 1 act, 1926; apparently expanded to 3 acts, 1927). Romeo and Juliet-like story of interracial love, involving the son of a black sharecropper and the daughter of a white southern planter, which ends in the shooting of the black man by the woman's father. Received honorable mention in the *Crisis* Contest Awards, Oct. 1926.

Peter Stith (drama, 1-act version, 1926). An earlier version of both his one-act play **Old Man Pete** (1934) and his three-act play, also entitled **Peter Stith** (1935). Concerns an old couple from the South who freeze to death in New York's Central Park because their children are ashamed of their country ways. Received honorable mention in the *Crisis* Contest Awards, Oct. 1926. Prod. by a group of black students at Oberlin under the auspices of the Dunbar Forum, Oberlin, OH, 1927.

Rocky Roads (comedy-drama, 3 acts, 1926). His first full-length play, written while a student at Oberlin. Concerns the obstacles that impede the course of love and happiness, as well as the professional career, of a young black medical doctor at the beginning of his practice in Alabama. First prod. by the Dunbar Forum at a high school in Oberlin, May 15, 1926. Copy of program in Williams, Ph.D. diss. (1972), pp. 82–83.

A Virginia Politician (tragedy, 1 act, 1927). A black maid, forced to yield to the sexual advances of a white Virginia politician who preaches against miscegenation, gives birth to his two children, with tragic consequences.

Bleeding Hearts (folk drama, 1 act, 1927). A sentimental play set in slavery times, depicting the hopelessness and despair of slave life under this system. Received honorable mention in the *Opportunity* Contest Awards, June 1927. Prod. at a drama festival in Columbus, OH, April 1935. Pub. in *SIX PLAYS*.

Silas Brown (folk tragedy, 1 act, 1927). Concerns the disintegration of a farm family because of the stinginess and sternness of the father toward his wife and son. Prod. by a group of black students at Oberlin, under the auspices of the Dunbar Forum, March 5, 1927.

Takazee (''A Pageant of Ethiopia'' [subtitle], full length, 1928). Dramatizes the history of Ethiopia in dialogue, pantomime, music, song, and dance, with special emphasis on the reign of King Menelik. Prod. by the Division of Recreation, Baltimore, MD, 1934, with a cast of over 1,000 people.

One Side of Harlem (drama, full length, 1928). The members of a Harlem family, who have migrated from the South, refuse to modify their southern rural customs, to the disdain and embarrassment of their neighbors, also from the South, who have adapted to the city's more sophisticated lifestyle.

Sirlock Bones (mystery-comedy, 1 act, 1928). A parody of the Sherlock Holmes detective stories, with a black detective as the hero. Prod. by the Morgan State Coll. Players, at the Apollo Theatre, New York, 1928.

Stock Exchange (musical, full length, 1928). A group of blacks organize their own stock exchange, and at first grow prosperous in their financial dealings, until the inevitable ''crash'' occurs.

Denmark Vesey (historical drama, 1 act, 1929). About the famous leader of a slave insurrection in South Carolina during the 1820s.

The Devil's Price (fantasy, 4 acts, 1930). Anti-dictatorship play, utilizing a Faustian theme, with angels and devils contending for the soul of the main character. Pub. in *SHADES AND SHADOWS*.

Drama Enters the Curriculum (didactic play, 1 act, 1930). Dramatic argument to show why drama should be a part of the college curriculum. Prod. at Morgan State Coll., Baltimore, 1930.

Everyman's Land (fantasy, 1 act, 1930). Two soldiers, one black, one white, who die on the battlefield of France during World War I, learn that in death they are both equal. Pub. in *SHADES AND SHADOWS*.

Hewers of Wood (mythical drama, 1 act, 1930). An angel releases the blacks from their ''destiny'' as hewers of wood and drawers of water for the white man after they have been tested by both the devil and the god of Ethiopia. Pub. in *SHADES AND SHADOWS*.

The Phantom Treasure (drama, 1 act, 1930). Concerns the search for a hidden treasure by two young black men. The treasure was believed to be buried by the slave grandfather of one of the men. Pub. in *SHADES AND SHADOWS*.

Shades and Shadows (melodrama, 1 act, 1930). Mystery drama in which an uncle is thwarted in his plans to put his nephew into an asylum. Pub. in *SHADES AND SHADOWS*.

The Tribal Chief (melodrama, 1 act, 1930). A Tibetan tribal chief, who condemns a man and woman to death for fornication, also meets his death by poetic justice. Pub. in *SHADES AND SHADOWS*.

The Man of God (drama, 3 acts, 1931). Concerns the plight of a prosperous minister when his wife and church members discover his involvement with a Sunday school teacher who has been helping with his sermons and other church work.

Bad Man (folk melodrama, 1 act, 1932). Overly sentimental play that is nevertheless significant as an early example of the use of the brute Negro ("bad nigger") as a symbol of black manhood and bravery. Prod. by the Morgan State Coll. Players, at a tournament of the Negro Intercollegiate Dramatic Association (NIDA), held at Virginia Union Univ., Richmond, VA, 1932. Pub. in *SIX PLAYS*; in *NegCarav* (Brown et al., 1942); and in *BlkThUSA* (Hatch, 1974).

Breeders (folk tragedy, 1 act, 1934). A slave girl commits suicide rather than marry the strapping mate her master has picked out for her after her true love has been slain for opposing the match. Prod. by the Columbus (OH) Experimental Theatre, Jan. 1938. Pub. by Walter H. Baker, 1934; in *SIX PLAYS*; in *NegCarav* (Brown et al., 1942); and in *BlkThUSA* (Hatch, 1974).

For Fatherland (melodrama, 1 act, 1934). Concerns one of Hitler's guards, who unsuccessfully tries to escape a purge of his organization by fleeing to Switzerland prior to World War II. In the end he is caught and subjected to Nazi punishment. Prod. by Yale Univ. School of Drama, New Haven, 1934.

The High Court of Historia (black history pageant, 1 long act, 1934/39). Written especially for prodn. during Black History Week, this pageant urges that black history be taught only from texts written by black scholars in order to teach race pride and to correct the fallacies that white historians have recorded about black people. Apparently first prod. by the Dillard Players' Guild, in the Theatre Workshop, Dillard Univ., New Orleans, Feb. 16, 1939. Pub. in *LAND OF COTTON*.

Nat Turner (black history play, 1 act [2 scenes], 1934). One of the earliest plays about the famous black insurrectionist. Won for Edmonds a scholarship to the Yale School of Drama, 1934. Won first prize in the Intercollegiate Drama Association (IDA) tournament at Petersburg, VA, 1935, where it was also first presented. Also prod. at the Columbus, Ohio [Drama] Festival, April 1935. Pub. in *SIX PLAYS* and in *NegHist13* (Richardson & Miller, 1935).

The New Window (folk melodrama, 1 act, 1934). Poetic justice is meted out to a mean and hated bootlegger who bullies his wife, mistreats his stepdaughter, and has murdered a man for interfering with his bootlegging. Pub. in *SIX PLAYS*.

Old Man Pete (folk melodrama, 1 act, 1934). The revised, retitled, and published version of his prizewinning one-act play, **Peter Stith** (1926), with no apparent change in plot. Pub. in *SIX PLAYS* and in *AmLitNA* (Dreer, 1950).

The Call of Jubah (folk tragedy, 1 act, 1935). In her grief and despair after the lynching of her nephew Jubah in a small southern town, Aunt Sarah imagines that she hears his voice calling her into the swamp, and she follows it to her death. No extant script.

Yellow Death (historical play, 1 act, 1935). "Written for special Negro History Week production to point out the fact that the Negro has played a heroic part, even if only a small one, in the fight against the dreaded scourge of yellow fever."—Pub. script. Prod. by the Morgan Coll. Players, at Douglass High School, Baltimore, Feb. 14, 1935. Pub. in *LAND OF COTTON*.

The Land of Cotton // Orig. title: **Sharecroppers** (drama, 4 acts, 1938). Social protest play, set in the Deep South, which "deals effectively with the theme of black and white sharecroppers uniting to fight injustice."—*Neg. YrBK., 1947*, p. 466. According to the author's commentary in *Neg. Hist. Bull.*, May 1943, p. 190:

The play was begun in the playwriting class in Yale University in 1935 where the author was in attendance on a fellowship granted by the General Education Board. Walter Prichard was the instructor. It was later finished and submitted for credit for the course. During 1938 two more revisions were made in Dublin, Ireland, where the author had gone to study. It won first prize in a national playwriting contest sponsored by the Foundation of Expressive Arts in Baltimore, Maryland. It is designed for production more in the social theatres than in the university theatres.

First prod. under its orig. title by the Civic Theatre Guild of the Spring Street YMCA at Ogden Theatre, Columbus, OH, May 29, 1938. Prod. under its present title by the People's Community Theatre of New Orleans, at the Longshoreman's Hall, March 20 and 21, 1941. Pub. in *LAND OF COTTON*.

Wives and Blues (romantic melodrama, 3 acts, 1938). Dramatization of a serialized story by Ralph Matthews, which appeared in the *Afro-American* newspaper, concerning the three wives who shape the life of lawyer-songwriter Leslie Kayne and the events that lead to his being convicted of murder.

Gangsters over Harlem (melodrama, 1 act, 1939). Plot revolves around the rivalry between members of two numbers-racket organizations in Harlem. First prod. by the Dillard Univ. Players' Guild, New Orleans, Feb. 16, 1939. Also presented at the Fourth Annual Conf. of SADSA, held at Talladega Coll., AL, April 28, 1939. Pub. in *LAND OF COTTON*.

Simon in Cyrene (biblical drama, 1 act, 1939; expanded to 3 acts, 1943). About the black man who bore the cross for Christ to Calvary. One-act version prod. 1939. Three-act version prod. by the Dillard Univ. Players, New Orleans, 1943.

G. I. Rhapsody (musical drama, full length, 1943). Coauthor with Wilbur Strickland and others. Army show, featuring skits, songs, dances, and musical numbers. Prod. by the Special Services Div., Ft. Huachuca, AZ, at the Univ. of Arizona Auditorium, Tucson, Dec. 29, 1943.

The Shape of Wars to Come (comedy, 1 act, 1943). Fantasy about war, set in the year 2500, when sexual roles are reversed; women are depicted as soldiers, while the men are left at home to raise the children. First prod. at Ft. Huachuca, AZ, 1943. Prod. at the tenth anniversary of the Dillard Players' Guild, at Dillard Univ., New Orleans, Spring 1945.

The Shadow Across the Path (fantasy, 1 act, 1943). Tragedy results when a shadow falls across the path of a mean, unjust, and unmerciful man. No extant script.

The Trial and Banishment of Uncle Tom (didactic play, 1 act, 1945). According to the author, "the grinning, black faced, subservient, knuckling stereotype" of Uncle Tom is tried and banished forever from drama and literature for his crime of perpetuating a false image of black people "and holding back the progress of the Negro stage."—*Neg.*

Hist. Bull., Jan. 1949, p. 93. Prod. by the Dillard Univ. Players' Guild, as a feature of its tenth anniversary celebration, New Orleans, Spring 1945; with the author in the role of the Judge.

Earth and Stars (drama, 3 acts, 1946; revised 1961). According to Darwin Turner, "the original version . . . explored problems of southern leadership during the reconversion following World War II. The revised version . . . brought the problem up to date by emphasizing the civil rights struggle of the 1960s.''—Intro. to pub. script, p. 378. The leading character, a minister, is reminiscent of Martin Luther King, Jr. First prod. during Negro History Week at Dillard Univ., Feb. 14–16, 1946. Has been prod. by numerous black schools and community theatre groups throughout the South. Pub. in the revised version in *BlkDrAm* (Turner, 1971).

Whatever the Battle Be ("A Symphonic Drama" [subtitle], full length, 1947/50). Selected incidents, in narration, pantomime, dance, and song, presenting the history of Florida A. & M. Univ. from its founding in 1887 to c. 1950. Prod. by the FAMU Playmakers and the Music Dept., at Tallahassee, on the eve of the inauguration services of the sixth president of the univ., 1950.

Prometheus and the Atom (fantasy, full length, 1948/55). The destructive use of the atomic bomb is related to the story of Prometheus in its concern with the misuse of a God-given power. Prod. at Florida A. & M. Univ., Tallahassee, late 1940s. Also presented by the same group in 1955.

Stage Works Since 1950:

Career or College (didactic play, 1 act, 1956). Dramatic debate concerning the advantages of going to college or going directly into a career, in which four college students justify their positions under the cross-examination of four lawyers. Prod. at FAMU, 1956.
FAMU's Objective IV (didactic play, 1 act, 1964). Dramatizes the importance of fine arts as one of Florida A. & M. Univ.'s educational objectives. Prod. at FAMU, 1964.
Down in the Everglades (drama, 1 act, 1964). A black man, lost in the Everglades, is discovered by an Indian girl who cannot speak English. Thinking that he has proposed marriage, she tells her father, the Chief, who threatens to kill the man if he does not go through with the ceremony. Presented by the FAMU Playmakers more than 40 times during their European tour, 1964. **Climbing Jacob's Ladder** (symphonic drama, 2 parts, 1967). Spectacular pageant depicting in narrative, drama, music, song, and dance the history of black involvement in the Methodist Church. Based on a black history of the church written by Dr. James A. Brawley, former president of Clark Coll., Atlanta. Written for and prod. at the National Methodist Conf., Dallas, TX, 1967.

Other Pertinent Writings:

"Four Negro Plays," *The Advisor*, Aug. 1929.

"Some Whys and Wherefores of College Dramatics," *Crisis*, March 1930, pp. 92–94.

"Some Reflections on the Negro in American Drama," *Opportunity*, Oct. 1930, pp. 303–5.

"The Tragic Atmosphere in John Webster," M.A. thesis, Columbia Univ., 1934.

"What Good Are College Dramatics?" *Crisis*, Aug. 1934, pp. 232–34.

"College Dramatics Blazing New Trails in the Theatre," *Afro-American* (Baltimore), Sept. 1, 1934.

"The Diary of a Dramatist in Eire [Ireland]," *Arts Q.*, Oct.-Dec. 1937.

"Negro Drama in the South," *The Carolina Play-Book* (Univ. of North Carolina), June 1940, pp. 73–78.

"The Crescent City, a Center of Amateur Drama," *Sepia Socialite*, May 1942.

"Amateur Drama in New Orleans," *The Neg. South*, March 1946.

"Towards Community Drama," *SADSA Encore*, Spring 1948.

"The Negro Little Theatre Movement," *Neg. Hist. Bull.*, Jan. 1949, pp. 82–86, 92–94.

"Some Objectionable Stereotypes and Themes in Negro Literature," *Florida A. & M. Univ. Bull.*, Dec. 1949, pp. 15–18.

"The Negro Playwright in the American Theatre," *NADSA Encore*, Spring 1950.

"The Negro Playwright and the South," *NADSA Encore*, 1952.

"Four Nineteenth Century European Playwrights of African Descent," *NADSA Encore*, Spring 1954.

"Who Are the Three Greatest American Playwrights?" *Q. Rev. of Higher Ed. Among Negs.*, July 1955.

"Program Adopted by S.E.T.C. for Unity and Action," *Southern Th. News*, Fall 1956.

"The Playmakers in Africa," with Irene C. Edmonds, *Inst. of International Ed. News Bull.*, May 1959, pp. 20–28.

"Report of the African Tour of the Florida A. & M. University Players," *NADSA Encore*, 1959/60.

"The Sense of Ghetto in the American Theatre" [a debate between Edmonds and others], *ETJ*, Special Issue, Aug. 1968, pp. 333–39.

"Black Drama in the American Theatre: 1700–1970," *The Am. Th.: A Sum of Its Parts*, ed. by Henry B. Williams. Samuel French, New York, 1971.

"Blacks in the American Theatre, 1700–1969," *Pan-African J.*, Winter 1974, pp. 297–322.

FURTHER REFERENCE: Williams diss. Hicklin diss. *The Development of Blk. Th. in Am.* (Sanders, 1988). Sandle diss. Taped interview in Hatch-Billops.

EDWARD, H.F.V. (Harry Edward) (1898–1973), Former British sprinting champion, who became an executive of *Crisis* magazine and an administrator of the Harlem Unit of the Federal Theatre. Participated in the pre-Olympic games of the Wilco Athletic Assn., held at Yankee Stadium, New York, during the 1920s. Worked for several months during the Depression as a temporary interviewer for the New York State Employment Service, where he became aware of the unemployment problem of blacks in Harlem. Joined the staff of *Crisis* as an advertising manager and book-keeper around 1930. There, stimulated by the presence of W.E.B. DuBOIS and visits of other noted and aspiring black writers of the period, he tried his hand at writing one play. Later joined the New York Negro Unit of the WPA Federal Theatre, housed at the Lafayette Theatre in Harlem, 1935–39, where he was in charge of personnel, promotion, and other administrative services of the unit.

Stage Work:

Job Hunters (docudrama, 1 act, 1931). Drama of urban black unemployment during the Depression, based on the author's observations while working as a temporary interviewer in the New York State Employment Service. The setting is a public employment office in Harlem where a student visitor, studying sociology at the Univ. of Pennsylvania, is allowed to work as a volunteer and observe first hand the helplessness of the employment official in locating adequate jobs for blacks and coping with hopelessness, starvation, and eviction as well. The play ends with a warning that "blood" and "force" may be the only solutions to this terrible situation. (This prediction was fulfilled a few years later by the Harlem riot of 1935.) Pub. in *Crisis*, Dec. 1931, pp. 417–30; and in *BlkThUSA* (Hatch, 1974), which includes critical commentary.

EDWARDS, LAURA L., Resident playwright with the Raleigh Negro Unit of the WPA Federal Theatre Project during the 1930s.

Stage Work:

Heaven Bound (morality play, full length, 1936). Black-oriented pageant of good versus evil, based on the oral tradition and utilizing many of the trappings of the medieval morality plays. The author, as reader, narrated the biblical episodes while pilgrims made their earthly progress across the stage, trying to resist the various temptations in their paths. Characters included St. Peter, St. John, the archangels Michael and Gabriel, Death, Mercy, and Victory. Among the scenic devices were the Hell-Mouth, which was a dreaded punishment for sinners; a large seven-foot cross under which a singer in white robes sang and dramatized spirituals and sacred songs; a golden stairway to the gates of heaven in the center of the stage, surrounded by clouds, in the midst of which was the heavenly choir of 60 voices. Prod. by the Raleigh Negro Unit of the WPA Federal Theatre Project, 1936, where it was seen by nearly 5,000 persons during its run of almost five months.

F

FELTON, HALEEMON SHAIK (Mrs. Nicholas G. Felton), Catholic actress-playwright and elementary school teacher who apparently taught at the St. Peter Claver School in New Orleans during the 1930s.

Stage Works:

EARLIEST PLAYS (all prod. at St. Peter Claver School, New Orleans, LA, dates as indicated): **The Diamond Necklace** (mystery drama, 2 acts, 1931). **College Blunders** (3 acts, 1931). **Drifting Souls** (religious play, 3 acts, 1933).

Backstage (3 acts, 1933). Prod. at Xavier Coll., New Orleans, June 19, 1933; revived 1937.

House of Darkness (drama, 3 acts, 1941). Deals with "the problem of insanity and the tragic consequences of it on a family."—Hicklin, Ph.D. diss. (1965), pp. 309–10. Prod. by Dillard Univ. New Orleans, 1941, during Negro History Week. Also taken to Talladega Coll. and Alabama State Coll.

FIGGS, CARRIE LAW MORGAN, Poet-playwright and teacher of the 1920s. Taught at Edward Waters College in Jacksonville, FL. Her books include *Poetic Pearls* (1920) and *Nuggets of Gold* (1921).

Collection/Stage Works:

SELECT PLAYS. Privately printed, Chicago, 1923. Contains: **Jeptha's Daughter, The Prince of Peace, Santa Claus Land,** and **Bachelor's Convention**. (No copy has been located.)

FISHER, RUDOLPH (1897–1934), New York City physician, who turned his hand to writing short stories and novels during the Harlem Renaissance while also pursuing a successful medical career. Although he was not a playwright, one of his novels was adapted as a popular play, which was produced two years after Fisher's death. Born in Washington, DC. Reared in Providence, RI, where he was educated in the public schools, and where he received his A.B. in English literature and biology, with honors (1919), and his M.A. (1920), both from Brown University. Studied medicine at Howard University Medical School (M.D. 1924), graduating with highest honors. After a year of internship at Freedman's Hospital in Washington, DC, and further medical study at the College of Physicians and Surgeons, Columbia University, he began to practice medicine in Harlem as an X-ray specialist just when the community was becoming a cultural and social center. While studying medicine, he began to pursue his second career as a writer of fiction. In 1925 he won a *Crisis* Contest Award with his first short story, "High Yeller," and published "The City of Refuge," another short story, in the *Atlantic Monthly*. His stories appeared with regularity in *Atlantic, American Mercury, Redbook, Survey Graphic, Story, Crisis Opportunity,* and other magazines, as well as in a number of black newspapers. Several have been anthologized in *The Negro Caravan, Black Voices,* and *Best Short Stories by Afro-American Writers, 1928–1950*. He also published two novels, *The Walls of Jericho* (1928), a satire on Harlem society; and *The Conjur Man Dies: A Mystery Tale of Dark Harlem* (1932), which was posthumously adapted as a play. A member of Phi Beta Kappa, Sigma Xi, and Delta Sigma Rho fraternities.

Stage Work:
(The) Conjur Man Dies (farcical mystery, 3 acts [15 scenes], 1936). Posthumous dramatization by ARNA BONTEMPS and COUNTEE CULLEN of the novel *The Conjur Man Dies: A Mystery Tale of Dark Harlem* by Fisher, who is usually credited erroneously as the adaptor. A black physician, investigating the murder of an African "conjure man" in Harlem, discovers that the corpse is not that of the supposed victim, but his assistant. When the real conjure man reappears, he is indeed murdered. Although primarily a mystery-drama with comic elements, the play also deals with the themes of voodoo and sorcery, as well as the problem of superstitions, among Harlem blacks. Considered the most popular Federal Theatre play among Harlem audiences, it was seen by more than 20,000 theatregoers, according to Hallie Flanagan, director of the federal program.— *Arena* (Flanagan, 1940), p. 62. First prod., two years after the author's death, by the Negro Unit of the Federal Theatre Project, at the Lafayette Theatre, New York, March 11–April 4, 1936, for 24 perfs.; dir. by J. AUGUSTUS SMITH and Joe Losey, with music perfd. by the WPA Orchestra, dir. by Joe Jordan. Went on tour with a traveling unit of the WPA Players as part of the New York City Recreation Dept.'s outdoor recreation program. Prod. in Cleveland, first by the Cleveland Federal Theatre, 1936, then by the Gilpin Players at the Karamu Theatre, Feb. 2–8, 1968. Unpub. scripts in Schomburg and TC/NYPL.
FURTHER REFERENCE: Ross diss.

FOSTER, (Mrs.) ESTELLE ANCRUM (1887–?), Boston musician and music school director. Founder-director of the Ancrum School of Music, 1922. Author of at least three musical works published in Boston by Presser: *Piano Composition* (1926), *Ancrum School Course in Sight Singing* (1926), and the following stage work.

Stage Work:
A Dream of Enchantment (musical play, 1926). Pub. by Presser, Boston, 1926.

FRANKLIN, JAMES T. See Appendix A.

FRENCH-CHRISTIAN, LILLIAN, Pageant writer of the 1920s.
Stage Work:
Milestones of a Race ("Negro historical pageant," 15 episodes, 1923). "Devoted to the interpretation of Negro spirituals in pictures and in song."—*Crisis,* May 1923, p. 70. Prod. in Parsons, KS, 1923, the music furnished by the Community Chorus, with over 100 singers.

FULLER, LORENZO. See Appendix A.

G

GAINES-SHELTON, RUTH (Ruth Ada Gaines Shelton) (1873–?), Public school teacher and early writer of church plays and plays for children. Born in Glasgow, MO, the daughter of an A.M.E. minister. Completed the Normal course at Wilberforce University, OH, in 1895. Taught in the public schools of Montgomery, MO, 1895–99. Married to William Obern Shelton, 1898; the mother of three children. According to *WWCA 1941–44* (p. 361), ''She started to write plays for Clubs, Schools, Churches about 1906 and has written and staged these plays for twenty years.'' In 1925 she was a prizewinner in the *Crisis* Contest Awards for her best-known play, **The Church Fight**.

Stage Work:
The Church Fight (comedy, 1 act, 1925). Some rebellious church members (including Brothers Ananias, Investigator, and Judas, and Sisters Sapphira, Instigator, Meddler, Experience, Take-It-Back, and Two-Face) hold a secret meeting to bring up ''charges'' against their pastor, Brother Procrastinator, because he has been there for 15 years and they are tired of looking at him. They are shocked when the pastor, whom they are afraid to confront, also shows up at the meeting. Won second prize in the *Crisis* Contest Awards, Oct. 1925. Apparently prod. and dir. by the author. Pub. in *Crisis*, May 1926, pp. 17–21; and in *BlkThUSA* (Hatch, 1974), which also includes critical commentary.

OTHER PLAYS (all one-acts, written and prod. between 1906 and 1925): **Lord Earlington's Broken Vow. Aunt Hagar's Children. The Church Mouse** (children's church play). **Gena, the Lost Child** (children's gypsy play). **Mr. Church** (church drama). **Parson Dewdrop's Bride** (church comedy).

GALE, BERESFORD. See Appendix A.

GARVEY, MARCUS. See Appendix B.

GIBSON, POWELL WILLARD (1875–?), Educator and playwright. Principal of the Douglass High School, Winchester, VA, pre–1920s.

Stage Work:
Jake Among the Indians ("A serio-comic play," 1917). About a black man's involvement with an Indian maiden and her obstinate father. Prod. by the Douglass High School, Winchester, VA, 1917. Privately printed, 1931; copy in Moorland-Spingarn.

GILBERT, MERCEDES, Actress of stage and screen, playwright, songwriter, author, and journalist. Born in Florida. Appeared in two silent pictures, *The Call of His People* (1922) and OSCAR MICHEAUX's *Body and Soul* (1924), in which Paul Robeson made his film debut; and a talking picture, *Moon over Harlem* (1939). A veteran of the Broadway stage, 1927–50, she appeared in *Bamboola* (1929) as Rhodendra Frost; *The Green Pastures* (1930) as Zipporah, the wife of Moses; LANGSTON HUGHES' *Mulatto* (1936), assuming the female lead following the death of ROSE McCLENDON; *How Come Lawd?* (1937); *The Searching Wind* (1944), in which she played the role of a dignified housekeeper; and the all-black versions of *Lysistrata* (1946) and *Tobacco Road* (1950). In 1941 she made her debut as a monologuist in a one-woman show at St. Martin's Community Theatre, New York, and in 1946 returned to the concert stage in another solo performance of music, comedy, drama, monologues, character sketches, and impersonations, in which she toured numerous colleges and universities during the spring and fall of that year. Between acting engagements, she also wrote a freelance newspaper column; a novel, *Aunt Sara's Wooden God* (1938); and the collection of poetry, stories, and plays cited below.

Collection:
SELECTED GEMS OF POETRY, COMEDY AND DRAMA. Christopher Pub. House, Boston, 1931; copies in Schomburg, Moorland-Spingarn, and TC/NYPL. Contains: **Environment** (1931).

Stage Works:
Environment (comic melodrama, 1 act, 1931). A black mother living in the ghetto tries to hold her family together and help them cope with the evil influences of urban life. Pub. in the author's *SELECTED GEMS*.

Ma Johnson's Harlem Boarding House (series of comedy sketches, 1938). Possibly written in the format of a radio serial.

In Greener Pastures (satire, 1 act, 1938). Parody of Marc Connelly's *The Green Pastures* (1930), in which Gilbert had appeared as an actress. Prod. by the Harlem YMCA, New York, 1938. Also presented in Jamaica, NY.

GILMORE, F. GRANT. See Appendix A.

GLANVILLE, MAXWELL. See Appendix A.

GRAHAM, OTTIE B. (1900–   ), Student of drama and dance, and writer of short stories and one-act plays during the 1920s. A product of the literary and dramatic activities of Howard University and *Crisis* magazine. Born in Virginia, the daughter of a minister. Educated in the Philadelphia public schools and at Howard University and Columbia University. While at Howard, she participated in the very first production of the Howard Players, *Simon the Cyrenian*, by white playwright Ridgely Torrence, presented in 1921; the following year she arranged the dances for *Danse Calinda*, a pantomime also written by Torrence. Awarded a prize of $50 by the Alpha Kappa Alpha sorority for "To a Wild Rose," designated as "the best short story written by a Negro student." This and another of her stories, "Blues Aloes," were published in *Crisis*, in May 1923 and August 1924, respectively.

Stage Works:

The King's Carpenters (1 act, 1921). Pub. in *The Stylus* (Howard Univ.'s literary magazine), May 1921, pp. 27–37; copies in Moorland-Spingarn and Schomburg.

Holiday (tragedy, 1 act, 1923). A successful mulatto actress who has given up her brownskinned daughter in order to "pass" for white, finally tells her daughter the truth, hoping to make up for all the years that they have lost. The daughter, however, rejects her mother for all the misery she has caused, and, in an act of rage and desperation, runs into a nearby ocean and drowns herself. The actress, grief-stricken and unable to be consoled, decides that now is the time to take that long overdue "holiday" that she has promised herself and rushes into the same ocean, calling to her daughter that they will now be able to have their holiday together. Pub. in *Crisis*, May 1923, pp. 12–17.

GRAINGER, PORTER. See Appendix B.

GREEN, EDDIE. See Appendix B.

GREEN, J. ED. See Appendix B.

GRIMKÉ, ANGELINA WELD (1880–1958), Educator, poet, playwright, and essayist. One of the outstanding women writers of the pre-Harlem Renaissance. Born in Boston. Her father, Archibald Henry Grimké, a Harvard-educated attorney, journalist, author, and consul to Santo Domingo, 1894–98, was one of two black sons of an aristocratic white Charleston, SC, slaveholder. Her great-aunt, Angelina Grimké (Weld), after whom she was named, and who helped her father to further his education, was a rebellious white woman who left the South (along with her sister) to become an abolitionist. Her mother, Sarah E. (Stanley) Grimké, was a white writer whose parents were prominent Bostonians. Angelina's parents separated early in life, and her mother died when she was 18. She was educated at Carleton Academy, Northfield, MN; Cushing Academy, Ashburnham, MA; the Girls' Latin School, Boston; and the Boston Normal School of Gymnastics, 1902. Taught English for many years in the public schools of Washington, DC, including Armstrong Manual Training School, 1902– c. 1916, and Dunbar High School, 1916–retirement. Began writing in 1913, contributing verses and essays to such periodicals as *Crisis* and *Opportunity*, attributing her inspiration for writing to her father, her uncle (Francis James Grimké, a prominent minister and author of sermons, verses, essays, etc.) and his wife (Charlotte Forten Grimké, a poet and diarist), with whom she lived for four years while her father served as consul in Santo Domingo. Her poetry and writings have been included in the leading anthologies of black literature since the Harlem Renaissance, beginning with COUNTEE CULLEN's *Caroling Dusk* (1927). She resided in New York during the last days of her life, until her death at age 78.

Stage Works:

Rachel (protest drama, 3 acts, 1916). Based on a plot by NAACP Executive Secretary Walter White, this play dramatizes the deep emotional impact on the life of a young, sensitive black woman of several incidents of racial violence and prejudice, which she learns about during her adolescence and young womanhood, apparently having been sheltered by her mother from all knowledge of racism prior to this time. When Rachel is a teenager, her mother reluctantly informs her that her father and one of her two brothers were brutally lynched by a white mob in the Deep South several years earlier, forcing the mother to flee from the South with her two remaining children, Rachel and a younger brother. Four years later, after Rachel has grown to young womanhood and has adopted a young boy in the neighborhood whose parents had died, she learns of two other incidents of racial prejudice that have occurred at the public school—one against her adopted son, the other against a young black girl who lives in the same apartment building. Each incident deepens Rachel's grief, until she comes to a strong emotional decision that she cannot allow this kind of racial prejudice to continue. She renounces her belief in God and refuses to marry the man she loves, who proposes to her near the end of the play, telling him that she will devote her entire life to loving and caring for black children and protecting them from the emotional and physical scars of racial prejudice. Called the first historically significant play by a black woman playwright. Hailed as a pioneering work in the use of racial propaganda to enlighten white Americans as to the plight of blacks in this country. First prod. by the Drama Committee of the NAACP, at the Myrtilla Miner Normal School, Washington, DC, March 3–4, 1916; dir. by Nathaniel Guy. With Rachel Guy in the leading role, Zita Dyson as the mother, and Barrington Guy in the principal juvenile role. Again prod. at the Neighborhood Playhouse in New York City, under the auspices of the NAACP, April 26, 1917, and at Brattle Hall, Cambridge, MA, May 24, 1917, under the auspices of the Sunday School of Bartholomew Church. Pub. by Cornhill Co., Boston, 1820; reprinted by McGrath, 1969. Also in *BlkThUSA* (Hatch, 1974), which includes commentary. REVIEWS AND OTHER COMMENTARY: Archer diss. *BlkPlots* (Southgate). *CLAJ* 6–1977; 6–1978. *Competitor* 1–1920; 4–1921. *Crisis* 4–1916; 6–1917; 7–1917; 6–1921. *Nation* 1–25–1922. *Neg&Dr* (Bond). *PlaysNegL* (Locke & Gregory). Stevenson diss.

Maria ("a partially revised four-act play, still in manuscript"). Described by Jean-Marie A. Miller as being set in "the South at the beginning of the twentieth century" and focusing on "the Southern black woman's powerlessness in protecting herself against the white man's lust."—*CLAJ*, June 1978. Unpub. script in Grimké Papers.

FURTHER REFERENCE: *AfrAmWW* Angelina Grimké Papers in Moorland-Spingarn. (Shockley). *CLAJ* 6–1978.

GUINN, DOROTHY C. , YWCA executive of the 1920s whose racial identity has not been verified. Possibly a member of the National Board of the association. According to the introduction to the published script (cited below, p. x), Guinn wrote the following pageant "in collaboration with her assistants, . . . to direct nationwide attention to the romantic story of the Negro."

Stage Work:
Out of the Dark (historical pageant, 4 episodes [with prologue and epilogue], 1924). The story of the Negro from slavery to modern times, with musical and dramatic interludes and tableaux. The Prologue introduces the Chronicler (Narrator), who states that the purpose of this pageant is to bring "out of the dark" the black man's record of progress in America. Episode I, "The Rape of a Continent," shows the taking of slaves from Africa. Episode II, "Slavery," depicts the horrors of this condition, but shows that even "out of the depths . . . we find men and women of note arising." Episode III, "A New Day Breaks," depicts the emancipation of slaves, which also brings "difficulties as arduous as those encountered in the days of slavery." Episode IV, "What of Today?," shows the contributions of blacks in music, art, literature, and science (all personified as characters). The pageant was "presented with great success in Bridgeport, Connecticut, and made an equally favorable impression in Atlanta, Georgia, where it was staged soon after."—All quotations from "Synopsis of the Pageant," in Richardson (cited below), pp. 307–9. Pub. by Women's Press, New York, 1924, and in *Plays&Pags* (Richardson, 1930).

GUNNER, FRANCES, Secretary to the YWCA in Brooklyn, NY, during the 1920s. According to playwright/anthologist WILLIS RICHARDSON, Gunner "experienced the difficulty encountered by others in acquainting the Negro with himself. She considered it especially unfortunate that Negro women knew nothing of those of their sex who have achieved so much as heroines of the critical period through which the race had to pass. This was what prompted her to write the pageant [below]."—Pub. script, p. x.

Stage Work:
The Light of the Women (black history pageant, short 1 act, pre–1930). Subtitled "A ceremonial for the use of Negro groups." The setting is the Temple of Service, where the Spirit of Service, flanked by Beauty and Truth, welcomes Queen Ethiopia to the temple. Ethiopia brings good news—news of "light among the women"—black women who have contributed to the progress of the race by the light that has shone from their souls in the spirit of service. Among the historical women represented are the Slave Mother, Sojourner Truth, Harriet Tubman, and Phillis Wheatley. Contemporary women (1930s) include the Mother, the Teacher, the Minister, the Doctor, the Nurse, and others. Apparently prod. by the Brooklyn, NY, YWCA, prior to its publication in *Plays&Pags* (Richardson, 1930).

GYNT, KAJ. See Appendix B.

H

HAMILTON, RONALD T., Columbus, OH, playwright of the 1930s. One of his stories appeared in *Best Short Stories by Afro-American Writers, 1924–1950* (Ford & Faggett, 1950).

Stage Work:
Crack of the Whip ("A Social Problem Play" [subtitle], 1 act [35 pp.], 1935). Deals with the problem of unemployment discrimination of blacks. After a vacuum cleaner firm fires all of its black salesmen, replacing them by whites, the fired salesmen form a new company, stealing their customers from the old firm. Written under the auspices of the Playwriting Dept. of the Civic Theatre Guild, Spring Street YMCA, Columbus, OH, mid–1930s. Prod. at the Columbus Drama Festival, April 1935. Also presented at the New Theatre League Conf., Chicago, Oct. 1935. Unpub. script in Schomburg.

HARRIS, HELEN WEBB, Washington, DC, public school teacher and playwright. Educated at Howard University during the early 1920s, where she became involved in the pioneer dramatic activity there. Her first play, written under the tutelage of Montgomery Gregory, professor of drama, was produced at Howard in 1922. She taught at Banneker Junior High School in Washington, where her second play was completed in 1941. Both of her works are historical plays for school production.

Stage Works:
Genefrede (historical play, 1 act, 1922). Concerns a tragic event in the life of Toussaint L'Ouverture's daughter, whose fiancé is executed by order of her famous father. Written while the author was a student at Howard Univ., and first prod. by the Howard Players, Washington, DC, May 1922. Winner of first prize, Howard Univ. Award. Pub. in *NegHist13* (Richardson & Miller, 1935).

Frederick Douglass (historical play, 3 acts, 1941). Episodes in the life of the famous black orator and antislavery leader, written for school prodn. Completed in Jan. 1941. First prod. at Banneker Junior High School, Washington, DC, c. 1944. Pub. in three installments in *Neg. Hist. Bull.*: Feb. 1952, pp. 97–102; March 1952, pp. 123–27; and April 1952, pp. 144–50.

HAYDEN, ROBERT E. (1913–1980), Eminent poet, anthologist, educator, editor, and playwright. Born in Detroit, MI. Educated at Wayne State University (A.B.) and the University of Michigan (M.A.), where he taught for two years, 1944–46, before beginning his long tenure as professor of English at Fisk University, 1946–69. Writer-in-residence and professor of English, University of Michigan, from 1969 to his death in 1980. Author of many volumes of poetry, including *Heart-Shape in the Dust* (1940), *The Lion and the Archer* (with Myron O'Higgins, 1948), *Figure of Time* (1955), *A Ballad of Remembrance* (1962), *Selected Poems* (1966), *Words in the Mourning Time* (1970), and *Angle of Ascent* (1975). Editor of *Kaleidoscope* (an anthology of black American poetry, 1967) and *Afro-American Literature: An Introduction* (with David Burrows and Frederick Lapides, 1971). Coeditor, with James E. Miller, Jr., and Robert O'Neal, of the following textbooks: *A Collection of Modern Stories* (1973), *The United States in Literature* (1973), *Person, Place, and Point of View: Factual Prose for Interpretation and Extension* (1974), *The Lyric Potential* (1974), *The Human Condition: Literature Written in the English Language* (1974), and *The United States in Literature: Glass Menagerie Edition* (1979). Poetry editor of *World Order*, an official periodical of the Baha'i faith, of which he is a prominent member. His individual poems, prose, and other writings have been published in numerous journals and anthologies. His "Stage Door Reviews" appeared in the *Michigan Chronicle*. Recipient of two Hopwood Awards for poetry from the University of Michigan, 1938 and 1942, and of the Grand Prize for Poetry at the First World Festival of Negro Arts held at Dakar, Senegal, 1965, for his volume of poetry, *Ballad of Remembrance*. Among the creative writing fellowships that he has received are a Julius Rosenwald Fellowship, 1947; a Ford Foundation Fellowship for travel and writing in Mexico, 1954–55; and a $10,000 fellowship from the Academy of American Poets, 1970s. He was the first black poet to be honored as Consultant in Poetry to the Library of Congress, 1976; and the recipient of an honorary Doctor of Letters from Brown University, Providence, RI, the same year. Following his death in 1980, the Michigan legislature passed a resolution honoring his memory.

Stage Works:

Go Down Moses (black history play, c. 1937). About Harriet Tubman and the Underground Railroad. Unpub. script in the Dept. of Rare Books and Special Collections, Univ. of Mich.

The History of Punchinello ("A Baroque Play" [subtitle] in blank verse, 1 act, 1948). Concerns the plight of a stereotyped black comedian whose longing for more serious acting roles is frustrated by racism, bigotry, and the commercial interests of his white manager. Utilizing masks and stylized dance movements for symbolic effect, it was prod. by the Fisk Univ. Stagecrafters, Nashville, TN, during the 1940s. Pub. in *NADSA Encore* (McQuiddy Co., Nashville), pp. 30–33.

In Memoriam Malcolm X (perfd. reading of his poem, 1974). Text from Hayden's poem "El-Hajj Malik El-Shabazz (Malcolm X)" (1969). Music by T. J. Anderson. Prod. in Avery Fischer Hall, New York, April 1974. Poem orig. pub. in *For Malcolm* (Randall & Burrows; Broadside Press, Detroit, 1969); revised in the author's collections *Words in the Mourning Time* (1970) and *Angle of Ascent* (1975).

Broadcast Works:
According to *Dark Symphony* (Emanuel & Gross, 1968, p. 481), "Hayden['s] . . . early works included radio scripts," the titles of which have not been discovered.

Other Pertinent Writings:
"Stage Show Reviews," *Michigan Chronicle*, Feb. 3, 1940, p. 12; Feb. 10, 1940, p. 12; Feb. 17, 1940, p. 10; Feb. 24, 1940, p. 10.
FURTHER REFERENCE: Hicklin diss.

HAZZARD, ALVIRA, Literary hobbyist of the 1920s. A member of the Saturday Evening Quill Club, a Boston writers' group.

Stage Works:
Mother Liked It (comedy, 2 acts, 1928). The plot revolves around the activities of an Indian prince. Pub. in *Sat. Eve. Quill*, June 1928, pp. 10–14; copy in Moorland-Spingarn.
Little Heads (1 act, 1929). Pub. in *Sat. Eve. Quill*, Jan. 1929; copy in Moorland-Spingarn.

HEYWOOD, DONALD (last name also frequently cited as both Heyward and Haywood) (1900–1951), Playwright, musical comedy librettist, screenwriter, composer, lyricist, producer, and performer. Born in Venezuela, of West Indian descent. Studied black music at Fisk University before beginning his show business career in New York, where he first performed in stage productions of *Ringside* (1928) and *Kilpatrick's Old Time Minstrels* (1930). Wrote a number of song-and-dance shows, 1923/32, before trying his hand at writing films and folk dramas, in which he was less successful. According to film historian Peter Noble, writing in *The Negro in Films* (1948), Heywood was "prominently associated with independent Negro films since 1932, when he wrote the screenplays of several Bud Pollard pictures." His best-known popular songs include "I'm Comin', Virginia" and "Harlem Moon."

Stage Works:

PLAYS
Ol' Man Satan (folk allegory, 3 acts [37 scenes], 1932). An abortive attempt to capitalize on the success of *The Green Pastures,* this crudely constructed drama sought to present the black concept of Satan and the afterlife through the telling of biblical and allegorical stories by a black mother, Mammy Jackson, to her small son. The stories are dramatized through a series of scenes involving the temptation and often defeat of well-known biblical and other characters by various tempters and temptresses, with Satan always as the central figure in the action. Produced by Shillwood Prodns. at the Forrest Theatre, New York, opening Oct. 3, 1932, for 24 perfs.; dir. by William A. Shilling. Cast included A. B. Comathiere (Satan), Georgette Harvey (Mammy [or Ma] Jackson), Edna Thomas (Maggie [Mary Magdalene]), Lawrence Chenault (Moses), Lorenzo Tucker

(Teacher), Bee Freeman (David's Temptresses), David Bethe (Disciples), Clyde Faison (Noah's Temptress), Florence Lee (Jezebel), and Wandolf Saunders (Racketeer). REVIEWS AND COMMENTARY: *BesPls 1932–23. Neg&Dr* (Bond). *NYT* 10–4–1932.

How Come, Lawd? (folk melodrama, 3 acts, 1937). God is called to account for the numerous misfortunes that thwart efforts of labor organizers to unionize Alabama cotton pickers and improve their working and living conditions. One of the pickers, Big Boy, becomes so stirred up emotionally by the rhetoric of the organizers that he confuses their work with God's work, and is unprepared for the violence that ensues when resentful whites attack and kill several blacks, including his girlfriend. At the end, Big Boy prays to God for answers. Prod. by the Negro Theatre Guild, at the 49th St. Theatre, New York, Sept. 30–Oct. 1, 1937, for 2 perfs.; dir. by Charles B. Adler. Cast included REX INGRAM (Big Boy), MERCEDES GILBERT (Mom), †J. HOMER TUTT (Pa), Hilda Rogers (Clorinda, Big Boy's girlfriend), and Alex Lovejoy (Slacks). REVIEWS AND COMMENTARY: *BesPls 1937–38. NYT* 10–1–1937.

MUSICALS

[NOTE: Librettos are listed first, followed by OTHER MUSICALS to which Heywood contributed. Musicals marked with a plus sign (+) are briefly annotated in Appendix B. Persons marked with an obelisk (†) are also listed in Appendix B.]

The Sheik of Harlem (musical comedy, full length, 1923). Book, music, and lyrics by Heywood and †IRVIN C. MILLER. A popular Harlem show, interspersed with comedy routines, involving a love story between a southern woman and a young Harlem man who disguises himself as a sheik. Prod. at the Lafayette Theatre, New York, 1923, with Irvin C. Miller, Quintard Miller, Billy Mills, Hattie Revas, and †WILL A. COOK.

Blue Moon (musical comedy, 1 act, 1926). Book and lyrics by Heywood and Irvin C. Miller. Prod. by Miller as a touring road show, 1926. Cast included William ("Babe") Townsend, Henrietta Lovelass, and Edna Barr.

Gingersnaps (musical comedy, full length, 1929). Book coauthored with J. Homer Tutt, †SALEM TUTT WHITNEY, and George Morris. Prod. at the Belmont Theatre, New York, opening Dec. 21, 1929, closing in early 1930; dir. and starred in by J. Homer Tutt.

Africana ("Congo Operetta" [subtitle], 2 acts, 1934). Book, music, and lyrics by Heywood. Title and some songs taken from Heywood's successful 1927 revue [see OTHER MUSICALS below]. Revolved around the generation and cultural gap that develops between an African king and his European-educated son when the son tries to bring about changes in his country's customs after his return home. Prod. at the Venice Theatre, New York, opening Nov. 26, 1934, for only 3 perfs.; dir. by °Peter Morrell. Integrated cast included Walter Richardson (King's son), Jack Carr (King), and °Gretchen Branch (Missionary's daughter).

Black Rhythm (musical show, 2 acts, 1936). Book, music, and lyrics by Heywood. A number of specialty acts held together by a thin plot revolving around an amateur night in Harlem. Prod. by Earl Dancer, at the Comedy Theatre, New York, Dec. 19, 1936, for 6 perfs.; dir. by Heywood and Dancer.

OTHER MUSICALS: + **Get Set** (musical revue, 2 acts, 1923). Music and lyrics by Heywood. Book by †JOE BRIGHT. Prod. by Harlem Producing Co., New York, 1923. Revived 1926. + **North Ain't South** (musical comedy, full length, 1923). Music by Heywood. Book by Salem Tutt Whitney, J. Homer Tutt, and †JESSE A. SHIPP. Prod. as a touring road show, 1923. + **Come Along Mandy** (musical comedy, full length,

1924). Music by Heywood. Book and lyrics by Salem Tutt Whitney and J. Homer Tutt. Prod. as a touring show, 1924. **Africana** // orig. title: **Miss Calico** (musical revue, 2 parts, 1926/27). Music and lyrics by Heywood. Conceived and prod. by Earl Dancer. Song-and-dance show, with comedy routines that boosted Ethel Waters to stardom. Prod. as a touring show under its orig. title in 1926 before opening on Bway at Daly's Sixty-Third Street Theatre, New York, July 11, 1927, for 72 perfs. **Great Temptations** (musical revue, full length, 1927). Prod. and possibly cowritten by Heywood and Jimmy Marshall, as a touring road show, 1927. **Hot Rhythm** (musical show, full length, 1930). Music and lyrics by Heywood, †PORTER GRAINGER, and Eubie Blake. With sketches by "Pigmeat" Markham, °Will Morrissey, °Ballard Macdonald, and °Edward Hurley. Prod. at the Times Square Theatre, opening Aug. 21, 1930, for 58 perfs. Featuring Gee Gee James, Mae Barnes, and Eddie Rector. +**De Gospel Train** // orig. title: **Jim Crow**, 1936; revived 1940. Book by J. Homer Tutt [earlier version coauthored with Salem Tutt Whitney]. Typescript in Schomburg. **Tropicana** (touring show, 1941).

Screen Works:
The Black King (film: scenario, 1932). A burlesque of the activities of Marcus Garvey, famed originator of the Back-to-Africa movement after World War I. Garvey is portrayed as an illiterate, ludicrous figure. One of several Budd Pollard pictures for which Heywood apparently wrote. Independent all-black film, prod. by Southland, 1932; dir. by Pollard. Cast included Vivian Babar, Harry Gray, Knolly Mitchell, and Jane Watkins. REVIEWS AND COMMENTARY: *NY Age* 7–16–1932.

Also contributed music and lyrics to **Murder on Lenox Avenue** (1941) and **Sunday Sinners** (1941), both prod. in Florida by °Goldberg; dir. by °Arthur Dreifuss. Appearing in both films were Mamie Smith, Norman Astwood, Gus Smith [J. AUGUSTUS SMITH], Alberta Perkins, and Alex Lovejoy.

Other Pertinent Writing:
"The Theatre Past and Present," *NY Amst. N.*, June 15, 1932.
FURTHER REFERENCE: Belcher diss. *BesPls 1927–28; 1930–31; 1931–32; 1934–35*. Hicklin diss. *NegMus&M* (Cuney-Hare). *Opportunity* 7–1938. *Time* 12–28–1936.

HICKS, LONNIE. See Appendix A.

HILL, ABRAM (Abraham Barrington Hill) (1911–1986), Playwright, black theatre organizer, director, drama critic, and one of the outstanding leaders of the Harlem theatre in the 1940s. Born in Atlanta, GA, the son of a railroad fireman on the Atlanta–Washington, DC, line. His family moved to New York in 1925. Educated at Roosevelt and DeWitt Clinton high schools, New York; City College of New York, where he pursued premedical courses (1930–32); and Lincoln University/PA, where he majored in English, studied drama, and wrote and directed plays (A.B. 1937). Also studied at Columbia University (playwriting), the Dramatic Workshop of the New School for Social Research (playwriting, on a Theresa Helburn scholarship), and Atlanta University Summer Theatre. After graduating from Lincoln, he was retained on the faculty for one semester as an assistant in drama. During the summers he also wrote and directed plays at a Civilian Conservation Corps (CCC) camp on Long Island, NY, and eventually became an assistant state supervisor of CCC camps. This experience led to his joining the WPA Federal Theatre in 1938, where he was given several special projects, including the reading and evaluation of black-oriented scripts and the writing of a "living newspaper" case history of the Negro people, **Liberty Deferred**. This play was never produced because of the dissolution of the Federal Theatre in 1939. Encouraged by the NAACP, Hill organized the Negro Playwrights Company in Harlem in 1940, but resigned after two months because of dissatisfaction with the progress of that organization. In the the same year, he cofounded with Frederick O'Neal the American Negro Theatre (ANT) and served as its artistic director and playwright in residence. While at ANT, he directed or codirected *Natural Man* (by THEODORE BROWNE, 1941), *Starlight* (1942), *Three's a Family* (1943), *Home Is the Hunter* (1945), *Tin Top Valley* (1947), and *John Loves Mary* (1947), in addition to his own plays listed below. ANT flourished until about 1948, producing a number of outstanding plays in the Harlem community and developing many of the theatrical stars of the next few decades, including Sidney Poitier, Harry Belafonte, Earle Hyman, *Ruby Dee, and such successful playwrights as *Ossie Davis and *Alice Childress. The triumph and highlight of Hill's career was the ANT production of his adaptation and direction of **Anna Lucasta** in 1944, which became an immediate success, taking many of its cast members to Broadway and Hollywood. In 1945 Hill was drama editor of the *New York Amsterdam News*. After the demise of ANT in 1948, he retired from the theatre and devoted his full energies to playwriting, teaching, lecturing, consulting, journalism, and traveling. In 1960 he directed a teenage production of *The King and I* at the Brooklyn Academy. For his contributions to the theatre, he has won a Schomburg Award and a Riverdale Children's Association Award for "promoting interracial understanding." In a 1984 letter to Bernard L. Peterson, Jr., he stated: "I have been quite busy with my files in putting together the plays that I have written. I am almost through and hope to get them published soon. . . . Some of these scripts are more than forty years old. Trying to put together a bit from here and there, some scenes or acts totally brittle or missing, was something of a mean task." Hill died in New York in October 1986, survived by his widow, Ruth Caston Mueller Hill, with whom "he moved high in borough-wide social and philanthropic circles for many notable years," according to the *NY Amsterdam News,* Oct. 18, 1986. Mrs. Hill (with the assistance of this writer) is currently compiling and editing eight of her late husband's plays for publication in a forthcoming collection.

Stage Works:

Stealing Lightning (dialect play, 1 act, 1937). Depression drama involving a feud between two families—one in comfortable circumstances, the other in dire need. This play and the following script were presumably prod. by the author at CCC camps in New York State in 1937. Unpub.

So Shall You Reap (fantasy, 3 acts, 1937). Labor problem play set in New York during the Depression era. Unpub. script in Schomburg.

Hell's Half Acre (drama, 3 acts [16 scenes], 1938). Described as "the dramatization of the intricate forces at odds in a small southern town when four [white] persons accused of murder [i.e., lynching] are finally brought to trial.''—*Neg&Dr* (Bond, 1940), p. 189. Based on the author's recollections of his great-grandmother's stories of slavery. First submitted as a one-act play in the Theatre Guild [playwriting] contest, but did not win a prize. On the basis of criticisms in that contest, Hill apparently rewrote the script as a three-act play. Prod. by the Unity Players in the Bronx, New York City, and by Joseph Ornato, 1938–39. Unpub. script in Schomburg and TC/NYPL. COMMENTARY: *BesPls 1938–39*.

Liberty Deferred ("living newspaper," full length, 1938). Coauthor, with JOHN SILVERA. Documentary of the history of blacks in America, from slavery to the 1930s. Written in 1938 for prodn. by the WPA Federal Theatre Project, but never prod. because of the demise of FTP. Unpub. scripts in FTP/GMU and TC/NYPL.

(On) Striver's Row ("A Comedy About Sophisticated Harlem" [subtitle], 3 acts, 1939). Satire of middle-class social snobbery and pretentiousness among the "Sugar Hill" residents of the Harlem community. Considered Harlem's most popular play. Revolves around the coming out party for the Radcliffe-educated daughter of a prominent family and the crisis she precipitates when she refuses to marry the wealthy young man whom her family has picked out for her. First prod. by the Rose McClendon Players, at the 124th St. Branch of the New York Public Library, Jan. 3–27, 1940, for 16 perfs.; dir. by the author. Cast members included Goldie McGirt, Frederick O'Neal, Betty Haynes, and Ruby Wallace [Ruby Dee]. Prod. by ANT, at the 135th St. Library Theatre (also called the ANT Playhouse), Sept. 11, 1940–Feb. 1, 1941, for more than 50 perfs.; dir. by the author. With Goldie McGirt, Clarice Taylor, Virgil Richardson, Ann Petry, James Jackson, Ruby Wallace Dee, Ruth Ford, Frederick O'Neal, Betty Haynes, Claire Leyba, Stanley Greene, Betty Humphries, Claude Sloan, Helen Martin, Blanche Kirkland, and Kenneth Mannigault. Prod. as a musical by the Harlem People's Theatre, at the Apollo Theatre, New York, March 1941, with Alice Childress and Louis Jordan. Again prod. by ANT, at the Elks Building in Harlem, Feb. 28–April 15, 1946, for about 30 perfs.; dir. by the author. Cast included Dorothy Carter (as Dolly Van Strivens, a society matron), Letitia Toole (as Tillie Petunia, a gossipy newspaperwoman), Jovette Sutton (as Cobina Van Strivens, a debutante), Stanley Greene (as Oscar Van Strivens, a professional businessman), Jacqueline Andre (as Ruby Jackson, a flamboyant domestic), Draynard Clinton, Isabel Sanford, *Oliver Pitcher, Hattie King Reavis, Verneda LaSelle, Hilda Haynes, Charles Henderson, Courtney Olden, Austin Briggs-Hall, Vivian Hall Dogan, Sally Alexander, and Fred Carter. Prod. by the New Heritage Repertory Co., 1975; dir. by *Roger Furman. With a cast of Actors Equity members. Prod. by the Morehouse-Spelman Players, Atlanta, GA, Nov. 1971; dir. by Carlton Molette. Revived by Molette at the Atlanta Univ. Summer Theatre, July 1974, and at a dinner theatre production at Southern Univ., Baton Rouge, LA, Feb. 1982. Revived by the New Heritage Theatre, 1984; dir. by Andre Robinson. Pub. in *Roots of Blk. Drama* (Hatch & Hamalian, 1989). Unpub. script in Schomburg. REVIEWS AND COMMENTARY: Abramson diss. *DBlkTh* (Woll). *NY Amsterdam N.* 4–14–1984. *NYT* 3–1–1946. *Opportunity* 2–1942. *PM* 12–1–1944; 3–3–1946.

Latin, Greek or Grits // Orig. title: **Booker T. Washington** (biographical drama, length unknown, 1939; revised 1983). About the famed founder of Tuskegee Inst. Written for FTP, but not prod. Scheduled for prodn. by Tuskegee Inst. in 1983/84. No record of the actual prodn.

Anna Lucasta (drama, 3 acts, 1944). Adaptn. for an all-black cast by Hill of °Philip

Yordan's play by the same title, originally written about a Polish family in Pennsylvania. With additional changes by the director, °Henry Wagstaff Gribble. Also prod. as a film (1958). Concerns the struggle of a prostitute to reclaim her life. This adaptn. concerns a naive young black man who has been sent up north by his father to Brooklyn, NY, with a large sum of money, to find a good wife. He falls into the clutches of the Lucasta family, who scheme to get their hands on his money (originally $800), using every unscrupulous device that they can think of—including bringing their prostitute daughter Anna home from her waterfront beat to marry the country hick. As a favor to her family, Anna consents, but when she meets and gets to know the young man, she falls in love with him. The situation is complicated when Anna's old sweetheart, a sailor, returns from sea, expecting to "shack up" with Anna while he is on leave. Historically significant as the longest-running play with an all-black cast up to its time; also, it was this play that brought many of the black stars of the postwar years to Broadway, films, and television. First prod. (in what has been called a tryout prodn.) by ANT in the basement of the 135th St. Library in Harlem, opening June 16, 1944, for five weeks. With Hilda Simms as Anna, Earle Hyman as Rudolph, the young man from the South, Lionel Monagas, ALVIN CHILDRESS, Letitia Tools, Alberta Perkins, Frederick O'Neal, Betty Haynes, John Proctor, Alice Childress, Martin Slade, Billy Cumerbatch, and Buddy Holmes. Prod. on Bway, with minor changes, at the Mansfield Theatre, Aug. 30, 1944– Nov. 30, 1946, for 957 perfs. Starring Hilda Simms in the title role, Earle Hyman as Rudolph, and Canada Lee as Danny, the sailor. A second company was formed, which presented the play in Chicago, first with Valerie Black as Anna, replaced by Hilda Simms (from the Broadway company), for 40 weeks, then went on the road. A third company went on tour in England. Revived on Bway, again at the Mansfield Theatre, Sept. 22– Oct. 18, 1947, for 32 perfs., with Isabelle Cooley as Anna and Sidney Poitier as Rudolph. During the course of the play's run, the actors who moved in and out of the cast included (in addition to the above): Ossie Davis, Ruby Dee, *Maxwell Glanville, Frank Silvera, RALF COLEMAN, FRANK WILSON, *Rosetta LeNoire, Georgette Harvey, and Roy Allen. Prod. as a film by United Artists, 1958, with Eartha Kitt as Anna, Sammy Davis, Jr., as Danny, and Henry Scott as Rudolph. The only published version of the Hill-Gribble adaptn. is abridged in *The Best Plays of 1944–45*. REVIEWS AND COMMENTARY: *AnthANT* (Patterson), photos. *BesPls 1943–44; 1944–45; 1947–48*. *BlkDr* (Mitchell). *BlkMagic* (Hughes & Meltzer). *Cath. World* 10–1944. *Commonweal* 9–15–1944. *Ebony* 12–1945; 12–1958. *Life* 10–9–1944. *Neg. Digest* 3–1945. *Neg. Hdbk. Neg. YrBK. 1947* (Guzman). *New Republic* 9–18–1944. *NYT* 5–6–1945. *New Yorker* 9–9–1944. *Newsweek* 9–11–1944. *Opportunity* Fall 1944. *Our World* 7–1953. *Phylon* 1st qtr. 1945. Pitts diss. *Spectator* 12–7–1947. *Th. Arts* 11–1944, photo; 4–1945, photo; 2–1948. *Th. Bk. of the Yr., 1944–45* (Nathan). *Time* 6–26–1944.

Walk Hard (drama, 3 acts, 1944). Adapt. from °Len Zinberg's novel *Walk Hard— Talk Loud,* about a black boxer's battle with racial prejudice and discrimination. First prod. by ANT at the Harlem Branch of the New York Public Lib., opening Nov. 10, 1944, for a six-week engagement; with an integrated cast of nine black and nine white actors. Prod. on Bway by Gustav Blum at an auditorium on the 50th floor of the Chanin Bldg. on East 42nd St., New York City, March 27–31, 1946, for 7 perfs., featuring Mickey Walker as the boxer, Maxwell Glanville, Joseph Kamm, and Leonard Yorr. Pub. in *BlkThUSA* (Hatch, 1974). Unpub. script in TC/NYPL. REVIEWS AND COMMENTARY: *BesPls 1945–46*. *NYT* 12–1–1944; 3–28–1946. *Phylon* 1st qtr. 1945; 2nd qtr. 1946. Pitts diss. *PM* 12–1–1944.

The Power of Darkness (drama, full length, 1948). Adaptn., for an all-black cast, of Leo Tolstoy's novel by the same title, with the locale transferred to the American South. Prod. by ANT at the Master Institute, New York, 1948. REVIEW: *Phylon* 2nd qtr. 1949.

Miss Mabel (drama, 2 acts, 1951). A black version of °G. R. Sheriff's novel. About a woman who poses as her own twin sister who has amassed a fortune, draws up a will in her sister's name, then murders her sister—hoping to provide generous financial gifts to her church and some of her needy friends, leaving only a small bequest for herself. Her crimes are uncovered, however, immediately after the reading of the will, and Miss Mabel is jailed for forgery and murder, in spite of her loyal friends' efforts to get her out of trouble. Unprod. and unpub.

Split Down the Middle (drama, full length, 1969). Pub. by Simon and Schuster, New York, 1970.

Beyond the Bush (drama, 1 act, 1970). About a romantic affair which takes place in the upper South, just below the Mason-Dixon line, involving a divorced, white landowner and a lower class black woman while her boyfriend is serving in Vietnam. Unprod. and unpub.

FURTHER REFERENCE: Abram Hill Folder in Schomburg. *AnthANT* (Patterson). *BlkDr* (Mitchell). *Current Biog.* 1945. *DBlkTh* (Woll). *DirBlksPA* (Mapp). Hicklin diss. *NegPlaywrs* (Abramson). Pitts diss. Taped interview in Hatch-Billops. *VoicesBTh* (Mitchell).

HILL, J. LEUBRIE. See Appendix B.

HILL, LESLIE PINCKNEY (1880–1960), Educator, poet, and pioneer playwright, for many years president of Cheyney State College in Pennsylvania. Born in Lynchburg, VA. Educated in the public schools of Orange, NJ, where he grew up; and at Harvard University (A.B. cum laude, 1903; A.M. 1904) while working as a waiter at a fraternity house. He was elected to Phi Beta Kappa and was a member of the debating team. Married Jane E. Clark, 1907. Taught and served as department head at Tuskegee Institute (1904–7) and Manassas (VA) Institute (1907–13) before becoming principal and later president of the Institute for Colored Youth in Cheyney, PA, later known as Cheyney Training School for Teachers, and finally as Cheyney State Teachers College, where he remained, until his retirement as president emeritus, from 1913 to 1951. Also served as visiting professor at UCLA for two summers and as administrator of the Mercy-Douglass Hospital in Philadelphia. Author of *The Wings of Oppression* (a volume of poetry, 1921), one poem of which, ''The Teacher,'' enjoyed great popularity, being translated into several languages and set to music. Another of his works, *What the Negro Wants* (ed. by Rayford Logan, 1944), sets forth the six major areas in which black people were striving for equality: (1) in the law and its administration, (2) in education, (3) in voting, (4) in employment, (5) in health and hospitalization, and (6) in the armed forces. Member of the Republican Party and the National Education Association. Founder of Camp Hope for underprivileged children in Delaware County; founder of the Association of Pennsylvania Teachers; founder and president of the board of the West Chester

Community Center; founder and past president of the Pennsylvania State Negro
Council. Recipient of honorary degrees from Lincoln University (PA) (Litt.D.
1929); Morgan State College (LL.D. 1939); Haverford College; and Cheyney
State Teachers College. Recipient of the Seltzer Award for distinguished service
to the Mercy-Douglass Hospital in Philadelphia, where he later died of a stroke
at age 70.

Stage Works:
Toussaint L'Ouverture (dramatic history, 5 parts [35 scénes], 1928). Written in blank
verse, apparently as a drama to be read rather than acted, depicting Toussaint L'Ou-
verture's period of leadership in Haiti. No record of prodn. Pub. by Christopher Pub.
House, Boston, 1928; xerographic reprints available from Univ. Microfilms International,
Ann Arbor, MI.

Jethro (historical musical pageant, full length, 1931). Dramatizes the life of the Ethiopian contemporary of Moses who gave to mankind the concept of representative government. First prod. by the State Teachers Coll. of Cheyney, PA, 1931, for three
performances, two in Cheyney and one at Harrisburg, PA. Again presented in 1934 at
The Playhouse in Wilmington, DE, "to an appreciative unsegregated audience of about
600 Negroes and white people, . . . by an all-student cast from the State Teachers College."—*Crisis,* July 1934, p. 203.

FURTHER REFERENCE: *Danb. NegGen* (Brawley). *Neg. Hist. Bull.* 3–1961. *WWCA
1950* (and earlier eds.).

HIRSCH, CHARLOTTE TELLER, Playwright. (Racial identity not verified.)
Stage Work:
Hagar and Ishmael (biblical episode, short sketch, 1913). Dramatizes an incident in
the Bible concerning Hagar, an Egyptian slave, and her son Ishmael, whose story is
related in Genesis xvi, xxi, and xxv. [Ishmael was the elder son of Abraham, the founder
of the Hebrew nation, by Hagar, who was given as a concubine to Abraham by his wife
Sarah, who was barren. However, some 13 years after Ishmael was born, Sarah herself
conceived a son, Isaac, who was acknowledged by God to be the true son of Abraham.
Abraham and Sarah, with God's approval, expel Ishmael and his mother to the wilderness
of Bersheeba, with God's promise that Ishmael, too, shall be the founder of a great
nation.] The play begins in the scorching desert into which they have wandered following
the expulsion. In their desperate situation, Hagar vows that her son shall "breed a race
to take great vengeance upon Isaac's seed."—Pub. script. [Ishmael later became the
ancestor of a group of Arab tribes, many of whom embraced Mohammedanism, or Islam,
one of the three great religions of the world.]

HODGES, GEORGE W. See Appendix A.

HOGAN, ERNEST. See Appendix B.

HOLIFIELD, HAROLD. See Appendix A.

HOPKINS, PAULINE ELIZABETH (1859–1930), Writer, novelist, editor,
playwright, and singer. Born in Cambridge, MA. Educated at the Girls High
School in Boston. Demonstrated her writing talents at an early age, winning $10

for the best essay in a competition sponsored by WILLIAM WELLS BROWN and the Congressional Publishing Society of Boston. Performed in recitals, concerts, and dramatic presentations with her family group, called the Hopkins Colored Troubadours, for which she wrote at least one musical drama. Worked as a stenographer for the Bureau of Statistics in Boston, 1885–89. Wrote for the *Colored American,* a monthly periodical, beginning in 1890, where her first stories, essays, and serialized novels were published. Her three novels (the latter two published as serials) are *Contending Forces: A Romance Illustrative of Negro Life North and South* (1900), *Of One Blood, or The Hidden Self* (1902), and *Winona: A Tale of Negro Life in the South and Southwest* (1902/3). She also wrote *A Primer of Facts Pertaining to the Goodness of Africa* (1905), a work of nonfiction. Her relationship with the magazine discontinued in 1904, when she was forced to resign to make a place for the nephew of Mrs. Booker T. Washington. In 1916 she became editor of the short-lived *New Era Magazine,* in which she published a serial about a modern-day Topsy, called "Topsy Templeton," and a number of biographical sketches before the magazine ceased publication. Unable to make a living through her writings, she again worked as a stenographer, for the Massachusetts Institute of Technology. She died in 1930, at the age of 71, from burns resulting from an accidental oil stove fire.

Stage Works:

Slaves' Escape; or, The Underground Railroad (historical musical drama, 3 acts, 1880). Orig. title: **Peculiar Sam; or, The Underground Railroad** (4 acts, 1879). The story of the Underground Railroad and how it assisted slaves to escape from slavery to freedom in the North. Prod. by the Hopkins Colored Troubadours, at Oakland Garden, Boston, July 5, 1880, where it ran for one week. Cast included the author, her mother and stepfather, the famous Hyers Sisters, and a chorus of over 60 voices.

One Scene from the Drama of Early Days (dramatization of the biblical story of Daniel). Unpub.

FURTHER REFERENCE: *AfrAmWW* (Shockley). *Blk. Am. Writers* (Rush et al.). Pauline Hopkins Papers in the Fisk Univ. Lib. and Research Center.

HOWARD, SALLY, New York City playwright.

Stage Work:

The Jackal (c. 1950). Although *Loften Mitchell liked Howard's play and called it "imaginative," it apparently created quite a controversy when it was produced by Ruth Jett at the Harlem Showcase at 290 Lenox Ave., where it had a limited run around 1950. According to Mitchell, *Harold Cruse panned the show "in vitriolic terms," which infuriated the producers and actors and may have caused the show to close prematurely.

HUEY, RICHARD. See Appendix A.

HUFFMAN, EUGENE HENRY. See Appendix A.

HUGHES, LANGSTON (James Langston Hughes) (1902–1967), Prolific poet, playwright, scriptwriter, essayist, and editor; often called the "Poet Laureate of Harlem" and the "Dean of Black American Professional Writers." One of the major figures of the Black, or Harlem Renaissance; the author of more than 35 books. Although best known as a poet, his literary output includes novels, short stories, autobiographies, histories of drama and entertainment, librettos and lyrics for operas and musicals, edited anthologies, histories of blacks in various fields, radio and television scripts, a screenplay, and numerous articles for newspapers and magazines. Born in Joplin, MO, the child of a broken home; his father was an expatriot. He was brought up by his mother and maternal grandmother in Lawrence and Topeka, KS, and Cleveland OH. After graduating from Cleveland's Central High School, he went to Mexico to visit his father during the summer of 1920, during which he wrote some of his early poems and short stories, which were published in the *Brownies' Book* and *Crisis* magazine. Attended Columbia University for one year, 1921–22, before abandoning his studies to travel in Africa and Europe, 1922–24. Completed his undergraduate education at Lincoln University (PA), where he received the B.A. in 1929. Correspondent for the Baltimore *Afro-American* newspaper, 1938–40; columnist for the *Chicago Defender,* 1943–67, and the *New York Post,* 1963–c. 1966. Playwright-in-residence at the Karamu Theatre, Cleveland, 1936 and 1939; resident poet, University of Chicago Laboratory School, 1949. Founder of three theatre groups: the Harlem Suitcase Theatre, 1938; the New Negro Theatre, Los Angeles, 1939; and the Skyloft Players, Chicago, 1941. His major volumes of poetry (more than 17 in all) include *The Weary Blues* (1926), *Fine Clothes to a Jew* (1927), *The Dream Keeper and Other Poems* (1932), *Shakespeare in Harlem* (with *Robert Glenn, 1942), *Fields of Wonder* (1947), *One-Way Ticket* (1949), *Montage of a Dream Deferred* (1951), *Ask Your Mama: 12 Moods for Jazz* (1961), and *The Panther and the Lash* (1967). Books of fiction include six novels, of which four are about a fictional character named Jesse B. Semple (*sic*)—*Not Without Laughter* (1930), *Simple Speaks His Mind* (1950), *Simple Takes a Wife* (1953), *Simple Stakes a Claim* (1957), *Tambourines to Glory* (1953), and *Simple's Uncle Sam*; and three volumes of short stories—*The Ways of White Folks* (1934), *Laughing to Keep from Crying* (1952), and *Something in Common and Other Stories* (1963). His two autobiographies are *The Big Sea* (1940) and *I Wonder as I Wander* (1956). Books of nonfiction include two photoessays—*The Sweet Flypaper of Life* (1955) and *Black Misery* (1969); two pictorial histories (both with Milton Meltzer)—*A Pictorial History of the Negro in American Entertainment* (1967) and *Black Magic: A Pictorial History of the Negro in American Entertainment* (1967). Books for children include *Popo and Fifina: Children of Haiti* (with ARNA BONTEMPS, 1932), *The First Book of Negroes* (1952), *The First Book of Rhythms* (1954), *The First Book of Jazz* (1955), *The First Book of the West Indies* (1956), and *The First Book of Africa* (1965). Edited anthologies include *Famous American Negroes* (1954), *Famous Negro Music Makers* (1955), *The Book of Negro Folklore* (with Arna Bontemps, 1959), *An African Treasury* (1960), *The Book of Negro Humor* (1966), *The Best Short Stories by Negro Writers* (1967), and *The Poetry of the Negro, 1746–1970* (1970/73). Member of Omega Psi Phi fraternity, ASCAP, and the National

Institute of Arts and Letters. Recipient of *Opportunity* Poetry Prize, 1925; Harmon Gold Medal for Literature, 1931; Guggenheim Fellowship for Creative Writing, 1935; Rosenwald Fellowship, 1942; American Academy of Arts and Letters Grant, 1947; Anisfeld-Wolf Award, 1953; and Spingarn Medal, 1960. Also awarded a Litt.D. from his alma mater, Lincoln University, in 1943.

Collections:

SCOTTSBORO LIMITED: Four Poems and a Play in Verse . Golden Stair Press, 1932. Contains: **Scottsboro Limited** (1931).

THE LANGSTON HUGHES READER. George Braziller, NY, 1958. Contains: **Glory of Negro History** (1958), **Soul Gone Home** (1954), and **Simply Heavenly** (1957).

FIVE PLAYS BY LANGSTON HUGHES. [*FIVE PLAYS*] Edited by Walter Smalley. Indiana Univ. Press, Bloomington, 1963. Contains: **Mulatto** (1930), **Soul Gone Home** (1937), **Little Ham** (1935), **Simply Heavenly** (1957), and **Tambourines to Glory** (1963).

Stage, Screen, and Broadcast Works:

PRIOR TO 1950

The Gold Piece (children's play, 1 act, 1921). Concerns two Mexican village children who make a great sacrifice to help an old woman with a blind son. Prod. by the Karamu Theatre, Cleveland, and by several school and children's groups during the 1920s. Pub. in *Brownies' Bk.*, July 1921, p. 191. Also in *NADSA Encore*, Spring 1949, pp. 30–32. COMMENTARY: Coleman diss.

Mulatto (tragedy, 2 acts, 1930). Based on his short story "Father and Son." Later adapt. into an opera, *The Barrier* (1950). Concerns the tragic conflict between a white plantation owner and his mulatto son in the Deep South. Written 1930. First prod. on Bway in a version adapt. by producer °Martin Jones at the Vanderbilt Theatre, Oct. 24, 1935, where it established a record of 373 perfs.—the longest run on Bway up to that time for a play by a black playwright. Toured for eight months in the United States, including a three-week stay in Chicago at the Studebaker Theatre, opening Dec. 25, 1936; dir. by Martin Jones. Cast included ROSE McCLENDON as Cora Lewis, the mother (and after her death, MERCEDES GILBERT); Stuart Beebe as Colonel Thomas Norwood, the plantation owner; and Morris McKenney as the son, Robert. First prod. in the author's orig. version by the Gilpin Players at the Karamu Theatre, Cleveland, March 8, 1938. Prod. in Italy, with Italian actors in blackface, as part of the repertory of the Compagnia del Teatro Italiano in Rome and Milan, during the 1950s, where it ran for two years. Also prod. in Buenos Aires in the late 1950s, where it ran for two years. Text of the orig. version pub. in *FIVE PLAYS*. Also in *Blk. Dr.* (Brasmer & Consolo, 1970). Text of the Martin Jones adaptn. used for the Bway prodn. pub. in *Three Neg. Plays* (Bigsby, 1964). Italian edition, *Mulatto, Drama in Due Atti e Tre Scene,* trans. by A. Ghireli, pub. by A. Mondadori, Milan, 1949. Spanish edition, *Mulato, Drama en Dos Actos,* trans. by J. Galer, pub. by Editorial Quetzal, Buenos Aires, 1954. Czechoslovakian edition, *Mulat,* trans. by B. Becher, pub. by Dilia Pubs., Prague, date unknown. Copies of all texts, including foreign eds., in Schomburg. REVIEWS AND COMMENTARY: *AnthANT* (Patterson). *BesPls 1935–36; 1950–51.* *BlkMagic* (Hughes & Meltzer). *CLAJ. Cleveland Plain Dealer* 10–17–1938. Coleman diss. *Drama Critique* Spring 1964. *NegPlaywrs* (Abramson). *NYT* 8–8–1935; 10–25–1935; 2–9–1937; 2–10–1937; 2–11–1937; 2–12–1937; 11–25–1939; 11–16–1967. *Phylon* 2nd qtr. 1950; 2nd qtr. 1955. *Th. Arts* 12–1935; 8–1942.

Cock o' de World (musical comedy, 3 acts, 1931). Adapt. by Hughes from a play by †KAJ GYNT. With lyrics by †Duke Ellington. Concerns the adventures of a black sailor who travels from New Orleans through the West Indies to Paris, where he encounters the racism of a white society and is forced to return home. Incomplete script in JWJ/YUL.

Scottsboro Limited (play in verse, 1 act, 1931). A bitter protest of the famous Scottsboro case of nine black youths accused of raping two white women in Alabama. Prod. at Webster Hall, New York City, during the winter of 1931. Pub. in *New Masses,* Nov. 1931, pp. 18–21, and in *SCOTTSBORO LIMITED.* COMMENTARY: Hicklin diss. *People's Theatre in Amerika* (Taylor).

The Emperor of Haiti // Original titles: **Troubled Island** and **Drums of Haiti** (tragedy, 3 acts, 1935). Concerns the heroic rise from slavery and the tragic downfall of the Haitian emperor Dessalines during the Napoleonic era. First prod. as *Troubled Island* by the Gilpin Players, at the Karamu Theatre, Cleveland, Nov. 18–23, 1936, for 6 perfs. Prod. as *Drums of Haiti* by the Roxanne Players, Detroit, c. 1937. (Revised under its present title, 1938.) Prod. in Harlem, under its present title, by the Manhattan Art Theatre, at St. Martin's Episcopal Church Theatre, for 4 perfs.; and at the Joseph P. Kennedy, Jr. Memorial Community Center Theatre, for 4 additional perfs., 1958. (Adapt. into an opera also called *Troubled Island,* 1949.) Again revised as a drama, 1963. Pub. under its present title in *BlkDrAm* (Turner, 1971) and in *Blk. Heroes* (Hill, 1989). Script of *Drums of Haiti* in JWJ/YUL. REVIEWS AND COMMENTARY: *Cleveland Plain Dealer* 11–19–1936; 4–22–1937. Hicklin diss.

Blood on the Fields (social drama, 3 acts, 1935). Migrant cotton workers attempt to organize a union to improve their working conditions. Incomplete script in JWJ/YUL.

Little Ham (comedy, 3 acts, 1935; also adapt. as a radio series). Play of Harlem life during the 1920s, revolving around the escapades of Hamlet Jones, a carefree, antiheroic Harlem "sporting" type. Copyrighted 1935. First prod. by the Gilpin Players at the Karamu Theatre, Cleveland, June 9–14, 1936, for 6 perfs. Revived by the Karamu Theatre, May 25–June 6, 1938, for 9 perfs. Pub. in *FIVE PLAYS*. Typescript of 65-episode radio program in JWJ/YUL. REVIEWS AND COMMENTARY: *Cleveland Call and Post* 4–2–1936; 6–4–1936. *Cleveland Gazette* 3–28–1936; 6–6–1936. *Cleveland N.* 3–26–1936. *Cleveland Press* 3–24–1936. *Cleveland Plain Dealer* 3–25–1938; 5–26–1938. Coleman diss. *NYT* 10–25–1935.

St. Louis Woman (adaptn., full length, 1936). Revision by Hughes of the orig. play by Arna Bontemps and COUNTEE CULLEN, for prodn. by the Federal Theatre Project. Microfilm copy of unpub. script in Schomburg.

Angelo Herndon Jones (drama, 1 act, 1936). Won first prize in the New Theatre League's contest of 1936 as the best play about the Herndon case, which dealt with a black man who was sentenced to the chain gang for 20 years because he led a protest against unemployment in the United States. Prod. by the Harlem Suitcase Theatre, New York City, May 1938. Pub. in *New Th. Mag.,* 1936. Script in JWJ/YUL.

No Left Turn (comedy, 1 act, 1936). Short play on the social life of a black man. First prod. by the Community Laboratory Theatre, a unit of the WPA Federal Theatre Proj., at the Karamu Theatre, Cleveland, 1936.

When the Jack Hollars, or Careless Love (folk comedy, 3 acts, 1936). Comedy of folk superstitions among poor black and white sharecroppers on a plantation in the Mississippi Delta region. First prod. by the Gilpin Players, at Karamu House, Cleveland, April 28–30 and May 1–4, 1936. Unpub. scripts in JWJ/YUL and Schomburg. COM-

MENTARY: Hicklin diss. *Neg. in Am. Th.* (Isaacs), photo. *Th. Arts* 8–1942, photo.

Joy to My Soul (farce, 3 acts, 1937). The plot turns on the well-worn situation of a wealthy bachelor waiting to meet for the first time his fiancée, whom he has courted through "lonely hearts" correspondence. He does not know that she is a buxom woman twice his age, who has been set up by a pair of crooks to fleece him of his money. First prod. by the Gilpin Players at the Karamu Theatre, April 1–11, 1937, for 9 perfs. Revived by the same group, May 24–June 4, 1969. Unpub. scripts in JWJ/YUL and Schomburg. Drafts and prodn. notes also in JWJ/YUL. COMMENTARY: Hicklin diss.

Soul Gone Home (fantasy, 1 act, 1937). Also prod. as an opera (1 act, 1954). The "spirit" of a dead son accuses his mother of causing his untimely death through her misconduct and neglect. First prod. by the Gilpin Players at Karamu House and by the Cleveland Federal Theatre, during the 1930s. Prod. by the Negro Arts Players at the Elks Theatre, New York, Aug. 25, 1952; by the Burlap Summer Theatre, at Club Baron, New York, July 9, 1953; and by the Greater New York Chapter of ANTA, at the Theatre De Lys, Oct. 27, 1959. Pub. in *One-Act Play Mag.*, July 1937, pp. 196–97; in *Contemp. One Act Plays* (Kozlenko, 1938); in *THE LANGSTON HUGHES READER*; in *SADSA Encore,* Spring 1949, pp. 33–35; and in *FIVE PLAYS,* which also includes commentary. Adapt. as an opera in one act by *Ulysses Kay; copy in JWJ/YUL. OTHER COMMENTARY: Coleman diss. *Drama Critique* Spring 1964. Hicklin diss.

Don't You Want to Be Free (musical pageant, 1 long act, 1937; revised 1963). First written in 1937 as a "poetry play"; revised in 1963 as a "Negro history play." Traces the history of blacks in America from slavery through the blues to the present (1930s in the orig.; 1960s in the revised version), combining poetry, dramatic sketches, spirituals, blues, work songs, and jazz. First prod. by the author at the Harlem Suitcase Theatre, opening in Feb. 1937, where it established a record run for the Harlem community of 135 perfs., presented mainly on weekends; dir. by Hilary Phillips. The cast featured Earl Jones, the father of James Earl Jones, in his stage debut. Presented briefly on Bway, under the sponsorship of the New Theatre League, at the Nora Bayes Theatre, June 10, 1938. Also prod. by the New Negro Theatre, a group founded by the author, in Los Angeles, 1939. Pub. in *One-Act Play Mag.*, Oct. 1938, pp. 359–93. Drafts and unpub. revisions, 1938–1963, in JWJ/YUL. Also in *BlkThUSA* (Hatch, 1974), which also includes commentary. Unpub. script of the revised 1963 (Emancipation Centennial) version, with music by Sammy Heyward, in Schomburg. OTHER COMMENTARY: *AnthANT* (Patterson), advertisement. *BesPls 1937–38. BlkDr* (Mitchell). *BlkMagic* (Hughes & Meltzer), photo, poster. Coleman diss. Hicklin diss. *NegPlaywrs* (Abramson). *Th. Arts* 8–1942, photo.

De Organizer (blues opera, 1 act, 1938). Music by †James P. Johnson. Undisguised labor propaganda, in support of efforts to organize a union of sharecroppers in the South. Apparently prod. by the Harlem Suitcase Theatre, New York, 1939. Unpub. scripts in JWJ/YUL and Schomburg.

Like a Flame (drama, 1 act, 1938). Dramatization by °Alice Holdship Ware of Hughes' poem "Tomorrow," which deals with attempts on the part of American tourists to persuade French night club owners to segregate black customers from white. Pub. by the New Theatre League, New York; copies in Moorland-Spingarn and TC/NYPL.

Em-Fuehrer Jones (satirical skit, 1 act, 1938). A parody of Eugene O'Neill's *The Emperor Jones,* with the white leading character modeled after Adolf Hitler. Prod. with the two following plays by the Harlem Suitcase Theatre, 1938. Unpub. scripts in JWJ/YUL and Schomburg. COMMENTARY: *AnthANT* (Patterson), advertisement.

Little Eva's End (satirical skit, 1 act, 1938). A parody of Harriet Beecher Stowe's character in *Uncle Tom's Cabin,* who became a symbol of white purity and innocence. Her ascension into Heaven following her untimely death was the most sentimental scene in the novel and formed the spectacular climax of the play. Hughes' skit apparently presented a new ending for Little Eva. A companion skit to the plays above and below, presented with them at the Harlem Suitcase Theatre, 1938.

Limitations of Life (satirical skit, 1 act, 1938). A parody of the 1934 Fanny Hurst film *Imitation of Life,* starring Louise Beavers as the faithful mammy and Claudette Colbert as the benevolent young white mistress. The skit reverses the racial roles of the film characters, making Mammy Delilah Weaver the mistress and Audette the faithful servant. A companion skit to the two plays above prod. on a triple bill with them at the Harlem Suitcase Theatre, 1938. First pub. in *Skits and Sketches,* second printed collection (New Theatre League, 1939). Reprinted in *BlkThUSA* (Hatch, 1974).

Front Porch (3 acts, 1938). Classified as either a social comedy or a social drama, depending on which of two alternative Act III endings is used. Concerns the social strivings of a middle-class black mother and her attempt to alienate herself and her family from the problems of the black working class. The front porch is a status symbol of the middle class. Written for and first prod. by the Gilpin Players, at the Karamu Theatre, Cleveland, Nov. 16–21, 1938, for 6 perfs. Unpub. scripts in JWJ/YUL and Schomburg. Drafts also in JWJ/YUL. REVIEWS AND COMMENTARY: *Cleveland Gazette* 11–19–1938; 12–3–1938. *Cleveland Plain Dealer* 11–17–1938. *Cleveland Press* 11–17–1938. Hicklin diss.

Way Down South (feature film, full length: screenplay, 1939). Coauthor with CLARENCE MUSE. A stereotypical melodrama of the old South, which tells the story of the devotion of a young white boy to the slaves on his deceased father's plantation. The plot revolves around the boy's attempt to save his favorite slave, Old Uncle Canton, from mistreatment by the plantation overseer, a Simon Legree–like character. The role of Uncle Canton was played by Hughes' coauthor, actor Clarence Muse, who decided that the best way to get a good film role was to write the part himself. Prod. by Sol Lesser, 1939. With Bobby Breen as the white boy. The Hall Johnson Choir sang 11 spirituals in this film.

Mule Bone (folk play, 3 acts, 1930s). Coauthored with ZORA NEALE HURSTON. Based on folk material collected by Hurston, some of which later appeared in her book *Mules and Men* (1935). Written during the 1930s. Sched. for prodn. by the Gilpin Players, Cleveland, but never prod. because of a literary quarrel between the coauthors, which Hughes reported in his autobiography, *The Big Sea* (1940). Excerpt (Act III) pub. in *Drama Critique* ("The Negro in the Theatre" issue), Spring 1964. Scripts of the three-act version in Hatch-Billops and JWJ/YUL. COMMENTARY: *Big Sea* (Hughes).

Trouble with the Angels (drama, 1 act, 1930s). Adapt. by °Bernard C. Schoenfeld from a short story of the same title by Hughes. Script submitted to the Karamu Theatre, Cleveland, for prodn. consideration during the late 1930s, but apparently never prod. Pub. by the New Theatre League, New York, date unknown; copy in Moorland-Spingarn.

Tropics After Dark (musical theatre work, 2 acts, 1940). Coauthored with Arna Bontemps. Music by Margaret Bonds. Prod. at the American Negro Exposition, Chicago, 1940. Unpub. script in JWJ/YUL.

Booker T. Washington in Atlanta (radio script, 1940). Commissioned by Tuskegee Inst. to celebrate the occasion of the issuance by the Post Office of the Booker T. Washington commemorative stamp in April 1940. Broadcast by CBS Radio on the "Pursuit of Happiness'' show, presumably in April 1940, featuring Rex Ingram. Pub. in *Radio Drama in Action* (Barnouw, 1945).

Cavalcade of the Negro Theatre (theatre script, 1940). Coauthored with Arna Bontemps. Pageant of black participation in the theatre from the mid-nineteenth century to 1940. Written for and presumably prod. at the American Negro Exposition, Chicago, July 4–Sept. 4, 1940. Mimeographed script, dated 1940, issued by Maxim Lieber, New York; copy in Moorland-Spingarn. [See also next entry.]

Jubilee: A Cavalcade of the Negro Theatre (radio script, 1941). Coauthored with Arna Bontemps. Adapt. from the above script. A narrated dramatization of black participation in the American theatre from the mid-nineteenth century to the 1940s, utilizing folk songs, spirituals, Creole melodies, popular songs, and specially written numbers by Duke Ellington and Tommy Dorsey. First prod. as a showcase prodn. by CBS, 1941. Prod. and recorded by the War Dept. and shortwaved overseas, 1943. According to *Negro Year Book, 1947* (Guzman, p. 448): "[This broadcast] brought the great luminaries of the world of music to its microphones in answer to the scores of requests made by fighting men overseas. Marion Anderson, the Charioteers, Lena Horne, the Mills Brothers, Noble Sissle's Band, Nicodemus, Jesse Cryer and other well-known figures were heard on this program." Unpub. script (without the music) in Schomburg.

The Sun Do Move // Orig. title: **Sold Away** (musical drama, 3 acts and prologue, 1941). The black people's journey from slavery to freedom, depicted through a series of dramatic scenes interspersed with spirituals and expository speeches. The title is an allusion to the famous sermon of John Jasper, a popular but unlettered Richmond, VA, black preacher of the nineteenth century. Sched. for spring prodn. under its orig. title by the Karamu Theatre, Cleveland, at the Brooks Theatre during the 1941–42 season, but was not prod. because of Pearl Harbor. First prod. by the Skyloft Players, Chicago, at the Good Shepherd Community House, Spring 1942. Presented during the 1940s at Parkway House, New York. Mimeographed by the International Workers Order, New York, 1942; copies in Schomburg and Moorland-Spingarn. Drafts and script also in JWJ/YUL.

Brothers (radio script, 1942). Patriotic program on heroic black seamen, written for the Writers War Board. Recorded in New York and released to local radio stations in 1942.

That Eagle (patriotic play with music, 1942). Wartime propaganda piece, utilizing Hughes' poetry set to music. Prod. for "The Canteen Show" at the Stage Door Canteen, 1942, where Hughes worked as a volunteer waiter. Song lyrics, "That Eagle," with music by Emerson Harper, pub. by Musette Pubs. REVIEW: *NYT* 9–4–42.

For This We Fight (radio script, with music, 1942/44). A black soldier narrates the history of black Americans to his son, explaining why they are willing to fight for their country. World War II patriotic program, written for and presumably prod. at a freedom rally at Madison Square Garden between 1942 and 1944. Song lyrics, "For This We Fight," with music by Haufrescht, pub. by Negro Freedom Rally. Unpub. script in JWJ/YUL.

Hotel Black Majesty (c. 1943). Drama set in a hotel lobby.

Popo and Fifina (children's play, 1943). Adaptn. of a book of the same title by Arna Bontemps about life in Haiti.

John Henry Hammers It Out (radio script with music, 1943). Prod. by NBC on a program entitled "Labor for Victory," with Paul Robeson and Kenneth Spencer. Hughes' contribution included lyrics for bridges and the final scene, "We'll Hammer It Out Together," with music by Earl Robinson.

Freedom's Plow (radio script, 1943). Patriotic program, presumably based on Hughes' long wartime poem by the same title, which narrates the role of black slaves in the building and spiritualizing of America. Prod. by the National Urban League and presented over the Blue Network in 1943, with Paul Muni and the Golden Gate Quartet. Pub. by Musette Pubs., 1943.

The Man Who Went to War (radio script with music, 1944). Recorded in New York, with Ethel Waters, Paul Robeson, Josh White, and the Hall Johnson Choir. Broadcast over BBC, spring 1944.

In the Service of My Country (radio script, 1944). Wartime patriotic script, written for the Writers War Board, presumably broadcast over radio station WNYC, Jan. 1944.

Pvt. Jim Crow (radio script, 1945). Pub. in *Negro Story Mag.*, May-June 1944, pp. 3–9.

Street Scene (folk opera, 2 acts, 1947). Libretto by Elmer Rice. Lyrics by Hughes. Musical score by °Kurt Weill. Based on Rice's play of the same title, which won the Pulitzer Pirze in 1929. Tragedy of tenement life in New York. Labeled by some "the first Broadway opera." Prod. on Bway at the Adelphi Theatre, Jan. 9–May 17, 1947, for 148 perfs.; dir. by °Charles Friedman. The integrated cast featured white singer/actors Polyna Stoska, Ann Jeffreys, and Norman Gordon; with Creighton Thompson and Juanita Hall as a black janitor and his wife. Revived by the New York City Opera Co., with William Dupree in the role of the janitor. Pub. by Chappell & Co., New York, 1948; copy of playscript in Schomburg. Cast recording by Columbia Records (OL4139). RE-VIEWS AND COMMENTARY: *Am. Plays and Playwrs.* (Lewis). *BesPls 1946–47; 1958–59; 1965–66. Cath. World* 2–1947. *Commonweal* 1–31–1947. *Musical Am.* 5–1959; 10–1959. *New Republic* 2–10–1947. *Newsweek* 1–20–1947. *New Yorker* 1–18–1947. *Sat. Rev. of Lit.* 2–1–1947. *Th. Arts* 3–1947. *Time* 1–20–1947.

Swing Time at the Savoy (radio script, 1949). Coauthored with Noble Sissle. Written for Lucky Millinder's Band. Prod. on NBC's "Summer Musical Series," 1949.

Troubled Island (opera, 4 acts, 1949). Musical score by William Grant Still. Based on Hughes' play *The Emperor of Haiti* (1935). Concerns the hectic rise and tragic fall of Dessalines, emperor of Haiti during the Napoleonic era. When prod. by the New York City Opera Co. at City Center, March 31, 1949, considered "America's first top-quality presentation of a full-length opera by Negroes."—*Langston Hughes* (Emanuel, 1967), p. 42. Pub. by Leeds Music Corp., New York, 1949; copies in Schomburg and TC/ NYPL. COMMENTARY: *BesPls/ 1948–49.*

OTHER STAGE WORKS BEFORE 1950: (all undated and unpub. scripts; copies in JWJ/YUL): **Adam and Eve and the Apple** (opera, 1 act: libretto). **At the Jazz Ball** (opera, 2 acts: libretto). Musical score by °Jan Meyerowitz. **Outshines the Sun** (drama). **Tell It to Telstar** (musical play, 1 act). Dancers, soloists, and a chorus are used to dramatize the common struggle for freedom that connects blacks to other oppressed peoples of the world. **Wide River** (folk opera: libretto). Music by Granville English. Adapt. from the play *The Shuffle Town Outlaws*, by William Norman Cox. Apparently incomplete.

SINCE 1950

(For descriptions of these plays, consult my earlier volume, *Contemporary Black American Playwrights and Their Plays*, Greenwood Press, Westport, CT, 1988).

The Barrier (opera; also called a musical drama, 2 acts, 1950). Libretto and lyrics by Hughes. Musical score by Jan Meyerowitz. Based on Hughes' play **Mulatto** (1930) and his earlier short story "Father and Son." **Just Around the Corner** (musical, 2 acts, 1951). Lyrics by Hughes. Book by °Abby Mann and °Bernard Drew. Music by °Joe Sherman. **The Wizard of Altoona** (musical, 3 acts, 1951). Music by °Elie Siegmeister. **Pennsylvania Spring** (1953). **Love from a Tall Building** (musical, also called an opera, 1 act, c. 1954). [Since this title was not included in my earlier volume, the following brief description is given: In the setting of a New York skyscraper, a woman threatens to jump from the building because she is convinced that "Joe" does not love her. The play involves the successful efforts on the part of the rest of the cast to convince her that she can live without Joe.] **Simple Takes a Wife** (folk comedy, full length, 1955). The orig. dramatic version of Hughes' novel *Simple Takes a Wife*, which in 1957 was expanded into the musical **Simply Heavenly** (1957), below. **St. James: Sixty Years Young** (historical play, 1 act, 1955). **The Ballot and Me** (historical pageant, 1 act, 1956). [History of black efforts to gain the vote.]. **Esther** (opera, 3 acts, 1957; also in a 1-act version, 1957). **Simply Heavenly** (musical comedy, 2 acts [17 scenes], 1957). Book and lyrics by Hughes. Music by David Martin. Based on Hughes' nonmusical play **Simple Takes a Wife** (1955), above, which in turn was based on his novel by the same title. **Glory of Negro History** (pageant, 1958). **Shakespeare in Harlem** (theatre work, full length, 1959). Adaptn. by *Robert Glenn of the poetry of Hughes, utilizing the music of †James Weldon Johnson. Although the title is based on a 1942 volume by Hughes, most of the poems were taken from his *Montage of a Dream Deferred* (1952). **Mr. Jazz** (musical theatre work, 1960). **Port Town** (opera, 1 act, 1960). Libretto by Hughes. Musical score by Jan Meyerowitz. **Ballad of the Brown King** (Christmas cantata; also called a Christmas song play, 2 acts, 1960). Music by †Margaret Bonds. [Much of the material in this show was worked into Hughes' **Black Nativity,** immediately below.] **Black Nativity** ("Christmas song play" [subtitle]; also called a gospel song play as well as a gospel pageant, 2 acts, 1961). [Includes material from **Ballad of the Brown King,** above.] **Gospel Glow** // Orig. title: **The Gospel Glory** ("A passion play" [subtitle]; also called a gospel song play, 1 long act [revised from its former 2-act version], 1962). [Title revised to distinguish it from **Tambourines to Glory,** immediately below.] **Tambourines to Glory** (gospel song play, 2 acts [12 scenes], 1963). Music by Jobe Huntley. Evolved from some of Hughes' poems that had been previously turned into gospel songs by Huntley, an earlier play written around these songs, and Hughes' novel *Tambourines to Glory.* **Jerico-Jim Crow** (song play, full length, 1963). [Also spelled Jericho in some listings.] **Beyond the Blues** (TV script with music, 1954). **The Prodigal Son** (gospel song play, 1 act, 1965). **Mother and Child** (theatre vignette, 1 act, 1965). Based on his short story by the same title (1934). **It's a Mighty Wind** (TV script with music, 1965). Easter program. **Soul Yesterday and Today** (theatre work, 1965). By Hughes and Bob Teague, arranged by *Rosetta LeNoire. **The Weary Blues** (theatre work with music, 1966). Authorized adaptn. by *Woodie King, Jr., of Hughes' poetry and prose. **Strollin' Twenties** (TV script, 1966). With music by Duke Ellington. Conceived and prod. by Harry Belafonte. **Ask Your Mama** ("Jazz-mood piece," 1969). Posthumous adaptn. of some of Hughes' works. **Langston Living** (ritual, 1974). Another posthumous adaptn. of his works. OTHER UNDATED PLAYS: **The American Negro Speaks** (opera). With contributions by Clarence Muse and †Jo Trent. **Five Foolish Virgins** (opera, 2 acts). Music by Jan Meyerowitz. **The Get-Away** (skit). **Killed but Not Dead** (incomplete). **The Man Next Door** (incomplete).

Other Pertinent Writings:

"Harlem Literati in the Twenties," *Sat. Rev. of Lit.*, June 22, 1940, pp. 13–14.

The Big Sea: An Autobiography. Knopf, New York, 1940.

"The Need for Heroes," *Crisis,* June 1941, pp. 184–85.

"Is Hollywood Fair to Negroes?" *Neg. Digest,* April 1943, pp. 16–21.

Famous American Negroes. Dodd, Mead, New York, 1954.

I Wonder as I Wander: An Autobiographical Journey. Rinehart, New York, 1956.

A Pictorial History of the Negro in America. With Milton Meltzer. Crown, New York, 1956. Retitled *Pictorial History of Black Americans.*

"The Need for an Afro-American Theatre," *Chicago Defender,* June 12, 1961; reprinted in *AnthANT* (Patterson, 1967).

"The Negro in American Entertainment," in *Am. Neg. Ref. Bk.* (Davis, 1966).

Black Magic: A Pictorial Hist. of the the Neg. in Am. Entertainment. [*Blk Mag* (Hughes & Meltzer, 1967)]

FURTHER REFERENCE: *AnthANT* (Patterson). *Bio-Bibliog. of Langston Hughes* (Dickinson). *Biog. Encyc. & Who's Who of the Am. Th.* (Rigdon). *BlkDr* (Mitchell). *BlkMagic* (Hughes & Meltzer). *BlkThUSA* (Hatch). *CLAJ* 6–1968 (Darwin T. Turner, "Langston Hughes as Playwright," pp. 297–309). Coleman diss. *Curr. Biog. 1940.* *DANB. Harl. Renais. Remembered* (Bontemps). Hicklin diss. *Langston Hughes* (Emanuel). *Langston Hughes: A Biog.* (Meltzer). Langston Hughes Papers (c. 1917–63) in State Historical Society of Wisconsin, Archives and Ms. Div., Madison, WI; other papers in American Acad. of Arts and Letters Lib., New York City. *Life of Langston Hughes,* 2 vols. (Rampersad). *NegPlaywrs* (Abramson). Primary source materials in JWJ/YUL, TC/NYPL, and Fisk Univ. Lib.

HUNTER, CHARLES A. See Appendix B.

HUNTER, EDDIE. See Appendix B.

HUNTER, OLIVIA, Playwright associated with Talladega College, AL, during the 1920s.

Stage Work:

An' de Walls Came Tumblin' Down (4 acts, 1926). Coauthored with °Lillian Voorhees (former assoc. prof. of public speaking and dramatic arts at Talladega Coll.). Dramatization of poems by PAUL LAURENCE DUNBAR. First prod. at Tougaloo Coll., MS, Dec. 1926. Prod. at Talladega Coll., AL, June 3, 1929. Unpub. script in Amistad Research Center, Dillard Univ., New Orleans, LA.

HUNTLEY, ELIZABETH MADDOX. See Appendix A.

HURSTON, ZORA NEALE (c. 1891–1960), Legendary folklorist, novelist, short story writer, playwright, and teacher. One of the major literary figures of the Black or Harlem Renaissance. Born and reared in the all-black town of Eatonville, FL, where her father was mayor, and which provided much of the material for her writing and research. Following the early death of her mother and the remarriage of her father, she left home at an early age. Her schooling was interrupted by frequent moves from the home of one relative to another. At 16, she worked for a year and a half as a maid for a white singer in a musical show. Following this experience, she worked in Baltimore as a waitress while completing her high school education at Morgan (now State) College Preparatory School, 1918. She later studied at Howard University 1921–24, where her efforts in English and writing were encouraged by Lorenzo D. Turner and Alain Locke, and where her first short story was published in *The Stylus,* the campus literary magazine. One of her stories and two plays were published in *Opportunity* magazine and won *Opportunity* literary awards. Encouraged by her early success, she left Howard at the end of her sophomore year to go to New York, where she continued to write, earning her expenses as secretary and later chauffeur to Fannie Hurst, the well-known white novelist. She also won a scholarship to Barnard College, where her interest was diverted from English to anthropology and folklore. After graduating from Barnard with an A.B. degree in 1928, she did graduate work in folklore and anthropology for four years at Columbia University under a Rosenwald Fellowship, doing her research in Harlem, 1928–32. During this period, she married Herbert Sheen, from whom she was divorced four years later. From 1936–38 she continued her research in Haiti, the British West Indies, and in her native state of Florida under a Guggenheim Fellowship and several private grants. Among her best-known works are *Jonah's Gourd Vine* (novel, 1934), *Mules and Men* (folklore, 1935), *Their Eyes Were Watching God* (novel, 1937), *Dust Tracks on a Road* (autobiography, 1942), for which she received a $1,000 Anisfeld-Wolf Award, and *Seraph on the Suwanee* (novel, 1948). Her stories and articles have appeared in such periodicals as *Opportunity, American Mercury, Negro Digest, New Republic,* and the *Saturday Evening Post.* In the 1930s, she was associated with the Federal Theatre Project. In the early 1940s, she worked as a scriptwriter for Paramount Pictures in Hollywood. She taught drama for a short period at North Carolina College in Durham. During the 1950s, she broke contact with her friends and moved to Ft. Pierce, FL, where she lived in obscurity, seclusion, and poverty until her death at age 69. Recipient of a Litt.D. degree from Morgan State College, 1939, and a Howard University (Distinguished) Alumni Award, 1943.

Stage Works:

Spears (1925). Received honorable mention in the *Opportunity* Contest Awards of 1925.

Color Struck (melodrama, 4 scenes, 1925; revised 1926). About the color complexes of a dark-skinned woman in Jacksonville, FL, who cannot accept the love of a black man who wishes to marry her because of her hatred of her own color. During the course of the play, she has an affair with a white man and gives birth, out of wedlock, to a mulatto child, on whom she lavishes her affections. The child becomes seriously ill and dies because the mother refuses to let a black doctor treat her while she frantically tries to locate a nearby white doctor. Received second prize in the *Opportunity* Contest Awards of 1925 and honorable mention (in the revised version) in the *Opportunity* Contest Awards of 1926. The revised version was published in *Fire!* (a periodical), 1926, pp. 7–14. COMMENTARY: Austin diss.

The First One (comedy, 1 act, 1926). A satire of the biblical story concerning Noah's curse on his son Ham, who is traditionally held to be the ancestor of the black race. In this play, which takes place after the Flood, Ham and his family are portrayed as demonstrating many of the traits and characteristics, such as ornate attire, laziness, tardiness, ability to sing and dance, and general mirthfulness, which have come to represent the black stereotype. Received honorable mention in the *Opportunity* Contest Awards, May 1926. Pub. in *Ebony and Topaz* (Johnson, 1927). COMMENTARY: Austin diss.

Fast and Furious (musical show, full length, 1931). Included sketches by Hurston, †Tim Moore,†Clinton Fletcher,†Jackie ("Moms") Mabley, and others. Hurston contributed three comedy sketches: "The Courtroom" starred Tim Moore as the Judge and Clarence Todd as the Prosecuting Attorney, with Jackie Mabley, Juano Hernandez, and Etta Moten also in the cast. "The Football Game" depicted a game between Howard Univ. and Lincoln Univ., with Tim Moore as Captain of Howard's Team, Clinton Fletcher as Captain of Lincoln's Team, and Juano Hernandez as Howard's Wrestler. "Poker Game" apparently depicted a game in which the stakes involve going to Heaven or Hell for the winner or loser. The players included Tim Moore, Clarence Todd, Russell Lee, and Maurice Ellis; other characters included the Devil and his assistants, Sojourners in Hell, the Lord, and various angels. Prod. at the New Yorker Theatre, Sept. 15, 1931, for 7 perfs.; prod. and dir. by °Forbes Randolph. COMMENTARY: *BesPls 1931–32. BlksBf* (Sampson). *DBlkTh* (Woll).

Sermon in the Valley (monologue, 1 act, 1931). Dramatization of a rural Negro sermon, interspersed with songs, chants, and responses from the congregation. Prod. by the Gilpin Players, Cleveland, at the Little Theatre (Public Hall) as a Theatre of Nations entry, March 29, 1931; revived Dec. 12, 1934, and Dec. 7, 1949, as one of the offerings in the Karamu Theatre's Festival week, where it ran in repertory for more than a month.

Great Day (orig. title) // revised as **From Sun to Sun,** and later as **Singing Steel** (dramatic arrangement of collected folklore, full length, 1932/34). Series of folk scenes and folk songs. Prod. and dir. by Hurston, under its orig. title, at the John Golden Theatre, New York, Jan. 10, 1932; and at the New School for Social Research, New York, March 29, 1932. Toured Florida as **From Sun to Sun,** 1933, playing at the Civic Auditorium in Orlando and at Rollins Coll. in Winter Park, among other locations. Prod. as **Singing Steel** at the Chicago South Parkway YMCA, Nov. 23–24, 1934.

The Fiery Chariot (1935). Unpub. script in Hurst Collection, Rare Books and Manuscripts, Univ. of Florida Lib., Gainesville.

Mule Bone (folk play, 3 acts, 1930s). Coauthored with LANGSTON HUGHES. Based on folk material collected by Hurston, some of which later appeared in her book *Mules and Men* (1935). Sched. for prodn. by the Gilpin Players, Cleveland, but was never prod. because of a literary quarrel between the coauthors. Excerpt (Act III) pub. in *Drama Critique* ("The Negro in the Theatre" issue), Spring 1964. Unpub. script in Moorland-Spingarn. COMMENTARY: *The Big Sea* (Hughes). *Yale/Theatre* Fall 1976.

Polk County (3 acts, 1944). Subtitled "A Comedy of Negro Life in a Sawmill Camp, with Authentic Negro Music." Coauthored with Dorothy Waring. Apparently prod. in New York by Stephen Kelen-d'Oxylion. Unpub. scripts in LC, JWJ/YUL, and TC/NYPL.

Other Pertinent Writing:
"Mimicry," in *Negro Anthology* (Cunard), p. 39.

FURTHER REFERENCE: Austin diss. *Big Sea* (Hughes). *Contemp. Auths.*, vols. 85–88. *Curr. Biog. 1942. DANB. Neg. Hist. Bull.* 4–1966. Speisman diss. *Tenn. Folklore Society Bull.*, vol. 19, 1953; vol. 20, 1955. *Yale Univ. Lib. Gazette,* vol. 20, 1955.

I–J

INGRAM, REX. See Appendix A.

JACKSON, WILLIAM, Actor-playwright associated with several black little theatre groups from 1926 to 1931. A native of Montclair, NJ. Attended Howard University and Lincoln College (now University) in Jefferson City, MO, before receiving the B.A. degree from Columbia University, 1923. Apparently he was at the beginning of his career when he won third place in the *Opportunity* literary awards of 1926. In the "Contest Spotlight" of that year, as published in *Opportunity* magazine, Jackson is quoted as saying that he was interested in "building small houses for people" as his future career, as well as in "building themes for plays." In 1926 he was associated with the Aldridge Players of New York and was in the cast of a program of three one-act plays by FRANK WILSON. The following year he performed with the New York branch of the Krigwa Players in a production of three one-act plays, two of which were written by EULALIE SPENCE. With Theophilus Lewis, drama critic and former literary editor of *Opportunity,* Jackson founded the Negro Experimental Theatre in New York in 1929. (This latter group is not to be confused with the Harlem Experimental Theatre, which was founded in New York by REGINA ANDREWS and others around the same time.)

Stage Works:

Four Eleven (1 act, 1927). Winner of third prize in the *Opportunity* contest of 1927. Prod. by the Bank Street Players at the Robert Treat School in Newark, NJ, April 29, 1927.

Burning the Mortgage (1 act, 1931). Prod. by the Harlem Players, New York, Feb. 2, 6, and 9, 1931.

JEANNETTE, GERTRUDE. See Appendix A.

JEFFERSON, W. J. See Appendix A.

JOHNSON, FENTON (1888–1958), Poet, short story writer, editor, and play-wright. Born in Chicago, where he was educated in the public schools and at the University of Chicago. Also studied at Northwestern University and Columbia University School of Journalism. Came into prominence during World War I with the publication of three volumes of poetry: *A Little Dreaming* (1913), *Visions of Dusk* (1915), and *Songs of the Soil* (1920). Credited with having written several plays that were presented at the old Pekin Theatre in Chicago during the 1920s, only one of which has been identified. Other writings include *Tales of Darkest America* (short stories, 1920) and *For the Highest Good* (essays, 1920).

Stage Work:
(Although Johnson wrote several plays, only one title has been located.)
The Cabaret Girl (1925). Prod. at the Shadow Theatre, Chicago, 1925. No extant script.

JOHNSON, FREDDIE. See Appendix B.

JOHNSON, GEORGE P. (Perry) (1887–19–?), Early black independent film-maker. The brother of film actor/producer Noble P. Johnson. Together they founded the Lincoln Motion Picture Company, incorporated in 1916 and located in Nebraska. This company operated until the early 1920s, turning out short feature films for black audiences. Johnson was living in Los Angeles in 1978.

Screen Work:
By Right of Birth (silent feature film: scenario, 1923). The story of Juanita Cooper, a California University coed of Indian ancestry. "After a series of villainous attempts to defraud her of her true identity and her fortune, . . . a happy family reunion is celebrated and Juanita comes into the fortune and happiness which is hers 'by right of birth.' "—*Blks. in Am. Movies* (Powers, 1974), p. 146. Prod. by the Lincoln Motion Picture Co., 1923.

JOHNSON, GEORGIA DOUGLAS (1886–1966), Poet, playwright, and one of the leading members of the Washington literati during the period of the Harlem Renaissance, more properly called the Black Renaissance. Born in Atlanta, GA. Educated at Atlanta University, Howard University, and the Oberlin Conservatory of Music. Taught school for a brief period in Atlanta before moving to Washington, DC, with her husband, Henry Lincoln Johnson, a lawyer who was appointed Recorder of Deeds by President Taft. There she wrote and published four volumes of poetry, *The Heart of a Woman and Other Poems* (1918), *Bronze* (1920), *An Autumn Love Cycle* (1928), and *Share My World* (1962). Although best known as a poet, she also wrote a novel, her husband's biography, numerous short stories, and about 30 one-act plays. For some 40 years, her Washington, DC, home, known as "Halfway House," located on S Street in the Northwest section, became a literary salon for black artists and intellectuals of the area, who met regularly on Saturday nights and dubbed themselves "The Saturday Nighters." Among the well-known figures attending these salons were LANGSTON HUGHES, Alain Locke, JEAN TOOMER, COUNTEE CULLEN, MAY MILLER, Sterling Brown, OWEN DODSON, ANGELINA GRIMKÉ, MARITA BONNER, and RICHARD BRUCE NUGENT. Johnson received honorable mention in the *Opportunity* Contest Awards of 1926 for her play **Blue Blood** and won first prize the following year for her play **Plumes**. Remained in Washington, DC, until her death at 80, still writing and publishing her work.

Stage Works:

Sunday Morning in the South (tragedy, 1 act, c. 1925). Concerns the appalling effect on an ailing black grandmother in a small town in the South of the arrest of her eldest grandson on a Sunday morning on the charge that a man of his color, size, and age attacked a white woman the previous night. Knowing that her grandson is innocent, the grandmother prepares to go to an influential white woman for help, but learns, before she can leave the house, that the young man has already been lynched by an angry white mob. In grief and horror, she collapses and dies. Throughout the play, the singing of hymns in a nearby black church can be heard in the background. Apparently not prod. or pub. during the author's life. Pub. in *BlkThUSA* (Hatch, 1974). Also reportedly written in a second version, with the singing of a white church in the background, but this version has not been located.

Blue Blood (drama, 1 act, 1926). The problems of miscegenation, incest, and black social snobbery are all treated in this play, which explores the reactions of a black couple (and their respective mothers) who learn on their wedding night that they are children of the same white father, a wealthy southern aristocrat. Received honorable mention in the *Opportunity* Contest Awards, May 1926. First prod. by the Krigwa Players, New York, for 3 perfs., April 20–27, 1927. Prod. by the Students' Literary Guild at Central YMCA, Brooklyn, NY, Feb. 28, 1928. Also prod. by numerous little theatre groups following its publication in *Representative One-Act Plays, Fourth Series* (Shay, 1927) and in *Fifty More Contemporary One-Act Plays* (Shay and Loving, 1928).

Plumes (folk tragedy, 1 act, 1927). Explores the superstitions and funeral practices of lower-class blacks during the 1920s. An indigent mother whose daughter is desperately ill struggles to decide whether to spend her $50 savings on an operation which the doctor insists that the daughter must have immediately, but which is not guaranteed to save her life, or to keep the money to pay for a grand funeral "with plumed horses" after her daughter's death. The mother makes her life-or-death decision on the basis of the "reading" of coffee grounds by a superstitious friend, who predicts that the operation will do no good. Won first prize in the *Opportunity* Contest Awards of 1927. First prod. by the Harlem Experimental Theatre, New York, 1928. Prod. by the Cube Theatre, Chicago, 1928. Pub. by Samuel French, New York, in 1927; in *PlaysNegL* (Locke & Gregory, 1927); in *Opportunity*, July 1927, pp. 200–201, 217–18; and in *Anth. of Am. Neg. Lit.* (Calverton, 1944).

Safe (drama, 1 act, c. 1929). About the aftermath of a lynching. Pub. in *Wines in the Wilderness* (Brown-Guillory, 1990). Unpub. script in FTP/GMU.

Blue-Eyed Black Boy (drama, 1 act, c. 1930). About a lynching that is successfully averted. Pub. in *Wines in the Wilderness* (Brown-Guillory, 1990). Unpub. script in FTP/GMU.

William and Ellen Craft (black history play, 1 act, 1935). Focuses on the preparations made for one of the most thrilling slave escapes through the Underground Railroad in the folklore of the abolitionist crusade. William and Ellen Craft were a slave husband and wife who made their dash to freedom disguised as master and slave. William, who could read and write, was quite dark in color; Ellen, a mulatto who could easily pass for white, was illiterate. The play dramatizes how Ellen is dressed in a man's suit thought to have been burned after the death of its owner; her hair is cut, and she is taught how to "walk along bigity like a white man." To keep her from having to write or speak during the journey, her right hand is bandaged and put into a sling, and she is instructed to pretend that she is sick with a toothache and nearly deaf, and that her "nigger slave" is taking her to a doctor in Philadelphia. The play ends with the brave couple leaving on their perilous journey, afraid that they might be betrayed by another slave who has discovered their secret. Pub. in *NegHist13* (Richardson & Miller, 1935).

OTHER STAGE WORKS (all unpub. 1-act plays, pre–1930s): Plays dealing with lynching: **And Still They Paused. Midnight and Dawn. A Bill to Be Passed** (about the need for an antilynching law). **Camel-Legs. Heritage. Miss Bliss. Money Wagon**. Plays dealing with other aspects of black life: **Jungle Love. Little Blue Pigeon. The New Day. One Cross Enough. Red Shoes. Well-Diggers. Scapegoat. The Starting Point** (about a father's sacrifice to prevent his son from going into racketeering): script in JWJ/JUL. **Sue Bailey.**

FURTHER REFERENCE: *Crisis* 12–1952 (Cedrick Dover, "The Importance of Georgia Douglas Johnson," pp. 633–36, 674). Hicklin diss. *WWCA 1950.*

JOHNSON, HALL (Francis Hall Johnson) (1888–1970), Musician, composer, choral conductor, and arranger, who has been called the greatest black American choir director. Founder and director of the famed Hall Johnson Choir. Born in Athens, GA. His father, who apparently emigrated from the West Indies, was an A.M.E. minister who became president of Allen University in Columbia, SC; his mother was a former slave who taught him many of the Negro spirituals that he later arranged for his famous choir. Educated at Knox Institute, Athens (graduated c. 1903); Atlanta University (1 year); Allen University (graduated 1908); Hahn School of Music, Philadelphia (violin lessons, c. 1908–12); the University of Pennsylvania School of Music (graduated, 1910), from which he also received the Simon Haessler Prize for the best composition for orchestra and chorus; the Institute of Musical Art, New York (1923–24); and the Philadelphia Music Academy (hon. Mus.D., 1934). Married Celeste Corpening, a musician, in 1912; she died in 1935. Became involved, beginning in 1914, in show orchestras, including that of Vernon and Irene Castle, and such musical revues as *Shuffle Along* (1921), with which he toured the nation. Organized the Hall Johnson Negro Choir in 1925, which performed extensively on radio and stage and in films. Arranged composed and directed music for °Em Jo Basshe's *Earth* (1927), and both the stage and film version of *The Green Pastures* (1930, 1935); musical arranger and director for the following films: *Lost Horizon* (1937), *Way Down South* (1939), *Swanee River* (1939), *Lady for a Night* (1941), *Tales of Manhattan* (1942), and *Cabin in the Sky* (1943). Organized the Negro Festival Chorus of Los Angeles, 1941, while working in motion pictures; and the Festival

Chorus of New York City, 1946. His best-known spiritual arrangements are *Honor, Honor* and *Ride on, King Jesus*. Member of ASCAP, 1952. Winner of two Holstein Prizes for composition, 1925, 1927; the Harmon Award, 1931; and a citation from the City of New York, 1954. Inducted into the Black Film-makers Hall of Fame, posthumously, 1975.

Stage Work:

Run, Little Chillun! // Orig. title: **Across the River, or Run Little Chillun** (a "Negro folk drama" with incidental music composed and arranged by the author, 2 acts [4 scenes], 1933). Revolves around a bitter clash between two opposing black religious groups: the New Day Pilgrims, a pagan cult that practices a form of voodoo and hedonism taken from the Bahamas, and the Hope Baptist Church, a fundamentalist Christian sect that is intolerant of all non-Christian worship. A crisis occurs when the married son of New Hope's Baptist minister, who is destined to take over his father's position, is seduced by a girl from the other group, who persuades him to leave his wife and his church and join her cult. What then ensues is a fervent effort on the part of the Baptists to win their prodigal son back to the fold. In the meantime, the chief prophet of the pagan cult, who also opposes the love affair, puts a curse on the girl. Victory is assured for the Baptists when the girl is struck down by lightning just as the errant son is repenting his sins and being received back into his church with great rejoicing. Although the plot has been dismissed as somewhat simplistic, Johnson's play was universally praised for the exciting religious worship scenes of each group—the singing, dancing, "speaking in tongues," voodoo, and orgiastic rituals of the New Day Pilgrims, and the spirituals, prayers, sermons, confessions, and other revival practices of the Hope Baptist Church. First prod. at the Lyric Theatre, New York, opening March 1, 1933, for 126 perfs.; dir. by °Frank Merlin. With Alston Burleigh and Fredi Washington in the leading roles, and featuring the Hall Johnson Choir. Prod. by the Los Angeles Federal Theatre in Los Angeles and Hollywood, CA, for 11 months, 1938–39. Prod. by the Federal Theatre and Music Projects, at the Alcazar Theatre, San Francisco, opening Jan. 12, 1939, for 17 weeks. Revived by °Lew Cooper at the Hudson Theatre, New York, opening Aug. 11, 1943, for 16 perfs.; dir. by CLARENCE MUSE. With Caleb Peterson and Edna Mae Harris in the leading roles. Unpub. scripts in LC, Schomburg, and Doheny Lib., Univ. of Southern California/Los Angeles. REVIEWS AND COMMENTARY: *AnthANT* (Patterson). *Arena* (Flanagan). *BesPls 1932–33; 1938–39; 1939–40; 1943–44. Dust Tracks on the Road* (Hurston). Hicklin diss. *List of Negro Plays* (WPA). *Neg&Dr* (Bond). *NegPlaywrs* (Abramson). *NY Herald Tribune* 8–12–1833. *NYT* 3–2–1933; 3–12–1933, 4–30–1939; 6–14–1939; 7–14–1943. *Opportunity* 4–1933; 5–1941. *Th. Arts* 4–1933; 5–1933; 8–1942; 10–1943. *Th. Bk. of the Yr. 1943–44* (Nathan).

Other Stage Work:

Son of Man (a religious cantata, 1946). **Fi-Yer** (a Negro operetta) and **Coophered** (an operetta; a portrayal of Negro life in the southland).

Other Pertinent Writing:

The Green Pastures Spirituals, Arranged for Voice and Piano. New York: Farrar and Rinehart, 1930.

FURTHER REFERENCE: *Current Biog. 1945. DirBlksPA* (Mapp). *Historical Neg. Biogs.* (Robinson). *MusBlkAms* (Southern). Ross diss. *WWCA 1950* and earlier eds.

JOHNSON, J. ROSAMOND. See Appendix B.

JOHNSON, WILLIAM (BILLY). See Appendix B.

JONES, WILLA SAUNDERS (Mrs. Charles E. Jones) (1901–1979), Playwright, producer, director, and musician, whose musical accomplishments included the piano, organ, singing, directing, and composing. Resided in Chicago since the early 1920s, where for 47 years she was the author and producer of an annual passion play, "reputed to be Chicago's oldest continuous cultural event."—*Jet,* March 26, 1970. As a member of the National Baptist Convention, she also directed its chorus of 1,000 voices, which sang at various conventions throughout the United States, from California to New York.

Stage Work:
Black Passion Play (full length, 1926/73). The life and suffering of Christ as interpreted through the black man's experience in the United States. Prod. annually in Chicago from 1926 to 1973.

OTHER PLAYS (not dated): **The Call to Arms. Just One Hour to Live—for the Dope Addict. The Life Boat. Up from Slavery.**

K–L

KELLY, BUENA V. See Appendix A.

LAMB, ARTHUR CLIFTON (A. Clifton Lamb) (1909–), College professor, drama director, and playwright, who taught for more than 25 years at Morgan State College (now University) in Baltimore, MD. Born in Muscatine, IA. Received the A.B. in dramatics, English, and Spanish from Grinnell College in 1931; the M.A. degree in playwriting from the State University of Iowa in 1940; and a Certificate in Television and Radio from New York University in 1948. Also pursued Ph.D. studies at the State University of Iowa, 1954. Taught English and drama at Shaw University (Raleigh), Prairie View State College (Texas), and Johnson C. Smith University (Charlotte, NC) before joining the faculty of Morgan, where he developed the theatre arts program and the courses in television and radio that were antecedents of the present program in telecommunications, and where he is now professor emeritus. He has also been guest director at the Atlanta University Summer Theatre (1941, 1943, and 1946) and vice president of the National Association of Dramatic and Speech Arts (NADSA) (1963–?). Recipient of the Henry York Steiner Prize in Playwriting at Grinnell in 1931; the Sergel Prize in regional playwriting at Iowa in 1939; and the Mister Brown Award for his pioneering achievements in theatre and television, at the National Conference on Black American Protest Drama and Theatre, April 1985. He is currently working on a novel, tentatively titled "First Family in the Promised Land."

Stage and Broadcast Works:
EARLIEST PLAYS: **The Faith Cure, Reachin' for the Sun,** and **She Dyed for a Prince** (all 1-acts, c. 1930). First prod. at Grinnell College, IA, around 1930, and also presented at several other colleges and high schools.

Shade of Cottonlips (1 act, 1931). Awarded the Henry Steiner Memorial Prize in Playwriting, Grinnell College, IA, 1931. First prod. at Grinnell College, May 18, 1933.

Prod. at North Carolina A. & T. College, Greensboro, and the New School for Social
Research, New York.

The Two Gifts ("A Christmas Play for Negroes" [subtitle], 1 act, 1935). Prod. by
the Maclean College Players, Chicago, Dec. 6, 1935. Pub. in *Grinnell Plays* (1935).

Black Woman in White // Former title: **Beebee** (drama, 3 acts [10 scenes], 1940).
Concerns the struggles of a black woman doctor. First prod. at the State Univ. of Iowa
under its former title, April 25, 1940. Prod. by the Rose McClendon Players, at the Rose
McClendon Workshop, New York, Aug. 13, 1941. Also prod. by a number of colleges
and universities, including Prairie View College, Johnson C. Smith Univ., Dillard Univ.,
and Morgan College, 1941–47. Was under option for Bway prodn. in 1964.

Millsboro Memorial (1 act, 1946). Prod. at the Tenth Annual Conf. of the Southern
Association of Dramatic and Speech Arts (SADSA), held at Tennessee A. & I. State
Univ., Nashville, April 10, 1946.

Portrait of a Pioneer (short radio play, 1949). Concerns the theatrical career of IRA
ALDRIDGE, the first black Shakespearean and classical actor of the nineteenth century.
Pub. in *Neg. Hist. Bull.*, April 1949, pp. 162–64.

Roughshod up the Mountain (comedy-drama, also called a musical, 3 acts, 1953).
Music by Herman Branch. The conflict between the "old Negro" and the new is dramatized in this struggle of an uneducated minister to keep his congregation from replacing
him with a young divinity school graduate. First prod. at the State Univ. of Iowa as part
of the author's Ph.D. studies in playwriting, 1953. Prod. at Tennessee A. & I. State
Univ., Nashville, June 25, 1956. Presented as the American entry in the Annual International Festival, at the Sarah Bernhardt Theatre, Paris, June 1946, followed by a tour
of Italy, Germany, Sweden, Ireland, and England.

Mistake into Miracle (90-minute teleplay, also adapt. as a full-length play, 1961).
Submitted as a TV script to the Hallmark Hall of Fame television scriptwriting contest,
and ranked among the 30 best scripts received, but not prod. on TV. Prod. as a stage
play at Morgan State Coll., Baltimore, Dec. 8, 1961.

LEDERER, CLARA. See BUNDY, FLORENCE, and CLARA LEDERER.

LIGHTS, FREDERICK L. See Appendix A.

LINDSAY, POWELL, Pioneer producer, director, theatrical organizer, play-
wright, screenwriter, author, and research official. Born in Philadelphia, PA.
Educated at St. Paul's College, Virginia Union University, and Yale University
School of Drama. Associated with LANGSTON HUGHES' Harlem Suitcase
Theatre in 1938/39; one of the founding members of the Negro Playwrights'
Company and director of that company's production of THEODORE WARD's
Big White Fog, 1940. Wrote and directed several black films produced in and
around New York City during the 1940s. Organized the Negro Drama Group in
1949, which "took a group of professional actors on Southern tours," producing
such non-black plays as *Night Must Fall* and *Murder Without Crime.—BlkDr*
(Mitchell, 1967), p. 216. A resident of Michigan since the 1960s, where he
organized and was executive director of the (new) Suitcase Theatre, an interracial
touring theatre group, while working as a research analyst with the Michigan

State Legislature in Lansing. Member of the Baha'i faith as well as numerous civic and youth organizations. Recipient of first prize, while still a student, in the Yale University Drama Tournament, New Haven, year unknown; and several awards, citations, and plaques for the Suitcase Theatre's contribution to national and international understanding—from the Michigan Education Association, the Michigan Association of Classroom Teachers, the Michigan State Legislature, the United States Congress, and drama societies in several countries in North America and Europe.

Stage Works:

PRIOR TO 1950

Young Man of Harlem (1938). Sched. to be prod. by the Harlem Suitcase Theatre, New York, 1938, but, according to *Loften Mitchell (ibid., p. 105), "It did not come off."

Flight from Fear (c. 1940).

SINCE 1950

This Is America (c. 1960s). Staged for the Panorama of Progress at the Michigan State Fairgrounds, presumably during the 1960s.

... **These Truths** ... (black history collage, 2 acts, 1970/74). International touring show, with annual revisions, documenting life in America. "Featur[ed] vignettes from Black history, and in the second act, works of the late poet Langston Hughes."—*Jet,* Sept. 24, 1970, p. 57. Taken on tour of Europe and the North American continent, including England, Wales, Belgium, the Netherlands, Germany, Finland, Denmark, Sweden, and Canada, as well as the continental United States, during which rave notices and numerous awards were received.

Screen Works:

According to actress *Ruby Dee, speaking of her film career prior to 1946, "I had a number of roles in films shot in and around New York—so called Negro films, if you will. . . . Powell Lindsay wrote and directed a number of films that I worked in."—Interview in *VoicesBth* (Mitchell), p. 216. Only one of Powell's films has been located: *Jivin' in Be-Bop* (musical revue, length unknown, 1947). According to Donald Bogle (*Blk. Am. Films & TV,* 1988, p. 121), this film is "interspersed with some dull-witted comic routines. There are only two redeeming factors here: namely Dizzie Gillespie and vocalist Helen Humes. Otherwise the proceedings are pretty dreary." Prod. and codir. by Leonard Anderson with SPENCER WILLIAMS. Cast includes Freddie Carter, Ralph Brown, Ray Snead, Dan Durley, Daisy Richardson, Panch and Dolores, Phil and Audrey. Gillespie performs many of his classics, such as "Night in Tunisia" and "Salt Peanuts."

Other Pertinent Writing:

"We Still Need Negro Theatre in America," *Neg. Hist. Bull.*, Feb. 1964, p. 112.
FURTHER REFERENCE: *Blk. Am. Writers* (Rush et al., 1975).

LIPSCOMB, G. D. (George Dewey) (1898–   ), College professor, biographer of George Washington Carver, prizewinning orator, and playwright of the 1920s. Born in Freeport, IL. Educated at Freeport High School and Northwestern University (A.B. 1921). While in high school, won first prize in the Illinois state oratorical contest and a scholarship to Northwestern. At Northwestern, he was the first sophomore to win the Kirk Prize for oratory; there also he represented the university in the Northern Oratorical League Contest and won the Sargent Prize in dramatic interpretation. Beginning in 1924, he taught for many years at Wiley College, Marshall, TX, where he was professor of languages and literature and director of the Department of Expression. Won first prize in the *Opportunity* Contest Awards, 1925, for his play **Frances**. Coauthor, with SHIR-LEY GRAHAM DuBOIS, of *George Washington Carver, Scientist* (1944). Member of Alpha Kappa Psi fraternity.

Stage Works:

Frances (melodrama, 1 act, 1925). Utilizes a popular nineteenth-century melodramatic plot to tell the story of a black Mississippi sharecropper who tries to persuade his niece Frances to sleep with a white landowner to pay off the uncle's mortgage on some land. In the nineteenth-century plot, the girl is usually saved by her heroic lover, thus preventing the ultimate tragedy. In this play, Frances' lover, a teacher and civil rights worker, is forced to leave town at 9:00 P.M., under threat of being lynched for hitting and insulting the white landowner. He persuades Frances to leave town with him, and she reluctantly agrees. In the meantime, Frances is able to resist the advances of the white man, thus causing a fight between her uncle and the landowner in which both men are killed, exactly at the hour of nine. Frances realizes that she has failed to meet her lover at the appointed hour and that he has gone away without her. Prod. by the Norman Players of Philadelphia, at St. Peter Claver's Auditorium, 1925. Received first prize in the *Opportunity* Contest Awards, May 1925. Pub. in *Opportunity*, May 1925, pp. 148–53.

Daniel (1 act, not dated). Unpub. script in Schomburg.

FURTHER REFERENCE: Austin diss. *WWCA 1938–40.*

LIVINGSTON, MYRTLE SMITH (1902–1974), Teacher and playwright. A product of the literary activity of *Crisis* magazine and the Black or Harlem Renaissance. Born in Holly Grove, AR; reared in Denver, CO, where she attended both the elementary and high schools. Studied pharmacy at Howard for two years, 1920–22, where she was also a member of the Rho Psi Phi medical sorority. Received the A.B. from Colorado State Teachers College/Greeley, 1927; and the M.A. from Columbia University, 1940. Married William Mc-Kinley Livingston, a physician, in 1925. The following year, won third prize in the *Crisis* Contest Awards for the play cited below. Taught in the public schools of Denver prior to accepting a position at Lincoln University in Jefferson, MO, where she taught health and physical education from 1928 to her retirement in 1972. There several of her plays and skits were reportedly produced by student groups, though none can now be located. Spent the remaining two years of her life sharing a condominium with her sister in Hawaii, where she died at age 72.

Stage Work:

For Unborn Children ("a plea against intermarriage" [pub. script], 1 act, 1925). Reflects the black woman's anger at the black man's reputed preference for white women. A young black man in the Deep South is dissuaded by his family from running away to the North with his white sweetheart. ("What is to become of us," his own sister asks him angrily, "when our own men throw us down?") Instead of running away, the young man surrenders himself to the white lynch mob and sacrifices his life (in what James V. Hatch has called "an incredible ending"—*BlkThUSA*, p. 184) for the sake of unborn children whose lives might be ruined by intermarriage. Recipient of third prize in the *Crisis* Contest Awards, Oct. 1925, and first pub. in *Crisis*, July 1926, pp. 122–25. Also pub. in *BlkThUSA* (Hatch, 1974), which includes commentary.

FURTHER REFERENCE: Austin diss. *BlkPlots* (Southgate).

LOVETTE, LOUISE J., Neophyte playwright of the 1940s, who adapted several African myths and folk stories for dramatic purposes.

Stage Work:

Jungle Justice ("A Play of African Life Based upon the African Myth, 'Three Rival Brothers'" [subtitle], 7 scenes, 1940). Three brothers have traveled many miles to the dwelling of their king on the eve of his daughter's (the princess') birthday. They remind the king that he has promised their father that one of them would have his daughter's hand in marriage. Each brings a rare and magical gift and asks the king to choose him as the princess' husband. As the play progresses, the princess dies, and each of the magical gifts plays an important part in bringing her back to life. In the end, the king decides that although each brother deserves his daughter, he cannot divide her among them. They must, therefore, withdraw their request, or the decision must be postponed until one of them has proved his superiority over the other two by a test that the king proposes. During the course of the play, several folk stories are told to entertain the court, making the point that although many choices are difficult to make, it is quite simple to choose between blood relationships and friendship. Pub. in *Neg. Hist. Bull.*, June 1940, pp. 139–41.

LYLES, AUBREY. See Appendix B.

M

McBROWN, GERTRUDE PARTHENIA. See Appendix A.

McCLENDON, ROSE (Rosalie Scott) (1884–1936), Outstanding dramatic actress, featured in many Broadway productions of the 1920s and 1930s. Born in New York City. Studied dramatics for three years at Sargent's Dramatic School. Married Dr. Henry P. McClendon. Was a member of the Lafayette Players and cofounder of the Negro People's Theatre, both in Harlem. Appeared in the following plays: *Justice* (1919), *Roseanne* (1924), *Deep River* (1926), *In Abraham's Bosom* (1927), *Porgy* (1927), *The House of Connelly* (1931), *Never No More* (1932), *Black Souls* (1932), *Brain Sweat* (1934), *Roll Sweet Chariot* (1934), *Panic* (1935), *Mulatto* (1935), and the CBS radio series "John Henry, Black River Giant."

Stage Work:
Taxi Fare (drama, 1 act, 1931). Coauthored with RICHARD BRUCE NUGENT. First prod. by the Harlem Players, at the 135th Street Library Theatre, New York, opening Feb. 2, 1931, for 4 perfs.
FURTHER REFERENCE: *DANB*. *NegGen* (Brawley).

McCOO, (Rev.) EDWARD J., Minister of the African Methodist Episcopal (A.M.E.) Church, who lived in Newport, KY, during the 1920s.

Stage Work:
Ethiopia at the Bar of Justice (black history pageant, 1 act, 1924). Opposition has demanded that Ethiopia (symbolic of the Negro and/or Africa) be brought before the bar of Justice, because she is "becoming too ambitious" and making too great "demands upon a civilization which she did not produce." In answer to Opposition's charges, the contributions and achievements of black men and women from ancient to modern times are presented before the court by an array of symbolic and historical witnesses, including Mercy, History, Crispus Attucks, a slave, veterans of various wars (Civil, Spanish, World

War I), Labor, Business, the Professions, Womanhood, the Church, Haiti, Liberia, the Declaration of Independence, Amendments to the Constitution (the Thirteenth, Fourteenth, and Fifteenth), the Anti-Lynch Law, Political Opinion, Prophecy, and Love. Ethiopia is vindicated, Justice prevails, and Opposition is denounced. First prod. in 1924 at the Quadrennial Conf. of the A.M.E. Church in Louisville, KY. Prod. in 1926 at the Sesqui-Centennial Conf. of the A.M.E. Church in Philadelphia. For many years this pageant enjoyed wide popularity and was frequently presented during Negro History Week. Privately printed by the author in Newport, KY, 1924; copy in Moorland-Spingarn. Pub. in *Plays&Pags* (Richardson, 1930).

McDONALD, WARREN A., Prizewinning playwright in the *Opportunity* Contest Awards of 1925 and 1926. Otherwise no biographical information has been located for McDonald, except that he was a native of Philadelphia. As he wrote in *Opportunity*'s June 1925 issue, "As yet I have not accomplished enough to furnish material even for a brief sketch." McDonald was also awarded honorable mention in the 1926 contest for his short story "A Matter of Inches."

Stage Works:

Humble Instrument (moralistic comedy, 1 act, 1925). A gambler who has recently won a large sum of money is counseled by his minister to give up gambling and try to live a better life. The gambler promises the minister that he will give up betting if the minister, an ex-gambler, can beat him at one game of dice. When he loses the game, even with a pair of loaded dice, the gambler keeps his promise to quit, believing that divine powers have influenced the outcome of the game. Winner of second prize in the *Opportunity* Contest Awards, May 1925. Considered for prodn. by the Federal Theatre Project, but was never prod. No extant script. Synopsis located in FTP/GMU.

Blood (melodrama, 1 act, 1926). A black woman becomes severely upset when she learns that her son has been beaten up by a member of the Ku Klux Klan, a hemophiliac who a year earlier had received a blood transfusion from her son. After the mother learns this distressing news, the Klansman comes to her for aid for his bleeding arm. Unable to feel compassion for the man who has beaten up her son, the mother allows the Klansman to bleed to death. Winner of third prize in the *Opportunity* Contest Awards, May 1926. Considered for prodn. by the Federal Theatre Project, but was never prod. No extant script. Synopsis located in FTP/GMU.

FURTHER REFERENCE: Austin diss.

MacENTEE, GEORGE, Playwright, director, and performer, associated with the WPA Federal Theatre Project during the 1930s. His racial identity has not been verified. FREDERICK BOND (*Neg&Dr*, 1940, p. 168) classifies him as white. Sterling Brown (in *AnthANT*, 1967, p. 105) calls him a Negro playwright, as does Ronald Patrick Ross (Ph.D. diss., 1972, p. 155). In any event, no biographical information has been located, except that he was the director of *Meek Mose* (1928) and performed in several non-black plays and musicals: *Wanted (1928), Gala Night* (1930), *Stepping Sisters* (1930), and *American Holiday* (1936).

Stage Work:

The Case of Philip Lawrence (drama, 3 acts, 1937). Described by Ross (ibid.) as a dramatization of "the difficulties which . . . the college educated black athlete . . . experienced in attempting to secure employment commensurate with his talents and training." The protagonist was apparently modeled after Olympic medalist Jesse Owens, who, after his 1936 victory in the Olympic Games in Berlin, became an international figure, but had difficulty finding work after graduating from college the following year. In the case of Philip Lawrence, he takes a job in a Harlem night club as master of ceremonies and becomes involved in a murder, for which he is about to be convicted on circumstantial evidence. He is saved in the nick of time when new evidence is uncovered which exonerates him. Prod. by the New York Negro Unit of the WPA Federal Theatre, at the Lafayette Theatre, opening June 7, 1937, and closing July 31, 1937, for a total of 55 perfs.; dir. by J. AUGUSTUS SMITH. With Maurice Ellis in the title role. Unpub. scripts in Schomburg and TC/NYPL. REVIEWS AND COMMENTARY: *BesPls 1936–37; 1937–38. Neg&Dr* (Bond). *NY Daily News* 6–9–1937. *NYT* 6–9–1937. Ross diss.

MACK, CECIL. See Appendix B.

MADDOX, GLORIA DENBY, Former student playwright at Fisk University, where she was also a member of the Fisk Stagecrafters and the Southern Association of Dramatic and Speech Arts (SADSA). After graduating from Fisk in the late 1940s, she became director of the Theatre of Wee Folks in Selma, AL. Lillian Voorhees, director of the Fisk Stagecrafters, said in 1951 that "Mrs. Maddox is especially interested in the possibilities for the dramatization of folk literature with . . . children."—Quoted in Sandle, Ph.D. diss. (1959), p. 255.

Stage Works:

Black Monday's Children (1 act, 1940s). Prod. by the Fisk Univ. Stagecrafters, 1940s. Unpub. script in the Amistad Research Center, Dillard Univ., New Orleans.

Rare Cut Glass (1 act, 1947). Prod. by the Fisk Univ. Stagecrafters, at the Eleventh Annual Conf. of SADSA, held at Arkansas State Coll., Pine Bluff, April 30, 1947.

MANNING, SAM. See Appendix B.

MATHEUS, (Dr.) JOHN FREDERICK (1887–1983), College foreign language teacher, prizewinning short story writer, and playwright. Born in Keyser, WV. Educated at Case Western Reserve University (A.B. cum laude, 1910), Columbia University (A.M. 1921), the Sorbonne in Paris (1925), and the University of Chicago (1927). Married to Maude Roberts in 1909. Professor of Latin and modern foreign languages, Florida A. & M. College (now University), 1911–22. Professor and head of the Department of Romance Languages, West Virginia State College (now University), 1922–53. His extensive travel included research in Haiti, summer of 1928; six months in Liberia as secretary to Dr. Charles S. Johnson, who was then the American member of the International Commission of Inquiry to Liberia, 1930; one year in Haiti as director of the English teaching program of the National Schools of Haiti, 1945–46; and visits to Europe, Cuba, and Mexico. Author of more than 50 short stories published in such anthologies as *The New Negro* (Locke, 1925), *Ebony and Topaz* (Johnson, 1927), *Readings from Negro Authors* (Cromwell et al., 1931), *365 Days: A Book of Short Stories* (Boyle et al., 1936), and *Negro Caravan, Caroling Dusk* (Cullen, 1927), *Anthology of American Negro Literature* (Calverton, 1944), and *A Rock Against the Wind* (Patterson, 1973). His reviews and criticism have appeared in numerous periodicals, including *Journal of Negro History, Negro History Bulletin, College Language Association Journal*, and *Opportunity* magazine. Memberships in numerous language and teachers' associations. Winner of the *Crisis* Contest Award, for one of his short stories; second prize in the *Opportunity* Contest Awards, 1926, for his play '**Cruiter**; a *Journal of Negro History* Award, 1936, for the best review of the year; and an achievement award from the Tau Chapter of Kappa Alpha Psi, 1951. Decorated by the Haitian government and conferred the title of "Officier de L'Ordre Nationale d'Honneur et Mérite." Recipient of an honorary Doctor of Letters degree from West Virginia State College, 1978. Died at age 96 in Tallahassee, Fl, where he lived for the last few years of his life.

Stage Works:

'**Cruiter** (folk drama, 1 act [2 scenes], 1926). Tired of their miserable existence as tenant farmhands, a young man and his sister are lured to an uncertain future in the North by a white recruiter for a wartime munitions factory. Won second prize in the *Opportunity* Contest Awards, May 1926. Pub. in *PlaysNegL* (Locke & Gregory, 1927); in *Anth. of Am. Neg. Lit.* (Calverton, 1944; in *ReadingsNA* (Cromwell et al., 1931); in *Blackam. Lit, 1760–Present* (Miller, 1971); and in *BlkThUSA* (Hatch, 1974).

Black Damp (drama, 1 act, 1929). Focuses on the hopes and aspirations of several coal miners, black and white, including a murderer, trapped together in a mine following an explosion. Pub. in *Carolina Mag.*, April 1929.

Tambour (folk comedy, 1 act, 1929). With musical setting by †Clarence Cameron White. According to Hatch & Abdullah (*Blk. Playrs., 1823–1977,* p. 159), "A Haitian peasant who has a passion for his drum . . . wins a victory over the chief of the army and . . . [the love of] a beautiful woman." Prod. by the Allied Arts Players, Boston, Oct. 1929; dir. by MAUD CUNEY-HARE. Unpub. script in Hatch-Billops.

Ti Yette (tragedy, 1 act [2 scenes], 1930). A race-conscious young mulatto, proud of his African ancestry, kills his own sister (Ti Yette) to prevent her from marrying a white man. Pub. in *Plays&Pags* (Richardson, 1930).

Ouanga (drama and libretto for an opera, 3 acts, 1941). Music composed by Clarence Cameron White. Based on the life of Dessalines, emperor of Haiti during the nineteenth century. Auditioned at the New School for Social Research, New York, 1941. Broadcast over radio station WINS, New York, June 1948. Premiered by the Burleigh Music Association, at Central High School, South Bend, IN, June 10 and 11, 1949. Prod. by the National Opera Co., at the Metropolitan Opera House, New York, 1956. Libretto in Hatch-Billops. For commentary by author, see Other Pertinent Writings below.

Other Pertinent Writings:

"Lady Windermere's Fan," *Dramatis Personae*, vol. 34 (1927), p. 11.

"The Theatre of José Joaquim Gamboa,"*CLA Bull.*, Spring 1951.

"*Ouanga*: My Venture in Libretto Creation," *CLAJ*, vol. 15, (1972), pp. 428–40.

FURTHER REFERENCE: Austin diss. Hicklin diss. *Neg&Dr* (Bond). *NegGen* (Brawley). Taped interview of Matheus in Hatch-Billops. *WWCA 1950.*

MEYER, ANNIE NATHAN. See Appendix A.

MICHEAUX, OSCAR DEVEREAUX (1884–1951), Flamboyant pioneer film producer, director, and novelist, who has been called "America's first legendary black filmmaker." Credited with more than 40 feature films produced between 1918 and 1948—only 7 of which are extant; also wrote five novels which were developed into (or from) film scenarios. Produced the first full-length, all-black silent film by a black company; also produced the first full-length, all-black talking picture. Born in a small farming community near Metropolis, IL, "the fourth son and the fifth child of a family of thirteen." His grandfather was a slave, and his father, in spite of his French-sounding name, was born in Kentucky, later moving to Illinois, where he became a rather prosperous farmer. His mother was a typical churchgoing farm wife, who "always declared emphatically that she wanted none of her sons to become lackeys." Concerned about the children's education, the family moved from the farm to Metropolis, a nearby river and factory town, that they might attend the local colored school. Oscar's older sister became a teacher, his eldest brother became a dining car waiter for a Chicago railroad company, and his two elder brothers joined the army. After a time, the family moved back to the farm, continuing to market their produce in Metropolis. Oscar, who did not like farm work, was sent to town to do the marketing, where he developed the art of salesmanship that was to serve him well as a book publisher and filmmaker. He left Metropolis at the age of 17, and after working at a number of odd jobs, visited his brother in Chicago, where he obtained a job as a Pullman porter. There he saved enough money to purchase some land in South Dakota, where he sought to establish himself as a ranger and farmer. However, this dream was wrecked by a disastrous first marriage and by financial reversals brought about by mortgaging his homestead. In an effort to recover his losses, he turned to writing and eventually financed the printing of his most autobiographical novel, *The Conquest,* in which many of the details of his early life, including those in this biographical sketch, up to his first marriage, are delineated. He paid for publication by taking advance orders for his book, and on the basis of these persuaded a group of prosperous neighbors to put up the cash for him and to sign a "guarantee of account" for the balance. Beginning with his second novel, *The Forged Note* (1915), he published under his own imprint, Western Book Supply of Lincoln, Nebraska, later shortened to Book Supply when he moved to New York. In *The Forged Note* he describes how he attempted to sell his first book in the Deep South, traveling by car from city to city; speaking at churches and schools; talking to fraternal, civic, and social groups; and going from house to house peddling his books wherever he could. His third novel, *The Homesteader* (1917), is a rewritten version of *The Conquest,* carrying the story forward in time and introducing more fictitious plot details, including an interracial romance and a happy ending for his love life. His life story was again rewritten as *The Wind from Nowhere* (1944) and further embellished with melodramatic situations designed to increase sales among both black and white readers. Other novels by Micheaux are *The Case of Mrs. Wingate* (1944), which deals with an interracial romance between a black woman and a white barber. *The Story of Dorothy Stanfield* (1946), a sequel to *Mrs. Wingate*, carries the interracial romance to marriage; and *The Masquerade* (1947) is an unauthorized adaptation (or, more properly, a plagiarized version) of Charles W. Chesnutt's novel *The House Behind the Cedars* (1905), apparently based on Micheaux's scenario for his 1923 film by the same title. His involvement in filmmaking came about through his desire to see his life story made into a major, full-length feature film, which he himself would direct. Failing to find an interested producer, he raised the necessary capital, formed his own film company, known as the Micheaux Film Corporation, and hired a white cameraman to shoot his early pictures while he learned the craft. He promoted his films in the same aggressive way that he had promoted his books, by traveling with scenarios or the original novels in hand to every city in the Midwest, East, and South that had a movie house, or where a white theatre would allow Negroes to attend, and persuaded theatre managers to book his films in advance of filming. Although many of these films were poorly produced, they represent a remarkable achievement considering his lack of financial backing and support; the inadequacy of equipment, facilities, and resources; the difficulties of obtaining distribution and bookings; and the general restrictions imposed by the racial climate of the times. An annual Oscar Micheaux Award was established by the Oakland Museum at Oakland, CA, which also sponsors the Black Filmmakers Hall of Fame. The ceremony is held each February in Oakland. Micheaux's seven extant films were exhibited at the Whitney Museum in New York City in 1984 as part of its American Filmmakers Series. These films are **Body and Soul** (1924), a silent film starring Paul Robeson; **The Exile** (1931), the first black total sound film; **Ten Minutes to Live** (1933); **Underworld** (1936); **Swing** (1938); **God's Stepchildren** (1938); and **Lying Lips** (1939). An Oscar Micheaux Theatre, supported by the National Endowment and the New York State Council on the Arts, was established in Buffalo, NY, around the mid–1980s. Micheaux died in 1951 at the age of 67, survived by his widow, Alice B. Russell, who appeared in many of his films. It is not known whether she was the true love of his life as depicted in many of his books and films. After his death, his widow never made any public comments concerning her husband or his films, thus helping to keep alive the mystery and many of the myths that he himself originated and helped to perpetuate.

Screen Works:
(All are 35mm feature-length films in black and white, prod. by the Micheaux Film Corp., dir. by Oscar Micheaux, and based on his scenarios, unless otherwise indicated.)

SILENT FILMS
(NOTE: Only one of Micheaux's *silent* films is extant—**Body and Soul,** which is marked with a double obelisk (‡) below.)

The Homesteader (biographical melodrama, 8 reels, 1918). Adapt. from Micheaux's novel by the same title and his first novel, *The Conquest* (1913). His first film and the first feature-length black film by a black company. Combines the story of the author's early life as a homesteader in South Dakota with an interracial love story. A young black man migrates from Chicago to South Dakota, where he claims and develops a tract of public land under the Homestead Act of 1862. He becomes prosperous and falls in love with a young woman whom he believes to be white. Thinking that he cannot marry her, he returns to Chicago and marries the daughter of a prominent black minister; this marriage proves to be an unhappy one because of the dominance of the wife's father. After the marriage fails, the young man returns to Dakota, where he becomes reunited with his true love and learns that she is of part-black heritage, which removes all barriers to their marriage. Filmed in Chicago in 1918, where it opened the following year. Cast included Charles Lucas in the title role; Iris Hall as the hero's true love; Charles S. Moore as the wife's father, a minister; and Evelyn Preer as the wife. [See also **The Exile** (1931) and **The Betrayal** (1948), which deal with the same same subject matter and theme.]

Within Our Gates (tragedy, 8 reels [reduced to 7], 1918). Publicized as "founded on the famous Leo M. Frank case as witnessed by the author," although it is doubtful that the author actually witnessed the Frank murder trial. [NOTE: The Frank case, which was widely reported in the black press, was the first recorded case of the lynching of a Jew in the United States and the first case of a southern white man who was actually found guilty of murder on the testimony of a black man. See also **The Gunsaulus Mystery** below, in which Micheaux has treated the Frank case more directly.] This film, which deals only thematically with the Frank case, concerns the lynching of a black sharecropper who is falsely accused, tried, and found guilty of the murder of a wealthy white landowner on the testimony of a "white folks' nigger." First prod. in Chicago, under the title **Circumstantial Evidence,** it was at first denied a permit from the Board of Censors because of the controversial lynching scene, which it was feared might set off a second Chicago riot (the first having occurred the previous year). After a change of title and removal of the lynching scene, the film was shown before a prominent group of Chicago citizens of both races, including the press and clergy, and as a result of their approval the permit was finally granted. It premiered in Chicago, Jan. 1920, billed as "The most sensational story on the race question since *Uncle Tom's Cabin*." It was shown in Detroit in Aug. of the same year, and next in Omaha, NB, after a two-month period of negotiations to obtain a permit. It was banned in many theatres in the South because of its controversial subject matter. The cast featured Evelyn Preer, Lawrence Chenault, and Charles D. Lucas.

The Brute (melodrama, 7 reels, 1920). The story of a beautiful black woman who is involved with a brutal underworld gambling kingpin who constantly mistreats her. The hero of the film is a black boxer, played by boxer Sam Langford, who becomes a symbol of black manhood. The film was considered too sensational because of its erotic love scenes, racial violence, and realistic scenes of low life in black drinking and gambling joints, and failed to gain the censors' approval in Chicago, where it was shot. It opened in Omaha, NB, in Nov. 1920; in New York City in Dec. 1920; and in Chicago in April 1921. Cast featured Evelyn Preer as the young woman and A. B. Comathiere as the gambling boss.

Symbol of the Unconquered // Also known as **The Wilderness Trail** (western melodrama, 7 reels, 1920). The story of a beautiful mulatto woman passing for white who inherits some oil-bearing land after her father's death and goes West to claim it. There she gets in trouble with a scoundrel who tries to keep her from claiming her inheritance by violent means. She is protected by a black prospector, who helps her to get her land, and with whom she falls in love. Opened in New York and Pittsburgh, Jan. 1921. Cast included Iris Hall as the young woman, Lawrence Chenault, and Leigh Whipper.

The Hypocrite (melodrama, 7 reels, 1921). Apparently not released as a separate film, although it received a New York State license in June 1921. It was incorporated into Micheaux's next film, **Deceit,** as a film-within-a-film.

Deceit (melodrama, 6 reels, 1921). Dramatizes Micheaux's difficulties in getting censor approval of his film **Within Our Gates** (1918), described above. The plot concerns a film producer's efforts to gain a license for his film, **The Hypocrite** (see above). Approval of the film is opposed by a group of ministers, who succeed in causing the film to be rejected without actually having seen it. The producer finally succeeds in having the film shown to a group of leading citizens, which permits the inclusion of a reduced version of **The Hypocrite** as a film-within-a-film. Following the showing, the film is approved and the license is granted by the censors. Prod. in New York in 1921, but did not open until March 1, 1923, apparently having had to wait two years for a New York State license. Cast of **Deceit** (the external film) included Narman Johnson as the film producer, Evelyn Preer as his secretary, and A. B. Comathiere as the leader of the delegation of ministers. Preer and Johnson also appeared in The Hypocrite (the internal film).

The Gunsaulus Mystery (melodrama, 8 reels, 1921). (Often cited incorrectly as *The Gonzales Mystery*.) Micheaux's second of three films on the Leo M. Frank case. [See also **Within Our Gates** (1918) and **Lem Hawkins' Confession** (1935), a remake of **The Gunsaulus Mystery** in sound.] Adheres closely to the details of the Frank case, except that Micheaux's interest is in vindicating the black man who is involved circumstantially in the case, and not in the real victim, Leo Frank. [NOTE: The Frank case was concerned with the alleged murder by a young Jew in Atlanta, GA, of a white woman whose sexually assaulted body was found partially burned in a furnace in the basement of a factory managed by Frank. According to established testimony, the woman, who worked in the factory, had gone to see Frank alone on the previous day to get her wages. It was alleged by the prosecution that Frank raped her, killed her, and intimidated a black janitor into helping him dispose of the body. After Frank was arrested, he reportedly tried to blame the crime on the janitor, who was found innocent. Frank was found guilty on circumstantial evidence and lynched by a white mob.] In the plot of Micheaux's film, a young black janitor is arrested and indicted for the murder of a white woman whose body he discovered in the cellar of the factory where he works. He is defended by a black attorney and author, who succeeds in exonerating the janitor and transferring suspicion of the crime to the white manager and foreman of the factory. The attorney writes a book about the case, in which he reveals the true circumstances of the murder, which were never revealed at the trial. Premiered in New York on April 18, 1921. Cast included Lawrence Chenault and Evelyn Preer, with Ethel Waters at the beginning of her film career.

The Shadow (mystery-melodrama, 7 reels, 1921). Opened in Oct. 1921.

The Dungeon (melodrama, 7 reels, 1922). A beautiful black woman, about to be married, is abducted by a notorious crook whose advances she has spurned. Through the use of hypnotism and drugs, she is forced to marry her abductor and is kept a virtual prisoner after her marriage. Her fiancé, having learned of the marriage, leaves town in utter dejection until he learns that the crook is running for Congress; then he returns to oppose him in the election. Meanwhile, the "wife" has learned that her abductor is a bluebeard who has murdered his previous wives, and she attempts unsuccessfully to escape. Her "husband" then locks her in a dungeon, where his other wives had been killed, and attempts to asphixiate her. She is saved in the nick of time by her fiancé, who also kills the abductor. Released in New York, May 22, 1922. Cast included William E. Fountaine, Shingzie Howard, J. Kenneth Goodman, and W.B.F. Crowell. When shown in Chicago, it was criticized by D. Ireland Thomas in the *Chicago Defender* (July 9, 1922) for featuring only light-skinned actors.

The Virgin of the Seminole (melodrama of the Northwest, 7 reels, 1922). Concerns the deeds of bravery of a black member of the Canadian mounted police, who apparently rescues a half-caste woman from the Indians, for which he receives a substantial reward and the love of the woman. Filmed in 1922; opened in New York, April 15, 1923. Cast included William E. Fountaine and Shingzie Howard.

The Ghost of Tolson's Manor (mystery-melodrama, presumably 7 reels, 1922). Prod. 1922; opened in New York, 1923. Cast included Andrew Bishop, Lawrence Chenault, Edna Morton, and Monte Hawley.

Uncle Jasper's Will // Orig. title: **Jasper Landry's Will** (melodrama, 6 reels, 1922). A sequel to **Within Our Gates,** apparently dealing with a will left by Jasper Landry, a sharecropper who was lynched for allegedly murdering a white plantation owner. Opened in New York, 1922. Cast included William E. Fountaine and Shingzie Howard.

The House Behind the Cedars (melodrama, 9 reels, 1923). Film version of Charles W. Chesnutt's novel of the same title (1905), from which film scenario Micheaux later adapted his own novelization entitled *The Masquerade* (1947). About a woman of mixed blood who marries a white man without him knowing her true racial identity. Fearing that she may be discovered, she eventually gives up her charade and returns to her own people, eventually finding love with a young black man whom she had previously spurned. Filmed in Roanoke, VA, in 1923, where the film made extensive use of local talent as extras. Released in New York, presumably in 1923. Cast included Shingzie Howard as the young woman, Lawrence Chenault as the white man whom she marries, and Douglas "C. D." Griffin as the young black man.

Birthright (black achievement film, 10 reels, 1924). Adapt. by Micheaux from °Thomas S. Stribling's novel by the same title (1922). The story of a black man's attempt, after graduating from Harvard, to build a college for blacks in the Deep South. Deals with the hostilities that he encounters from both blacks and whites, intertwined with a story of unrequited love on the part of a black woman who thinks that she is not good enough for him because of his high ambition and educational accomplishments. Filmed on location in Roanoke, VA, 1922. Released in New York, Feb. 1, 1924. †J. HOMER TUTT as the young man, and Evelyn Preer as the woman who loves him. Also in the cast were †SALEM TUTT WHITNEY, Lawrence Chenault, and W.B.F. Crowell. The film was quite successful and was later remade in a talking version by the same title (1939).

‡**Body and Soul** (melodrama, 5 reels, 1924). (No relation to the John Garfield film of the same title, made in 1947, also featuring black actor Canada Lee.) Micheaux's only extant silent film. A cautionary tale exposing black religious cult leaders, bootleggers, and gamblers who exploit the black community. Made in two versions; one portrays a thoroughly corrupt black minister "who associates with the proprietor of a notorious gambling house, extorts money from him, betrays a girl of his parish, forces her to steal . . . her mother's savings, forces the girl to leave home, and finally kills the girl's brother when he comes to his sister's protection."—New York State licensing record. In the second version, made to satisfy the censors, the minister (played by Paul Robeson) is

portrayed as playing a double role; he is really a detective posing as a disreputable minister in order to expose the activities of a ring of criminals. The first version was completed in 1924, but Micheaux did not receive a New York State license until 1925. In addition to Paul Robeson, the cast included Julia Theresa Russell and MERCEDES GILBERT.

A Son of Satan (melodrama, about 7 reels, 1924). Apparently a re-release of **The Ghost of Tolson's Manor** (1922), or a sequel to that film, since Captain Tolson also appears as a character in this melodrama. The New York State license records indicate that "this picture is filled with scenes of drinking [and] carousing and shows masked men becoming intoxicated. It shows the playing of crap for money, a man [Captain Tolson] killing his wife by choking her, the killing of the leader of the hooded organization [Ku Klux Klan] and the killing of a cat by throwing a stone at it." The film was presented in Chicago, Jan. 1925, and was favorably reviewed by D. Ireland Thomas (*Chicago Defender*, Jan. 31, 1925), who wrote that while some viewers objected to it because "it shows up some of our race in their true colors," the film was basically an honest portrayal of black life. Thomas also praised the "all-star cast," which included Andrew Bishop, Lawrence Chenault, Emmett Anthony, Edna Morton, and Shingzie Howard.

Marcus Garland (melodrama, feature length, 1925). Based on the life of Marcus Garvey, father of the Back-to-Africa movement. Released in 1925. Cast included Salem Tutt Whitney and Amy Birdsong.

The Conjure Woman (melodrama, feature length, 1926). Adaptn. of Charles W. Chesnutt's story by the same title (1899). Released in 1926. Cast included Evelyn Preer and Percy Verwayen.

The Devil's Disciple (melodrama, feature length, 1926). Dealt with compulsory prostitution (white slavery) in New York City. Released in 1926. Cast included Evelyn Preer and Lawrence Chenault.

The Spider's Web (melodrama, 7 reels, 1926). Based on "The Policy Players," a story of unknown authorship. About a beautiful young woman from Harlem who visits her aunt in a small Mississippi town, where she is forced to ward off the sexual advances of a well-to-do young white man. She is saved by the black hero, a Secret Service agent from Chicago, who is investigating a case in Mississippi. The woman, accompanied by her aunt, returns to Harlem, where her aunt becomes addicted to playing the numbers and is implicated in the murder of her numbers writer. The Secret Service agent is called to investigate the case, and he again saves the day by uncovering the real murderer, proving the aunt's innocence, and winning the love of the woman. Released in New York in 1927. Cast included Evelyn Preer as the woman, Lorenzo McLane, Edward Thompson, and Grace Smythe.

The Broken Violin (melodrama, 7 reels, 1927). Ostensibly based on Micheaux's *House of Mystery*, presumably a novel which never materialized, but which Micheaux probably intended to create after making the film. The story of a violin prodigy whose alcoholic father, after losing his wages in a gambling game, comes home drunk, demanding money from his wife, and when she refuses, smashes the daughter's violin over the mother's head. His punishment occurs when he is killed by a passing truck, after which the prodigy goes on to achieve a successful musical career and finds happiness in love. Released in 1927. Cast included J. Homer Tutt, Ardell Dabney, Alice B. Russell, and Ethel Smith.

The Millionaire (melodrama, 7 reels, 1927). Advertised as "the screen version of [Micheaux's] own novel, The Millionaire," which, as in the case of the above film source, was probably never actually written, and certainly never published. After making his fortune in South America, the millionaire-hero of this film becomes the target of a ring of crooks who try to swindle him out of his money by tricking him into marriage with one of their own women. The millionaire, however, not only eludes marital entrapment, but also succeeds in reforming the woman. Shot in Chicago, where one of the film's locations was the Plantation Cafe. Premiered in New York, Feb. 15, 1928. Cast included Grace Smith, J. Lawrence Criner, Cleo Desmond, and Lionel Monagas.

Dark Princess (presumed to be a full-length melodrama, 1928). Cited in *WWCA 1928–29* as one of Micheaux's films, although no plot or prodn. information has been located. May have been based on, or suggested by, W.E.B. DuBOIS's novel by the same title (also 1928), about a young black medical student who, because of racial discrimination at home, goes to Berlin to secure a hospital internship, and there falls in love with an Indian princess.

A Fool's Errand (presumed to be a full-length melodrama, 1928). Cited in *WWCA 1928–29* as one of Micheaux's films, although no plot or prodn. information has been located. May have been based on, or suggested by, EULALIE SPENCE's one-act play by the same title (1927), which received second prize in the National Little Theatre Tournament held at the Frolic Theatre in New York, 1927. In that play, a group of nosy neighbors assume that the daughter of a church member is pregnant, and try to force her into marriage.

Thirty Years Later (melodrama, 7 reels, 1928). Based on HENRY FRANCIS DOWNING's *The Racial Tangle*, which was scheduled to be prod. as a play in 1928 by the Quality Amusement Corp., a stock company of the [New York] Lafayette Players. Concerns the mulatto son of a white father and black mother who is brought up to believe that he is white. Only after he falls in love with a black woman, who refuses his marriage proposal on racial grounds, is he told of his black heritage. He becomes proud of his black blood, and when he again proposes, the woman accepts. Opened in New York in 1928. Cast included William Edmondson as the leading man, and Mabel Kelly as the woman. With A. B. Comathiere, Ardella Dabney, and Gertrude Snelson also in the cast.

The Wages of Sin (melodrama, full length, 1929). Adapt. from "Alias Jefferson Lee," a story of unknown authorship. About two brothers of opposite moral character. The good brother, a film producer, agrees upon his mother's death to take care of his morally unprincipled brother by giving him a job. Not long after he begins working for the film company, the brother begins stealing funds, spending them on women and parties, soon pushing the company into financial difficulty and forcing his brother to fire him. When he recovers from his financial difficulties, the good brother has a change of heart and rehires his brother, who, the second time around, almost destroys the company. An unexpected turn of events, however, brings the story to a satisfactory conclusion. Opened in Chicago in 1928, where it was apparently filmed, but was closed by the censors' board. Cast included Lorenzo Tucker, William Clayton, Jr., Bessie Gibbens, Gertrude Snelson, Ethel Smith, and Alice B. Russell (Mrs. Oscar Micheaux).

When Men Betray (melodrama, feature length, 1929). A re-release of **Wages of Sin** (above), revised and retitled in order to satisfy the board of censors. With the same cast as above.

Easy Street (melodrama, 5 reels, 1930). Apparently a crime story set in a metropolitan city. Opened in New York, where a license was granted on Aug. 1, 1930. Cast included Richard B. Harrison (known for his portrayal of "De Lawd" in *The Green Pastures*) and Alice B. Russell.

SOUND FILMS

(NOTE: Only those films marked with a double obelisk (‡) are extant.)

A Daughter of the Congo (melodrama, 9 reels, 1930). Adapt. from *The American*

Cavalryman: A Liberian Romance, a novel by Henry Francis Downing. Micheaux's first partly-sound film. An adventure, set in the not-so-mythical Republic of Monravia in the Belgian Congo (actually Monrovia, Liberia). The beautiful mulatto daughter of a wealthy family has been kidnapped as a baby and brought up in the jungle of the Belgian Congo by savages. After she grows to womanhood, she is again abducted by Arab slavehunters while she is bathing in a brook. She is rescued by a black cavalry officer who had been sent by the U.S. Army to Monravia to operate a military police force. After her rescue, she is taken to a mission school, where, according to Micheaux's press book, "she succumbs to learning readily and soon becomes the most popular maid in Monravia, in spite of the inclination, very often, to revert to the wild life of the jungle from which she is rescued." Opened in New York on April 5, 1930. With Lorenzo Tucker as the cavalryman and Katherine Noisette as the mulatto woman. Theophilus Lewis, reviewer for the *NY Amsterdam News* (April 16, 1930), accused the film of "persistent[ly] vaunting . . . intraracial color fetishism," stating that "half the characters wear European clothes and are supposed to be civilized, while the other half wear their birthday suits and some feathers and are supposed to be savages. All of the noble characters are high yellows; all the ignoble ones are black."

Darktown Review // Also known as **Darktown Scandals Review** (feature film, 1930/ 31). Film version of one of †IRVIN C. MILLER's nightclub floor shows, featuring Miller in the cast. Prod. in 1931. With the Club Alabam Stompers, the Dixie Jubilee Singers, the Harlem Strutters, Sara Martin, and Maude Mills.

Black Magic (musical revue, feature length, 1932). Another nightclub revue.

‡**The Exile** (melodrama, 70 minutes, 1931). Based partly on Micheaux's first film, **The Homesteader** (1918), which was in turn based on his 1917 novel by the same title, with added nightclub scenes featuring singing and dancing. The first total sound film by a black company. The story of a young Chicago man who breaks off his engagement when he learns that his fiancée, who has come into possession of a large mansion formerly owned by whites, has turned it into a notorious cabaret in order to pay for its upkeep. Disgusted with city life, he goes to the wilderness of South Dakota to claim and develop a large tract of land and establish a new life. There he falls in love with a beautiful young woman whom he believes to be white, and assumes that he can never marry her because of racial barriers. He later discovers, however, that she is of part-black heritage, and this obstacle to their happiness is removed. Filmed in New York City, using singers, dancers, and musicians from the famed Cotton Club, Connie's Inn, the Blackbirds, DONALD HEYWOOD's Band and Leonard Harper's Chorines. Premiered successfully in New York in 1932, but when it opened in Pittsburgh, where the South Dakota scenes were shot, it was closed in the middle of the showing by the censors, who objected to what they assumed to be interracial love scenes. Cast included Stanley Murrell in the leading role, Eunice Brooks, A. B. Comathiere, and Katherine Noisette. One of Micheaux's extant films.

‡**Ten Minutes to Live** (crime melodrama, feature length, 1932). With Lawrence Chenault, Willor Lee Guilford, and William Clayton, Jr. One of Micheaux's extant films.

Veiled Aristocrats (melodrama, feature length, 1932). Based on °Gertrude Sanborn's novel by the same title (1923), about the mulatto descendants of a southern white aristocratic family, who are described in the novel as "worthy men and women caught by a mad fate in a prison of prejudice." Apparently an interracial love story, which ends happily when the white lover is discovered to be a "veiled aristocrat." Cast included Lorenzo Tucker and Barrington Guy.

The Girl from Chicago (crime melodrama, feature length, 1932). A remake in sound of Micheaux's **The Spider's Web** (1926). A beautiful Chicago woman receives a teaching position in a small Mississippi town, where she goes to live with her aunt. Coincidentally, a handsome young Secret Service agent from New York is also assigned to a case in the same town and also lodges with the aunt. Naturally the two young out-of-towners become romantically involved. A well-to-do young white man attempts to sexually assault the girl from Chicago, and the situation is saved by the Secret Service agent. The white man is subsequently arrested and sent to prison. Following the incident, the aunt decides to move to New York City, accompanied by her niece, and the secret agent, whose home is also in New York, also returns to the big city. The aunt becomes addicted to playing the numbers and has almost lost her life savings when she "hits" for more than $10,000. When she rushes to the numbers broker's office to claim her winnings, she finds him dead in front of his open safe. She grabs her rightful winnings and flees, but is soon arrested and indicted on a murder charge. The secret agent is assigned to the case, succeeds in proving the aunt innocent, and catches the real murderer. Meanwhile, as the aunt's legal difficulties are being untangled, the romance between the young couple has developed into true love, and the film ends happily for all. Prod. in 1932, with Carl Mahon as the agent, Starr Calloway as the niece, and Eunice Brooks as the aunt.

The Phantom of Kenwood (mystery melodrama, feature length, 1933).

Ten Minutes to Kill (mystery melodrama, feature length, 1933). Apparently a re-release of, or a sequel to, **Ten Minutes to Live** (1932).

Harlem After Midnight (melodrama, feature length, 1934). A depiction of both the sordid and exotic aspects of Harlem life, mainly in nightclubs and cabarets, including drinking, gambling, erotic love scenes, and criminal activities. According to the producer's press book, it was billed as "Gangdom in Action Again—but from a new angle—the Angle of the Kidnaper!" Viewers were promised "An Epidemic of high-yallers and sugar-cured browns straight from Harlem and sizzlin' hot!" Filmed in 1934, with the following cast: Lorenzo Tucker, Dorothy Van Engle, Bee Freeman, Alfred ("Slick") Chester, Rex Ingram, Lawrence Chenault, A. B. Comathiere, and Count Le Shine.

Lem Hawkins' Confession (crime melodrama, feature length, 1935). A remake in sound of **The Gunsaulus Mystery** (1921). A successful young attorney and novelist is contacted by his former sweetheart (whom he did not marry because he was told that she was a wicked woman—charges that proved later to be untrue), asking him to defend her brother, who has been indicted on a murder charge. The lawyer takes the case and successfully defends the brother by obtaining a confession from a person who had actually witnessed the crime. Through his involvement in this case, the lawyer finds that the charges of bad character against his former sweetheart are unfounded, and the two rekindle their old romance on a firmer foundation for future marriage. Premiered in 1935 with the following cast: Clarence Brooks as the lawyer, Dorothy Van Engle as the sweetheart, Alex Lovejoy, Laura Bowman, Lionel Monagas, Henrietta Loveless, Bee Freeman, Alice B. Russell, Andrew Bishop, and Flournoy E. Miller.

Temptation (seduction film, feature length, 1936). Sex melodrama in the manner of Cecil B. DeMille. About the romantic and professional involvements of a black model with the underworld, and her difficulties in extricating herself from these involvements. Prod. in 1936, featuring Andrew S. Bishop, Ethel Moses, Lorenzo Tucker, Hilda Rogers, and "Slick" Chester. The nightclub sequences featured the Pope Sisters, the Kit Kat Club Orchestra, Dot and Dash (tapdancing team), the Six Sizzlers (orchestra), Taft Rice, Lillian Fitzgerald, and Raymond Kallund.

‡**Underworld** (crime thriller, feature length, 1936). All-black version of the typical Hollywood gangster movie of the 1930s. A black college graduate who goes to Chicago becomes involved with the underworld through association with a racketeer and his "gun moll." He experiences the world of mobsters and low-life characters, including alcohol, drugs, violence, prostitution, gambling, and other sordid activities. Filmed in 1936; opened in 1937. Cast included Oscar Polk as the gangster, Bee Freeman as his sweetheart, Sol Johnson, Alfred "Slick" Chester, Ethel Moses, Larry Seymour, Lorenzo Tucker, and Angel Gabriel. One of Micheaux's extant films.

‡**God's Stepchildren** (melodrama, feature length [70 minutes], 1938). Based on the story "Naomi Negress," of unknown origin, which dealt with the problem of "passing" for white. Naomi, a fair-skinned girl, the product of a white mother and a black father, is abandoned by her real mother and brought up as a black child. Deeply resentful of her life in a black environment, she becomes rebellious and is placed in a convent until she comes of age. She falls in love with a white man and almost marries him, but then learns that he is her stepbrother. She then marries a wealthy black man, but after having a child by him she abandons both and begins to pass for white. She next marries a white man, who discovers that she is black. Finally, in disgrace and despair, she commits suicide. Prod. in 1938, with the following cast: Jacqueline Lewis (Naomi, as a child), Gloria Press (Naomi, as a woman), Alice B. Russell, Ethel Moses, Carman Newsome, Alec Lovejoy, and Laura Bowman. An extant film.

‡**Swing** (musical, feature length, 1938). A musician and his girlfriend travel from Birmingham to Harlem, visiting nightclubs and musical spots along the way. Prod. in 1938, with Cora Green, Hazel Diaz, Carman Newsome, Dorothy Van Engle, Alec Lovejoy, and Amanda Randolph. An extant film.

Birthright (drama, feature length, 1939). A remake of his silent film by the same title (1924), which deals with a Harvard graduate who tries to build a black college in his home town in Tennessee in spite of tremendous opposition from both blacks and whites. The woman who loves him and gives him the most support does not believe that she is either socially or morally fit to be his wife. Prod. 1939, with Alec Lovejoy, Laura Bowman, Ethel Moses, Carman Newsome, and George Vessey.

The Notorious Elinor Lee (melodrama, feature length, 1939). About a black gun moll who is assigned by her gangster friends to persuade a black boxing champion to throw an important fight, but who changes her mind when she gets to know the boxer. Co-prod. by black aviator Col. Hubert Julian, also known as the Black Eagle. The film's world premiere, held in New York in Jan. 1940, was a gala celebration, with all the customary Hollywood effects, including searchlights, policemen, red-carpeted sidewalks, and the arrival of black cinema's most glamorous personalities in chauffeured limousines and formal attire. Cast included Edna Mae Harris as Elinor Lee, Robert Earl Jones as the boxing champion, Carman Newsome, Gladys Williams, and Ella Mae Waters.

‡**Lying Lips** (melodrama, feature length, 1939). A nightclub singer is convicted of murdering her aunt because she is the sole beneficiary of an insurance policy which she (the singer) had recently purchased. The plot involves the efforts of two detectives to save her from life imprisonment, to which she has already been sentenced. Prod. in 1939 by Col. Hubert Julian; featured many of the cast members who appeared in **The Notorious Elinor Lee,** including Edna Mae Harris as the singer and Carman Newsome and Robert Earl Jones as detectives. An extant film.

The Betrayal (melodrama, feature length, 1948). Micheaux's last film, based on his semi-autobiographical novel, *The Wind from Nowhere* (1944), a rewritten version of *The*

Homesteader (1917), which had been the basis of his first film by the same title (1918). Tells the story of a pioneer in South Dakota, intermingled with the story of a disastrous marriage and an interracial love story. Prod. independently by Micheaux, billed as "the greatest photoplay of all time." Released by Astor Pictures; widely reviewed by the press when it premiered in downtown New York at the Mansfield Theatre. Cast included Leroy Collins as the homesteader, Myra Standon, Verlie Cowan, Harris Gaines, Yvonne Machen, and Alice B. Russell.

Other Pertinent Writings:
(All novels from which biographical information can be inferred.)
The Conquest: The Story of a Negro Pioneer, by the Pioneer. Lincoln, NB: Woodruff Press, 1913; reprinted by McGrath.
The Forged Note: A Romance of the Darker Races. Lincoln, NB: Western Book Supply, 1915.
The Homesteader. Sioux City, IA: Western Book Supply, 1917; reprinted by McGrath.
The Wind from Nowhere. New York: Book Supply, 1944.
The Case of Mrs. Wingate. New York: Book Supply, 1945.
The Story of Dorothy Stanfield. New York: Book Supply, 1946.
FURTHER REFERENCE: *Am. Film Inst. Catalog . . . , 1921–1930* (Munden). *Blks. in Am. Film & TV* (Bogle). *BlksB&W* (Sampson). *DANB. TomsCoons* (Bogle). *WWCA 1928–29.*

MILLER, ALLEN C. See Appendix A.

MILLER, FLOURNOY E. See Appendix B.

MILLER, IRVIN C. See Appendix B.

MILLER, MAY (Mrs. John Sullivan) (1899–), Poet, teacher, playwright, and anthologist. Born in Washington, DC, the daughter of Kelly Miller, the well-known scholar, writer, professor, and dean at Howard University from 1907 to 1925. During her childhood and early youth, she became acquainted with many famous artists, writers, and intellectuals who visited her home, including W.E.B. DuBOIS, PAUL LAURENCE DUNBAR, and others, and was greatly encouraged to write by her father and his friends. Educated at Howard University, from which she graduated. She participated in the activities of the Howard Players and won a drama prize for one of her early plays, which was also produced at her commencement in 1920. She became a member of GEORGIA DOUGLASS JOHNSON's literary salon, called "The Saturday Nighters." Johnson was also a family friend who became one of her mentors. After completing her education at Howard, she continued to study at American University and Columbia University. For 20 years, from about 1922 to 1942, she taught English, speech, and dramatics at the Frederick Douglass High School of Baltimore, MD, and also served as supervisor of English in the junior high schools of that city. During the mid–1920s, she began to be associated with the New Negro literary movement in Washington, and submitted her plays in the *Opportunity* literary contests of

1925 and 1926, where one play received third prize and another honorable mention. Other scripts were produced by various drama groups in North Carolina, Baltimore, and Washington, DC. During the 1930s, she collaborated on two drama anthologies with playwright and fellow Washingtonian WILLIS RICH-ARDSON (see collections below). By 1943, married to John Sullivan, she retired from teaching and drama and began to devote full time to her literary career as a poet in her native Washington, DC. She served as poetry coordinator for the Friends of Art in the District of Columbia Program for the Public Schools. With the establishment of the District of Columbia Commission on the Arts and Humanities, she was named by the mayor to become a member representing the literary segment. Under her chairmanship, two collections of verse by children were published—one for the children of seven Washington public schools, and another for the children of the Bluefield, WV, public schools. During the 1960s and 1970s, Miller has served as poet-in-residence at Monmouth College, 1963; the University of Wisconsin, 1972; Bluefield State College, 1974; Exeter Academy, 1973–76; and Southern University, 1975. Since 1959 she has published eight volumes of verse: *In the Clearing* (1959), *Poems* (1962), *Lyrics of Three Women* (with Katie Lyle and Maude Rubin, 1964), *Not That Far* (1973), *The Clearing Beyond* (1974), *Dust of Uncertain Journey* (1975), *Halfway to the Sun* (1981), and *The Ransomed Wait* (1983). In 1983 she was living and writing in Washington, DC, where she was a member of the Folger Library Poetry Advisory Committee.

Collections:

(Although Miller was named as editor only for the second collection, she asserts that she collaborated with Richardson on both volumes—hence, they are included here.)

PLAYS AND PAGEANTS FROM THE LIFE OF THE NEGRO. [*PLAYS&PAGS*] Ed. by Willis Richardson [with May Miller]. Washington, DC: Associated Publishers, 1930. Contains: **Riding the Goat** (1928) and **Graven Images** (1930), by Miller.

NEGRO HISTORY IN THIRTEEN PLAYS. [*NEGHIST13*] Ed. by Willis Richardson and May Miller. Washington, DC: Associated Publishers, 1935. Contains: **Christophe's Daughters, Samory, Harriet Tubman,** and **Sojourner Truth** (all 1935), by Miller.

Stage Works:

Pandora's Box (adapt. of the Greek classic myth, 2 acts, 1914). Pub. in two install-ments in *School Progress for Teachers, Parents, and Pupils* (a Philadelphia magazine), July 1914 and Jan. 1915.

Within the Shadow (1920). Winner of the Howard Univ. Drama Award (first prize), 1920. Prod. by Howard Univ. students at Howard's commencement, upon the author's graduation, Washington, DC, 1920.

The Bog Guide (drama, 1 act, 1925). In the setting of an African swamp, this play concerns the vengeance taken by an African girl for the mistreatment of her English mulatto father by his family, which caused him to live in exile in Africa until his death from a tropical disease. Her father had been the offspring of a white Englishman and a mulatto woman, and as the son of this mixed marriage, his racial background was eventually exposed by his cousin when both fell in love with the same Englishwoman. The cousin, now remorseful for his mistreatment of the girl's father, has come to Africa in search of him to bring him back to England. Upon discovering that his cousin is dead, the Englishman asks the daughter to return with him instead (not knowing that she also has the same disease from which both her father and mother had died, and that she is also near death). Nevertheless, the African girl pretends that she is willing to accompany her father's cousin back to England, but while serving as his guide through the African marshlands, she leads him into a treacherous mire, where they both sink to their deaths in the wet, soggy ground. Winner of third prize in the *Opportunity* Contest Awards, May 1925. Prod. by the Intercollegiate [Drama] Association at the Imperial Elks Auditorium, on West 129th St. in New York City, May 5, 1926. Pub. in *Wines in the Wilderness* (Brown-Guillory, 1990). COMMENTARY: Austin diss. *NY Age* 5–1–1926.

The Cuss'd Thing (drama, 1 act, 1926). This play, set in a Harlem apartment, dramatizes the conflict that arises between a musician and his wife concerning the playing of popular or secular music. The wife, who is pregnant, objects to the music on religious grounds. The husband wishes to take a job as a show musician for a popular black musical then playing on Broadway. When the husband announces his plans to take the job, the wife has a dream of impending death and soon goes into labor, losing her baby. Consequently, the husband, believing that this event is an omen, abandons his plan to accept the musician's job. Received honorable mention in the *Opportunity* Contest Awards, May 1926. Unpub. script in the author's personal collection.

Stragglers in the Dust (c. 1929). Unpub. script in the author's personal collection.

Scratches (drama of black ghetto life, 1 act, 1929). Set in a Washington, DC, pool hall in 1915, this play, whose characters are typical pool hall hustlers and gamblers, deals with a game of pool in which the stakes are a matter of life or death. The tense situation is turned around when the main tough guy villain demonstrates unexpected magnanimity toward his intended victim. Pub. in *Carolina Mag.*, April 1929, pp. 36–44, and in *Wines in the Wilderness* (Brown-Guillory, 1990).

Riding the Goat (folk comedy, 1 act, 1930). This comedy, set in Baltimore, revolves around an impending parade by the members of a black fraternal lodge, and contrasts the love of ritual and parades among the older blacks with the attitude of the younger, more educated generation, who do not share this predilection for fraternal pomp and pageantry. A young physician, who is disdainful of lodge activities, is persuaded by the woman he loves to become an active participant in the parade in order to win the confidence and better serve the people of the community in which he practices medicine. Prod. by the St. Augustine Coll. Players of Raleigh, NC, at the Eighth Annual Festival of the Carolina Dramatic Association, held at the Univ. of North Carolina at Chapel Hill, March 28, 1928; also presented by St. Augustine at its commencement, May 25, 1931. Prod. by the Krigwa Players, at Albert Auditorium, Baltimore, Feb. 16, 1932. Pub. in *PLAYS&PAGS* and in *Wines in the Wilderness* (Brown-Guillory, 1990). COMMENTARY: *Carolina Play-Book* 6–1935.

Graven Images (children's play, 1 act, 1930). In the setting of an arena before the Tabernacle in Egypt, this play deals with the origin of prejudice in the Bible, when Miriam, the sister of Moses, spoke out against her brother for his marriage to a Cushite (or Ethiopian) woman. A subplot concerns the playful worship of idols by a group of children. Pub. in *PLAYS&PAGS* and in *BlkThUSA* (Hatch, 1974). COMMENTARY: *Blk. World* 4–1976.

Nails and Thorns (1933). Apparently a biblical drama involving the Crucifixion. Winner of third prize in a drama contest at Southern Univ., Baton Rouge, LA, in 1933. Unpub. script in the author's personal collection.

Christophe's Daughters (black history play, 1 act, 1935). Concerns the plight of the two daughters of Henry Christophe—the revolutionary general who briefly reigned as king of Haiti (1811–20)—during the final days of his tragic downfall. One daughter's view is sadly retrospective as she looks back at the progress made by her father; the other prepares herself to give up her status as a princess and seems to sense the justice of the peasant uprising that will soon depose her father. Pub. in *NEGHIST13*.

Samory (black history play, 1 act, 1935). The story of the African Sudanese conqueror of the 1880s who successfully forestalled French efforts to colonize his native town. Pub. in *NEGHIST13*.

Harriet Tubman (black history drama, 1 act, 1935). About the famed black heroine who led many groups of slaves to freedom through the Underground Railroad. The subplot involves a love story between two slaves and emphasizes the wisdom and courage of Harriet. Prod. by Dillard Univ., New Orleans, during the 1935–36 season. Pub. in *NEGHIST13* and in *Blk. Heroes* (Hill, 1989).

Sojourner Truth (black history play, 1 act, 1935). About the former New York slave named Isabella Baumfree who changed her name and devoted her life to traveling and preaching. The play dramatizes one of the occasions in which her preaching was effective in persuading a group of hostile white youths to cease their racially motivated activities. Pub. in *NEGHIST13*.

Freedom's Children on the March (dramatized folk ballad, 1943). Prod. at the commencement program of Frederick Douglass High School, Baltimore, June 1943.
FURTHER REFERENCE: Austin diss. *NegGen* (Brawley). Ross diss.

MITCHELL, ABBIE (Mrs. Will Marion Cook). See Appendix B.

MITCHELL, JOSEPH S. (1891–?), Boston lawyer and amateur playwright. Born in Auburn, AL. Educated at Talladega College (A.B. 1913), Harvard Law School (1913–14), and Boston University (L.L.B. 1917). Began his law practice in Boston in 1917 and was still practicing in 1944. Member of the Saturday Evening Quill, an organization of literary hobbyists in Boston who published their writings in an annual called the *Saturday Evening Quill*. According to Fannie Ella Frazier Hicklin (Ph.D. diss., 1965), his plays deal with a variety of problems faced by blacks in the South and North, such as lynching, discrimination in employment, and "passing." Member of Alpha Phi Alpha; Worshipful Master, Union Lodge, Prince Hall Masons; and member of numerous political and legal organizations.

Stage Works:
Son Boy (drama, 1 act, 1928). Although the specific plot is not known, this play is set on a plantation in the Deep South and deals with reactions of blacks to the racist attitudes of whites in the small Southern town. Pub. in *Sat. Eve. Quill* (Boston), June 1928, pp. 38–65.

Help Wanted (1 act, 1929). Dramatizes the hardships that arise from race prejudice in industry. Pub. in *Sat. Eve. Quill*, April 1929, pp. 62–71.

The Elopement (1 act, 1930). Pub. in *Sat. Eve. Quill*, April 1930.
FURTHER REFERENCE: Hicklin diss. *WWCA 1941–44*.

MITCHELL, LOFTEN. See Appendix A.

MONTGOMERY, FRANK. See Appendix B.

MORGAN, EDWIN J. See Appendix A.

MOSS, CARLTON ("Ritz") (1910–), Screenwriter/producer, playwright, radio scriptwriter, actor, and critic. Born in Newark, NJ. Educated in the public schools of North Carolina and at Morgan State College, Baltimore, where he received his bachelor's degree during the late 1920s. There he came under the tutelage of early playwright and drama director RANDOLPH EDMONDS, who persuaded him to go to New York to pursue a career in the theatre and radio. In 1931 one of his plays was produced by the Harlem Players. During 1931–32 several of his radio scripts were produced by NBC. He also wrote and acted in a radio series, "Community Forum," which was aired on station WEVD. Also performed in a number of plays, presumably with the Lafayette Players, and in some of the early films of OSCAR MICHEAUX. In 1934 he was drama director of the Harlem YMCA, under a federal program sponsored by President Franklin D. Roosevelt's New Deal. In 1935 he was one of the principal black consultants to the WPA Federal Theatre and was later appointed a director of the Harlem Unit, after the two white directors, John Houseman and Orson Welles, were replaced by three blacks. His Federal Theatre position required him to go to black community organizations to win audiences for the Negro Unit's productions. While with the Federal Theatre, 1935–39, Moss also wrote at least one original show, which was produced by the Philadelphia Unit. During World War II, he served with the Information and Education (I&E) Div. of the War Dept., where he was an information specialist, consultant, and writer of documentary films and stage shows for the armed forces. During this period, he wrote **The Negro Soldier,** considered one of the best documentaries on the participation of black servicemen in the war. For this accomplishment, the Schomburg Collection placed him on its Honor Roll for Race Relations in 1943. Since the war, he has devoted most of his creative talents to the writing and producing of film biographies of famous black Americans, several produced by his own firm, Artesian Productions, and others by Fisk University in Nashville, where for many years he was resident writer/producer and cinema professor. He has also lectured in comparative culture at the University of California at Irvine. His articles and film criticism have appeared in *Freedomways* and several film publications.

Stage Works:
Summertime (musical, 2 acts [12 scenes], 1929). Written and prod. by Moss. Lyrics and music by Dick Handel. Featured Thelma Hall, Russell White, and Walker L. Smith.
Sacrifice (1 act, 1931). Coauthored with RICHARD HUEY. Prod. by the Harlem Players, at the 135th Street Library Theatre, New York, Feb. 2–13, 1931.

[Untitled Pageant] (1935). Depicted the history of blacks in America. Staged at the Wadleigh Annex Theatre, New York City, 1935.

Prelude in Swing (musical doc., full length, 1939). Text by Moss. Choreography and direction by Malvena Fried. A dramatic history of black American music from Africa to the United States, utilizing a dance group, a choral group, and a swing orchestra. Written for and prod. by the Philadelphia Negro Unit of the WPA Federal Theatre Proj. in early June 1939; was still receiving good reviews and playing to enthusiastic audiences when the Federal Theatre was terminated by Congress on June 30, 1939. (Although Moss was then director of the Harlem Unit, he was loaned to the Philadelphia Unit to do this show.)

Salute to Negro Troops (patriotic stage show, 1942). Prod. at the Apollo Theatre in Harlem, 1942.

Broadcast Works:

"Careless Love" (series of weekly radio scripts, half hour, 1931). Broadcast over station WAEF, Baltimore, 1931. Performed by FRANK WILSON, Edna Lewis Thomas, Clarence Williams, Eva Taylor, and "The Southernaires" Quartet.

OTHER WORKS: Also wrote **Folks from Dixie, Noah,** and "scores" of other radio plays for NBC, 1932–33.

Screen Works:

PRIOR TO 1950

The Negro Soldier (doc. film, 40 min., 1943). Script by Moss, who also narrated the film and served as technical advisor. Prod. in 1932 by the U.S. Army Signal Corps; dir. by Capt. Stuart Heisler, under the supervision of the well-known Hollywood director (then Col.) Frank Capra. Considered one of the best doc. films to be prod. during World War II. Depicted the black serviceman's contributions to this and earlier wars, and was highly praised for its contribution toward racial tolerance. According to one description:

The major portion of this film is given over to shots of Negro troops in training camps throughout the country from Fort Custer to Huachuca. A thread of dramatic continuity is conveyed through a Negro mother who reads a letter from her son at her church service detailing his routine from induction to his preparation for Officers' School. The role of the mother is played by Bertha Wolford and the son by Lieutenant Norman Ford. Several excellent Negro composers and arrangers were associated on the musical staff of the production. [*Negro Year Book 1947* (Guzman), p. 453]

The film was widely shown, not only in all-black theatres and army camps, but in thousands of predominantly white theatres throughout the United States, including the Deep South.

Team Work (short doc. film, 1944). A sequel to the author's **The Negro Soldier** (above). Showed the black soldier's contribution to the United States' military, naval, and air forces in the European battles during World War II. Prod. by the War Dept., under the author's supervision, 1944.

SINCE 1950

(For most information on these scripts, consult my earlier volume, *Contemporary Black American Playwrights and Their Plays,* Greenwood Press, Westport, CT, 1988.)

Frederick Douglass: The House on Cedar Hill // Also called by subtitle alone (biographical film, 17 min., 1953). **George Washington Carver** (biographical film, 12 min., 1959). **Paul Laurence Dunbar** (biographical film, 22 min., pre–1972). OTHER

UNDATED FILMS: **Two Centuries of Black American Art. All the World's a Stage. Gift of the Black Folks**.

Other Pertinent Writing:
"The Negro in American Films," in *AnthANT* (Patterson, 1967), pp. 229–47.
FURTHER REFERENCE: *Contemp. Blk. Am. Playwrs.* (Peterson).

MURRAY, JOHN, Playwright, apparently associated with the Karamu Theatre in Cleveland, OH.

Stage Work:
The Prince of Mandalore (comedy, pre–1950). Three black men, traveling through the South, evade southern segregation laws by posing as an Indian prince and his official entourage. Prod. at the Karamu Theatre, Cleveland, prior to 1950.

MUSE, CLARENCE (1889–1979), Actor, composer, director, and screen-writer, best known for his portrayal of dignified servant roles in over 200 Hollywood films from 1929 to 1976. Born in Baltimore, MD. Educated at Dickinson College in Carlisle, PA, from which he received a degree in international law in 1911. Putting aside his plans for a law career, he entered show business immediately after his graduation, performing as a quartet singer and entertainer in Palm Beach and Jacksonville, FL. In 1912 he was one of the cofounders of the Freeman-Harper-Muse Stock Company (with George Freeman and Leonard Harper), at the Globe Theatre in Jacksonville, which in its first year put on a play entitled *Stranded in Africa,* in which Muse played the role of King Gazu. By 1915, married to his first wife Ophelia Muse, he and she were performing in vaudeville—mainly in black theatres on the East Coast—billed as the team of Muse and Muse. The two Muses formed a stock company at the Franklin Theatre in New York City known as the Muse and Pugh Stock Company (with Willard[?] Pugh). After a short engagement, this company moved to the Crescent Theatre in New York, where the group's name was changed to the Crescent Players. The Crescent produced a number of plays, the first of which was *Another Man's Wife,* in which Muse played a comic philanderer and his wife played a stereotypical "poor little orphan girl." In 1915 he joined the Lincoln Players, where he performed in a number of "tab shows" (i.e., tabloid, or short musical, shows, often presented between films) at the Lincoln Theatre, but was lured away from the Lincoln to the Lafayette Players in 1916, at a weekly salary of $90, to replace Charles Gilpin, who quit the company following a salary dispute. As one of the stars of the Lafayette Players, he performed at the Lafayette Theatre for the next seven years in such plays as *Fine Feathers, The Master Mind, Escape,* and *Dr. Jekyll and Mr. Hyde*—a dual role which he played in whiteface makeup. In 1920 Muse was one of the founders and a member of the board of the Delsarte Film Corp., in New York, which produced the film *Toussaint L'Ouverture,* written by and starring Muse, presumably with members of the Lafayette Players. In 1921 this company made another all-black film, *The Custard Nine,* shot in Vicksburg, MI. He moved to Chicago in 1921, where he was associated with the Royal Gardens Theatre, with which group he produced and directed a number of black shows, including *Hoola Boola* (1922) and *Rambling Around* (1923). He produced and directed *The Charleston Dandies* (1926), *The Chicago Plantation Revue* (1927), and *Miss Bandana* (with Jackie "Moms" Mabley in her acting debut, 1927), which toured the TOBA (Theatre Owners and Booking Association) circuits. At some point in his career (dates unknown), he directed and served as production supervisor of the opera *Thais,* which was performed in Chicago and St. Louis with a cast of 190 black actors and singers, with Muse playing the part of the priest. In 1929 he went to Hollywood, at the invitation of Fox Studios, to appear as the 90-year-old Uncle Napus in an all-black plantation film musical, *Hearts in Dixie,* for which he received a salary of $1,250 a week, under a 12-month contract. He remained in Hollywood for the rest of his career, where he became the "pet actor" of director Frank Capra, who treated him kindly and with great sensitivity, using him in many of his films. While making films, Muse also starred in the play *Porgy* and a re-creation of *Dr. Jekyll and Mr. Hyde* with the Lafayette Theatre which came to Hollywood before the group disbanded in 1932. With the WPA Federal Theatre Project (FTP), Muse directed HALL JOHNSON's *Run, Little Chillun* in Los Angeles and Hollywood in 1938–39, a production that was revived on Broadway in 1943 after the demise of WPA/FTP. As a member of ASCAP, he is credited with a number of songs, the best known of which is "When It's Sleepy Time Down South," written with °Otis and Leon Rene as the title song for a stage show in which Muse played the role of a butler. By one count, he appeared in 219 films between 1929 and 1976, the best known of which are *Huckleberry Finn* (1931), *The Count of Monte Cristo* (1934), *Broadway Bill* (1934), *Show Boat* (1936), *Way Down South* (which he cowrote with LANGSTON HUGHES, 1939), *Tales of Manhattan* (1942), *Porgy and Bess* (1959), *Buck and the Preacher* (1972), and *Car Wash* (1976). Recipient of an honorary Doctor of Humanities degree from Bishop College, 1972. Elected to the Black Filmmakers Hall of Fame, 1973. Died on his ranch in Perris, CA, on the day before his ninetieth birthday, survived by his third wife, a daughter, and a son.

Screen Works:

Toussaint L'Ouverture (feature film, full length: screenplay, 1920). Subtitled "The Abraham Lincoln of Haiti." Based on a story by Col. Charles Young, dramatized by Muse. Romantic tragedy of the famed Haitian revolutionary general (1743–1803) who fought to overthrow slavery in his country, until his arrest, imprisonment, and death. According to the producer, the film featured "The Glamour of beautiful Haiti, the Hypnotic influence of the AFRICAN Voodoo, the thrill of true Patriotism, the tender touch of Love and Duty, all blended in radiant romantic Tragedy that creeps into your heart."— *Crisis,* Oct. 1928, p. 297. Prod. by the Delsarte Film Corp., New York, 1920, featuring Muse, Inez Clough, Susie Sutton-Brown, and Spahr Dickey.

The Sport of Gods (biographical film: screenplay, 1921). Based on a story by PAUL LAURENCE DUNBAR. Prod. 1921.

Spirit of Youth (feature film, 1937). Wrote music and lyrics only, with °Elliot Carpenter. The story of Joe Louis' life, in which Louis played himself. Muse costarred in the film and served as Louis' acting and dialogue coach. Prod. 1938. REVIEWS: *NYT* 2–8–1938. *Time* 1–31–1938.

Way Down South (feature film, full length, 1939). Screenplay by Langston Hughes, based on a story by Muse. Stereotypical melodrama of the old South, which tells the story of the devotion of a young white boy to the slaves on his deceased father's plantation. The plot revolves around the boy's attempt to save his favorite slave, Old Uncle Canton, played by Muse, from mistreatment by the plantation overseer, a Simon Legree character. Prod. by °Sol Lesser, 1939; dir. by °Bernard Vorhaus. With Bobby Breen as the boy. The Hall Johnson Choir sang 11 spirituals, cowritten by Muse and Hughes. COMMENTARY: *Th. Arts* 8–19–1942, photo.

Broken Strings (feature film, full length, 1940). Screenplay coauthored with °Bernard E. Ray and °David Arlen. Melodrama which "focus[es] on a concert violinist in conflict with himself and his son (a bright kid who prefers swing music to his father's classics)."— *Blks. in Am. Films & TV* (Bogle, 1988). Independently prod. and dir. by Ray, starring Muse as the violinist/father. Cast includes Stymie Beard (originally of the "Our Gang" comedy series) as the son, Sybil Lewis, and William Washington.

Other Pertinent Writings:

Way Down South. By Clarence Muse and David Arlen. Pub. by David Graham Fisher, Hollywood, CA, 1932; Copy in Schomberg. [Not to be confused with Muse's film by the same title (1939), coauthored with Langston Hughes. This book chronicles Muse's theatrical career, telling of his experiences on the TOBA circuit. Full of interesting anecdotes on black musical stars of the period.]

The Dilemma of the Negro Actor. Pamphlet, 1934.

FURTHER REFERENCE: *BlksB&W* (Sampson). *BlksBf* (Sampson). *Blks. in Am. Films & TV* (Bogle). *DirBlksPA* (Mapp). *TomsCoons* (Bogle).

N

NORFORD, GEORGE E. (1918–   ), Journalist; broadcasting executive, producer, and writer; playwright. Born in New York City. Educated at Columbia University and the Free School for Social Research. For many years vice president of the Westinghouse Broadcasting Company, where he "coordinat[ed] the Broadcast Skills Bank designed to expand job opportunities for minority group members."—*BlkMagic* (Hughes & Meltzer, 1967), p. 297. Former theatrical editor of *Opportunity* magazine; former associate editor of *Negro Digest*; first black producer of network TV programs at NBC. Author of short stories and reportedly at least six plays (of which only one has been located). Member of the Rose McClendon Theatre Workshop, 1930s; one of the organizers of the Negro Playwrights' Company, 1940s; member of the National Academy of Television Arts and Sciences (NATAS); and board member of numerous business and civic organizations, including Westinghouse Broadcasting Co. Currently resides in New York.

Stage Work:

Joy Exceeding Glory // Retitled **Head of the Family** (satirical comedy, 3 acts, 1939; revised 1950). The tranquility of a Harlem family is wrecked when the maternal head of the family (the wife is the breadwinner) joins Father Faithful's religious cult and goes around trying to convert others, including her skeptical husband. Only when her son embraces communism and gets into trouble with the law does she begin to cast off her religious fervor and folly, to try to cope with her family problems as wife and mother. First prod. under its orig. title by the Rose McClendon Workshop Theatre, at the New York Public Library, 124th Street Branch, Oct. 17–21 and 26–28, 1939. Prod. in the revised and retitled version by the Theatre Guild, New York, 1950, and tried out at the Westport Country Playhouse, but never reached Bway.

Other Pertinent Writings:

"On Stage," *Opportunity*, Summer 1947, pp. 164–67, 174–75; Fall 1947, pp. 210–14.

FURTHER REFERENCE: Hicklin diss. George Norford Scrapbook in Schomburg.

NORMAN, DORA COLE. See Appendix A.

NUGENT, RICHARD BRUCE (Richard Bruce Nugent; Bruce Nugent) (1905–   ), Art-deco illustrator, short story writer, scenarist, poet, and playwright; a product of the Black or Harlem Renaissance. Born in Washington, DC, the son of socially prominent parents, and educated there at Dunbar High School. After his father's death, he moved with his mother to New York City, where he held a number of ordinary jobs (including bellhop, elevator operator, and errand boy) and received his first training in art as an apprentice with a catalog house. To prevent her son from becoming an artist, his mother sent him back to Washington to live with his grandparents. There, however, he came under the influence of the Washington literati and was invited to attend the salons of GEORGIA DOUGLAS JOHNSON, where he met a number of writers, including Alain Locke of Howard University, who included Nugent's writings and drawings in two of his anthologies, and LANGSTON HUGHES, who helped Nugent to get his first poems published in COUNTEE CULLEN's anthology *Caroling Dusk* (1927) and *Opportunity* magazine. Nugent returned to New York, where he was introduced to anthropologist/author/playwright ZORA NEALE HURSTON, novelist/playwright WALLACE THURMAN, and painter Aaron Douglas. He became an apprentice to Douglas, helping him to execute his commissioned murals and accompanying him to art classes under Winold Reiss. Within a few years, Nugent had published a number of his art-deco drawings in several periodicals, and became known for his voluptuous, erotic, and geometric style, which was strongly influenced by Erté and Beardsley. Throughout his life, Nugent continued to paint, draw, and write, but he is best remembered for his early works, which reflect a distinctive, unconventional, and highly stylized quality.

Stage Works:

Sahdji, an African Ballet (dance drama: scenario, 1 act, 1925). Written as Richard Bruce, in collaboration with Alain Locke (whose name also appears on the copyright notice, although not listed originally as a collaborator). Ballet music score by †William Grant Still. Based on Nugent's short story, "Sahdji," written as Bruce Nugent, which originally appeared in *New Neg.* (Locke, 1925). A tribal chanter (as narrator) interprets the ballet; all other action is dance-pantomime. Tells the story of an African chief whose wife has a romantic affair with his apparent successor while the chief is away on a hunting trip. The chief is killed in the hunt, and the wife reluctantly, but dutifully, according to tribal custom and her marriage vows, commits suicide (by plunging a dagger into her breast) as part of the funeral rites for her husband, while her lover looks on in helpless grief. First prod. by Howard Univ., Washington, DC, late 1920s. Prod. by the Eastman School of Music, Rochester, NY, 1932. Pub. in *PlaysNegL* (Locke & Gregory, 1927). Pub. by the Eastman School of Music, Univ. of Rochester, Rochester, NY, 1961 (47 pp.). Manuscript score of William Grant Still's ballet, "in which is laid autobiographical comment in longhand by Alain Locke and Bruce Nugent, who collaborated on the scenario for this dance-drama," is located in JWJ/YUL.—*Crisis*, July 1942, p. 223.

Taxi Fare (drama, 1 act, 1931). Coauthored with ROSE McCLENDON. First prod.

by the Harlem Players, at the 135th Street Library Theatre, New York, opening Feb. 2, 1931, for 4 perfs.

FURTHER REFERENCE: *Caroling Dusk* (Cullen). *When Harlem Was in Vogue* (Lewis).

O

OTTLEY, ROI (1906–1960), Author, journalist, and radio scriptwriter. Born in New York City of British West Indian immigrant parents. Educated in the public schools of New York and at St. Bonaventure College, the University of Michigan, and St. John University Law School, with writing courses at CCNY and Columbia University. Journalist for the *New York Amsterdam News,* beginning in 1931, rising to one of the editors by 1935, a position he held for two years. Joined the New York City Writers Project as an editor in 1937, directing research on Negro life, which resulted in two books: *New World A'Coming* (1943), a best-seller that became the basis of a popular radio series by the same title, and *Black Odyssey: The Story of the Negro in America* (1948). Other books include *No Green Pastures* (1952) and *Lonely Warrior: Life of Robert S. Abbott* (1955). Ottley was unsuccessful in realizing his ambition of becoming a radio commentator in spite of his successful radio series. The position "was closed to him," he believed, "because . . . of the white man's reluctance to take the Negro intellectual . . . (as compared with Negro entertainers) seriously."—*The Negro Vanguard* (Bardolph 1959), p. 250. Beginning in the 1940s, "Ottley . . . made extensive stays abroad, but always preferred the American motherland."—Ibid., p. 281. His numerous articles were published in the *Pittsburgh Courier* and the *Baltimore Afro-American;* book reviews in the *Herald Tribune* and *New York Times.*

Broadcast Works:

"**New World A'Coming**" (two series of radio programs, from half-hour scripts by Ottley and others, 1944/46). Conceived by Ottley and based on his best-selling book by the same title (1943). The series, though not a strict adaptation of Ottley's book, tried to be true to its general themes and purposes. The first series, broadcast March 5, 1944–May 27, 1945, had as its subtitle "A series of vivid programs on Negro life, based on *New World A'Coming,* by Roi Ottley." The second series, broadcast Oct. 8, 1945–May 7, 1946, was subtitled "Dramatizing stories of men and events which affect the lives of all minorities in our democracy.'' Each series consisted partly of dramatizations of various literary works by and about blacks, original radio scripts, and programs of black music. Broadcast as a public service by station WMCA, New York, 1944–46; dir. by Mitchell Grayson. Narrated in part by Canada Lee; with various guest stars. The program won the Schomburg Award in 1945. The first series, recorded on Phonodiscs by NBC Recording Div., New York, is located in Schomburg. Radio scripts of both series, reproduced from typewritten copy, are also located in Schomburg. [See also next entry, and OWEN DODSON, for other scripts in these series.]

The Negro Domestic (radio script, half hour, 1944). By Ottley. From the **"New World A'Coming"** series, described above, first broadcast on station WMCA, New York, March 1944. Pub. in *Radio Drama in Action* (Barnouw, 1945).

FURTHER REFERENCE: *Afro-Am. Encyc. Dict. Catalog of the Schomburg Collection. Neg. YrBk. 1947.*

OWSLEY, TIM. See Appendix B.

P

PAWLEY, THOMAS D., III (1917–   ), Distinguished professor of speech and theatre, playwright, director, and author; for many years head of the Dept. of Speech and Theatre at Lincoln University in Jefferson City, MO. Born in Jackson, MS. Received the A.B. (with distinction) from Virginia State College, 1937; the A.M. and Ph.D. in theatre arts from the University of Iowa, 1949; with postdoctoral studies at Columbia University and the University of Missouri. Married; the father of two sons. Has had a lengthy teaching and directing career, which has included the following institutions: teacher and director, Atlanta University Summer Theatre, 1939–41, 1943; teacher and director, Prairie View State College, 1939–40; professor and chairman, Dept. of English, Speech and Theatre, Lincoln University (MO), 1958–77, then chairman, Div. of Humanities and Fine Arts, 1967–77, and finally dean of the College of Arts and Sciences, 1977–83. Appointed Curator's Distinguished Professor of Speech and Theatre at Lincoln University in 1983. He has been visiting professor at the University of California/Santa Barbara, 1968; Northern Illinois University/DeKalb, 1971; University of Iowa/Iowa City, 1976; and University of Missouri/Columbia, 1980. Coauthor, with William Reardon, of *The Black Teacher and the Dramatic Arts* (1970). Author of numerous articles on theatre, listed at the end of this entry. His poetry has appeared in *Phylon* and *Crisis*, and his book reviews in the *Quarterly Journal of Speech* and the *Central States Speech Journal*. Member of numerous professional organizations, among which are the National Association of Dramatic and Speech Arts (NADSA), the American Educational Theatre Association (AETA), the American Theatre Association (ATA), Dramatists Guild, Alpha Phi Alpha fraternity, and the Speech and Theatre Association of Missouri. Consultant to the Guggenheim Foundation, 1981, 1982. Recipient of the following honors and awards: Shields-Howard Creative Writing Award, Virginia State College, 1934; National Theatre Conf. Fellowship, 1947–48; first prize, Jamestown (VA) Corp. Playwriting Contest, 1954, for his play **Messiah;**

elected to Outstanding Educators of America, 1970; Outstanding Teacher Award, Speech and Theatre Assn. of Missouri, 1977; elected to the College of Fellows, ATA, 1978; NADSA Outstanding Service Award, 1984.

Groups of Related Plays:

["Master's Thesis Plays"]. Title of thesis unknown. Includes the following plays, the first two prod. by the Dept. of Theatre Arts, Univ. of Iowa City, April 21, 1939; dir. by Prof. Hunton D. Sellman: **Jedgement Day** (1938), **Smokey** (1939), and **Freedom in My Soul** (1939).

"EXPERIMENTAL PRODUCTIONS OF A GROUP OF ORIGINAL PLAYS." The author's Ph.D. diss., Univ. of Iowa, Iowa City, 1949; copy in the Univ. of Iowa Lib.

Stage Works:

PRIOR TO 1950

Jedgement Day (folk comedy, 1 act, 1938). Set in the home of Minerva and Zeke Potter, this play concerns the harrowing experience of a disbelieving, errant husband (Zeke), whose minister has warned him that he will be punished in the deepest pit of Hell on the "day of Jedgement" for his sinful ways. The punishment occurs in a dream, involving Satan, the archangels, and the minister who warned him of his impending doom. The first of three plays written by Pawley for his master's thesis, and first prod. at the Univ. of Iowa, at Iowa City, April 21, 1938. See ["Master's Thesis Plays"] above. Pub. in *NegCarav* (Brown et al., 1941); in an Italian translation by Gerardo Guerrieri, pub. in the periodical *Sipario* (1950s) and prod. over several radio stations in northern Italy; and also pub. in *Humanities Through the Black Experience* (Klotman et al., 1977).

Smokey (melodrama, 1 act, 1938). Set in a small southern town, this play is a character study of a quiet, mild-mannered, rather well-liked black farmhand who murders a southern white plantation owner, apparently with neither motivation nor regret. He is finally lynched by a mob of poor whites while trying to escape with another cellmate from the local jail. The second of three plays written by Pawley for his master's thesis; first prod. at the Univ. of Iowa, at Iowa City, April 21, 1938, with the author in the title role. See ["Master's Thesis Plays"] above. Also prod. at Atlanta Univ. Summer Theatre, 1939.

Freedom in My Soul (drama, 1 act, 1939). The third of three plays written by Pawley for his master's thesis at the State Univ. of Iowa, 1939. See ["Master's Thesis Plays"] above.

Crispus Attucks // Alternate title and current subtitle: **Son of Liberty** (historical tragedy, 3 acts [5 scenes], 1947). About the black man who was the first person to die in the American Revolution, dealing mainly with the motives that led Attucks to fight against the Tories in Boston. According to Fannie Ella Frazier Hicklin:

Attucks and the other revolutionary zealots are depicted as ordinary men, following ordinary tasks, but gradually fired to rebellion because of the personal effects of British domination. Attucks desires revenge because a British officer's horse trampled his son to death; he also anticipates the crumbling of slavery with the expulsion of the British. [Hicklin Ph.D. diss., 1965, pp. 315–16]

First prod. by the Dept. of Speech and Dramatic Arts, at the Univ. of Iowa, March 18–19, 1948. Unpub. script included in the author's Ph.D. diss., "EXPERIMENTAL PRODUCTIONS OF A GROUP OF ORIGINAL PLAYS" (1949) [see Groups of Related Plays above]. Revised for the American Bicentennial, 1976. A film treatment was also done by *Whitney LeBlanc, 1976.

SINCE 1950

(For descriptions of these plays, see my earlier volume, *Contemporary Black American Playwrights and Their Plays,* Greenwood Press, Westport, CT, 1988.)

F.F.V. ("First Family of Virginia") (drama, full length, 1963). **The Tumult and the Shouting** (drama, 2 acts, 1969). **The Eunuchs** (comedy, 2 parts, 1977). **The Long Lonesome Ride of Charley Young** (1984).

Other Pertinent Writings:

"I Am a Fugitive from a Play," *Bulletin*, National Theatre Conf., July 1948; reprinted in *SADSA Encore*, 1949, pp. 15–17.

"Stagecraft in Negro Colleges," *Neg. Coll. Q.*, Dec. 1946, pp. 193–99; reprinted in *SADSA Encore*, 1948, pp. 18–19.

"Theatre Arts and the Educated Man," *Central States Speech J.*, Spring 1957, pp. 5–11.

"The Black Theatre Audience," *Players*, Aug.-Sept. 1971, pp. 257–61; reprinted in *Theatre of Blk. Ams.* (Hill, 1980).

"The First Black Playwrights," *Blk. World*, April 1972, pp. 16–24.

"Neo-Stereotypes in the Black Theatre," *Encore*, 1973.

"Dunbar as Playwright," *Blk. World*, April 1975.

"Sheppard Randolph Edmonds" [a memoir], *Encore*, Sept. 1984.

FURTHER REFERENCE: *BlkThUSA* (Hatch, 1974). *Contemp. Blk. Am. Playwrs. and Their Plays* (Peterson). Hicklin diss.

PAYTON, LEW (1873–?), Stage performer, musical comedy librettist, and playwright of the 1930s. Was resident playwright with the Federal Theatre Project in Chicago during the 1930s. Appeared in a number of New York stage productions, including *Harlem* (1929), *Boundary Line* (1930), *Solid South* (1930), *Never No More* (1932), *Bridal Wise* (1932), and *Jezebel* (1933).

Collection:

DID ADAM SIN? And Other Stories of Negro Life in Comedy-Drama and Sketches. Privately printed, Los Angeles, 1937. Copies in TC/NYPL, Moorland-Spingarn, Hatch-Billops, and the following southern college libraries: Alabama State Univ., Tuskegee Inst., Atlanta Univ., and Fisk Univ. Contains: **Did Adam Sin?, A Bitter Pill, A Flyin' Fool, Some Sweet Day, Two Sons of Ham,** and **Who Is de Boss?**

Stage Works:

PLAYS

Did Adam Sin? (melodrama of Harlem life, 3 acts, 1936). Deals with the oppressive effect of poverty on a black family during the Depression, which leads the family members into lives of crime in order to survive. Prod. by the Chicago Negro Unit of the WPA Federal Theatre, opening April 30, 1936, and closing on May 14, after a run of two weeks. Pub. in *DID ADAM SIN?* COMMENTARY: Ross diss.

A Bitter Pill (drama of racial prejudice, 1 act, 1937). A tragic incident is depicted in which a black man stands up for his rights in a small southern town and is killed. Pub. in *DID ADAM SIN?*

A Flyin' Fool (comedy, 1 act, 1937). A black couple go up for the first time in an airplane. Pub. in *DID ADAM SIN?*

Some Sweet Day (comedy, 1 act, 1937). About a black family whose matriarchal head is blind, but who manages to hold the family together in peace and harmony. Pub. in *DID ADAM SIN?*

Two Sons of Ham (comedy, 1 act, 1937). A series of vaudeville sketches for two black comedians, reminiscent of Bert Williams and George Walker. Pub. in *DID ADAM SIN?*

Who Is de Boss? (comedy, 1 act, 1937). A satire of the early Hollywood movies, in which the servants of famous film personalities are cast together in a film. Pub. in *DID ADAM SIN?*

MUSICAL

The Chocolate Dandies // Orig. title: **In Bamville** (musical comedy, 2 acts [12 scenes], 1924/25). Book by Payton and †NOBLE SISSLE. Music and lyrics by Sissle and Eubie Blake. (For plot synopsis, see Appendix B.) Toured on the road as **In Bamville,** 1924, before opening on Bway, under its present title, at the Colonial Theatre, Sept. 1, 1924, for 96 perfs., closing in 1925. Cast featured the authors and Valaida Snow. Josephine Baker also appeared as a comedy chorus girl, and Lena Horne was in the chorus line.

PITTS, LUCIA MAE. See Appendix A.

PRATT, RACHEL BROCK, Former student playwright at Wilberforce University, OH; a graduate of the class of 1921.

Stage Work:
The Way of the World ("Race Play," 1921). Prod. by Wilberforce Univ., Wilberforce, OH, 1920/21.

PRICE, DORIS, Student playwright of the 1930s, who studied with Kenneth Rowe at the University of Michigan. Lennox Robinson, who wrote the introduction to the anthology in which two of her plays are included, considered her a playwright of promise and regretted that the commercial theatre would not be interested in producing her plays because they were all one-acts.

Stage Works:
The Bright Medallion (drama, 1 act, 1932). The play is set in the black district of a small Texas town. After finding a shiny medal from World War I, a disreputable black man begins to wear it, pretending that he won it for bravery in the war. To prove his valor, he rescues an infant from a burning house, which results in his death. Pub. in *Univ. of Michigan Plays* (Rowe, 1932).

The Eyes of the Old (drama, 1 act, 1932). To escape from her uneventful "existence" under the constant scrutiny of her aged grandmother, a young black girl elopes, hoping to find a better life. Pub. in *Univ. of Michigan Plays*, vol. 3 (Rowe, 1932).

Two Gods: A Minaret (folk play, 1 act, 1932). A very brief play dealing with a popular theme, God's battle with Satan for the black man's soul. Pub. in *Opportunity*, Dec. 1932, p. 380.

R

RANDLE, ANNIE. See Appendix A.

RAZAF, ANDY. See Appendix B.

REID, IRA DeA. (DeAugustine) (1901–1968), Leading black American sociologist; educator, author, actor, and playwright. Born in Clifton Forge, VA. Educated at Morehouse College (A.B. 1922), the University of Pittsburgh (M.A. 1925), and Columbia University (Ph.D. 1929). Taught in high schools in Texas and West Virginia during the 1920s. For several years associated with the Urban League, first as industrial secretary of the New York office, 1925–28; then as director of research for the national body, 1928–34. Also asst. editor of *Opportunity,* published by the Urban League. First marriage to Gladys Russell Scott, 1925, by whom he had a daughter. Following her death, he married Anne Cook, 1958. (Dr. Cook, who received her Ph.D. from Yale Drama School, was director of drama at Atlanta University during the 1930s and later was drama director at Howard University.) Ira DeA. Reid was professor of sociology at Atlanta University, 1934–46, where he was also the second editor of *Phylon,* an Atlanta University journal of race and culture founded and first edited by W.E.B DuBOIS. He was professor and chairman of the Dept. of Sociology and Anthropology, Haverford College, PA, 1947–66, when he retired as professor emeritus. Also taught at New York University School of Social Work, Columbia University, and Pennsylvania State University. As a nonprofessional actor, he performed with the Harlem Experimental Theatre in New York, the Atlanta University Summer Theatre, and the Morehouse/Spelman Players, also in Atlanta. The author of numerous sociological studies, including the following books: *The Negro Immigrant* (1939), *The Negro in New Jersey* (1930), *Negro Youth: Their Social and Economic Background* (1939), *In a Minor Key* (1940), and *Sharecroppers All* (coauthor, 1940). His popular article, "Mrs. Bailey Pays the Rent," about a Harlem rent party, was published in *NegCarav* (Brown et al., 1941). Social Board Consultant, 1937–41; hon. member of Phi Beta Kappa (Haverford); member of numerous professional sociological associations, including the American Sociological Society; editor of the *American Sociological Review*; member of Omega Psi Phi fraternity. Died in Haverford, PA, of emphysema; survived by his widow, Anne Cooke Reid, and his daughter by his first marriage.

Stage Work:

John Henry (folk legend, 2 scenes, 1937). About the legendary black railroad worker who outdistanced all other workers in the laying of railroad tracks with his famous hammer. Not much is known about Reid's version of this story except what has been reported by Sterling Brown (*Neg. Poetry and Dr.*, 1937, p. 122): "Ira D. Reid's John Henry has a first scene, laid in a camp shack, of great gusto. The second, which deals with the contest between hero and steam drill, suffers because of stage limitations." Prod. by the Atlanta Univ. Summer Theatre, Summer 1937, dir. by Anne Cooke, who later became Mrs. Ira DeA. Reid.

FURTHER REFERENCE: *DANB*.

RICHARDSON, THOMAS (deceased), Protest playwright and theatre manager of the 1930s, described by *Loften Mitchell as "a veteran of numerous theatrical ventures."—*BlkDr* (1967), p. 105. In 1938, on a "fellowship" from Paul Robeson, he supervised the activities of the Harlem Suitcase Theatre, as executive director, until it disbanded in 1939. According to Mitchell:

Robeson gave the Harlem Suitcase Theatre enough of a fellowship for the group to employ the brilliant Thomas Richardson to work with the group as artistic director on a full-time basis. Richardson, now deceased, had an enviable record of working with community theatre groups and he promptly brought to the Suitcase such talented people as OWEN DODSON, Canada Lee and other professionals. [*VoicesBTh* (Mitchell, 1975), p. 158; capitals added].

After leaving the Suitcase Theatre, Richardson organized the Negro Repertory Players in Washington, DC, 1939.

Stage Works:

Place: America (A Theatre Piece) (living newspaper-style play, 51 pp., 1939). "Based on the history of the National Association for the Advancement of Colored People [NAACP]."—Pub. script. Dramatizes the civil rights struggles of blacks in America, both in the South and the North. Prod. by the Negro Community Theatre of Richmond, VA, Saturday, July 1939. Pub. by the NAACP, New York, 1939; copies in Schomburg and Moorland-Spingarn, as well as in the libraries of Talladega Coll., Atlanta Univ., and Fisk Univ.

Dead Men Don't Dance and Protest // Orig. title: **Protest** (experimental mass chant, post–1940). Utilizes drama and Lawrence Gellert's *Negro Songs of Protest* to expose racial injustices experienced by blacks. Apparently prod. after 1940; no record of the actual prodn.

RICHARDSON, WILLIS (1889–1977), Pioneer playwright and drama anthologist; retired United States civil service clerk; also an essayist, poet, and short story writer. Historically significant as the first black American author to have a serious, nonmusical play produced on Broadway. Born in Wilmington, NC, where he lived until 1898, when his parents moved to Washington, DC. After graduating from Dunbar High School in 1910, he became a clerk in the U.S. Dept. of Engraving and Printing, where he remained until his retirement in 1954. Married to Mary Jones in 1914; the couple had three children. Influenced by early black playwrights MARY BURRILL (his high school English teacher) and ANGELINA GRIMKÉ, he studied playwriting by correspondence from 1916 to 1918. His earliest plays were published mainly in *Crisis* and *The Brownies' Book,* both magazines affiliated with the NAACP. He also edited two major drama anthologies, publishing works of several playwrights included in this volume. Twice winner of *Crisis* Contest Awards, in 1925 and 1926, and winner of the Schwab Cup at Yale University in 1928. Much of his work deals with the lives of urban blacks and shows the influence of the folk tradition of Ridgely Torrence and Paul Green. Member of GEORGIA DOUGLAS JOHNSON's Washington, DC, literary group, "The Saturday Nighters." One of the founders of the Washington branch of the Krigwa Players. Died in Washington at age 88.

Collections:

PLAYS AND PAGEANTS FROM THE LIFE OF THE NEGRO. [PLAYS & PAGS] Editor. Associated Pubs., Washington, DC, 1930. Contains; **The Black Horseman** (1929), **The House of Sham** (1929), and **The King's Dilemma** (1926).

NEGRO HISTORY IN THIRTEEN PLAYS. [NEGHIST13] Coeditor, with MAY MILLER (SULLIVAN). Associated Pubs., Washington, DC, 1935. Contains: **Antonio Maceo** (1935), **Attucks, the Martyr** (1935), **The Elder Dumas** (1935), **Near Calvary** (1935), and **In Menelik's Court** (1935).

THE KING'S DILEMMA AND OTHER PLAYS FOR CHILDREN. [KING'S DILEMMA] Exposition Press, New York, 1956. Contains: **The Dragon's Tooth** (1921), **The Gypsy's Finger Ring** (1956), **The King's Dilemma** (1926), **Man of Magic** (1956), **Near Calvary** (1935), and **The New Santa Claus** (1956).

Stage Works:

PRIOR TO 1950

The Deacon's Awakening (social problem play, 1 act, 1920). On the theme of women's suffrage. About a church deacon who plans to bring all women members before the church board for disciplinary action if they attend the meetings of the Voting Society. He changes his mind when he discovers that his own wife and daughter are active participants in the society. Prod. in St. Paul, MN, 1921. Pub. in *Crisis,* Nov. 1920.

    The Children's Treasure (children's play, 1 act, 1921). Pub. in *Brownies' Bk.*, June 1921.

    The Dragon's Tooth (children's play, 1 act, 1921). Fairy tale in which some children try to steal a magic dragon's tooth on which is written the secret of the future. Pub. in *Brownie's Bk.,* June 1921, and in *KING'S DILEMMA.*

    The Chip Woman's Fortune (folk drama, 1-act version, 1922). Historically significant as the first serious play by a black author to be presented on Bway. Because of a debt that has been reported to his employer, a store porter loses his job in a small southern community. He tries to borrow the money from an old woman who earns a meager living by picking up and selling chips of wood and bits of coal in the street, believing that she has a small fortune stashed away. First prod. by the Ethiopian Art Theatre of Chicago (also called the Chicago Folk Theatre) in the following cities: Chicago, Jan. 29, 1923; Washington, DC, April 23, 1923, New York City, first at the Lafayette Theatre in Harlem, May 7, 1923, then on Bway at the Frazee Theatre for one week beginning May 17, 1923. Prod. more recently by the Afro-American Studio of Acting and Speech, New York, 1973. Pub. in *Fifty More Contemp. One-Act Plays* (Shay, 1928); in *AnthANT* (Patterson, 1967); in *BlkDrAm* (Turner, 1971). Also revised as a full-length play, 1927.

Mortgaged (race-propaganda play, 1 act, 1924). Concerns two rival brothers, one devoted to uplifting the race by making a contribution, the other seeking to make money by exploitation of his own people. Prod. by the Howard Univ. Players, Washington, DC; was Howard's first play by a black playwright, other than their own students, to be prod. there. Prod. by the Dunbar Dramatic Club of Washington in a drama tournament at Plainfield, NJ, May 1925, where it gained fourth place. Prod. by the Krigwa Players of Washington at Armstrong Auditorium, Washington, DC, May 7, 1927; by the Morgan Players of Morgan Coll., Baltimore, April 8, 1930; by Bishop Coll., Marshall, TX, Jan. 14, 1932; by Florida A. & M. Coll., Tallahassee, Jan. 27, 1932; and by the Douglas High School Players, Baltimore, Feb. 7, 1934. Pub. in *ReadingsNA* (Cromwell et al., 1931) and *NewNegRen* (Davis & Peplow, 1975).

Compromise (folk drama, 1 act, 1925). About the continuous compromises that blacks often had to make in their relationships with whites in the Deep South. Several tragedies have been suffered by a black family at the hands of their white neighbors for which no legal justice can be obtained; but after his sister is made pregnant by the son of the white family, the black son decides to take justice into his own hands. First prod. by the Gilpin Players at Karamu House, Cleveland, OH, Feb. 25, 1925; was the first play by a black playwright to be prod. by this group. Prod. by the Krigwa Players of New York City at the 135th St. Library in Harlem, May 3, 10, and 17, 1926; and by the Krigwa Players of Washington, DC, Jan. 27 and Feb. 15, 1932. Prod. by the Howard Univ. Players, Washington, DC, April 8, 1936. Pub. in *Crisis*, July 1927, in *New Neg.* (Locke, 1925), and in *Ujsag* (Vasarnap, Hungary), April 5, 1931.

The Broken Banjo (folk tragedy, 1-act version, 1925). A man who plays the banjo and loves it more than any person or thing, and who has secretly killed a man for breaking it, is turned in to the police by a disgruntled brother-in-law who had witnessed the murder. Received first prize in the *Crisis* Contest Awards of 1925. Prod. by the Krigwa Players of New York, Aug. 1, 1925, and May 3, 10, and 17, 1926; and by the Krigwa Players of Washington, DC, at Garnet-Patterson Auditorium, Jan. 11, 1928. Prod. by the Dixwell [House] Players at Yale Univ. Theatre, New Haven, March 27, 1928, where the author won the Schwab Cup. Also presented by the following groups: Hampton Inst., Hampton, VA, March 25, 1930; Clark Coll., Atlanta, GA, April 10, 1930; Shaw Univ. Players, Raleigh, NC, Oct. 12, 1931; Bishop Coll., Marshall, TX, Jan. 14, 1932; Florida A. & M. Univ., Tallahassee, March 28, 1933; St. Phillip's Jr. Coll., San Antonio, TX, March 16, 1934; and Atlanta Univ. Summer Theatre, Summer 1934. Pub. in two installments in *Crisis*: Feb. 1926, pp. 168–71, and March 1926, pp. 225–28; in *PlaysNegL* (Locke & Gregory, 1927); in *ReadingsNA* and in *Blk. Wrs. of Am.* (Barksdale & Kinnamon,

1972). "Revised Acting Version" (unpub. script) in Schomburg. Also expanded into a three-act play, 1965.

Fall of the Conjurer (1 act, 1925). Received honorable mention in the *Opportunity* Contest Awards, May 1925.

The New Generation (1 act, 1926). Unpub. script in Moorland-Spingarn.

The Bootblack Lover (folk drama, 3 acts, 1926). A young woman is in love with a bootblack who is looked down upon by her family and friends because of his lowly profession. Won first prize in the *Crisis* Contest Awards, Oct. 1926. Unpub. scripts in Moorland-Spingarn and Hatch-Billops.

The Chasm (c. 1926). Written in collaboration with EDWARD CHRISTOPHER WILLIAMS. Prod. by the Krigwa Players of Washington, DC, at Dunbar High School, Washington, around 1926. Unpub. script in Moorland-Spingarn.

The King's Dilemma (children's play, 1 act, 1926). Set in the last kingdom of the world's domain, this play concerns the friendship between a young white prince and the black boy whom he chooses as a companion, and the king's efforts to break up the companionship. First prod. in the Washington, DC, public schools, where it won the Public School Prize, May 21, 1926. Pub. in *PLAYS&PAGS* and in *KING'S DILEMMA*.

Rooms for Rent (domestic comedy, 1 act, 1926). An unmarried woman living in a boardinghouse becomes the subject of malicious gossip by the other roomers. Prod. by the Negro Art Players, New York, Dec. 1926. Unpub. script in Schomburg.

Flight of the Natives (drama, 1 act, 1927). Concerns the escape of a number of slaves from a southern plantation, whose flight is threatened by the treachery of a slave informer and the brutality of an oppressive master. First prod. by the Krigwa Players of Washington, DC, at the Armstrong Auditorium, Feb. 11, 1928; and at Douglass High School, Baltimore, May 2, 1930. Pub. in *Carolina Mag.*, April 1927 (Univ. of North Carolina, Chapel Hill); in *PlaysNegL,* and in *BlkThUSA* (Hatch, 1974).

The Idle Head (drama, 1 act, 1927). Concerns the plight of an unemployed, rebellious youth in the Deep South who, in his effort to help his struggling mother, a washerwoman, steals a valuable pin that a white woman has forgotten to remove from her laundry, Pub. in *Carolina Mag.*, April 1929, and in *BlkThUSA*.

The Chip Woman's Fortune (folk drama, 3-act version, 1927). Unprod. version of his one-act play by the same title.

The Wine Seller (folk comedy, 3 acts, 1927). Deals with the problems of a family of bootleggers during Prohibition.

The Peacock's Feather (domestic satire, 1 act, 1928). On the theme of social snobbery among middle-class blacks. Prod. by the Krigwa Players, at Garnet-Patterson Auditorium, Washington, DC, Jan. 11, 1928. Unpub. scripts in Schomburg, Moorland-Spingarn, and Hatch-Billops.

The Black Horseman (historical drama, 1 act, 1929). Glorifies the image of the black hero during a period in Africa's imperial history when great kings ruled magnificent kingdoms and both Rome and Carthage vied to gain power in Africa. Prod. by Shaw Jr. High School, Washington, DC, June 6, 1931; and by the Playground Athletic League, Baltimore, MD, Oct. 12, 1931. Pub. in *PLAY&PAGS*.

The House of Sham (drama, 1 act, 1929). A cautionary tale about a prominent upper-class black family whose extravagant lifestyle and petty social strivings must come to an end as they discover that the father has been engaging in fraudulent business practices and is now being threatened with exposure and financial ruin. Prod. by many high schools during the 1930s. Pub. in *PLAYS&PAGS* and *AmLitNA* (Dreer, 1950).

Antonio Maceo (historical tragedy, 1 act, 1935). Concerns the assassination of the black Cuban revolutionary general who led a successful rebellion against Spain. Pub. in the author's *NEGHIST13*.

In Menelik's Court (historical play, 1 act, 1935). Drama of love and intrigue, set in the palace of Menelik, Emperor of Abyssinia (Ethiopia), in 1898. A young captain of the palace guard thwarts the plan of an enemy group to abduct the Emperor's daughter, and as reward for his heroism wins the princess' hand in marriage. Pub. in *NEGHIST13*.

Attucks, the Martyr (historical drama, 1 act, 1935). Dramatizes the heroism of Crispus Attucks, the escaped slave who is credited with being the first man to be killed in the American Revolution. Pub. in *NEGHIST13*.

The Elder Dumas (historical play, 1 act, 1935). A portrait of Alexandre Dumas père, the prolific French mulatto novelist who is best remembered for such works as *The Three Musketeers* and *The Count of Monte Cristo,* in which the criticism outweighs the praise. Dumas is portrayed as operating a writing factory, supplying the main idea of a book and letting his assistants work on the mechanics, and as taking credit for the creative work of others. Pub. in *NEGHIST13*.

Near Calvary (biblical play, 1 act, 1935). A portrayal of the bravery of Simon, the black man who carried the cross for Christ to Calvary when Jesus was too exhausted to continue. Simon is shown through the eyes of his relatives, who also face danger as followers of Jesus. Broadcast over the Voice of America, July 7, 1936. Pub. in *NEGHIST13* and *KING'S DILEMMA*.

Hope of the Lonely (folk drama, 1 act, 1940s). Concerns the attempts of a Georgia sharecropper and his family to accumulate the money that they need to move ''up North.'' Unpub. script in Hatch-Billops.

Miss or Mrs. (comedy, 1 act, 1941). In a school system where only single women are employed as teachers, a group of gossips try to determine whether one of the teachers is married or single. Prod. by the Bureau of Engraving Dramatic Club, Washington, DC, May 5, 1941. Unpub. script in Hatch-Billops.

SINCE 1950

The Gypsy's Finger Ring (children's play, 1 act, 1956). The gypsy's ring permits children to see into the future. Pub. in *KING'S DILEMMA*. **Man of Magic** (fantasy, 1 act, 1956). Envisions a future race through a character who is neither black nor white. Pub. in *KING'S DILEMMA*. **The New Santa Claus** (Christmas play for children, 1 act, 1956). Portrays a Santa Claus who is different from the one that children have been led to expect. Pub. in *KING'S DILEMMA*. **The Flight of the Natives** (historical drama, 3-act version, 1964). An expansion of his one-act play of the same title (1927). Unpub. script in Hatch-Billops. **The Broken Banjo** (domestic tragicomedy, 3-act version, 1965). An expansion of his one-act play by the same title (1925). **The Visiting Lady** (social comedy, 3 acts, 1967). About a neighborhood gossip who goes from house to house ·spreading her malicious news. Unpub. script in Hatch-Billops.

[NOTE: Unpub. scripts for the following plays (all pre–1970s) are located in the collections indicated: **The Amateur Prostitute** (social comedy, 3 acts). A scheming mother tries to force the son of a prosperous family to marry her daughter. In Schomburg and Hatch-Billops. **Bold Lover** (domestic drama, 1 act). A middle-class black mother tries to coerce her daughter to marry a man she does not love. In Schomburg and Hatch-Billops. **The Brown Boy** (1 act). In Schomburg. **The Curse of the Shell Road Witch** (folk drama, 1 act). Possibly based on ''The Shell Road Witch,'' a short story by M.

Budd, pub. in *Crisis*, June 1914. About superstition and religion among rural blacks. **The Dark Haven** (folk melodrama, 1 act). A black man gets the best of an enemy by trickery. In Schomburg and Hatch-Billops. **Family Discord** (domestic drama, 3 acts). A black youth shocks his family by bringing home a "white" bride, only to discover that she is really black. In Hatch-Billops. **Imp of the Devil** (domestic drama, 1 act). About an incorrigible child. In Schomburg and Hatch-Billops. **The Jail Bird** (1 act). In Schomburg and TC/NYPL. **Joy Rider** (domestic drama, 1 act). The son of a well-to-do family marries his brother-in-law's mistress. In Schomburg and TC/NYPL. **The Man Who Married a Young Wife** (domestic comedy). An old man tricks a young woman into marriage by pretending to be rich. In Schomburg. **The Nude Siren** (domestic comedy, 1 act). About a self-righteous prude whose hypocrisy is brought to light when his secret vice is discovered. In Schomburg and Hatch-Billops. **The Pillar of the Church** (domestic play, 1 act). An overly religious father does not allow his daughter to complete her education. In Schomburg and Hatch-Billops. **A Stranger from Beyond** (folk drama, 1 act). A dying mother is saved by a mysterious stranger who disappears into the night. In Hatch-Billops. **Victims** (folk drama, 1 act). Subtitled "The Deep Regret." A woman borrows some money on the strength of a future job, which she does not get. In Hatch-Billops.]

Other Pertinent Writings:
"The Hope of a Negro Drama," *Crisis*, Nov. 1919, pp. 338–39.
"The Negro and the Stage," *Opportunity*, Oct. 1924, p. 310.
"Propaganda in the Theatre," *Messenger*, Nov. 1924, pp. 353–54.
"Characters," *Opportunity*, June 1925, p. 183.
"The Unpleasant Play," *Opportunity*, Sept. 1925, p. 282.
Introduction to *The Broken Banjo*, *Crisis*, Feb. 1926, p. 167.
"Poetry and Drama," *Crisis*, July 1927, p. 158.
FURTHER REFERENCE: Austin diss. *Blk. World* 4–1975 (Bernard L. Peterson, Jr., "Willis Richardson: Pioneer Playwright," pp. 40–54, 86–88). Hicklin diss. Monroe diss. *Th. of Blk. Ams.*, vol. 1 (Hill).

ROGERS, ALEX C. See Appendix B.

ROSEMOND, HENRI CH. (Chrysostone), Haitian author, who in the mid–1940s was residing in Brooklyn, NY. He was described in a book review in *Crisis* (June 1945, p. 179) as one of the "political exiles from the 'tyranny' of President Elie Lescott," who (in the play cited below) brings "serious charges against the present Haitian administration."

Stage Work:
Haiti Our Neighbor ("A Play in One Act and Twelve Scenes" [subtitle], 1944). Melodrama of Haitian life based on historical facts concerning that country's struggle for independence. Among the aspects of Haitian life covered are political instability and one-man rule, bitter poverty and low standards of living, illiteracy, class and color divisions, and the widespread practice of voodooism. As reviewed in *Crisis* (ibid., p. 180), the reviewer considered the play "neither good theatre nor easy reading as drama," and felt that the playwright's criticisms of Haiti were "rendered less effective by frequent vulgarity and sportiveness." He conceded that "parts are interesting, but the [play] is frequently marred by typographical errors and faulty English." Pub. by the Haitian Pub. Co.,

Brooklyn, NY, 1944; copies in Moorland-Spingarn, Hatch-Billops, and the libraries of Tuskegee Inst., Atlanta Univ., and South Carolina State Coll.

ROSS, JOHN M. (McLinn), University drama professor, director, and playwright, who taught for many years at Fisk University, Nashville, TN, and later at Talladega College, AL, and Arkansas A. & M. College. Born in Boston. Received the A.B. degree from Morehouse College and the M.F.A. from Yale University, where he was the first black to attend the School of Drama and to receive the master's degree in fine arts. Most of his plays were produced at Fisk University, where for many years he was a prominent figure in black educational theatre circles and earned a reputation as a promising playwright. He has served as director and consultant with the Fisk Stagecrafters, the Atlanta University Players, the Woodmont Summer Theatre, and the Hampton Institute Theatre Workshop. He is also credited with having written a textbook on stage lighting.

Stage Works:
Doc's Place (1935). Typescript in Moorland-Spingarn. **Rho Kappa Epsilon** (tragicomedy, 3 acts). Prod. and possibly printed at Fisk Univ., Nashville, TN, 1935. **One Clear Call** (tragicomedy of black life, 1936). Prod. and possibly printed at Fisk Univ., Nashville, 1936. **Strivin'** (satire on the black middle class, 1937). Prod. at Fisk Univ., Nashville, 1937. **Wanga Doll** (Louisiana folk drama, 3 acts [6 scenes], 1945/46). Considered Ross' most successful play. Prod. by the Fisk Univ. Stagecrafters, Nashville, 1945–46. Apparently printed at Dillard Univ., New Orleans, 1954. **The Purple Lily** (1947/48). Prod. by the Fisk Univ. Stagecrafters, Nashville, 1947–48. **The Sword** (tragedy, 1948). Set in the mid–1850s. Prod. at Arkansas A. M. & N. Coll., Pine Bluff, AR, 1948. **I Will Repay** (tragedy, 3 acts, 1963). Prod. at Arkansas A. M. & N. Coll., Pine Bluff, 1963. **House or No House** (satire, 3 acts, 1967). Prod. by Arkansas A. M. & N. Coll., Pine Bluff, 1967. **Aztec Qzin** (tragedy, 3 acts, 1968). Prod. by Arkansas A. M. & N. Coll., Pine Bluff, 1968.

ROXBOROUGH, ELSIE, Promising young playwright and theatrical director of the 1930s. "The daughter of former Senator and Mrs. Charles Roxborough of Detroit, . . . [and] niece of John Roxborough, one of the managers of Joe Louis."—*Crisis,* updated clipping, 1930s. Educated at the University of Michigan. Reportedly the author of several short plays. Directed the Roxanne Players, which produced LANGSTON HUGHES' *Drums of Haiti* (later retitled *The Emperor of Haiti*), around 1937. Hughes wrote that she was "the girl I was in love with then."—*Dark Symphony* (Emanuel & Gross, 1968), p. 194. She reportedly "disappeared, passing for white," around 1938.—Ibid.

Stage Work:
Wanting (1 act, 1930s). Prod. by the Theatre Guild Players, Detroit, MI, 1930s.

S

SAMPSON, JOHN PATTERSON (J. P. Sampson) (1837–?), A.M.E. church-man, public lecturer, and playwright. Elder of the New England Conference of the African Methodist Episcopal Church. Two of his lectures are located in the Schomburg Collection: "The Importance of Evangelical Unity in Sunday School Work, Regardless of Denomination" (not dated) and "How to Live a Hundred Years" (1909). One of the earliest black authors to have a play published in the United States.

Collection/Stage Works:

PLAYS, POEMS AND MISCELLANY (not dated); copy in Schomburg. Contains: **Jolly People** (drama) and possibly one or more additional plays, as indicated by the title.

The Disappointed Bride; or, Love at First Sight (3 short acts [20 pp.], 1883). "One of three extant plays written by Negroes during the nineteenth century."—Belcher, Ph.D. diss. (1945), pp. 327–28. Pub. by Hampton School Steam Press, Hampton, VA, 1883; no copy has been located.

SCHUYLER, GEORGE S. (Samuel) (1895–1977), Prominent radical jour-nalist, author, and satirist. Born in Providence, RI. Educated in the public schools of Syracuse, NY, where he grew up. Dropped out of school at age 17 and enlisted in the U.S. Army, remaining for seven years with the black 25th Infantry, 1912–19, and receiving his discharge as first lieutenant. After a number of odd jobs and living as a hobo, he took a position as asst. editor for the *Messenger*, 1923–28, while also writing freelance columns for the *Pittsburgh Courier*, the *Nation*, and *American Mercury*. Married to Josephine (Schuyler), a white woman, around 1929. Their only child, Phillipa Duke Schuyler, born in 1933, was a composer, pianist, and writer and one of America's best-known musical child prodigies of the twentieth century; she was killed at the height of her fame in an airplane crash in 1967, after which her grieving mother committed suicide, having devoted her life to the nurture of her daughter. George Schuyler wrote two novels, *Black*

No More (a satire on color, 1931), which was adapted as a drama by MELVIN B. TOLSON, and *Slaves Today* (1932); as well as an autobiography, *Black and Conservative* (1966). He died in New York City at age 82.

Stage Work:
The Witch Hunt (anticommunist skit, 5 pp., 1948). A satire of communism, of which Schuyler was a virulent opponent, based on the Witches' Scene in Shakespeare's *Macbeth*. Pub. in *Plain Talk*, Jan. 1948, and in the author's autobiography, *Black and Conservative* (Arlington House, New Rochelle, NY, 1966).

Other Pertinent Writing:
"Ethiopian Nights Entertainment," *Messenger*, Nov. 1924, pp. 342–43.
FURTHER REFERENCE: *Blk. Am. Lit.* (Whitlow). *Crisis* 10–1965. *Neg. Digest* 12–1946. *Our World* 4–1951.

SEEBREE, CHARLES. See Appendix A.

SEILER CONRAD, Playwright, associated with the Negro Youth Theatre, a subunit of the Negro Theatre Project in New York City during the 1930s.

Stage Work:
Sweet Land (social drama, full length, 1937). A drama of "Negro oppression in the Deep South, especially as it affects the lives of sharecroppers."—Adubato, Ph.D. diss. 1978), p. 127. Two black veterans who have served in France during World War I return to their home in the South, hoping to find better conditions after the war. One is a so-called good nigger, who is able to adjust to his former life as a sharecropper without difficulty; the other is more rebellious and attempts to form a sharecroppers' union to improve working conditions for both blacks and whites. After the lynching of the more rebellious veteran, his docile friend is converted and begins to dedicate himself to fighting against racial prejudice in order to make this a "sweet land." Prod. by the Negro Youth Theatre of WPA/FTP at the Lafayette Theatre in New York City, Jan. 1937; dir. by Vanzella Jones. With ALVIN CHILDRESS as the rebellious veteran and Doe Doe Green as his docile friend. REVIEWS AND COMMENTARY: *Brooklyn Eagle* 1–20–1937. *New Masses* 2–2–1937. *NY Sun* 1–20–1937. *NY World Telegram* 1–20–1937.

OTHER PLAYS: **Darker Brother** (1938). Prod. by the Gilpin Players, Cleveland, OH, 1938. **End of the World** (pre–1950).

SÉJOUR, VICTOR (Juan Victor Séjour Marcon et Ferrand) (1817–1874), French mulatto actor, poet, and playwright. Born in New Orleans, LA, the son of a black father from Santo Domingo and a Creole quadroon mother. His father owned a cleaning establishment. Victor was educated at Saint Barbe Academy, where he demonstrated an exceptional talent for writing poetry, and at age 17 was invited to read one of his original poems before the (Creole) Society of Artisans. His parents sent him to France to continue his formal education, where he published his first poem in 1841, at the age of 24—a heroic poem entitled "Le Retour de Napoleon" (The Return of Napoleon). He was soon admitted into the literary circles of Paris, where he became acquainted with Emile Augier and Alexandre Dumas père, also a mulatto. Because of these friendships he developed a passion for the theatre, and began to turn his talents to acting and the writing of plays. By age 35, he had become one of the most popular French actors and playwrights of the nineteenth century. He wrote more than 21 plays, all in French, the majority produced and published in Paris. He wrote no plays about blacks or mulattoes, or on an American theme, and only one of his plays, **Le Martyre du Coeur** ("The Martyrdom of the Heart," 1858), includes a black character (a Jamaican). One of his short stories, "La Mulâtre" (The Mulatto, 1935), dealt with slavery in the French colonies. Séjour was honored with the title Chevalier, and made a member of the Légion d'Honneur, in 1860. He died in Paris of tuberculosis at age 57.

Stage Works:

Diégarias (drama, 5 acts, in heroic verse, 1844). Revenge play on the theme of anti-Semitism, set in Spain during the sixteenth century, involving Diégarias, a persecuted Jew who has kept the secret of his ethnic identity even from his daughter. First prod. at the Théâtre Français, Paris, opening July 23, 1844. Presented by the New Orleans Theatre, LA, Jan. 18, 1847. Pub. by Imprimérie de Boule, Paris, 1861; copies in Schomburg and TC/NYPL.

La Chute de Séjan ("The Fall of Sejanus") (drama in heroic verse, 5 acts, 1844). Possibly an adaptn. of Ben Jonson's *Sejanus His Fall* (1603). About the power struggle between Tiberius, Emperor of Rome, and his trusted minister Sejanus, who plans a coup against the emperor. First prod. in 1844, presumably in Paris. Pub. in Paris (publisher and date unknown).

La Tireuse de Cartes ("The Lady Who Pulls the Cards," or "The Fortune Teller") (drama, 5 acts, 1850). His second play on the theme of anti-Semitism. The story of an unfortunate Jewish mother whose only daughter has been kidnapped by her prospective husband, who refuses to return her. The mother vows to kill the abductor and reclaim her daughter. The daughter is brought up as a Christian and does not learn of her ethnic heritage until her mother finally locates her. First prod. at the Théâtre de la Porte-Saint-Martin, Paris, opening Dec. 22, 1850. Pub. by Michel Lévy Frères, Paris, 1860; copies in Schomburg, TC/NYPL, and LC. Also pub. in *Théâtre Contemporain Illustré* (Calman Lévy, Paris, 18–?); copy in Schomburg.

Richard III (drama, 5 acts, 1852). Concerns the bloody rise and fall of the diabolical English king whose history was also treated by Shakespeare. Considered to be Séjour's masterpiece and one of his greatest successes. First prod. at the Théâtre de la Porte-Saint-Martin, Paris, Sept. 28, 1952. Presented in the United States by the New Orleans Theatre, May 1, 1853. Pub. by D. Giraud et J. Dagneau, Paris, 1852; copy in TC/NYPL. Pub. as a literary supplement to *La Semaine* (New Orleans, 1853); copies in Schomburg and LC. Also pub. by Michel Lévy Frères, Paris, 1870 (new edition); copy in Schomburg. [See also **Les Enfants de la Louve** ("Children of the She-Wolf," 1865).]

Les Noces Vénitiennes ("Venetian Weddings") (romantic drama, 5 acts, 1855). Dramatizes the enmity and rivalry between two powerful and influential fifteenth-century Venetian families. First prod. at the Théâtre de la Porte-Saint-Martin, Paris, March 7, 1855. Pub. by Michel Lévy Frères, Paris, 1855; copies in Schomburg and TC/NYPL. Also in *Théâtre Contemporain Illustré* (Calman Lévy, op. cit.). Translated into English as *The Outlaw of the Adriatic; or, The Female Spy*, pub. in London by the adaptor, 1859.

L'Argent du Diable (''The Devil's Money'') (comedy, 3 acts, 1856). Coauthor with Adolphe Jaime fils. Presented by the New Orleans Theatre, April 12, 1857. Pub. by Michel Lévy Frères, 1858; copies in Schomburg and TC/NYPL.

Le Fils de la Nuit (''Son of the Night'') (romantic drama, 3 acts [plus prologue in 2 scenes], 1856). Based on an event in Italian history concerning the assassination of a Venetian magistrate and its effect on one of the members of his family. First prod. at the Théâtre de la Porte-Saint-Martin, Paris, opening July 11, 1856. Pub. by Michel Lévy Frères, 1856; copies in Schomburg and TC/NYPL.

André Girard (melodrama, 5 acts, 1858). A story of parental and filial love and loyalty. Pub. by Michel Lévy Frères, Paris, 1858; copy in TC/NYPL. Translated into Portuguese by J. J. Annaya, 1869.

Le Martyre du Coeur (''The Martyrdom of the Heart'') (drama, 5 acts, 1858). Coauthor, with Jules Brésil. The only drama in Séjour's canon that includes a black (Jamaican) character—a trusted servant who is sent to Paris when his master is on his deathbed to deliver an inheritance to the master's estranged daughter. Pub. by Michel Lévy Frères, 1858; copies in Schomburg and TC/NYPL. A Turkish translation was made by Mohammed Fakri, at Constantinople (now Istanbul), in 1854.

Le Paletot Brun (''The Brown Overcoat'') (comedy, 1 act, 1858). A widowed countess, having fallen in love with a young pianist, wishes to drop her current suitor, the Baron, without coming out and telling him so. First prod. at the Théâtre de la Porte-Saint-Martin, Paris, Dec. 28, 1858. Presented in the United States by the New Orleans Theatre, July 9, 1859. Prod. in the United States Off-Bway at the Circle-in-the-Square, Dec. 6–17, 1972, for 15 perfs., on a bill of three one-act plays, in the English translation of *Townsend Brewster, presented under the collective prodn. title *Please Don't Cry and Say No*. Pub. by Michel Lévy Frères, Paris, 1859; copy in Schomburg. Also in *Théâtre Contemporain Illustré* (Michel Lévy Frères, Paris, 1860). Pub. in an English translation by Pat Hecht, in *BlkThUSA* (Hatch, 1974). The English translation by Brewster is unpub.

Les Grands Vassaux (''The Chief Vassals'') (drama, 5 acts, 1859). First prod. at the Théâtre Imperial de L'Odeon, Paris, opening Feb. 16, 1859. Pub. by Michel Lévy Frères, Paris, 1859; copies in Schomburg and TC/NYPL. In *Théâtre Contemporain Illustré* (Calman Lévy, op. cit.).

Compère Guillery (''Comrade Guillery,'' or ''Friend Guillery'') (drama, 5, acts [9 scenes], 1860). Prod. in Paris, presumably in 1860. Pub. by Michel Lévy Frères, Paris, 1860. In *Théâtre Contemporain Illustré* (Calman Lévy, op. cit.).

Les Massacres de la Syrie (''The Syrian Massacres'') (drama, 8 scenes, 1860). First prod. at the Théâtre Impérial du Cirque, Paris, opening Dec. 28, 1860. Pub. by J. Barbré, Paris, 1860?

Les Mystères du Temple (''The Mysteries of the Temple'') (drama, 5 acts, 1862?). Pub. by Calman Lévy, Paris, c. 1862; copy in Schomburg. In *Théâtre Contemporain Illustré* (Calman Lévy, op. cit.). Also in *La Renaissance* (New Orleans, LA, Sept. 21, 1862), along with a favorable critical analysis by Paul de Saint-Victor.

Les Volontaires de 1814 (''The Volunteers of 1814'') (drama, 5 acts [14 scenes], 1862). Erroneously described by the *DAB* as ''the only work [by Séjour] based upon an American theme—that of the brave defenders of New Orleans against the English.'' James V. Hatch points out, in *BlkThUSA* (p. 25), that ''this play does not concern itself with the siege of New Orleans, but with Napoleon in Europe.'' T. A. Daley, writing in *Phylon* (1st qtr. 1943, pp. 13–16), states that ''Séjour's 'volunteers' were the good French peasants . . . who voluntarily sacrificed themselves to cover Napoleon's retreat across the

Rhine in 1814 when he was hard pressed by the Austrians and Prussians.'' First prod. at the Théâtre de la Porte-Saint-Martin, Paris, opening April 22, 1862. Pub. by Michel Lévy Frères, 1862; copy in Schomburg. In *Théâtre Contemporain Illustré* (Calman Lévy, op. cit.).

Le Marquis Caporal (''The Marquis Corporal'') (drama, 5 acts [17 scenes], 1864). First prod. at the Théâtre de la Gaiété, Paris, opening Oct. 13, 1864. Pub. by Michel Lévy Frères, Paris, 1865; copy in Schomburg.

Les Fils de Charles Quint (''The Sons of Charles the Fifth'') (drama, 5 acts, 1865). One of his greatest successes. Prod. (no record of theatre or date). Pub. by Michel Lévy Frères, Paris, 1865; copy in TC/NYPL. In *Théâtre Contemporain Illustré* (Calman Lévy, op. cit.).

Les Enfants de la Louve (''Children of the She-Wolf'') (drama, 5 acts, with a prologue, 1865). Coauthor with Théodore Barrière. Based on Shakespeare's *Henry VI, Part III*. Although written 13 years after his *Richard III* (1852), this play deals with political events leading directly to those of the earlier work, including the development of the character of Richard III. Pub. by Michel Lévy Frères, Paris, 1865; copies in TC/NYPL and Schomburg. In *Théâtre Contemporain Illustré* (Calman Lévy, op. cit.).

La Madone des Roses (''The Madonna of the Roses,'' or ''Our Lady of the Roses'') (drama, 5 acts, 1868). Coauthor with Théodore Barrière. First prod. at the Théâtre de la Gaiété, Paris, opening Dec. 5, 1868. Pub. by Michel Lévy Frères, Paris, 1869; copy in Schomburg. Also in *Théâtre Contemporain Illustré* (Calman Lévy, op. cit.).

OTHER STAGE WORKS: **Le Vampire** (''The Vampire'') (fantastic drama, 5 acts, 1874) and **Cromwell** (drama, 5 acts, 1874). Both contracted for prodn. at the Gaiété, Paris, in 1874, but were cancelled because of the author's death.

FURTHER REFERENCE: *DANB*. *Neg. Hist. Bull.* 5–1942 (A. E. Perkins, ''Victor Séjour and His Times,'' pp. 163–66). *Phylon* 1st qtr. 1943 (T. A. Daley, ''Victor Séjour,'' pp. 5–16). E. B. Young diss.

SHIPP, JESSE A. See Appendix B.

SILVERA, FRANK (Alvin) (1914–1970), Distinguished producer and director of stage, screen, and broadcasting, who has been called ''An 'Everyman' of the Theatre'' because of ''his ability to portray a wide range of parts far beyond the racial stereotypes,'' including ''Mexicans, Spaniards, Italians as well as white and black Americans.''—*Great Negroes Past and Present* (Adams, 1964), p. 134. Born in Kingston, Jamaica, B.W.I. Educated at Boston High School in Massachusetts, graduating in 1934; Northwestern Law School, 1934–35; the Old Vic School in London, 1948; and the Actors' Studio in New York City, 1950. Associated with the Boston Federal Theatre, with which he appeared in 30 productions, 1935–39, and the New England Repertory Theatre, 1939–40. During World War II, he wrote and directed radio shows while stationed at the Great Lakes Naval Training Station. Later appeared in the American Negro Theatre's production of *Anna Lucasta* on Broadway, 1945, and in London, 1947–48. His acting credits, too numerous to list in full, include: stage performances in *A Hatful of Rain, Camino Real,* and *King Lear*; screen appearances in *Mutiny on the Bounty, The Magnificent Seven,* and *Viva Zapata*; radio performances in such shows as *Perry Mason, Counterspy*, and *Two Billion Strong;* and television appearances on *The High Chaparral, Captain Video*, and *The Untouchables*. Throughout his varied and integrated show business career, Silvera maintained an active interest in black theatre. He produced and directed *James Baldwin's *Amen Corner*, which opened at the Robertson Playhouse in Los Angeles on March 4, 1964, and moved to Broadway in New York on June 9, 1964. He was also a member of the board of directors of the New York–based New Playwrights Company, and founder of the Theatre of Being in Los Angeles. He taught for two semesters at California State College in Los Angeles. Member of Actors Equity Association, with service on Equity's Ethnic Committee; American Federation of Theatre and Radio Artists (AFTRA); and Screen Actors Guild (SAG). Died of accidental electrocution, while working on a garbage disposal at his home in Pasadena, CA, at age 56.

Stage Work:
Unto the Least ("A Drama of Negro Life" [subtitle], 3 acts [4 scenes], c. 1938). Afro-American adapt. of Gorki's *The Lower Depths*, depicting the miserable lives of a group of social outcasts, in this version impoverished blacks. Apparently written for prodn. by the Boston WPA Federal Theatre, but was not prod. Unpub. script (Boston, c. 1938) in Schomburg.

Other Pertinent Writing:
"Toward a Theatre of Understanding," *Neg. Digest*, April 1969, pp. 33–35.
FURTHER REFERENCE: *Biog. Encyc. & Who's Who* (Rigdon). *DirBlksPA* (Mapp).

SILVERA, JOHN, Actor and playwright, who was active with the Federal Theatre Project in New York City during the 1930s. His writing has appeared in *Crisis* (see below).

Stage Work:
Liberty Deferred ("living newspaper" chronicle, full length, 1938). Coauthored with ABRAM HILL. Documentary of the history of the black man in America, from slavery to the 1930s. Commissioned by the Federal Theatre and completed in 1938, but never prod. Unpub. scripts in TC/NYPL and FTP/GMU. [See also Hill's entry.]

Other Pertinent Writing:
"Still in Blackface," *Crisis,* March 1939, pp. 76–77, 89.
FURTHER REFERENCE: *NegPlaywrs* (Abramson).

SINCLAIR, PAUL. See Appendix A.

SISSLE, NOBLE. See Appendix B.

SMITH, J. AUGUSTUS (also known as Augustus Smith, Gus Smith, J. A. Smith, and even erroneously as Augustus J. Smith) (1891–1950), Actor, director, producer, and playwright, who in 1936 became one of the three black directors of the Harlem Unit of the WPA Federal Theatre Project (FTP), after John Houseman and Orson Welles left the unit. Born in Gainesville, FL. Made his stage debut as performer with the Rabbit's Foot Minstrels at age 14; afterwards toured with vaudeville and minstrel shows, including R. L. Scott's Black American Troubadours, 1910, and later with the Black Swan Troubadours, 1922. Appeared in the silent film version of *Uncle Tom's Cabin* (1907). Starred in a three-act play entitled *Going White* (c. 1923) by †FLOURNOY E. MILLER. Prod. the musical *Oh Honey* (1924), in which he also starred and for which his wife, Genee Jones, was director of the orchestra. The couple also performed together in *Hello Dixie* (1925). Wrote three plays during the 1930s, two of which were produced by FTP; also produced and directed *Walk Together Children* (1936), *The Case of Philip Lawrence* (1937), *Conjure Man Dies* (1937), *Haiti* (1938), and *Androcles and the Lion* (1938) for FTP. Performed on Broadway with Canada Lee in *On Whitman Avenue* (1946), and two years later performed in *A Long Way from Home* and *Grandma's Diary* (both 1948).

Stage and Screen Works:

Louisiana (folk drama, 3 acts plus prologue, 1933; also prod. as a film). One of several plays during the 1930s that dealt with the conflict between Christianity and voodoo worship within the black community. In this drama, the pastor of Flat Rock Washfeet Baptist Church has been blackmailed for many years by a tavern keeper who knows that he once served time in prison. When the pastor's niece comes to town, the tavern keeper makes advances to her, knowing that the pastor is helpless to do anything about it. A contest develops between the pastor and Aunt Hagar, a voodoo priestess, to avert the advances of the tavern keeper. As described by *The Best Plays of 1932–33,* "Between the forces of God and those of Aunt Hagar's Voodoo controls [the tavern keeper] is blinded by lightning and sunk in quicksand." Although John Mason Brown liked the play and remarked that "this is the stuff out of which real folk plays can be made" [*AnthANT* (Patterson), p. 60], Hicklin felt that "Mr. Smith [was] not convincing in making the voodoo seem inherent in the lives of the people; thus the triumph over the Baptist beliefs and practices seems forced and superimposed, utilized for sensationalism and bizarre effect rather than for genuine reflection of Negro life in a backward community."—Hicklin, Ph.D. diss. (1965), p. 231. Prod. by the Negro Theatre Guild, at the 48th St. Theatre in New York City, Feb. 27, 1933, for 8 perfs.; dir. by Samuel J. Parks. With the author (Rev. Amos Berry), Laura Bowman (Aunt Hagar), Morris McKenney (Thomas Catt, the tavern keeper), and Edna Barr (Myrtie, the niece). Also adapt. into an all-black film, with Laura Bowman recreating her role as the voodoo priestess, and presumably other members of the orig. cast. COMMENTARY: *AnthANT* (Patterson). *BesPls 1932–33.* Hicklin diss.

Turpentine (social drama, 3 acts [10 scenes], 1936). Coauthored with °Peter Morrell. An exposé of the evils of the southern labor camp system. As described by Fannie Hicklin (Ph.D. diss., op. cit.): "Set in the turpentine camps of Florida, [the play] . . . is the stark revelation of the squalor, the impoverishment, the hunger of an underpaid people coerced by unscrupulous overseers. The workers rebel; labor organizers attempt to gain more fair terms from the owners." Prod. by the Harlem Unit of the WPA Federal Theatre, at the Lafayette Theatre, New York City, June 26–Sept. 5, 1936, for 68 perfs.; dir. by °Em Jo Basshe and the author, who also starred in the prodn. Cast included Muriel McCrory, Louis Sharp, and Alberta Perkins. Also prod. by the Gilpin Players, Cleveland, OH, Jan. 13–18, 1937. No script has been located, although one was reportedly in LC. REVIEWS

AND COMMENTARY: *Arena* (Flanagan). *BesPls 1932–33; 1936–37. Cleveland Plain Dealer* 1–15–1937. Hicklin diss. *Neg&Dr* (Bond). *NegPlaywrs* (Abramson). *NYT* 6–27–1936. *Opportunity* 1–1927. Ross diss.

Just Ten Days (melodrama, full length, 1937). Deals with black poverty and homelessness during the Depression. According to Ronald Ross (Ph.D. diss., 1972, p. 87):

The plot . . . focused on the plight of a black family which faced eviction from their home unless they were able to raise seventy-five dollars in "just ten days." The Joneses . . . had inexplicably borrowed money from an old nemesis (also black) and . . . had turned over the mortgage as collateral on the loan. Finally rescued in the end by charitable neighbors, the Joneses escape [from their predicament].

Prod. by the mobile theatre division of the Harlem Unit of the New York FTP, "which toured the streets of Harlem where thousands of Negro children awaited to be entertained" (Ross, p. 27). Toured for one month, from Aug. 10 to Sept. 10, 1937. No extant script.
FURTHER REFERENCE: Hicklin diss. *NegPlaywrs* (Abramson). Ross diss.

SPENCE, EULALIE (1894–1981), High school teacher, pioneer playwright, and drama director of the 1920s and 1930s. Born on the island of Nevis in the British West Indies. Immigrated to the United States in 1902 with her father and seven sisters, establishing residence in Brooklyn, NY. Attended Wadleigh High School and completed the Normal Dept. of the New York Training School for Teachers. Took courses in English and speech during the 1920s at the College of the City of New York (CCNY) and Columbia University, where she studied playwriting under Pulitzer Prize–winning playwright Hatcher Hughes. Later received the B.A. in speech from Teachers College in 1937 and the M.A. in speech from Columbia University in 1939. Also was a student at the short-lived National Ethiopian Art Theatre School in 1924. Taught speech and directed the dramatic society at the Eastern District High School in Brooklyn until her retirement; one of her most successful students was director Joseph Papp of the New York Shakespeare Festival Public Theatre. Directed the Dunbar Garden Players at St. Mark's Church in New York, 1929. Wrote many one-act plays of domestic life, several of which were awarded prizes by *Crisis* and *Opportunity* magazines in their annual literary contests. Won the Samuel French prize for **Fool's Errand,** the best unpublished play in the National Little Theatre Tournament of 1927. Active with the Krigwa Players' Little Negro Theatre, which produced several of her plays. Died in New York at age 87.

Stage and Screen Works:
Brothers and Sisters of the Church Council (c. 1920).

Being Forty (comedy, 1 act, 1924). Prod. by the National Ethiopian Art Players at the Lafayette Theatre, Oct. 15, 1924, on double bill with ELOISE BIBB THOMPSON's *Cooped Up*. Prod. by the Bank Street Players at the Robert Treat School, Newark, NJ, April 29, 1927.

Foreign Mail (comedy, 1 act, 1926). Winner of second prize in the *Crisis* Contest Awards, Oct. 1926. Prod. by the Krigwa Players in New York City at *Crisis* magazine's

"Prize Night," Oct. 25, 1926, and at the 135th St. Library Theatre for 3 perfs., Jan. 7, 19, and 24, 1927; dir. by CHARLES BURROUGHS. Also presented by the same group, for 3 additional perfs., April 20, 25, and 27, 1927. Pub. by Samuel French, New York, 1927.

The Starter ("A Comedy of Harlem Life" [subtitle], 1 act, 1926). An idealistic young man, who works as an "elevator starter," attempts to propose on a Harlem park bench to his more realistic sweetheart; but he gets cold feet when she begins to talk about the practical financial responsibilities of married life. Tied for third place in the *Opportunity* Contest Awards, June 1927. Apparently prod. by a number of amateur groups following its publication in *PlaysNegL* (Locke & Gregory, 1927).

Her (drama, 1 act, 1927). Prod. by the Krigwa Players at the 135th St. Library Theatre in Harlem, for 3 perfs., Jan. 7, 19, and 24, 1927; again presented April 20, 25, and 27, 1927; dir. by Charles Burroughs.

(The) Fool's Errand (comedy, 1 act, 1927). An unmarried woman is assumed to be pregnant by the busybody members of a church auxiliary because someone has discovered baby clothes among her personal possessions. First prod. by the Krigwa Players, New York, for 3 perfs., April 20, 25, and 27. Also presented at the National Little Theatre Tournament, held at the Frolic Theatre, New York City, May 2, 1927, where it won the Samuel French prize of $200 as the best unpub. play in the tournament. This prize was accepted by W.E.B. DuBOIS to pay for prodn. expenses and was not received by Spence. The resulting dispute led to the demise of the Krigwa Players, possibly preventing Spence from having any of her plays published by *Crisis* magazine. Pub. by Samuel French, New York, 1927, as a result of winning the national tournament.

The Hunch (comedy of Harlem life, 1 act, 1927). A young woman about to be married to a man whom she has only recently met learns from a former suitor that her sweetheart is already married; instead of expressing her gratitude, she vents her hatred upon her informer, accusing him of spoiling her happiness. Won second prize in the *Opportunity* Contest Awards, June 1927. Performed by the Krigwa Players of Washington, DC, June 1927. Pub. in *Carolina Mag.*, May 1927.

Undertow (melodrama, 1 act, 1927). Domestic triangle, set in Harlem, involving a confrontation among a husband, his wife, and the other woman, who has borne an illegitimate child by the husband. This confrontation leads to the accidental killing of the wife. Won third prize, jointly with the author's **Hot Stuff** (below), in the *Crisis* Contest Awards of 1927. Pub. in *Carolina Mag.*, April 1929, and in *BlkThUSA* (Hatch, 1974).

Hot Stuff (1 act, 1927). Won third prize, jointly with the author's **Undertow** (above), in the *Crisis* Contest Awards of 1927, and in *Wines in the Wilderness* (Brown-Guillory, 1990).

Episode (domestic comedy, 1 act, 1928). A lonely wife yearns for her husband's companionship, but he is more interested in sports and playing his cornet. Pub. in *The Archive,* April 1928, and in *Wines in the Wilderness* (Brown-Guillory, 1990).

La Divina Pastora (drama, 1 act, 1929). Set in Trinidad, this play concerns a blind woman, about to be married, who seeks a cure at the shrine of the Lady of a Thousand Miracles. Prod. by the Lighthouse Players of the New York Assn. for the Blind, at the Booth Theatre, March 1929.

The Whipping (comedy, 3 acts, 1934; also a screenplay, 1934). Dramatization of a novel by Roy Flannagan. Concerns a southern woman who gains fame as a result of publicity that she has been whipped for misconduct by the Ku Klux Klan. Sched. for prodn. by Century Play Co. in Bridgeport, CT, but did not open. Rewritten as a screenplay and sold to Paramount Pictures for $5,000 in 1934. Prod. under the title *Ready to Love,* starring Ida Lupino and Richard Arlen, with locale changed to New England during the time of the Puritans, and the stocks and ducking pond substituted for the original whipping.

Other Pertinent Writings:
"A Criticism of the Negro Drama," *Opportunity,* June 1928, p. 180; *Carolina Mag.,* April 1929.
"Negro Art Players in Harlem," *Opportunity,* Dec. 1928, p. 381.
FURTHER REFERENCE: Austin diss. Monroe diss. *List of Negro Plays* (FTP). Taped interview in Hatch-Billops.

STREATOR, GEORGE, Journalist and playwright. Former business manager, then managing editor, of *Crisis* magazine, 1933–34. (He resigned with W.E.B. DuBOIS in 1934.) While at *Crisis,* Streator wrote the two plays cited below as well as drama reviews of *Four Saints in Three Acts,* the all-black production of Gertrude Stein's opera (*Crisis,* April 1934) and of *Stevedore,* a militant labor play of the 1930s, which starred Leigh Whipper and Rex Ingram (*Crisis,* July 1934). In the early 1950s, Streator was editor of the *Pilot,* an official publication of the National Maritime Union.

Stage Works:
New Courage and A Sign (two very short 1-act plays, 1934). Both deal with racial prejudice in New Jersey. **New Courage** concerns the reactions of white passengers to integrated seating on a Jersey City bus. A lone black woman passenger, seated next to a white man, is heckled throughout her trip by the other white passengers. When she reaches her stop, she courageously takes down the bus driver's number before alighting. **A Sign** concerns a white clergyman's condoning of the recent lynching of a black man in order to curry favor with the state's racist governor and to please the southern element of his congregation. He considers the lynching "a sign that God will and does punish," and plans to make this the text of his Sunday sermon. Both plays pub. on the same page in *Crisis,* Jan. 1934, p. 9.

Other Pertinent Writings:
See biographical sketch above.

T

TANNER, WILLIAM H. See Appendix A.

THOMPSON, ELOISE BIBB (Eloise A. Bibb) (1878–1928), Pioneer playwright, screen-scenarist, poet, and short story writer. Born in New Orleans, the product of a middle-class family; her father was a United States Customs inspector. Attended Oberlin College's Preparatory Academy (1899–1901), after which she taught for two years in the public schools of New Orleans, 1901–3. Received the B.A. in 1907 from Howard University's Teachers' College, after which she became head resident at Howard's Social Settlement House, 1908–11. Her first book of poetry, *Poems,* was published in 1895 by Monthly Review Press of Boston, the same press that published her good friend ALICE DUNBAR-NELSON's first book. Married Noah Davis Thompson, a devout Catholic widower with one son, in Chicago, IL, Aug. 4, 1911; her husband, a journalist, had previously been married to the daughter of John H. Murphy, owner of the Baltimore *Afro-American* newspaper. The newly married couple moved to Los Angeles, where Noah pursued his journalism career and Eloise continued to write and publish her poetry and articles in a Catholic periodical, *Tidings,* and in other magazines and newspapers on the West Coast. By the 1920s, her writings were being published in *Opportunity* magazine, and she had written a number of plays that were produced in Los Angeles, Chicago, and New York City. The couple moved to New York City in 1927, where Noah became business manager of *Opportunity.* Eloise died the following year at the age of 50.

Stage and Screen Works:

A Reply to the Clansman (film scenario for a full-length feature, 1915). A rebuttal to the film *The Birth of a Nation* (1915) by D. W. Griffith, which had been based on the racist play *The Clansman* (1905) by Rev. Thomas Dixon, a justification of the actions and attitudes of the Ku Klux Klan. Submitted for production consideration to Griffith, who thought the scenario "to be good box office attraction as well as a good story.

However, after saying he would produce the film with a $500,000 budget, Griffith later reneged on his oral commitment.''—*Black World,* April 1976, pp. 33–34. Also submitted to Cecil B. DeMille, who ''stated that it would not be good box office even though it was a good story.''—Ibid. Unprod.

A Friend of Democracy (1920).

Caught (drama, 1 act, 1920). Prod. by the Playcrafters, at the Gamut Club, Los Angeles, 1920. Prod. by the Ethiopian Folk Players, Chicago, 1925. COMMENTARY: *BesPls 1925–26.*

Africanus (drama, 1 act, 1922). Prod. by the Frank Egan Dramatic School, at the Grand Theatre, Los Angeles, 1922.

Cooped Up (domestic drama, 1 act, 1924). A love-smitten roominghouse keeper attempts to break up the marriage of a newlywed couple who are roomers in her establishment in order that she can win the love of the young husband. She persuades another of her roomers, a local romeo, to make love to the wife, and counsels the young wife to go through with the affair. Thinking that she has succeeded in her duplicity, the roominghouse keeper confesses her love to the husband, who spurns her. The young couple are reunited before the proposed affair can take place. Received honorable mention in the *Opportunity* Contest Awards of 1925. Prod. by the National Ethiopian Art Players, at the Lafayette Theatre, Oct. 15, 1924, and by the Ethiopian Art Players in Chicago, 1925. Prod. by the Intercollegiate Association, at the Imperial Elks Auditorium in Harlem, May 5, 1926; and by the New Negro Art Theatre, at the Lincoln Theatre, in Nov. 1928. COMMENTARY: *Messenger* 11–1924.

FURTHER REFERENCE: *AfrAmWW* (Shockley, 1988). Austin diss. *Opportunity* 2–1925.

THURMAN, WALLACE (1902–1934), Novelist, magazine editor and founder, playwright, and film scenarist, whom the *DANB* has called ''a kind of *enfant terrible* of the Harlem Renaissance.'' Born in Salt Lake City, UT, where he finished high school and was a premedical student at the University of Utah (1919–20). After spending a few years in Los Angeles writing for a black newspaper and trying to establish his own magazine, the *Outlet* (which failed after six months), he came to New York in 1925, realizing that an important literary movement was taking place that he wished to become a part of. He became acquainted with the important artists and writers who were at the center of the movement, and soon found himself one of their number. He supported himself by taking a job as reporter and editor for the *Looking Glass,* a short-lived periodical in which he published his adverse criticism of Alain Locke's *The New Negro* (1925), one of the landmark literary anthologies of the renaissance, in which the work of many important writers was included. It was this criticism that began to alienate him increasingly from the more conservative Harlem literati, whom he disparagingly called the ''Niggerati,'' a term of his own coinage. Among the many magazines with which Thurman was associated during his short life were the *Messenger* (a radical monthly, as editor, in 1926, where he published some of his early work and that of LANGSTON HUGHES, ZORA NEALE HURSTON, and others), *The World Tomorrow* (a liberal white monthly, as circulation manager, in 1926), *Fire!!* (an experimental quarterly that he cofounded in 1926, devoted to the work of the younger black artists, which published only one highly controversial issue), *Harlem* ("a forum of Negro life," which he cofounded and published at his own expense in 1928, and which expired after only two issues), and *True Story* magazine (and other McFadden publications, for which he worked briefly as a ghost-writer in 1929). He also contributed articles to *New Republic, Independent, Bookman,* and *Dance Magazine.* In 1929 his "instant success" finally came with the Broadway production of his best-known play, **Harlem,** and the publication of his first novel, *The Blacker the Berry,* about the divisive color complexes within black society. [It should be noted at this point that Thurman was very dark-skinned, and that much of his disdain for "black society" sprang from what he perceived to be its rejection of him because of his color. His novel, which drew its title from a well-known Negro aphorism, "The blacker the berry, the sweeter the juice," is largely autobiographical.] It was the publication of this novel that brought Thurman into a long association with the Macaulay Publishing Company, where he became its first black reader and eventually its first black editor-in-chief. Macaulay also published his two other novels, *Infants of the Spring* (1932) and *The Interne* (1932), written in collaboration with °A. L. Furman, a relative of the publisher. It was his editorial position at Macaulay, coupled with his earlier work with McFadden Publications, that also led to Thurman's writing two film scenarios for Foy Productions Ltd., which were made into Hollywood "B" movies in 1934, for which he received a large sum of money and even went to Hollywood for lengthy story discussion sessions. However, because of his rather hectic lifestyle, which included excessive drinking of gin, these sessions in Hollywood proved too exhausting, and it was discovered that he had a terminal case of tuberculosis from which he collapsed in June 1934. He was hospitalized for the final six months of his life in the incurable ward of City Hospital on New York's Welfare Island, a place which he despised and about which he had written disparagingly in *The Interne.* He died on December 22, 1934, at age 32.

Stage Works:

Harlem // Orig. titles: **Cordelia the Crude** and **Black Belt** ("A Melodrama of Negro Life in Harlem" [subtitle], 3 acts, 1929). By Wallace Thurman in collaboration with °William Jourdan Rapp. Based on Thurman's short story, "Cordelia the Crude, a Harlem Sketch," published in the single issue of the short-lived periodical *Fire!!* (1926). This play combines many of the persistent themes found in the literature of the Harlem Renaissance, including the devastating effect of the Depression on the black family; the color and ethnic prejudices among blacks; the migration of blacks from the South to find a better life; and the portrayal of Harlem as both a romantic, wild, and exotic playground and as a den of debauchery in which are found gambling, racketeering, prostitution, sexual promiscuity, drinking, drugs, and murder. The plot concerns an impoverished South Carolina family, the Williamses, who migrate to Harlem, where they hope to find happiness and opportunity, but are forced instead to give "rent parties" in order to survive. Their daughter, Cordelia, succumbs to the corrupting influence of wild city life and becomes involved with a West Indian and then with a racketeer, who is eventually murdered. At the end of the play, after the murder is solved, Cordelia continues to pursue her wild life. First prod. on Broadway at the Apollo Theatre [not to be confused with the Apollo Theatre in Harlem], opening Feb. 20, 1929, for 93 perfs.; staged by °Chester Erskin. With Isabell Washington (Cordelia Williams), Billy Andrews (the racketeer), Richard Landers (the West Indian), Inez Clough (Ma Williams), and LEW PAYTON (Pa Williams). The Broadway company moved from the Apollo to the Times Square Theatre on 42nd St., April 29, 1929, but went on strike the following day because of verbal disputes, and on May 11, 1929, the show was closed. A second company, which had been formed earlier, took the show on the road, and returned to Broadway at the Times Square Theatre on 42nd St., Oct. 21, 1929, for 16 perfs. Unpub. script in JWJ/ YUL. REVIEWS AND COMMENTARY: *BesPls 1928–29; 1929–30*. Monroe diss. Hicklin diss. *Neg&Dr* (Bond). *NegPlaywrs* (Abramson). *NY Age* 9–1–1928. *NYT* 2–21–1929; 3–3–1939. *Sat. Rev. of Lit.* 6–22–1940. *Th. Mag.* 5–1929; 6–1929.

Jeremiah the Magnificent (drama, 3 acts, 1930). Coauthored with William Jourdan Rapp. According to Fannie Hicklin, this play "depicted Northern modes of discrimination and the abortive efforts to eliminate the evil by migration to Africa."—Hicklin, Ph.D. diss. (1965), p. 289. As Hicklin goes on to say:

The Marcus Garvey idea of a back-to-Africa movement as a solution to the race problem is projected in *Jeremiah the Magnificent* (1933). . . . [The] three-act play shows Jeremiah Saunders busy in the promotion of an International Fraternity of Native Sons and Daughters of Africa. . . . A young Negro graduate of Harvard is in sympathy with Jeremiah's organization. However, a conspiring lawyer and a secretary enter the movement for self-aggrandizement. Rapp and Thurman [the authors] thus revealed intraracial problems and universal problems of greed and selfishness simultaneously with the problem of interracial problems. [Ibid., p. 260]

Presented by the Repertory Playhouse Associates, at the Negro Repertory Theatre, New York(?), beginning Dec. 3, 1933. Unpub. script in Schomburg.

Screen Works:
According to Dorothy West (*Blk. World,* Nov. 1970, pp. 84–85), Thurman wrote two film scenarios, both of them made into "B" pictures by [Bryan] Foy Productions Ltd. in 1934: **High School Girl,** "which had a fair run at the Astor," and **Tomorrow's Children,** "a film on sterilization which was generally banned in New York."

Other Pertinent Writings:
"Negro Artists and the Negro," *New Republic,* Aug. 31, 1927, pp. 37–39.
"Nephews of Uncle Remus," *Independent,* Sept. 4, 1927, p. 296.
Further Reference: *The Big Sea* (Hughes). *Blk. World* 11–1970 (Dorothy West, "Elephant's Dance: A Memoir of Wallace Thurman," pp. 77–85). *DANB. Harl. Ren. Remembered* (Bontemps). *NegGen* (Brawley). Primary source materials (including Wallace Thurman Folders) in JWJ/YUL and Schomburg.

TILLMAN, KATHERINE DAVIS, One of the earliest published black American women playwrights, writing between 1890 and 1910. No biographical information has been located.

Stage Works:
Fifty Years of Freedom; or, From Cabin to Congress (drama, 5 acts, 1910) // Orig. title: **Thirty Years of Freedom** (drama, 4 acts, 1893). About the life and accomplishments of Benjamin Banneker, early black astronomer, mathematician, scientist, and inventor,

who was commissioned by President George Washington (at the suggestion of Thomas Jefferson) to lay out the streets of the District of Columbia (the U.S. capital). Unpub. script, **Thirty Years of Freedom,** located in Moorland-Spingarn. **Fifty Years of Freedom,** pub. by A.M.E. Book Concern, Philadelphia, 1910; copy in Schomburg.

Aunt Betsy's Thanksgiving (1 act, c. 1910). A mother who many years earlier abandoned her infant daughter, leaving her in the care of the child's grandmother, returns home as a wealthy woman to share her riches with her daughter and the grandmother who had cared for her. Pub. by A.M.E. Book Concern, Philadelphia, c. 1910; copy in Schomburg.

TOLSON, MELVIN B. (Beaunorus) (1900–1966), Poet, teacher, politician, and playwright. Born in Moberly, MO. Attended Fisk and Lincoln (MO) universities; received his M.A. from Columbia University. Taught English and directed drama at Wiley College (TX) for 20 years. Became professor of creative literature at Langston University (OK), where he directed the Campus Dust Bowl Theatre and served four terms as mayor of Langston. After retiring from Langston in the 1960s, he spent his remaining years in a specially created post in humanities at Tuskegee Institute (AL). Best known as a poet, Tolson received numerous fellowships, prizes, and awards for his poems, which have been widely published and anthologized. His major poems are "Dark Symphony," which won the National Poetry Contest and was subsequently published in *Atlantic Monthly,* and *Libretto for the Republic of Liberia* (commissioned in 1947, published in 1953), for which he was named Poet Laureate of Liberia.

Stage Works:
(All prior to 1950; unpub. scripts reportedly in Manuscript Div./LC)
The Fire in the Flint (drama, full length). Adaptn. of Walter White's 1924 novel by the same title.
Black No More (drama, full length). Adaptn. of GEORGE SCHUYLER'S 1931 novel by the same title.
The Moses of Beale Street ("Negro miracle play," with music, full length, pre–1941). Coauthored with Edward Boatner.
Southern Front (drama, full length, 1947).
Black Boy (drama, full length). Adaptn. of RICHARD WRIGHT's 1945 autobiographical novel.
FURTHER REFERENCE: *DANB. From the Dark Tower* (Davis). *Melvin B. Tolson* (Joy Flesch, 1972). Melvin B. Tolson Papers in Manuscript Div./LC.

TOOMER, JEAN (Nathan Eugene Toomer) (1894–1967), Mulatto poet, short story writer, essayist, novelist, and playwright. Historically significant as one of the most original and influential talents of the so-called Harlem Renaissance. Born in Washington, DC, of a prestigious family; his grandfather was P.S.B. Pinchback, the famous black politician of the Reconstruction who served as acting governor and later state senator of Louisiana. His father, Nathan Toomer, deserted his mother, Nina Pinchback Toomer, while Jean was still an infant. After graduating from Dunbar High School in Washington in 1914, Toomer enrolled at the University of Wisconsin for one semester, where he studied agriculture. (He was rejected for the draft in World War I because of a hernia and weak eyesight.) He enrolled for brief periods at a number of other colleges and universities in Massachusetts and Chicago, studying agriculture and physical training, before attending the City College of New York (CCNY, later CUNY), 1917–18. Began his career in 1918 with the publication of poetry and a variety of other writings in such magazines as *Opportunity, Crisis,* the *Double Dealer, Broom, Secession,* and the *Little Review.* Served for one semester as principal and teacher at a small industrial school in Sparta, GA, where he gathered much of the material for his only published book, *Cane,* a collection of poems, stories, sketches, and an informal drama, contrasting black experience in two vastly different sections of the United States: his native, urban Washington, and the rural South. Although the public reception of his book was disappointing, it was enthusiastically received by the literary and artistic community, and established him as an important black writer—a distinction he deplored, because he did not wish to be identified as a black man. One of his famous proclamations on his racial identity, written in *Essentials* (1931), a privately printed volume of aphorisms and definitions, has been widely quoted: "I am of no particular race, I am of the human race, a man at large in the human world, preparing for a new race." Although Toomer became one of the major celebrities of the Harlem Renaissance, he was still unable to interest publishers in his work, which they considered too avant-garde. During the 1920s, he began increasingly to isolate himself from blacks, forming literary friendships with white writers, among whom were Hart Crane and Waldo Frank. He became interested in mystical philosophy through the writings of Gurdjieff and Ouspensky, and reflected this interest in several of his writings between 1928 and 1931. By the 1930s, he had virtually crossed the color line and was twice married to white women. His first marriage, in 1931, was to Margery Latimer, a novelist and descendant of Anne Bradstreet; Margery died in childbirth in 1933. In 1934, he married Marjorie Content, daughter of a prominent Wall Street broker. Following this marriage, he embraced the Quaker religion and lived with his wife in a Quaker community in Doylestown (Bucks County), PA, where he remained for the rest of his life. He died in complete obscurity in a Philadelphia nursing home at age 73. After his death, a trunkful of unpublished manuscripts was discovered (including plays, novels, poems, and essays), which became the basis of the Jean Toomer Collection housed at Fisk University in Nashville, TN.

Stage Works:

Balo ("A sketch of Negro life" [subtitle], 1 act, 1922). Experimental folk play, dealing with the racial, psychological, and religious nuances of black life in rural Georgia, based on the author's experiences while a teacher there. Considered a less mature work than the author's **Kabnis,** and therefore presumed to be his earliest play. Written 1922. Prod. by the Howard Univ. Players, Washington, DC, 1923–24. Pub. in *PlaysNegL* (Locke & Gregory, 1927) and in BLKTHUSA (Hatch, 1974). COMMENTARY: See Krasny below.

Natalie Mann (drama, 1 act, 1922). Argues for the liberation of young black middle-class women from the conventions and mores of black middle-class society. Inspired by the style and thought of George Bernard Shaw's plays. Written 1922. Unpub. script in the Jean Toomer Collection, Fisk Univ., Nashville.

Kabnis (experimental drama, 1 long act [6 scenes], 1923). Semi-autobiographical play about a black intellectual from the North who searches for his identity in the Deep South, where he has accepted a teaching position. According to Darwin Turner: "Although he has pilgrimaged to the region which he posits for his ancestral home, he cannot identify himself with any Negroes who live successfully in that region. He cannot merge with uneducated Negroes because they discern his cultural dissimilarities." Failing to find intellectual, religious, or romantic fulfillment, Kabnis waits for a revelation from a character named Father John, who lives in a basement and has not spoken for years. Father John is the symbol of the archetypal wise old man, or spiritual ancestor of the black race. When he finally pronounces his long-awaited utterance, Father John says: "O th sin th white folks 'mitted when they made the Bible lie." Thoroughly disillusioned by this mundane pronouncement, Kabnis consoles himself with a night of debauchery and resolves to give up his intellectual pursuits and begin his apprenticeship as a blacksmith. Rejected for prodn. because of its avant-garde style. First pub. in *Broom* (a periodical), 1923. Pub. in the author's collection, *Cane* (1923).

The Sacred Factory (expressionistic drama, full length, 1927). Thematically and stylistically akin to Elmer Rice's *The Adding Machine*. A revelation of the frustrations and unfulfilled lives of the black middle classes, as contrasted with the uneventful and mechanical existence of lower-class blacks. Considered by Darwin Turner (*CLAJ*, June 1967, p. 317) to be Toomer's "most artistically successful drama." Written 1927. Unprod. Unpub. script in the Jean Toomer Collection, Fisk Univ.

The Gallonwerps (expressionistic play, full length, 1928). Rewritten as a drama from an earlier satirical novel by Toomer that had been rejected by publishers. Develops a concept of Gordon Craig (the famous actor-director), who suggested that human actors should be replaced by gigantic marionettes in order that the director can overcome their limitations in achieving his or her artistic ideals. In this play, the Gallonwerps are such giant marionettes, being manipulated by master puppeteer Prince Klondike, an expert practitioner in the art of deception. Not only is he a trickster, but he does it in such a way that his victims enjoy being tricked. The trick that Klondike plays on the Gallonwerps is to kidnap their son from his nurse while the family and others are assembled at a meeting in which Mr. Gallonwerp (the father) is expounding his philosophical ideas—a meeting that Klondike had helped him to arrange. Unprod. Unpub. script in the Jean Toomer Collection, Fisk Univ.

A Drama of the Southwest (realistic drama, 1935). Based on the author's experiences in New Mexico. Unprod. Unpub. script in the Jean Toomer Collection, Fisk Univ.

OTHER STAGE WORKS: Michael J. Krasny of San Francisco State Coll. states that Toomer wrote a play called **Topsy and Eva,** after the characters from *Uncle Tom's Cabin,* which he calls "a later work," and the only other play by Toomer that was prod.—*Neg. Am. Lit. Forum*, Fall 1973, p. 103. Darwin Turner states that Toomer continued to write dialogues after he abandoned writing dramas for stage prodn. His Socratic dialogues were pub. in the *New Mexico Literary Sentinel* in 1937 and 1941. Turner cited another satirical drama by Toomer, about a man who "consoles himself with the sympathetic companionship of a robot who serves as a maid" after the man is deserted by his wife, a typical clubwoman who is addicted to her meetings.—*CLAJ*, June 1967, p. 317.

FURTHER REFERENCE: *CLAJ* 6–1967 (Darwin T. Turner, "The Failure of a Playwright," pp. 308–18). *DANB.* Jean Toomer Papers (1920–50) in Jean Toomer Collection, Fisk Univ. Lib., Nashville, TN. *The Merrill Studies in Cane* (Frank Duncan, ed., Charles E. Merrill, Columbus, OH, 1971). *Negro American Literature Forum* Fall 1973 (Michael Krasny, "Design in Jean Toomer's *Balo*," pp. 103–4).

TOWNS, GEORGE A. (1870–1961), University professor, author, poet, and playwright. Educated at Atlanta University (1894) and Howard University (1900). Taught at Atlanta University 1895–1930, and at Ft. Valley State College, Georgia, 1930–1938. His writings were published in *Phylon* and *Opportunity*.

Stage Work:
The Sharecroppers (social drama, 1930s). According to *The Negro and the Drama* (Bond, 1940, p. 191), Towns' play struck "a dynamic blow at the exploitation of tenant farmers," but was not successful on the stage. Prod. at Ft. Valley State Coll., GA, during the late 1930s. Also presented at the Southern Association of Speech and Dramatic Arts (SADSA), held at Wiley Coll., Marshall, TX, April 24, 1941.
FURTHER REFERENCE: Primary source material in George Alexander Towns Collection, Robert W. Woodruff Lib., Clark Atlanta University Research Center.

TOWNSEND, (Mrs.) WILLA A., Writer of church plays during the 1920s. Apparently resided in Nashville, TN.

Stage Works:
Because He Lives ("A Drama of the Resurrection," 3 parts, 1924). Pub. by the Sunday School Publishing Board of the National Baptist Convention, Nashville, TN, 1925; copy in Moorland-Spingarn.
   A Song in the Night ("Christmas pageant-program for Sunday Schools," music included, 1920s?). "Arranged by Mrs. W. A. Townsend." Pub. by the Sunday School Publishing Board, Nashville, TN, not dated.

TROY, HENRY. See Appendix B.

TURNER, LUCY M. See Appendix A.

TURPIN, WATERS E. (Edward) (1910–1968), English professor, novelist, critic, drama director, and playwright. Born in Oxford, MD. Educated at Morgan State College, and Teachers College, Columbia University (Ph.D.). Taught English at Storer College, WV (where he also coached football), and at Lincoln University, PA, before joining the English faculty of Morgan State College (now University) in 1950, where he was a distinguished professor, author, and scholar until his death in 1968. During this period, he was also asst. director of dramatics and served for two years as chairman of the Humanities Division. Author of three novels: *These Low Grounds* (1937), "a poignant story of four generations of a black family on Maryland's Eastern Shore"; *O Canaan!* (1939), "a realistic treatment of black migration from the South to Chicago during the Great Depression"; and *The Rootless* (1957), "a historical treatment of black slavery as presented on a Maryland plantation in the eighteenth century."—Plot summaries of novels by Nick Aaron Ford, *CLAJ*, March 1969, p. 252. Turpin's scholarly articles and criticism have appeared in *CLA Journal* and *Negro History Bulletin*. Member of the College Language Association (CLA). Recipient of a Rosenwald Fellowship for creative writing.

Stage Works:

Let the Day Perish (domestic drama, 3 acts, 1950s). About the attempts of an impoverished Harlem family to survive during the Depression by resorting to illegal activities. Written for and prod. by the Ira Aldridge Players, Morgan State Coll., Baltimore, during the 1950s; dir. by the author.

St. Michael's Dawn (historical drama, 3 acts, 1950s). About the life of Frederick Douglass. Written for and prod. by the Ira Aldridge Players, during the 1950s; dir. by the author.

Other Pertinent Writing:

"The Contemporary American Negro Playwright," *CLAJ*, vol. 9, 1954, pp. 12–14. **FURTHER REFERENCE:** *CLAJ* 3–1969 (Nick Aaron Ford, "Tribute to Waters Turpin," pp. 281–82).

TUTT, J. HOMER. See Appendix B.

V–W–Y

VOTEUR, FERDINAND, Playwright, who in 1939 was associated with the Rose McClendon Players in New York City.

Stage Works:

My Unfinished Portrait (drama, 3 acts [7 scenes], 1915). Apparently an autobiographical play, which is cited in many sources (incorrectly) as *The Unfinished Symphony*. Pub. by Bruce Humphries, Boston, 1915.

A Right Angle Triangle (drama, full length, 1939). A play about black urban life. Prod. by the Rose McClendon Players' Workshop Theatre, New York, late May 1939.

WARD, THEODORE (Ted) (1902–1983), Prolific pioneer playwright, best known for his **Our Lan'** (1941), one of the earliest plays by a black American playwright to be produced on Broadway, in 1947. The author of more than 30 plays, of which 19 are extant. Winner of an AUDELCO Outstanding Pioneer Award for his contributions to the growth and development of black theatre, 1975. Born in Thibodaux, LA. His father was a schoolteacher and traveling salesman of books and patent medicines. Grew up and received his early schooling in New Orleans and St. Louis, MO. Ran away from home at 13, after the death of his mother, and worked his way to Chicago by doing odd jobs, including bootblack, barber shop attendant, and bellhop. Lived for a while in Seattle, WA, and in Salt Lake City, UT, where he continued his education at the University of Utah. There his writing talents were discovered and rewarded with a Zona Gale Fellowship for creative writing. On this fellowship, he studied for two years at the University of Wisconsin, where he wrote, acted in plays, and was a staff writer at station WIDA in Madison. Returned to Chicago during the thirties as drama instructor for Abraham Lincoln Center. There he wrote his first full-length play, **Big White Fog,** which was first produced by the Negro Unit of the Chicago Federal Theatre in 1938. Moved to New York City during the forties and was one of the founders and executive director of the Negro Playwrights Company. Wrote news and radio scripts for the War Department during World War II. Returned to Chicago in the fifties, where he continued to write, but remained relatively quiescent until the mid–1960s, when interest in his work was revived during the new black theatre movement of that decade. According to *Black World* (Dec. 1967):

After a long silence, playwright Theodore (Ted) Ward has surfaced in Chicago as head of the South Side Center of the Performing Arts, Inc., with the Louis Theater and School of Drama as its locus. Operating under a grant, Ward has leased and refurbished a movie house on Thirty-fifth Street, renamed it the Louis Theater, and programmed a new version of his 20-year-old play, *Our Lan'*, as the opening production. . . . Future productions planned for the new theater include two other Ward plays, *Candle in the Wind* and *Of Human Grandeur*.

Since the sixties, Ward has conducted writing seminars in Chicago and New Orleans, where he was playwright-in-residence at the Free Southern Theatre. In addition to the Zona Gale Fellowship and AUDELCO Outstanding Pioneer awards mentioned, Ward was recipient of a Theatre Guild Award for **Our Lan'**, 1947; Negro of the Year Award, 1947, by the Schomburg Collection of the New York Public Library; Guggenheim Foundation Fellowship for creative writing, 1947; National Theatre Conference Award, 1947–48; Rockefeller Foundation grant, 1978; and DuSable Writers' Seminary and Poetry Festival Award, 1982. Died in Chicago at age 80 after a short illness.

Stage Works:

PRIOR TO 1950

Sick and Tiahd // Alternate title: **Sick and Tired** (drama, 1 act, 1937). Concerns a black Mississipi Delta farmer who strikes a white creditor during an argument concerning his debt, resulting in the creditor's accidental death. The farmer refuses to flee, stating that he is "sick and tiahd" of being cheated and mistreated by "white folks." First prod. at the Abraham Lincoln Center, Chicago, 1938. Prod. at DuSable High School, Chicago, where it won second prize in a citywide contest sponsored by the New Theatre League. Unpub script, revised in 1964, in Hatch-Billops.

Big White Fog (tragedy, 3 acts, 1938). Set in Chicago during the Depression years, this play depicts how members of a black Chicago family who have migrated from the Deep South are frustrated, disillusioned, and eventually destroyed in their attempts to escape poverty, prejudice, and injustice in a white industrial city described metaphorically as "nothing but a big white fog and we can't see no light nowhere!"—Pub. script. According to Fannie Ella Frazier Hicklin (Ph. D. diss., 1965, p. 286): "The play grimly depicts many problems: the temptation of easy money through exorbitant rents and prostitution, the economic difficulties during the Depression, the intra-family conflicts, color consciousness within the race, the appeal of Garveyism [Back-to-Africa Movement] and of Communism in solving the race problems." Considered one of the best black plays to arise out of the WPA Federal Theatre, for which it was written. Prod. by the Negro Unit of the Chicago Federal Theatre, at the Great Northern Theatre, April 7–May 30, 1938. Prod. by the Negro Playwrights Company, at the Lincoln Theatre in Harlem, Oct. 22–Dec. 14., 1940, for 64 perfs.; dir. by Powell Lindsay, and starring Canada Lee. Excerpt (Act III only) pub. in *NegCarav* (Brown et al., 1941). Complete script pub. in

BlkThUSA (Hatch, 1974). REVIEWS AND COMMENTARY: *Blk. Dr.: An Anth*. (Brasmer & Consolo). *Th. Arts* 8–1942; 6–1947. *NYT* 10–23–1940; 5–8–1941. *Opportunity* 6–1938; 1–1941.

Falcon of Adowa (drama, 1938). Set in Ethiopia during the Italian invasion of that country, this play concerns the defection of an Ethiopian who has been collaborating with the Italians. Unpub, script in Hatch-Billops.

Even the Dead Arise (fantasy, 1 act, 1938). Concerns the uprising from their graves of black heroes of the past, who refuse to rest quietly as long as injustice prevails. Prod. Chicago, 1938. Unpub. script in Hatch-Billops.

Skin Deep (drama, 1 act, 1939). Deals with the problems of color prejudice. Prod. Cleveland, 1939.

Our Lan' (historical drama, 2 acts, 1941). Concerns the struggles by a group of freed slaves to settle on some land off the coast of Georgia after the Civil War. They were killed by federal troops when they refused to vacate the land. Written in 1941. One of the most successful black plays of the 1940s, and one of the earliest plays by a black playwright to be produced on Bway. Winner of the Theatre Guild Award, 1947. Prod. by Associated Playwrights, Inc., at the Henry Street Settlement Playhouse, New York, opening Feb. 26, 1947, for one week. Prod. New York, April 18–27, 1947. Prod. on Bway, under the auspices of the Theatre Guild, at the Royal Theatre, New York, Sept. 27–Nov. 1, 1947, for 41 perfs.; dir. by Eddie Dowling. With Muriel Smith, *Louis Peterson, William Vessey, Julie Haydon, J. AUGUSTUS SMITH, and Valerie Black. Prod. by the author at the South Side Center of the Performing Arts, Chicago, 1968, for a 10-month run. Script of the Bway version pub. with extensive commentary in *A Theatre in Your Head* (Rowe, 1960). Script of the revised orig. version pub. in *BlkDrAM* (Turner, 1971). REVIEWS AND COMMENTARY: *Am. Mercury* 1–1948. *BlkDr* (Mitchell). *Crisis* 10–1947. *Freedomways* 3rd qtr.–1947. *Harl. Q.* Fall/Winter–1950. *Phylon* 2nd qtr.–1947. *Sat. Rev. of Lit.* 10–1947. *Th. Bk. of the Yr. 1947–48* (Nathan).

Deliver the Goods (defense propaganda play, 3 acts, 1941). Written in support of America's war efforts during World War II. Concerns the difficulties in getting war supplies to the troops overseas, because of fascists and corrupt labor bosses. Prod. by Greenwich House, New York, 1942. Unpub. script in Hatch-Billops.

Shout Hallelujah! (social drama, 3 acts, 1941). About the tragic conditions of poverty and disease in a West Virginia coal mining town. Apparently pub. in *Masses and Mainstream*, May 1948. Unpub. script in Hatch-Billops.

Of Human Grandeur // Orig. title: **John Brown** (historical drama, 4 acts, 1949; revised and retitled, 1963). The story of John Brown, focusing on his conflicts with members of his family. First prod., under its orig. title, in an arena prodn. by the People's Drama, at Eldridge Street Theatre, New York, 1950. Excerpt (Act I, scene 4 only) pub. under its orig. title in *Masses and Mainstream,* Oct. 1949. Complete unpub. script in Hatch-Billops.

SINCE 1950

(All unpub. scripts in Hatch-Billops.) **Throwback** (drama, 1 act, 1951). A black man kills a white man for molesting his wife. Prod. by the Skyloft Players, Chicago, 1951. **Whole Hog or Nothing** (drama, 1 act, 1952). Black American servicemen, fighting in the South Pacific during World War II, must also combat white racism. Prod. Chicago, 1952. **The Daubers** (drama, 3 acts, 1953). Deals with the problem of drug addiction within an upper-middle-class black family. Prod. by the Experimental Black Actors Guild

(X-Bag), Chicago, 1952, for a two-month run on weekends only. Excerpt (1 scene) in *Blk. Scenes* (Childress, 1971). **John de Conqueror** (folk opera, 2 acts, 1953). Concerns a colony of former Jamaican slaves living in Biloxi, MS, on the Gulf of Mexico. Rather than submit to slavery by whites, they are led into the sea to their deaths by their leader, John the Conqueror. **Madison //** Orig. title and present subtitle: **Creole** (musical, 2 acts, 1956). Adapt. from "The Heroic Slave," a short story written by Frederick Douglass in 1853. Concerns the heroism of a slave leader, Madison, who leads an insurrection aboard the S.S. *Creole*, in which the slaves gain control of the ship and sail to their freedom in Nassau. **Charity** (musical, 3 acts, 1960). The story of Blind Tom, the most famous of the slave entertainers, who was born blind, exploited by his master, and made into a national attraction. **Big Money** (musical comedy, 2 acts, 1961). A man's life is changed drastically, and he is exploited by friends and pursued by the police, after he suddenly comes into possession of a small fortune. **The Bell and the Light** (musical, 2 acts, 1962). A group of slaves who have continued to depend on the good treatment of a benevolent master discover that their only salvation is through freedom. **Challenge** (1 act, 1962). Pub. in *Mainstream,* Feb. and March 1962; copy in Moorland-Spingarn. **Candle in the Wind** (historical drama, 4 acts, 1967). Concerns the events leading up to the murder of a black senator from Mississippi during the Reconstruction period in 1875. Prod. by the South Side Center of the Performing Arts, Chicago, 1969. Prod. by the Free Southern Theatre, New Orleans, 1978, on a grant from the Rockefeller Foundation.

Other Pertinent Writings:
"Why Not a Negro Drama for Negroes by Negroes?" *Current Opinion,* vol. 72 (1972), pp. 639–40.
"The South Side Center of the Performing Arts, Inc.," *Blk. Th.* no. 2 (1969), pp. 3–4.
"Interview with Playwright Ted Ward," *Afrika Must Unite,* vol. 2, no. 15 (1973), pp. 9–11.
FURTHER REFERENCE: *NegPlaywrs* (Abramson). *Freedomways* 1st qtr. 1975 (James V. Hatch, "Theodore Ward: Black American Playwright," pp. 37–41). Hicklin diss. *Pan African J.* Winter 1974. Taped interview (5 tapes) in Hatch-Billops. Theodore Ward Folder in Schomburg.

WASHINGTON, CAESAR G., Playwright, associated with the National Ethiopian Art Theatre in New York City, which grew out of the Ethiopian Art Theatre in Chicago during the 1920s.

Stage Work:
The Gold Front Stores, Inc. (comedy, 3 acts, 1924). About a fraudulent scheme devised by two grocery store owners to swindle a not-too-bright young man out of his money. The drama critic for the *New York Age* (March 8, 1924, p. 6) found considerable fault with the play and criticized the white director, Raymond O'Neill, for "neither understand[ing] Negro life nor the proper handling of a colored cast." Theophilus Lewis, drama critic for the *Messenger* (April 1924, p. 109), praised it as a commendable first effort by a black playwright and termed it "clever in conception but not so cleverly worked out." It was produced by the National Ethiopian Art Theatre and presented at the Lafayette Theatre in New York City, opening March 3, 1924; dir. by O'Neill. Starring Abbie Mitchell and Edna Thomas.

WATTS, AL F. See Appendix B.

WEBER, AMY L., Playwright, associated with the Mansfield Players, whose plays were entered in the National Little Theatre Tournament for two consecutive years, 1927 and 1928.

Stage Works:
Off Col'uh ("Off Color") (1927). Presented by the Mansfield Players in the National Little Theatre Tournament, New York, May 7, 1927; with vaudeville performer Tom Fletcher in the cast.

Wine of Life (1928). Presented by the Mansfield Players in the National Little Theatre Tournament, New York, May 7, 1928.

WELLS, FRANK B., Playwright, associated with the Washington, DC, Federal Writers Project during the mid–1930s. In 1938 he was living in Brooklyn, NY.

Stage Work:
John Henry ("Negro Legend in 9 scenes, Prologue and Epilogue" [subtitle], 1936). A dramatic version of the John Henry legend, based on the research and conclusions of Guy B. Johnson as set forth in his book, *John Henry: Tracking Down a Legend,* with music borrowed "freely from the great body of Negro music to provide additional musical symbolism wherever necessary."—Author, quoted in Ronald Patrick Ross, Ph.D. diss. (1972), p. 193. The plot, as presented by the National Service Bureau in *A List of Negro Plays* (1938), is as follows (capitalization in the original):

JOHN HENRY, a young and passionate slave burning to be free, enlists the aid of supernatural powers to help him purchase his freedom from a plantation OWNER. It is his own ingenuity however, and not black magic, that secures him his freedom. Cheated at the death of the Master, John Henry kills the OVERSEER and escapes. From the ranks of the army to driving steel on the railroad, John Henry finds his ambition to be a free landowning individual eluding him. His career is varied and colorful, living as he does during the time when the Negroes were exploited by Carpetbaggers and consequently so bitterly hated in the South. Eventually he is promised a clear title to a piece of land if he drives steel faster than can a new pneumatic drill. John Henry, in a frenzy of ambition and a spectacular physical exhibition, does beat the machine, but death brought about by overexertion prevents him from collecting the final reward.

Prod. by the Negro Unit of the Los Angeles Federal Theatre Project, where it was "considered by some critics as the most important Negro play since the production of The Emperor Jones fifteen years earlier."—*LA Herald-Express,* Oct. 1, 1936. The production played from Sept. 30 to Oct. 18, 1936. FTP script in the Doheny Lib. of the Univ. of Southern California/Los Angeles. COMMENTARY: Ross diss.

WHIPPER, LEIGH. See Appendix B.

WHITNEY, SALEM TUTT. See Appendix B.

WILLIAMS, CLARENCE. See Appendix B.

WILLIAMS, EDWARD CHRISTOPHER (E. C. Williams; Edward C. Williams) (1871–1929), Washington, DC, educator, librarian, author, and playwright. He was principal of the "M" Street High School in Washington during the second decade of the century. Apparently became librarian of Howard University during the 1920s, and later became librarian at Northwestern University. While at Howard, WILLIS RICHARDSON sought his help in getting some of his plays produced, and Williams put him in touch with Alain Locke and Montgomery Gregory, who were in charge of the Howard Players. At that time, however, according to Richardson, "The President of Howard University was a white man . . . and they couldn't get his consent."—Interview quoted in *BlkThUSA* (Hatch, 1974), p. 233. Nevertheless, Richardson and Williams were able to collaborate on one play, **The Chasm** (1921). Williams is the author of a number of articles in *The Messenger* and *Crisis* magazines.

Stage Works:
The Chasm // title also listed in some sources as *The Chase* (c. 1921). Coauthor with Willis Richardson (see commentary in biographical sketch above). Unpub. script in Moorland-Spingarn.
The Exile (full length [63 pp.], pre–1929). Unpub. script in Moorland-Spingarn.
The Sheriff's Daughter (1 act [14 pp.], pre–1929). "Adapted from the short story by Charles W. Chesnutt."—*Dict. Catalog of the Moorland Collection*. Unpub. script in Moorland-Spingarn. Correspondence with Charles W. Chesnutt is among Chesnutt's Papers in Fisk Univ. Lib.—*Dir. of Afro-Am. Resources* (Schatz, 1970), p. 302.
FURTHER REFERENCE: *Neg. Hist. Bull.* 3–1970.

WILLIAMS, SPENCER (Jr.) (1893–1969), Actor and pioneer motion picture performer-writer-director, best known for his TV role as Andy on the "Amos 'n Andy" series. [Not to be confused, as he often was, with Spencer Williams (1889–1956), the song-writer, musician, and musical comedy composer/lyricist.] Born in Vidalia, LA, across the river from Natchez, MS. Served for nine years in the army during and following World War I (1914–23), traveling extensively in Europe and the Far East. Twice married; the father of one daughter (c. 1921). Went to Hollywood after leaving the service, where in 1928 he got bit parts in *The Thief in the Dark* and *Steamboat Bill, Jr.* In 1929 he worked at the Al Christie Studios as an actor and writer of continuity and authentic Negro dialogue (or, more precisely, Negro dialect) for the Octavus Roy Cohen film comedy series, based on Cohen's stories published in the *Saturday Evening Post* (see specific titles below)—all stereotypical burlesques of black middle-class life, written primarily for white audiences. Appeared in *Georgia Rose* (1930), *The Virginia Judge* (1937), *Bad Boy* (1939), *Toppers Take a Bow* (1941), and a number of °Jed Buell's all-black westerns, including *Bronze Buckaroo* (1928), *Harlem on the Prairie* (1938), **Harlem Rides the Range** (which he cowrote with †FLOURNOY E. MILLER, 1939), and *Two Gun Man from Harlem* (1939). During the 1940s, he wrote, directed, and performed in several serious dramatic films on the black religious experience, which have been of increasing interest to black-genre-film buffs: **The Blood of Jesus** (1941), **Go Down Death** (1944), and **Of One Blood** (1940s); also wrote and directed **Marching On** (a wartime documentary, c. 1945) and **Juke Joint** (a comedy, 1947). Other film acting and directing credits of the 1940's include *A Girl in Room 20* (1945), *Dirty Gertie* *from Harlem USA* (1946), *Beale Street Mama* (1946), and *Jivin' in BeBop* (1947). After the war, he cofounded a school in Tulsa, OK, where he taught radio and photography to veterans under the G.I. Bill. From 1951 to 1953, he performed in the "Amos 'n Andy" television series, playing the role of Andy, the portly, ever-gullible, childlike victim of Kingfish's outlandish moneymaking schemes. After the demise of "Amos 'n Andy," Williams lived on social security and a veteran's pension until his death at age 76.

Screen Works:

Tenderfeet (short film, 1928). Written, dir. by, and starring Williams. Independently prod. by Midnight Prodns., costarring Mildred Washington.

Wrote continuity and dialogue for the following short, two-reel dialect comedies of black bourgeoisie society in the Octavus Roy Cohen film series, prod. at the Al Christie Studios in Hollywood in 1929: **The Melancholy Dame** (about a Birmingham nightclub owner whose wife is jealous of his attentions to one of the entertainers); **Hot Biscuits** (centering around the then-popular game of miniature golf); **Music Hath Charms** (concerning the rivalry between two musicians as to which one shall lead a band); **Brown Gravy** (about the rivalry between two black church choirs in Memphis); **The Lady Fare** (script in LC); **The Widow's Bite; The Framing of the Shrew** (script in LC); and **Oft in the Silly Night**—all costarring Williams. COMMENTARY: *Variety* 12–12–1928. *NY Amsterdam N.* 12–5–1928.

Harlem Rides the Range (black western, 1939). Cowritten with Flournoy E. Miller. About the misadventures of two comic cowboys trying to locate a lost mine. Costarring Miller and Williams.

Son of Ingagi (melodrama, 1940). Script by Williams. A poorly made monster gorilla film. Prod. independently by °Richard B. Kahn, 1940; starring Williams as a stock detective. Incomplete print in LC.

The Blood of Jesus (religious melodrama, 7 reels, 1941). Written and directed by Williams, who stars as a man who has accidentally killed a girl with a shotgun and prays successfully that she come back to life. Independently prod. in Texas by °Alfred Sack on a budget of less than $5,000, 1941; distributed by Ideal Pictures, which billed the film as "undoubtedly the most powerful all-Negro motion picture ever produced."—*Catalog of Ideal Pictures* (1968). Print in LC.

Go Down Death (religious morality, 70 min., 1944). Written and dir. by Williams, who portrays a minister of the gospel persistently plagued by temptations of the flesh. Featured a large cast of amateurs and singers. Independently prod. in Texas by Alfred Sack, 1944; distributed by Ideal Pictures and billed as "Saturday sinners and Sunday saints clash in the battle of Good against Evil."—*Catalog of Ideal Pictures* (1968). Print in LC.

Of One Blood (religious melodrama, feature length, c. 1945). Written and directed by Williams. Similar in theme to *The Blood of Jesus* and *Go Down Death*. The third of seven such religious films made by the author, which were shown at churches and before other community groups throughout the South.—*Ebony,* Oct. 1961, p. 68. Prod. by Alfred Sack, around 1945; costarring Williams as a deaf mute who is in reality an undercover agent for the FBI. Print in LC.

Marching On (World War II doc., c. 1945). About the contribution of black soldiers in the armed forces. Written and directed by Williams. Prod. by Alfred Sack, mid–1940s.

Juke Joint (comedy, feature-length, 1947). Described by Donald Bogle (*Blks. in Am.*

Films & TV, 1988, pp. 123–24) as "a series of skits and routines connected here by a plot which gives each actor a chance to showcase his/her particular talent or aptitude." Written and dir. by Williams. Featuring Williams and July Jones. Prod. by Alfred Sack Amusement Enterprises, 1947. Print in LC.

FURTHER REFERENCE: *BlksB&W* (Sampson). *Blks. in Am. Films & TV* (Bogle). *DirBlksPA* (Mapp). *Ebony* 10–1961. *From Sambo to Superspade* (Leab). *TomsCoons* (Bogle).

WILSON, FRANK (Francis H. Wilson) (1886–1956), Stage and screen actor and singer, pioneer playwright and screenwriter. Born in New York City, the date of his birth usually given as 1891. Worked as a mail carrier in New York City and for 12 years was active in Harlem theatrical circles as an actor, baritone singer, and vaudeville organizer while writing plays for what came to be known as the Lafayette Players. The group, first known as the Anita Bush Players, presented plays at the Lincoln Theatre, 1914/16, then moved to the Lafayette Theatre, where the name was changed. According to Henry T. Sampson (*BlksBf*, 1980, p. 452):

While carrying the mail around Harlem, [Wilson] came across what he regarded as excellent material for black plays. His first dramatic [*sic*] was produced at the Lincoln Theatre on West 135th Street near Lenox Avenue. For three years he wrote an average of one playlet every six or eight weeks for the theatre. . . . Wilson's debut as a legitimate actor was in or about 1917 as a member of the Lafayette Players Stock Company in a play titled "Deep Purple" at the Lafayette Theatre, Seventh Avenue and 131st Street.

His theatrical training apparently came after World War I when he attended a dramatic class organized by Franklin P. Sergent of the American Academy of Dramatic Art; he also studied for three and a half years under Anno Wolter, who took over the work started by Sergent. Wilson entered the professional theatre as a supporting actor with the Provincetown Players, playing in the original stage productions of *The Emperor Jones* (1925), supporting both Charles Gilpin and Paul Robeson; *All God's Chillun Got Wings* (1924); and *In Abraham's Bosom* (1926), in which he succeeded Jules Bledsoe in the leading role, establishing himself as one of the outstanding black actors of the period. Some of his numerous other stage appearances include *Justice* (1920), *Porgy* (1927), *Roll Sweet Chariot* (1930), *Blood Stream* (1932), *They Shall Not Die* (1934), *Memphis Bound* (1945), the American Negro Theatre's productions of *Anna Lucasta* (1946) and *The Washington Years* (1947), *Let My People Free* (1948), *The Big Knife* and *How Long Till Summer* (1949), and *Take a Giant Step* (1953). Among his film credits are *The Emperor Jones* (1933), *The Green Pastures* (1935), *Watch on the Rhine* (1943), and *Beware* (1946). According to musicologist/playwright MAUD CUNEY-HARE, Wilson was "an earnest and serious actor of artistic ideals" as well as "a singer of Negro songs of which he [made] effective use in his own plays."—*NegMus&M* (1936), p. 71. He died in Jamaica, NY, at the age of 70.

Stage Works:

EARLIEST PLAYS: The following dramatic sketches were written by Wilson for prodn. at the Lincoln and Lafayette theatres, between 1914 and 1923, by the acting company that came to be known as the Lafayette Players. Originally known as the Anita Bush Players when they performed at the Lincoln, the group changed its name when they moved to the Lafayette Theatre in 1916: **Back Home Again, Colored Americans, Confidence** [see also next entry], **The Flash, The Frisco Kid, The Good Sister Jones, Happy Southern Folks, The Prison Life, Race Pride,** and **Roseanna**.

Confidence (play of black life, 1 act, pre–1916). According to the *New York Age* (Nov. 1920, p. 6), this play was first prod. at the Lincoln Theatre by the Anita Bush Players, prior to that group's leaving the Lincoln in 1916. Prod. by the Players' Guild, at the Harlem YMCA, Jan. 3, 1920. Prod. by the Lafayette Players at the Lafayette Theatre in Harlem, Nov. 22, 1920. Cast included Edna Lewis Thomas and Lionel Monagas. Prod. by the Acme Players, at the Lafayette Theatre, Harlem, May 12, 1922. Also prod. by other units of the Lafayette Players in Philadelphia, Washington, DC, and other cities.

Sugar Cane // Orig. title **Sugar Cain** (drama, 1 act, 1920; rev. 1926). A beautiful black woman named Sugar is violated by a white man in the Deep South, and subsequently becomes the mother of his child; the play concerns the reactions of the woman's parents, and of the young black man who loves her, to her tragic situation. Written 1920. Won first prize as *Sugar Cain* in the *Opportunity* Contest Awards, 1926. According to John Gilbert Monroe (Ph.D. diss., 1980, pp. 134–35):

When first published in *Opportunity*, . . . the play was titled *Sugar Cain*. In December 1926 it was announced that ''Sugar-Cain'' was being readied for Broadway and would star Abbie Mitchell, Rose McClendon, Evelyn Ellis, Ida Anderson, and Barrington Carter. See *Amsterdam News*, 1 Dec. 1926, p. 10. The play was never produced on Broadway. A revised version of this play was pub. under the title *Sugar Cane*.

Prod. as *Sugar Cain* by the Aldridge Players, at the 135th St. Library in Harlem, July 12, 1926. Pub. as *Sugar Cain* in *Opportunity*, June 1926, pp. 181–84, 201–3. Revised as *Sugar Cane*, and pub. in *PlaysNegL* (Locke & Gregory, 1927).

The Heartbreaker (drama, presumably 1 act, 1921). Prod. by the Lafayette Players at the Lafayette Theatre in Harlem, Jan. 10, 1921. Cast included Edna Lewis Thomas, H. L. Pryor, and Lionel Monagas. Prod. by the Acme Players at the Harlem YMCA, May 25, 1923.

Pa Williams' Gal (drama, 2 acts, 1923). Described by John Gilbert Monroe (op.cit., p. 25), as a ''comedy drama about a death bed promise.'' No other clues to its plot have been located, except ''that the problems of race did not figure significantly in the play.''— Ibid. Prod. by the Lafayette Players at the Lafayette Theatre, Sept. 10, 1923. The cast included Richard B. Harrison, Rose McClendon, and the author in leading roles.

A Train North (drama, 1 act, 1923). Prod. by the Acme Players, at the Harlem YMCA, May 25, 1923.

Color Worship and **Flies** (two 1-act dramas, 1926). Prod. by the Aldridge Players, at the 135th St. Library in Harlem, July 12, 1926.

Meek Mose // Revived as **Brother Mose** (social drama, with music and spirituals, 3 acts, revised as a ''Comedy of Negro Life,'' 1928). Concerns a docile black leader who is highly criticized by his flock for advising them to give in to white demands to move from their homes to a tract of swampland in order to make room for the building of a new factory. Brother Mose is vindicated when oil is discovered on the swamp tract, thus proving the truth of the biblical promise that "the meek shall inherit the earth." First prod. by Lester A. Walton at the Princess Theatre, New York City, opening Feb. 6, 1928, for 32 perfs. The prodn. was historic in that it was the first play prod. on Bway by a black producer. Cast included Charles H. Moore in the title role, J. Lawrence Criner, Laura Bowman, Sidney Kirkpatrick, and Susie Sutton. Went on tour following its Broadway run, after playing one week at the Lafayette Theatre following its regular show. Revived by the WPA, and presented by the Works Division of the New York Dept. of Public Welfare, beginning July 25, 1934, and presented at various locations in New York City, including Central Park. Also toured (or possibly produced by other WPA groups) in Newark, Boston, and Salem, MA. The cast of the New York WPA prodn. included J. AUGUSTUS SMITH alternating with Augustus Jenkins in the title role, Laura Bowman (from the orig. prodn.), Alberta Perkins, and Canada Lee (in his acting debut). Pub. as *Brother Mose* (U.S. National Service Bureau Publication No. 7, mimeographed, 1937). REVIEWS AND COMMENTARY: *BesPls 1927–28. Blk. Manhattan* (Johnson). Hicklin diss. *List of Neg. Plays* (WPA/FTP). *Neg&Dr* (Bond). *NegPlaywrs* (Abramson). *NY Age* 2–11–1928. *NY Amsterdam N.* 2–8–1928. *NYT* 2–4–1928. Ross diss.

The Wall Between (drama, full length, 1929). Sched. for Bway prodn. by Jack Goldberg, but apparently was never prod.

Walk Together Chillun // Also known as **Walk Together Children** (social drama, with Negro spirituals, 3 acts, 1936). A plea for black unity and solidarity, in the context of a labor dispute between upstate New York blacks and a group of southern black workers who have been brought up from Georgia by whites to supply cheap labor. First prod. by the New York Negro Unit of FTP, at the Lafayette Theatre in Harlem, opening Feb. 2, 1936, for 19 perfs., with an attendance of 10,530 people. With J. Augustus Smith and Oliver Foster in the leading roles. Historic in that it was the first FTP prodn. in New York City. REVIEWS AND COMMENTARY: *BesPls 1935–36. List of Neg. Plays* (WPA/FTP). *Neg&Dr* (Bond). *New Masses* 3–1937. *NYT* 2–5–1936. Ross diss.

Screen Works:

Paradise in Harlem (all-black film, feature length presumed, 1939). Based on a scenario by Wilson. Independently prod. by Jack Goldberg, 1939; dir. by °Joseph Seiden. With Wilson, Mamie Smith, Edna Mae Harris, SIDNEY EASTON, Norman Astwood, Alex Lovejoy, George Williams, and Merritt Smith.

Murder on Lenox Avenue (all-black film, feature length presumed, 1941). Based on a scenario by Wilson. Lyrics and music by DONALD HEYWOOD. Independently prod. in Florida by Goldberg, 1941; dir. by °Arthur Dreifuss. With Mamie Smith, Alex Lovejoy, Dene Larry, Norman Astwood, Gus Smith (J. Augustus Smith), Edna Mae Harris, Alberta Perkins, and George Williams.

Sunday Sinners (all-black film, feature length presumed, 1941). Based on a scenario by Wilson. Lyrics and music by Donald Heywood. Independently prod. in Florida by Goldberg, 1941; dir. by Arthur Dreifuss. With Mamie Smith, Norman Astwood, Edna Mae Harris, Alex Lovejoy, Cristola Williams, Sidney Easton, Earl Sydnor, Gus Smith, and Alberta Perkins.

Other Pertinent Writing:

"The Theatre Past and Present," *NY Amsterdam News,* June 15, 1932.

FURTHER REFERENCE: *BlkDr* (Mitchell). *BlkMagic* (Hughes & Meltzer). *BlksBf* (Sampson). *Contemp. Am. Playwrs.* (Mantle). *DirBlksPA* (Mapp). Primary source materials in TC/NYPL, LC, and Schomburg (which also includes a Frank Wilson Folder).

WOOD, CHARLES WINTER (1870–1952), Actor, director, playwright, best known for his Broadway portrayal of "de Lawd" in *The Green Pastures* (1935), in which he replaced Richard B. Harrison when the noted actor became ill and subsequently died during the run of the play on Broadway. Born in Nashville, TN. Educated at Beloit College (B.A. 1895, M.A. 1898), Chicago Theological Seminary (D.D. 1898), Chicago University (1899), and Columbia University (1901–4). Taught at Tuskegee Institute (AL), 1898–1901, where he also directed the Tuskegee Players and "served Tuskegee as assistant to Booker T. Washington and Robert E. Morton [Washington's successor] for more than twenty-eight years." A well-known actor and dramatic reader, he served frequently in plays and recitals in Chicago and New York and at Tuskegee. He is credited with having organized in Chicago, in 1883, "the first Colored Professional Stock Company in America. It was composed entirely of Colored men and women versed in the art of drama and played Richard III, Hamlet and other Shakespearean plays."—*WWCA 1930–32*. This information is at least partly in error, since Wood was only 13 years old in 1883. [The first professional black stock company of record was indeed established in Chicago—the Pekin Stock Company of record, established by Robert Motts at his Pekin Theatre in 1906. There is no record, however, that Wood was associated with the Pekin Theatre.]

Stage Works:
College Life and **In Defense of Him** (both pre–1928). Prod. at Tuskegee Inst., Beloit Coll., and in Atlanta, GA.—*WWCA 1928–29*.

WOODS, G. A. See Appendix A.

WRIGHT, RICHARD (1909–1960), Major American novelist, short story writer, essayist, and autobiographer, best known for his naturalistic novel, *Native Son* (1940), which has become a classic of American literature. Also a playwright, screenwriter, and radio scriptwriter. Born on a plantation near Natchez, MS. His father deserted the family when Richard was six years of age, leaving him and his younger brother in the care of his sickly mother. Although the details of his early life are vague and often contradictory, he was apparently shuttled from one southern town to another, living with various relatives, and even spent a period of time in an orphanage. When the family moved to Jackson, MS, he apparently received his only two years of formal education in the public schools, where he was assigned to the fifth grade at age 13, and two years later graduated from the ninth, at 15. He tried to support himself by doing odd jobs, but soon became acquainted with the realities of being a black youth in the Deep South, and by age 17 had become involved in petty criminal activities for which he was forced to flee to Memphis, TN, in order to avoid prosecution and imprisonment. Memphis proved to be a turning point in his life, because there he was introduced by a white coworker to the writings of H. L. Mencken, Sinclair Lewis, and Theodore Dreiser, which sparked his ambition to become a writer. At age 19, he moved on to Chicago, where he worked at several menial jobs while learning how to write. By age 21, he was working as a clerk in the Chicago post office at night and reading and writing by day. During the Depression he was on relief, and during this period (1934), he joined the Communist Party of the United States, remaining a member for 10 years. He became a writer with the WPA Federal Writers Project and wrote publicity for both the Federal Negro Theatre and the white Federal Experimental Theatre. As a member of the literary left, he published his first writings in the *Daily Worker* and *New Masses* in 1937. His first important book was published in 1938, a collection of short stories entitled *Uncle Tom's Children,* which won him a $500 prize. In 1939 he received a Guggenheim Fellowship in creative writing and a Spingarn Medal from the NAACP. *Native Son,* published in 1940, was a Book-of-the-Month Club selection, the first book by a black author to achieve this distinction. It brought him international fame and recognition and was adapted as a play in 1941, in collaboration with white playwright Paul Green. The success of *Native Son* was repeated with the publication of his fictionalized autobiography, *Black Boy,* in 1945. After his break with the Communist Party in 1934, he published the story of his disillusionment in *The God that Failed* (1950). In 1946, after World War II, Wright became an expatriot and moved to Paris with his Jewish wife Ellen, whom he married in 1940, and their five-year-old daughter. His later books include *The Outsider* (1953), *Black Power* (1954), *The Color Curtain* (1956), *White Man, Listen!* (1957), and *The Long Dream* (1958). He died of a heart attack in Paris at the age of 51. Following his death in 1960, two of his works were published posthumously, *Eight Men* (1961), a collection of stories, and *Lawd Today* (1963), a novel.

Stage, Screen, and Broadcast Works:

Native Son (drama, prologue & 10 scenes, 1941; also produced in 2 film versions, 1951 and 1987). Adapt. by °Paul Green and Richard Wright from the novel by Wright (1940). A protest drama that, for the first time on the Broadway stage, presented the portrait of a so-called brute Negro, the kind stereotypically referred to as a ''bad nigger,'' showing the economic and sociological forces in American society that molded his character. Tells the story of Bigger Thomas, a rebellious black youth who grew up in the rat-infested slums of Chicago, hating white people, black people, his family, and himself. As explained by Darwin Turner in his introduction to *Black Drama: An Anthology* (Brasmer & Consolo, 1970, pp. 11–12):

He envies, fears, and hates white people who control the society . . . and deny opportunity and free movement to black people. Bigger, however, also hates Negroes because they occupy inferior positions. To stave off awareness of his impotence to assist his family, he even erects a wall of hate between himself and them. But, because he cannot completely conceal his impotence from himself, he hates himself.

Bigger is employed as a chauffeur by the Daltons, a white liberal family, in spite of their knowledge that he has spent some time in reform school and the statement from his social worker that ''he is of unstable equilibrium as to disposition.'' His duties include driving their daughter Mary, a liberated and free-thinking radical, wherever she wishes to go. Mary takes advantage of her ''white prerogatives'' by trying to communicate with Bigger on a personal level, discussing with him the racial situation, and introducing him socially to her friends. One night when she has drunk too much, Bigger struggles to get her up to her room and has to pick her up physically and take her to bed. After they are in the bedroom, Mary becomes confused and calls out her mother's name, almost terrorizing Bigger, who accidentally smothers Mary by putting his hand over her mouth to keep her from revealing his presence in the room. The rest of the play involves Bigger's efforts to conceal the crime, his flight, capture, trial, and execution. Prod. by °Orson Welles and °John Houseman, as a Mercury Production, at the St. James Theatre, New York, March 24–June 28, 1941, for 114 perfs.; dir. by Welles. With Canada Lee as Bigger Thomas, Anne Burr as Mary Dalton, and Evelyn Ellis as Bigger's mother. "Following its original run," according to *BesPls 1942–43*, "it was taken over by other producers, reduced to the proportions of a popular-priced drama, and sent on tour. A second New York engagement was played at the Majestic Theatre, New York," Oct. 23, 1942–Jan. 2, 1943, for 84 perfs., with Canada Lee in his orig. role, and many members of the orig. cast. Prod. by the Players' Workshop, New York, opening Oct. 19, 1974; dir. by Clay Stevenson. Prod. by the American Theater Experiment, at the Perry St. Theatre, New York, March 21–April 16, 1978, for 16 perfs., in repertory; dir. by Dick Gaffield. With Bo Rucker as Bigger Thomas. Prod. in an independent film version, 1951, filmed in Argentina by Argentina Sono Films, with screenplay by Wright, who also starred as Bigger Thomas; dir. by Pierre Chenal, who was also in the cast. Prod. as a major motion picture by Cinecom International Films, 1987; starring Victor Love as Bigger Thomas, with Caroll Baker, Akosua Busia, Matt Dillon, John Karlen, Elizabeth McGovern, John McMartin, Geraldine Page, David Rasche, Lane Smith, and Oprah Winfrey as Bigger's mother. Orig. dramatization pub. by Harper, New York, 1941; abridged in *The Best Plays of 1940–41*; full script in *BlkThUSA* (Hatch, 1974). Revised dramatization by Paul Green in *Blk. Dr.* (Brasmer & Consolo, 1970). Copy of Wright's screenplay for the 1951 film version in Schomburg. REVIEWS AND COMMENTARY: *BlkDr* (Mitchell). *Ebony* 4–1959. Hicklin diss. *Human Relations in the Th.* (Gassner). *Lib. J.* 7–1951. *Life* 4–7–1941. *Mod. Blk. Men* 1–1987. *Neg. Digest* 2–1943. *Neg. in Films* (Noble). *NegPlaywrs* (Abramson). *New Republic* 7–2–1951. *Newswk.* 7–9–1951. *NYT* 3–25–1941; 4–6–1941; 10–24–1942; 11–1–1942; 12–7–1942; 4–11–1943. *Opportunity* 2–1942. *Our World* 12–1950. *Sat. Rev.* 7–7–1951. *Th. Arts* 5–1941; 6–1941; 7–1941; 10–1941; 7–1942; 8–1942; 12–1942. *Th. Bk. of the Yr.*, *1942–43* (Nathan). *Time* 4–7–1941.

   Fire and Cloud (radio play, 1 act, 1941). Adaptn. by °Charles K. O'Neill of a short story by Richard Wright. About a southern Negro bread riot. Pub. in *American Scenes* (Kozlenko, 1941).

   The Long Dream (drama, 3 acts, 1960). Adaptn. by °Ketti Frings of the novel by Richard Wright (1958). About a wealthy black undertaker in a southern town who has achieved his wealth through support of illegal activities in the black community and through his friendship with the town's chief of police. Prod. at the Ambassador Theatre in New York, opening Feb. 17, 1960, for 5 perfs.; dir. by Lloyd Richards, and starring Al Freeman, Jr. REVIEWS AND COMMENTARY: *BesPls 1959–60*. *BlkDr* (Mitchell). *BlkMagic* (Hughes & Meltzer). *Crisis* 3–1962. *Th. Arts* 3–1960.

   Daddy Goodness (comedy, 3 acts [5 scenes], 1968). Adapt. by Wright from *Papa Bon Dieu*, a play by °Louis Sapin, made relevant to the life of Father Divine. About the resurrection of a man from the "dead," who was in reality only "dead drunk," and the exploitation of this situation to proclaim him as the Messiah. First prod. by the American Theatre Assn., Paris, France, Feb. 19, 1959. Prod. by the Negro Ensemble Company, at St. Mark's Playhouse, New York, opening June 4, 1968, for 64 perfs.; dir. by *Douglas Turner Ward. With Moses Gunn as Daddy Goodness. Prod. in a musical version, 1980, which closed before reaching Bway, starring Clifton James. REVIEWS AND COMMENTARY: *Blk. Th. #1*, 1968. *Liberator* 7–1968.

OTHER PLAYS: **The Burkes** (incomplete script, 1937). **The Farmer in the Dell** (late 1940s). On the difficulty of adapting *Native Son* for the stage. **3314** (incomplete adaptn. of Wright's *Lawd Today*.

Other Pertinent Writings:
"Negro Tradition in the Theatre," *Daily Worker*, Oct. 15, 1937, p. 5.
"How Bigger Was Born," *Sat. Rev.*, June 1, 1940, pp. 3–4.
"Birth of Bigger Thomas," *Crisis*, Sept.1942, pp. 24–29.
FURTHER REFERENCE: *Blk. Am. Writers* (Rush et al.). *DBlkTh* (Woll). Hicklin diss. *NegPlaywrs* (Abramson). *Runthrough* (John Houseman, New York: Curtis, 1972). *The Unfinished Quest of Richard Wright* (Michel Fabre, New York: Morrow, 1973).

YERBY, FRANK. See Appendix A.

APPENDIX A

OTHER EARLY BLACK AMERICAN PLAYWRIGHTS AND THEIR PLAYS

All undated plays are pre–1950. Playwrights marked with an asterisk (*) are included in my earlier volume, *Contemporary Black American Playwrights and Their Plays* (Greenwood Press, Westport, CT, 1988), where more information regarding their early and contemporary plays can be located. The following abbreviations are occasionally used in this appendix: Am. (American), Aud. (Auditorium), Exp. (Experimental), N.Y. (New York City), Pr. (Press), Sq. (Square), Th. (Theatre).

Other Early Black American Playwrights and Their Plays

PLAYWRIGHT	PLAY	PRODUCTION	PUBLICATION	LOCATION OF SCRIPT OR PUBLICATION
BLACK, JEAN BELCHER	*The Pit* (1 act, 1949)		*SADSA Encore* 1949	
*BREWSTER, TOWNSEND (1924–)	*The Choreography of Love* (comic opera libretto, 1 act, 1946)	Queens Coll., N.Y. c.1945 & WNYC-Radio, N.Y. 2–16–1946		
	Letter and Lottery (harlequinade, 1 act, 1948)	Queens Coll. Community Th., N.Y. Fall 1948		
	Andromeda (musical: bk. & lyrics, 1 act, 1949)			
	Look Eastward (musical, 2 acts, 1949)			
	Rough and Ready (lyric comedy: bk. & lyrics, 2 acts, 1949)			
CAMP, HARRY	*The Prodigal Son* (c.1932)	Harlem Exp. Th. 1932		
*CAMPBELL, DICK (1903–)	*The Watchword Is Forward* (civil rights play, 1 act, 1942)	Madison Sq. Garden, N.Y. 6–16–1942		Moorland-Spingarn
CARTER, JEAN (Emma Loyal Lexa)	*Country Gentlemen* (1950)		Exposition Pr., 1950	

206

Author	Title	Production	Publication	Location
*CHILDRESS, ALICE (1920–)	*Florence* (drama, 1 act, 1949)	ANT, N.Y. 1949 & Club Baron, Harlem 9-1950	*Masses and Mainstream* 10-1950 & *Wines in the Wilderness* (Brown-Guillory, 1990)	
	Just a Little Simple (musical, full length, 1950)	Club Baron, Harlem 9-1950		
COGMAN, GEORGE	*Little Stone House* (c.1932)	Harlem Exp. Th. 1932		
COLEMAN, WARREN	*Juba* (1 act, mid-1930s)			FTP/GMU
COLES, EROSTINE	*Festus De Fus!* (1 act, 1930s)	Atlanta Univ. Summer Th. 1930s		
	Mimi La Croix (1 act, 1934)	Atlanta Univ. Summer Th. 1934		
COOK, S. N.	*Out in the Streets* (temperance play, 1 act, 1875)		Happy Hrs. Co. 1875 & Am. Temperance Pub. Co.	TC/NYPL Moorland-Spingarn
COOPER, ANNA JULIA (1859–1964)	*Christmas Bells* (children's play, 1 act, 16 pp.)			Not located
*DAVIS, OSSIE (1917–)	*Goldbrickers of 1944* (variety show, full length, 1944)	Liberia 1944 (U.S. armed forces)		
	Alexis Is Fallen (1947)			
	They Seek a City (adaptn., 1947)			

PLAYWRIGHT	PLAY	PRODUCTION	PUBLICATION	LOCATION OF SCRIPT OR PUBLICATION
	Point Blank (1949)			
	The Mayor of Harlem (1949)			
	The Last Dance for Sybil (c.1950)			
DIXON, PHELON	*His Cross* (full length, 1927)	Imperial Elks Aud., N.Y. 4-8-1927		
DORSEY, ROBERT	*Get Thee Behind Me, Satan* (c.1932)	Harlem Exp. Th. 1932		
FRANKLIN, JAMES T.	*Retribution* (3 acts, 1890s)			
*FULLER, LORENZO	*A Temporary Island* (musical, full length, 1948)	Prod. N.Y. 1948		
GALE, BERESFORD	*The Hand of Fate; or, Fifty Years After* (4 acts)	A.M.E. Sunday School Union, Nashville, TN		
GILMORE, F. GRANT	*The Problem* (military drama, 1915)		H. Conolly, N.Y. 1915	
*GLANVILLE, MAXWELL	*Swing Wedding* (skit, 1945)	Champaign, IL, USO 1945 & Harlem YMCA 1947		
HICKS, LONNIE	*Scufflin'* (musical, 1939)			Moorland-Spingarn

HODGES, GEORGE W.	*Bring Dat College Home* (1927)	135th St. Lib., N.Y., by Atlanta Univ. Club 4-8-1927	
HOLIFIELD, HAROLD	*Cow in the Apartment* (c.1948)	115th St. People's Th., N.Y. c.1940	
	J. Toth (fantasy, 1950/51)	Council of Harlem Th., early 1950s	
HUEY, RICHARD	*Sacrifice* (1 act, 1931) (with CARLTON MOSS)	135th St. Lib. Th., N.Y. 2-1931	
HUFFMAN, EUGENE HENRY	*Hoo-dooed* (1932)	Philharmonic Aud., Los Angeles 4-1932	
	The Imposter		
	The Last Chord		
	St. Peter Is Out		
	Unto Us a Child Is Born		
*HUNTLEY, ELIZABETH MADDOX	*Legion, the Demoniac* (1950)		*AmLitNA* (Dreer, 1950)
INGRAM, REX (1895–1969)	*Drums of the Bayou* (1935)	Prod. 1935, starring auth.	
*JEANNETTE, GERTRUDE (1948–)	*This Way Forward* (dramatic comedy, 2 acts, 1948)	ANT Workshop, Harlem 1949	
JEFFERSON, W. J.	*Mandy* (1 act, 1927)	Krigwa Players, N.Y. 1-1928	

PLAYWRIGHT	PLAY	PRODUCTION	PUBLICATION	LOCATION OF SCRIPT OR PUBLICATION
KELLY, BUENA V.	*Forty Years of Progress* (pageant, 3 episodes, 1942)	Tindley Temple, Philadelphia 1942	Guide Quality Printery, Norfolk, VA 1942	
*LIGHTS, FREDERICK L. (1922–)	*All over Nothin'* (domestic play, 1 act, c.1948)	Yale School of Drama, New Haven c.1948		
	The Underlings (adapt., 1 act, c.1948)	Yale School of Drama, New Haven c.1948		
*McBROWN, GERTRUDE PARTHENIA	*Bought with Cookies* (children's radio play, 1 act, 1949)		*Neg. Hist. Bull.* 4-1949	
MEYER, ANNIE NATHAN	*Black Souls* (1932)	Prod. 1932	Reynolds Pr., Bedford, MA 1932	
MILLER, ALLEN C.	*The Unending War* (historical drama, 3 acts, 1928)			Schomburg
	The Opener of Doors (1932)	FTP	*Neg. One-Act Plays* (1923)	
*MITCHELL, LOFTEN (1919–)	*Blood in the Night* (drama, 3 acts, 1938)	People's Th. Workshop, N.Y. 3-22-1946		
	Cocktails (satirical comedy, 1 act, 1938)	Pioneer Drama Group, Harlem 1938		
	Shattered Dreams (1938)	Pioneer Drama Group, Harlem 1938		

	Title	Production	Publication	Repository
[MITCHELL, LOFTEN, continued]	*Crossroads* (drama, 1 act, 1938)			
	The Cellar (drama, 2 acts, 1947)	People's Th., Harlem 10-1947		
	The Bancroft Dynasty (domestic drama, 3 acts, 1947)	People's Th., Harlem 1948		
MORGAN, EDWIN J.	*The Return* (1920)	Varsity Dramatic Club, NYU 1920		
NORMAN, DORA COLE	*The Niche* (1 act, 1921)	Player's Guild, Harlem YWCA 2-22-1921		
PITTS, LUCIA MAE	*Let Me Dream*			
RANDLE, ANNIE	*The Voice on the Wire* (1919)			
*SEEBREE, CHARLES (1914–1986)	*My Mother Came Crying Most Pitifully* (fantasy, 3 acts, 1949)			Hatch-Billops
SINCLAIR, PAUL	*Color-Blind* (1 act, 1934)		*The Stylus*, Howard Univ. 6-1934	
TANNER, WILLIAM H.	*The Birth of Freedom and the Present Age* (1919)		Privately printed, Dayton, OH 1919	
TURNER, LUCY M.	*The Exodus* (3 acts, c.1931)		Privately printed, E. St. Louis, IL c.1931	Moorland-Spingarn

PLAYWRIGHT	PLAY	PRODUCTION	PUBLICATION	LOCATION OF SCRIPT OR PUBLICATION
WOODS, G. A.	*Pitfalls of Appearances* (thesis play, 1 act, 1921)	Players' Guild, Harlem YWCA 2-11-1921		
YERBY, FRANK (1916–)	*No Majesty* (1940)	Florida A.&M. Univ. 1940		

APPENDIX B

ADDITIONAL MUSICAL LIBRETTISTS AND BRIEF DESCRIPTIONS OF THEIR SHOWS

This appendix is divided into two parts. The first lists the major musical librettists whose shows were written prior to 1950. The second gives brief annotations of these shows. More complete information on these librettists and shows will be included in my forthcoming volume, *Encyclopedia of the Black American Musical Stage*, now in progress.

THE LIBRETTISTS

All musicals listed below, except those in brackets, are annotated in the second part of this appendix.

ANDERSON, ALFRED

Captain Rufus (book with J. Ed. Green, 1907, revived 1914).

BRIGHT, JOE

Get Set (book, 1923/26).

BROOKS, MARION A.

Panama (book with Charles A. Hunter, 1908). [Also wrote *Ephraham Johnson from Norfolk* (book with Flournoy E. Miller, 1908).]

COLE, BOB

A Trip to Coontown (book, music, and lyrics with William [Billy] Johnson, 1897/1901). *Darktown Circus Day* (book, 1903). *The Shoo-Fly Regiment* (book, 1905/7). *The Red Moon* (book; lyrics with J. Rosamond Johnson and Joe Jordan, 1908/9). [Also contributed sketches to *Black Patti's Troubadours* (1896) and *The Creole Show* (1899).]

COOK, WILL A.

In the Jungles (book with Al F. Watts, 1911).

COOK, WILL MARION

Clorindy, the Origin of the Cakewalk (orig. concept and music [no book], 1898). *Jes Lak White Folks* (book; lyrics with PAUL LAURENCE DUNBAR, 1900).

CREAMER, HENRY S.

Old Man's Boy (book with Alex C. Rogers, 1913/14). *Strut Miss Lizzie* (book; lyrics with J. Turner Layton, 1921).

DUDLEY, S. H.

The Black Politician (book with °S. B. Cassion, 1904/8). *Dr. Beans from Boston* (book with Henry Troy, 1911/12). [Also contributed comedy material to *His Honor, the Barber* (1909/11).]

GARVEY, MARCUS

Brown Sugar (book with Sam Manning, 1927).

GRAINGER, PORTER

Lucky Sambo (book, music, and lyrics with Freddie Johnson, 1925). [Also wrote *De Board Meetin'* (script and music with Leigh Whipper, 1925) and *We's Risin'* (script with Whipper, 1927).]

GREEN, EDDIE

Blackberries of 1932 (book with °Lew Posner, 1932).

GREEN, J. ED.

Captain Rufus (book with Alfred Anderson, 1907; revived 1914). [Also wrote scripts for *Fred Douglass's Reception* (1896), *Queen of the Jungle* (with Bob H. Kelly, c. 1900), *The Hoosier Detective*, and *Jack's Return from Africa* (both c. 1900).]

GYNT, KAJ

Rang Tang (book, 1927).

HILL, J. LEUBRIE

The Darktown Follies (book, music, and lyrics with Alex C. Rogers, 1911/16), which was based on Hill's earlier musicals, *My Friend from Dixie* (1911) and *My Friend from Kentucky* (1913). [Also wrote *A Blackville Corporation* (adapt. from *Bandanna Land*, 1910, 1915).]

HOGAN, ERNEST

Rufus Rastus (book, 1905/7).

HUNTER, CHARLES A.

Panama (book with Marion A. Brooks, 1908).

HUNTER, EDDIE

The Eddie Hunter Company (book only, 1922). *How Come?* (book only, 1923). *My Magnolia* (book with Alex C. Rogers, 1926). *4–11–44* (book, 1926/27). [Also wrote vaudeville sketches, including *Goin' to the Races, The Battle of Who Run, Subway Sal, Why Husbands Leave Home, The Gentleman Burglar,* and *The Railway Porter* (all 1909/ 1920).]

JOHNSON, FREDDIE

Lucky Sambo (book, music, and lyrics with Porter Grainger, 1925).

JOHNSON, J. ROSAMOND

The Cannibal King (book with PAUL LAURENCE DUNBAR, 1901).

JOHNSON, WILLIAM (Billy)

A Trip to Coontown (book, music, and lyrics with Bob Cole, 1897/1901).

LYLES, AUBREY

All books with Flournoy E. Miller, except where indicated. *The Man from 'Bam* (1906; revived 1920, 1923). *The Oyster Man* (1907). *The Husband* (1907/8). *The Colored Aristocrats* (1909). *Who's Stealin'* (1914). *Runnin' Wild* (1923/24). *Negro Nuances* (with Miller and Abbie Mitchell, 1924). *Rang Tang* (vaudeville sketches with Miller, 1927). *Keep Shufflin'* (1928). *Shuffle Along* (1921; revised and revived 1930, 1933, 1952). *Sugar Hill* (revised version by Lyles of the 1931 book by Miller, 1947, 1950). [Also wrote with Miller *The Flat Below* (play, 1924) and *Honey* (book, 1924).]

MACK, CECIL

Swing It (book; lyrics with Milton Reddie, 1937).

MANNING, SAM

Brown Sugar (book with Marcus Garvey, 1927).

MILLER, FLOURNOY E.

All books with Aubrey Lyles, except where indicated. *The Man from 'Bam* (1906; revived 1920, 1923). *The Husband* (1907/08). *The Oyster Man* (1907/9). *The Colored Aristocrats* (1909). *Who's Stealin'* (1914). *Shuffle Along* (1921; revised and revived 1930, 1933, 1952). *Runnin' Wild* (1923/24). *Negro Nuances* (with Lyles and Abbie Mitchell, 1924). *Rang Tang* (vaudeville sketches with Lyles, 1927). *Keep Shufflin'* (1928). *Black-birds of 1930* (book alone, 1929/30). *Sugar Hill* (book alone, 1931; revised and revived by Aubrey Lyles, 1947, 1950). [Also wrote *Ephraham Johnson from Norfolk* (book with Marion Brooks, 1908), *Happy Sam from 'Bam* (book, 1912), *The Flat Below* (play, with Lyles, 1922), *Goin' White* (play, 1923), *Honey* (book with Lyles, 1924), *Pudden Jones* (play, 1925), and *Get Lucky* (book with Quintard Miller, 1934/35).]

MILLER, IRVIN C.

Mr. Ragtime (book and lyrics, 1912/15). *Broadway Rastus* (several editions, book, 1915/18). *Put and Take* (book, 1921). *Liza* (book, 1922). *Dinah* (book, 1927). [Also wrote and prod. the famous *Brown Skin Models* revues (1927/42, 1954), *Blue Moon* (book and lyrics with Donald Heywood, 1926), and *Desires of 1927* (book, 1926/27).

MITCHELL, ABBIE (Mrs. Will Marion Cook)

Negro Nuances (book with Flournoy E. Miller and Aubrey Lyles, 1924).

MONTGOMERY, FRANK

In Ethiopiaville (book, lyrics, and music, 1913). *Raisin' Cain* (book and music, 1923).

OWSLEY, TIM

Shades of Hades (book, 1922/23).

RAZAF, ANDY

Hot Chocolates (book and lyrics, 1929; revived 1935).

ROGERS, ALEX C.

Abyssinia (book and lyrics with Jesse A. Shipp, 1906/7). *Bandanna Land* (book and lyrics with Shipp, 1908/9). *Mr. Lode of Koal* (book with Shipp, 1909/10). *The Darktown Follies* (book and lyrics with J. Leubrie Hill, 1911/16). *Old Man's Boy* (book with Henry Creamer, 1913/14). *Baby Blues* (book and lyrics, 1919/20). *My Magnolia* (book with Eddie Hunter, 1926). [Also wrote *This and That* (book and lyrics with Shipp, 1919) and *Jasper Lee's Revenge* (playlet, which was originally part of *Follies of the Stroll,* 1920).]

SHIPP, JESSE A.

The Policy Players (book, 1899/1900). *The Sons of Ham* (book, 1899/1900). *In Dahomey* (book only; lyrics with PAUL LAURENCE DUNBAR; music with Will Marion Cook and others, 1902/5). *Abyssinia* (book and lyrics with Alex C. Rogers, 1906/7). *Bandanna Land* (book and lyrics with Rogers, 1908/9). *Mr. Lode of Koal* (book with Rogers, 1909/10). *North Ain't South* (book with Salem Tutt Whitney and J. Homer Tutt, 1923). [Also wrote *Mooching Along* (book with Cecil Mack and James P. "Jimmy" Johnson, 1925) and *Darktown Affairs* (book with Garland Howard and others, 1929).]

SISSLE, NOBLE

The Chocolate Dandies (book with LEW PAYTON; music and lyrics with Eubie Blake and others, 1924/25).

TROY, HENRY

Darkydom (book, 1914/15). *Dr. Beans from Boston* (book with S. H. Dudley, 1911/12).

TUTT, J. HOMER

(Book and other contributions with Salem Tutt Whitney unless otherwise indicated.) *Blackville Strollers* (books, music, and lyrics, 1908). *The Mayor of Newtown* [also *Newton*](book, music, and lyrics, 1909/12). *How Newtown Prepared* (book, lyrics, and staging; music with Whitney and Taylor L. Corwell, 1916). *Darkest Americans* (book and lyrics, 1918/19). *Children of the Sun* (book, 1919). *Bamboula* (book, 1921). *Up and Down* (book, lyrics, and music, 1922). *North Ain't South* (book with Whitney and Jesse

A. Shipp, 1923). *Come Along Mandy* (book and Lyrics, 1924). *Deep Harlem* (book, 1929). *Gingersnaps* (book and lyrics with DONALD HEYWOOD, 1929). *De Gospel Train* (book, c. 1936/40). [Also with Whitney wrote *The Wrong Mr. President* (book and lyrics, 1913), *His Excellency the President* (book and lyrics, 1913/15). *Oh Joy!* (book, lyrics, and music, 1922).]

WATTS, AL F.

In the Jungles (book with Will A. Cook, 1911).

WHIPPER, LEIGH

Runnin' de Town (book, 1930). [Also wrote *We's Risin'* (coauthor with Porter Grainger, 1927) and *Yeah-Man* (book with Billy Mills, 1932).]

WHITNEY, SALEM TUTT

Book and other contributions with J. Homer Tutt, unless otherwise indicated. *Blackville Strollers* (book, music, and lyrics, 1908). *The Mayor of Newtown* [also *Newton*] (book, music, and lyrics, 1909/12). *How Newton Prepared* (book, lyrics, and staging; music with Tutt and Taylor L. Corwell, 1916). *Darkest Americans* (book and lyrics, 1918/19). *Children of the Sun* (book, 1919). *Bamboula* (book, 1921). *Up and Down* (book, lyrics, and music, 1922). *North Ain't South* (book with Tutt and Jesse A. Shipp, 1923). *Come Along Mandy* (book, 1924). *Deep Harlem* (book, 1929). *De Gospel Train* (book, c. 1936/40). [Also wrote *Silas Green from New Orleans,* the longest-running black show (book, music, and lyrics [alone], c. 1902/1931); and in collaboration with Tutt wrote *The Wrong Mr. President* (book and lyrics, 1913), *His Excellency the President* (book and lyrics, 1913/15), and *Oh Joy!* (book, lyrics, and music, 1922).]

WILLIAMS, CLARENCE

Bottomland (book, lyrics, and music, 1927).

THE MUSICAL SHOWS

The following pages present brief descriptions of some of the major book musicals by black American writers before 1950. Production dates are given in parentheses. A span of several years usually indicates a seasonal show with frequent revisions and changes of cast. The names of librettists or writers of musical books included in the Biographical Directory are written in all capitals. Librettists whose names are in all capitals and preceded by an obelisk (†) are included in the first part of this appendix. More information on these shows and hundreds of others is given in my forthcoming *Encyclopedia of the Black American Musical Stage,* now in the process of completion.

Abyssinia (1906/7). Book and lyrics by †JESSE A. SHIPP and †ALEX C. ROGERS, based on contributions by Bert Williams and George Walker. Music by †WILL MARION COOK. Successful Williams & Walker show in which a group of black Americans visit the ancient land of their ancestors (Abyssinia, now called Ethiopia), experiencing a number of misadventures brought about by cultural misunderstandings.

Alabama Bound (1931). Book by †IRVIN C. MILLER. A sequel to his seasonal show, *Broadway Rastus* (1915/28), which follows Rastus and one of his buddies on a "hoboing" adventure from New York to Alabama, where they use their wits to secure necessities of life along the way.

Baby Blues (1919/20). Book and lyrics by †ALEX C. ROGERS. Music by C. Luckeyth Roberts. About a gold-digging woman who marries a good-for-nothing man who has received a large inheritance.

Bamboula (1921). Book by †SALEM TUTT WHITNEY and †J. HOMER TUTT. Music and lyrics by Edgar Powell and James Vaughan. After hearing a melody that he believes to be of African origin, a fanatical music professor travels with an entourage to Africa to prove his theory.

Bandanna Land (1908). Book and lyrics by †ALEX C. ROGERS and †JESSE A. SHIPP. Music by †WILL MARION COOK. With contributions by Bert Williams and George Walker. Successful Williams & Walker show revolving around a real estate scam by blacks to move into a white neighborhood and create such a disturbance that their neighbors buy back their homes at twice the price.

Blackberries of 1932 (1932). Book by †EDDIE GREEN and °Lee Posner. Music and lyrics by DONALD HEYWOOD and °Tom Peluso. Stereotypical song and dance revue imitative of Lew Leslie's successful Blackbirds revues. [See next entry.]

Blackbirds of 1930 (*Lew Leslie's Blackbirds of 1930*) (1929/30). Book by †FLOURNOY E. MILLER. Music by Eubie Blake. Lyrics by Andy Razaf. Sixth edition of Lew Leslie's famous Blackbirds (a series of revues with all-black casts, which first appeared in 1926); this edition is significant because of its all-black authorship.

The Black Politician (1904). Book by †S. H. DUDLEY and °S. B. Cassion. Music and lyrics by James Reese Europe and Cecil Mack. About a mayoral election campaign that is sabotaged by two schemers who hope to gain control of one candidate's campaign funds.

Blackville Strollers (1908). Book, music, and lyrics by †SALEM TUTT WHITNEY and †J. HOMER TUTT. One-act musical, written for the Black Patti Troubadours, revolving around a group of traveling players who call themselves the Blackville Strollers, under the management of Miss Sureta Walkback, a comic old maid played by J. Homer Tutt.

Bottomland (1927). Book, music, and lyrics by †CLARENCE WILLIAMS. About a singer who leaves her southern home in Bottomland hoping to find fame and fortune in Harlem.

Broadway Rastus (1915/28). Seasonal show in several editions, with books mainly by †IRVIN C. MILLER. The original show upon which Miller's *Put and Take* (1921) was based, built around the activities and exploits of a character named Rastus, who constantly dreams about getting rich.

Brown Sugar (1927). Book by †MARCUS GARVEY and †SAM MANNING. About a beautiful girl who is courted by two suitors—one a rich prince from India, the other an ordinary mechanic.

The Cannibal King (1901). Book by PAUL LAURENCE DUNBAR and J. ROSAMOND JOHNSON. Lyrics by Johnson and Bob Cole. Music by †WILL MARION COOK. A black headwaiter at an elite white hotel suddenly becomes rich and now tries to educate his people in the social graces to make them acceptable in high society.

Captain Rufus (1907; revived 1914). Book by †J. ED. GREEN and †ALFRED ANDERSON. Music by H. Lawrence Freeman, Joe Jordan, and Tim Brymn. Military comedy set in the Philippines, about a phony captain named Rufus.

Children of the Sun (1919). Book by †SALEM TUTT WHITNEY and †J. HOMER TUTT. Music by James Vaughan. An archeologist sets out from a well-known black university to locate the original site of the "Children of the Sun," where, according to legend, a golden treasure will also be discovered.

The Chocolate Dandies (orig. title: *In Bamville,* 1924/25). Book by †NOBLE SISSLE and LEW PAYTON. Music and lyrics by Sissle and Blake. Additional music by Spencer Williams and Chris Smith. A race horse owner dreams that his horse has won a fortune that enables him to live like a king and win the girl that he loves—until he wakes up.

Clorindy, the Origin of the Cakewalk (1898/1901). Concept, orig. sketch, and music by †WILL MARION COOK. Lyrics by PAUL LAURENCE DUNBAR, who also wrote a libretto that was never used. Successful musical of the 1890s, which was the first to introduce Broadway to the cakewalk, a black dance that had become a staple of the minstrel tradition.

The Colored Aristocrats (1909). Book by †Flournoy E. MILLER and †AUBREY LYLES. Music by Sidney Perrin. Satire of social snobbery and hypocrisy among middle-class blacks.

Come Along Mandy (1924). Book and lyrics by †SALEM TUTT WHITNEY and †J. HOMER TUTT. Music by DONALD HEYWOOD. Concerns a dispute over boundary lines between two pieces of property, which is complicated when the deeds to both parcels of land are stolen.

Darktown Circus Day (1903). Book by †BOB COLE. Short musical comedy written for the Black Patti Troubadours, in which a number of specialty acts are assembled around a thin circus plot.

The Darktown Follies (evolved from three separate musicals: *My Friend from Dixie, My Friend from Kentucky,* and *Here and There,* 1911/16). Book, music, and lyrics by †J. LEUBRIE HILL and †ALEX C. ROGERS. About a Kentucky man who tries to desert his shrewish wife and family in order to marry a Washington, DC, society matron. A highly successful Harlem show, which in 1913 started the vogue of white audiences going uptown to see it. Its finale was purchased by Florenz Ziegfeld for inclusion in his *Follies*.

Darkydom (1914/15). Book by †HENRY TROY. Lyrics by Henry Creamer and Lester Walton. Music by †WILL MARION COOK and James Reese Europe. A series of sketches and specialty acts centering around the comedy team of Miller & Lyles, who play two crosstie inspectors for a railroad company.

Deep Harlem (1928/29). Conceived and produced by Earl Dancer. Book by †SALEM TUTT WHITNEY and †J. HOMER TUTT. Lyrics by Tutt and Henry Creamer. Music by Joe Jordan. Portrays in song and dance the black odyssey from Africa to Harlem.

De Gospel Train (orig. title: *Jim Crow,* 1936; revived 1940). Book by †J. HOMER TUTT [and †SALEM TUTT WHITNEY, who collaborated on the earlier version]. Musical settings by DONALD HEYWOOD. Concerns the fate of the passengers of a "Jim Crow" railroad car headed from the South to Washington, DC.

Dinah (1927). Book by †IRVIN C. MILLER. Lyrics and music by Tim Brymn. Song and dance show loosely built around the story of a man who steals his niece's inheritance, which was to be invested in a dance hall. This show introduced a popular black dance called the Black Bottom.

Dr. Beans from Boston. (1911/12). Book by †S. H DUDLEY and †HENRY TROY. Music by Will H. Vodery. Lyrics by Henry Creamer. A lovesick ex-minstrel, with the aid of a confederate, impersonates a druggist in order to gain access to a love potion, which he dispenses to his beloved until the real Dr. Beans shows up to complicate the plot.

The Eddie Hunter Company (1922). Book by †EDDIE HUNTER. Music by Will Fountain. Tabloid musical concerning the arrest of a forger at an elegant social affair, his imprisonment and escape.

4–11–44 (title changed to *Struttin' Hannah from Savannah,* 1926; revived 1927). Book by †EDDIE HUNTER. A henpecked husband steals money from his wife in order to bet on the numbers, then falls asleep while hiding from her, dreaming that she has had him arrested for theft.

Get Set (1923). Book by †JOE BRIGHT. Music and lyrics by DONALD HEYWOOD and Porter Grainger. A revue in which Ethel Waters appeared, revolving around the efforts of the wife of a Kentucky soldier of fortune to get into Chicago society.

Gingersnaps (1929). Book and lyrics by †J. HOMER TUTT and DONALD HEYWOOD. Music by Heywood. Variety show consisting mainly of song and dance numbers, comedy routines, and sketches, with apparently very little plot.

Hot Chocolates (orig. title: *Connie's Hot Chocolates,* 1929; revived 1935). Book and lyrics by †ANDY RAZAF. Music by Thomas ("Fats") Waller and Harry Brooks. This revue, which began as a nightclub floor show, included Waller and Razaf's hit song, "Ain't Misbehavin'," which later had a broadway show named after it.

How Come? (1923). Book by †EDDIE HUNTER. Lyrics by Hunter, Will Vodery, Henry Creamer, and Ben Harris. Broadway song and dance show that attempted to imitate the success of *Shuffle Along* (1921). Centered around the thin plot of the embezzlement of funds from a business venture by one of the partners.

How Newtown Prepared [also *Newton*](1916). Book, music, and lyrics mainly by †SALEM TUTT WHITNEY, †J. HOMER TUTT, and Taylor L. Corwell. Colonel George Washington Bullion forms a volunteer army of the old black veterans of Newtown and leads them off to foreign wars, where they experience many tribulations until they realize that they are fighting on the wrong side against the Allies and must be rescued and returned to the U.S.A.

The Husband (1907/8). Book and lyrics by †FLOURNOY E. MILLER and †AUBREY LYLES. Music by Joe Jordan. Domestic comedy which was the first show written by Miller & Lyles. The noted actor Charles Gilpin appeared in the 1909 edition.

In Dahomey (1902/5). Book by †JESSE A. SHIPP. Lyrics by PAUL LAURENCE DUNBAR and Shipp. Music by †WILL MARION COOK and others. The most successful Williams & Walker musical, which not only played on Broadway, but also became a London hit after a command performance at Buckingham Palace. In this show, two con men, played by Williams & Walker, lead a group of dissatisfied black Americans back to Africa, where they hope to colonize some land. There they have many terrifying experiences, making them happy to return home.

In Ethiopiaville (1913). Book, lyrics, and music by †FRANK MONTGOMERY. The plot turns on the theft of a jewel case and its eventual recovery by a down-and-out minstrel man posing as a detective.

In the Jungles (1911). Book by †WILL A. COOK and †AL F. WATTS. Music by †WILL MARION COOK and Alex C. Rogers. Sketch written for the Black Patti Troubadours, dealing with an attempt by a missionary society to rescue a young woman who has been lost in the jungles.

Jes Lak White Folks (1900). Book by †WILL MARION COOK. Lyrics by Cook and PAUL LAURENCE DUNBAR. A black soldier dreams that his daughter has all the opportunities and privileges that white folks' daughters have, until he discovers that troubles go along with affluence.

Keep Shufflin' (1928). Book by †FLOURNOY E. MILLER and †AUBREY LYLES. Lyrics by Henry Creamer and †ANDY RAZAF. Music by James P. Johnson and Thomas ("Fats") Waller. Two "lazy bones" dream of a scheme to provide wealth and plenty for the whole world, but the damage to the economy is so great that the money becomes worthless.

Liza (orig. title: *Bon Bon Buddy, Jr.,* 1922). Book by †IRVIN C. MILLER. Music by Maceo Pinkard. Successful song and dance musical built around the plot of embezzlement of funds that were to be used to erect a monument to the town's deceased mayor. This musical was the first to introduce the Charleston (the popular black dance of the twenties) to Broadway, although *Runnin' Wild* (1923) is generally credited with this distinction.

Lucky Sambo (orig. title: *Aces and Queens,* 1925). Book, music, and lyrics by †PORTER GRAINGER and †FREDDIE JOHNSON. The story of an oil stock swindle, combined with a love story; the swindlers are eventually jailed and the lovers united.

The Man from 'Bam (1906/7; revived 1920, 1923). Book by †FLOURNOY E. MILLER and †AUBREY LYLES. Music by Joe Jordan and Will Vodery. After winning a fortune on the horses, an Alabama man becomes estranged from his wife because he does not share his winnings with her. In the next race he loses his fortune, while she becomes rich by winning on another horse.

Mayor of Newtown [also *Newton*](1909/12). Book, lyrics, and music mainly by †SALEM TUTT WHITNEY and †J. HOMER TUTT. The mayor desires to bring modern ideas to Newtown, but is violently opposed by many of the older citizens, including the former mayor.

Mr. Lode of Koal (1909/10). Book by †JESSE A. SHIPP and †ALEX C. ROGERS. Music by †J. ROSAMOND JOHNSON and others. A coalworker daydreams that he is about to be made king of a savage island kingdom whose former king has been overthrown. While preparations are made for the coronation, he is kept a virtual prisoner and has a number of harrowing experiences before waking up to discover that it is all a dream.

Mr. Ragtime (1912/15). Book and lyrics by †IRVIN C. MILLER. Music by Will Dorsey. Miller's first musical show, set in the interior of the Dumas Hotel in New Orleans, which is occupied by an assortment of hotel employees, guests, and visitors who provide the entertainment and variety acts for the show.

My Magnolia (1926). Book and lyrics by †ALEX C. ROGERS and †EDDIE HUNTER. Music by C. Luckeyth Roberts. Song and dance revue, with a thin story line about a southern girl who goes to New York to try to make it in show business.

Negro Nuances (1924). Book by †ABBIE MITCHELL, †FLOURNOY E. MILLER, and †AUBREY LYLES. Music and lyrics by †WILL MARION COOK. A review of black musical history from Africa to America, and from slavery to freedom.

North Ain't South (1923). Book by †SALEM TUTT WHITNEY, †J. HOMER TUTT, and †JESSE A. SHIPP. Music by DONALD HEYWOOD. About a group of southern black singers and dancers who travel north with the expectation of making it in the theatre. After much difficulty in finding work, they go back home with the realization that north ain't south.

Old Man's Boy (1913/14). Book by †ALEX C. ROGERS and †HENRY S. CREAMER. Song and dance show, presented as a play-within-a-play. The performers are rehearsing for a show that is presented in the final act.

The Oyster Man (1907). Book by †FLOURNOY E. MILLER and †AUBREY LYLES. Lyrics by †HENRY CREAMER and Lester A. Walton. Music by Will H. Vodery, in collaboration with Ernest Hogan. A sequel to *Rufus Rastus* (1905/7), revolving around the adventures of Rufus as an oyster vendor who is mysteriously transported to a mythical sea island, where he has a number of memorable experiences.

Panama (1908). Book by †MARION A. BROOKS and †CHARLES A. HUNTER. Music by Tim Brymn and H. Lawrence Freeman. The inhabitants of a small Kentucky town are swindled out of their money when they invest in a nonexistent piece of land in Panama.

The Policy Players (final metamorphosis of several abortive Williams & Walker musical shows, including *Senegambian Carnival, Dollar Bill and Silver King, A Lucky Coon,* and *4–11–44*, 1899/1900). Book by †JESSE A. SHIPP. Music by †WILL MARION COOK. Concerns a lottery winner who wishes to enter high society; a swank affair is arranged, at which he is introduced as the Ex-President of Liberia.

Put and Take (1921). Book by †IRVIN W. MILLER. Music by SPENCER WILLIAMS, Perry Bradford, and Tim Brymn. A reworking of Miller's successful touring show, *Broadway Rastus,* which had appeared in three earlier editions (1915/19) before this version opened on Broadway. Although it included blackface comedy, this musical was criticized as being ''too white'' for a black show because it tried to avoid many of the stereotypes of the minstrel stage.

Raisin' Cain (1923). Book and music by †FRANK MONTGOMERY. A musical odyssey of the black man from Africa (Senegambia) to New York, with a passing review of the best black musicals from the Williams & Walker shows of the turn of the century to *Shuffle Along* (1921).

Rang Tang (1927). Book by †KAJ GYNT. Music by Ford Dabney. Lyrics by Jo Trent. Based on vaudeville routines of †FLOURNOY E. MILLER and †AUBREY LYLES, who portray two debt-ridden barbers who escape their creditors in Jimtown by stealing a plane and flying to Africa, where they become involved in a series of jungle misadventures.

The Red Moon (1908/9). Book by †BOB COLE. Lyrics and music by Cole, †J. RO-SAMOND JOHNSON, and Joe Jordan. Romantic operetta involving a part-black, part-native American Indian woman and a young black man. The woman is rescued from her father's reservation, where the father has taken her after abducting her from her mother's house.

Rufus Rastus (1905/7). Book by †ERNEST HOGAN and William D. Hall (racial identity unknown). Lyrics by Lester A. Walton and Frank Williams. Music by Hogan, Joe Jordan, and Tom Lemonier. An unlucky character who cannot even raise the money to pay his rent accidentally comes into possession of a small fortune.

Runnin' de Town (1930). Book by †LEIGH WHIPPER. Music and lyrics by J. C. Johnson. About an ongoing feud between two rival fraternal groups and the efforts to bring about an end to their dispute.

Runnin' Wild (1923/24). Book by †FLOURNOY E. MILLER and †AUBREY LYLES. Lyrics by Cecil Mack. Music by James P. Johnson. The musical usually credited with introducing the popular black dance creation, the Charleston, to Broadway audiences, although *Liza* (1922) was actually the first. In this Miller & Lyles show, two swindlers are forced to flee town to avoid prosecution, but they return in disguise, posing as mediums.

Shades of Hades (1922/23). Book by Tim Owsley. Music and lyrics by Dave Payton. About a woman's attempt to cure her husband of jealousy by causing him to lose his memory; the memory loss, however, is not permanent.

The Shoo-Fly Regiment (1905/7). Book by †BOB COLE. Lyrics and music by Cole, †J. ROSAMOND JOHNSON, and James Weldon Johnson. About the role and heroism of black soldiers in the Spanish-American War; called the first true black operetta because of its well-written book and musical score.

Shuffle Along (1921; revived 1930, 1933, and 1952). Books mainly by †FLOURNOY E. MILLER and †AUBREY LYLES. Music and lyrics mainly by †NOBLE SISSLE and Eubie Blake. The best-known, most sensational, and most influential musical up to the 1920s, which set the pattern for black musicals for many years after. The thin plot had its setting in Jimtown in Dixieville on election day, and concerned the rivalry between two ignorant storekeepers (Miller & Lyles), both running for mayor of the town.

The Sons of Ham (1899/1900). Book by †JESSE A. SHIPP. Music mainly by †WILL MARION COOK. Based on production ideas by Bert Williams and George Walker. Two bums, played by Williams & Walker, are mistaken for twin brothers who are heirs to a large fortune.

Strut Miss Lizzie (1921). Book by †HENRY S. CREAMER. Lyrics and music by Creamer and J. Turner Layton. Musical conductor was Joe Jordan. Song and dance show, fashioned after *Shuffle Along* (1921), which glorified the "Creole" or fair-skinned beauty.

Sugar Hill (alternate title: *Meet Miss Jones,* 1931; revived 1947, 1950). Books mainly by †FLOURNOY E. MILLER and †AUBREY LYLES. Music mainly by James P. Johnson. Lyrics by Jo Trent. About the activities of a group of Harlem racketeers combined with a sketch of life in upper-middle-class Harlem society.

Swing It (1937). Book by †CECIL MACK. Lyrics by Mack and Milton Reddie. Music by Eubie Blake. Some entertainers from a Mississippi show boat try to find a better life in New York's Harlem, where they finally put on the show of shows.

A Trip to Coontown (1897/1901). Book, music, and lyrics mainly by †BOB COLE and †WILLIAM (BILLY) JOHNSON. Musical farce fleshed out with vaudeville specialty acts, featuring the character of Willie Wayside, a tramp, played by Cole. The plot revolved around the efforts of a bunko artist to swindle an old man out of his pension. Usually cited as the first black musical comedy.

Up and Down (1922). Book, lyrics, and music by †J. HOMER TUTT and †SALEM TUTT WHITNEY. Whitney & Tutt, as two con men, are being pursued across the country by a man who has lost money on one of their get-rich-quick schemes and wishes to get revenge.

A Chronology of Plays and Dramatic Works Classified by Genre

The following is a chronology of black-authored and coauthored plays and dramatic works for each decade from the 1820s to 1950, classified under the three major genres with which this book is concerned: stage works, screen works, and works for broadcasting. Cross-references are provided for the authors whose main entries are included in the Biographical Directory, as well as for those other playwrights and librettists listed in Appendixes A and B. Authors in the main directory will be indicated by the use of all capitals (e.g., OWEN DODSON). Authors listed in the two Appendixes will be followed by either (A) or (B) to indicate the appropriate appendix. Musicals will be indicated by (M), operas and operettas by (O). Adaptations will be indicated by (adapt.)

1820–1829

Stage Work:

Tom and Jerry; or, Life in London (adapt.) and *King Shotaway // The Drama of King Shotaway* (1823), [MISTER BROWN]

1830–1839

No plays or dramatic works.

1840–1849

Stage Works:

La Chute de Séjan and *Diégarias* (1844), V. SÉJOUR
The Black Doctor (adapt., 1847), I. ALDRIDGE
Titus Andronicus (adapt., 1849), I. ALDRIDGE

1850–1859

Stage Works:

La Tireuse de Cartes (1850), V. SÉJOUR

Richard III (1852), V. SéJOUR

Les Noces Vénitiennes (1855), V. SÉJOUR

L'Argent du Diable (1856) and *Le Fils de la Nuit* (1856), V. SÉJOUR

The Escape; or, A Leap for Freedom (1857), W. W. BROWN

André Girard (1858), V. SÉJOUR

Le Martyre du Coeur and *Le Paletot Brun* (1858), V. SÉJOUR

Les Grands Vassaux (1859), V. SÉJOUR

1860–1869

Stage Works:

Compère Guillery and *Les Massacres de la Syrie* (1860), V. SÉJOUR

Les Mystères du Temple and *Les Volontaires de 1814* (1862),V. SÉJOUR

Les Marquis Caporal (1864), V. SÉJOUR

Experience; or, How to Give a Northern Man a Backbone (1865), W. W. BROWN

Les Fils de Charles Quint and *Les Enfants de la Louve* (1865), V. SÉJOUR

La Madone des Roses (1868), V. SÉJOUR

1870–1879

Stage Works:

Cromwell and Le Vampire (1874), V. SÉJOUR

Out in the Streets (1875), S. N. Cook (A)

Slaves' Escape; or, The Underground Railroad // Peculiar Sam; or, The Underground Railroad (1879/80), P. E. HOPKINS

1880–1889

Stage Work:

The Disappointed Bride; or, Love at First Sight (1883), J. P. SAMPSON

1890–1899

Stage Works:

The Stolen Calf (1891), P. L. DUNBAR

Dessalines (1893), W. E. EASTON

Thirty Years of Freedom (1893), revised as *Fifty Years of Freedom* (1910), K. D. TILL-MAN

Dream Lovers (O, 1896), P. L. DUNBAR

A Trip to Coontown (M, 1897/1901), B. Cole (B) and W. Johnson (B)

Clorindy, the Origin of the Cakewalk (M, 1898/1901), W. M. Cook (B) and P. L. DUNBAR

Robert Herrick // Herrick, Uncle Eph's Christmas, and *Winter Roses* (1899), P. L. DUNBAR

The Sons of Ham (M) and *The Policy Players* (M) (1899/1900), J. A. Shipp (B)

Retribution (1890s), J. T. Franklin (A)

1900–1909

Stage Works:

The Author's Evening at Home (1900), A. M. DUNBAR-NELSON

Jes Lak White Folks (M, 1900), W. M. Cook (B) and P. L. DUNBAR

On the Island of Tanawana (M, 1900), P. L. DUNBAR

The Cannibal King (M, 1901), P. L. DUNBAR and J. Rosamond Johnson (B)

In Dahomey (M, 1902/5), J. A. Shipp (B) and P. L. DUNBAR

Caleb, the Degenerate (1903), J. S. COTTER, SR.

Darktown Circus Day (M, 1903), B. Cole (B)

The Black Politician (M, 1904), S. H. Dudley (B)

Rufus Rastus (M, 1905/7), E. Hogan (B)

The Shoo-Fly Regiment (M, 1905/7), B. Cole (B)

Abyssinia (M, 1906/7), J. A. Shipp (B) and A. C. Rogers (B)

Lord Earlington's Broken Vow, Aunt Hagar's Children, The Church Mouse, Gena, the Lost Child, Mr. Church, Parson Dewdrop's Bride (1906/25), R. Gaines-Shelton

Captain Rufus (M, 1907, 1914), J. Ed. Green (B) and A. Anderson (B)

The Oyster Man (M, 1907), F. E. Miller (B) and A. Lyles (B)

The Husband (M, 1907/8), F. E. Miller (B) and A. Lyles (B)

Bandanna Land (M, 1908), A. C. Rogers (B) and J. A. Shipp (B)

Blackville Strollers (M, 1908), S. T. Whitney (B) and J. H. Tutt (B)

Panama (M, 1908), M. A. Brooks (B) and C. A. Hunter (B)

The Red Moon (M, 1908/9), B. Cole (B)

The Colored Aristocrats (M, 1909), F. E. Miller (B) and A. Lyles (B)

Mayor of Newtown [also *Newton*](M, 1909/12), S. T. Whitney (B) and J. H. Tutt (B)

The Chastisement and *Caesar Driftwood* (1900s), J. S. COTTER, SR.

1910–1919

Stage Works:

Aunt Betsy's Thanksgiving (1910), K. D. TILLMAN.

Mr. Lode of Koal (M, 1910/11), J. E. Shipp (B) and A. C. Rogers (B)

Christophe (1911), W. E. EASTON

The Darktown Follies (evolution of several separate musicals, 1911/16), J. L. Hill (B) and A. C. Rogers (B)

Dr. Beans from Boston (M, 1911/12), S. H. Dudley (B) and H. Troy (B)

In the Jungles (M, 1911), W. A. Cook (B) and A. F. Watts (B)

The Star of Ethiopia (1911), W.E.B DuBOIS

Mr. Ragtime (M, 1912/15), I. C. Miller (B)

The Exiles, Melic Ric, The Pulcherian War Loan, The Sinews of War, The Statue and the Wasp, Which Should She Have Saved? (pre–1913), H. F. DOWNING

The Arabian Lioness; or, *The Sacred Jar* (1913), H. F. DOWNING

Hagar and Ishmael (1913), C. T. HIRSCH

In Ethiopiaville (M, 1913), F. Montgomery (B)

Lord Eldred's Other Daughter (1913), H. F. DOWNING

Old Man's Boy (M, 1913/14), A. C. Rogers (B) and H. Creamer (B)

Back Home Again, Colored Americans, Confidence, The Flash, The Frisco Kid, The Good Sister Jones, Happy Southern Folks, The Prison Life, Race Pride, Roseanna (1914/23), F. WILSON

Darkydom (M, 1914/15), H. Troy (B)

Incentives and *Voodoo* (1914), H. F. DOWNING

Pandora's Box (adapt., 1914), M. MILLER

Broadway Rastus (M, 1915), I. C. Miller (B)

Memories of Calvary (1915), O. W. BUSH

My Unfinished Portrait (1915), F. VOTEUR

The Problem (1915), F. G. Gilmore (A)

An Hawaiian Idyll (O, 1916), A. M. DUNBAR-NELSON

How Newtown Prepared [also *Newton*](M, 1916), S. T. Whitney (B), J. H. Tutt (B) [and T. L. Corwell]

Rachel (1916), A. W. GRIMKÉ

Jake Among the Indians (1917), P. W. GIBSON

Mines Eyes Have Seen (1918), A. M. DUNBAR-NELSON

Aftermath (1919), M. BURRILL

Baby Blues (M, 1919/20), A. C. Rogers (B)

The Birth of Freedom and the Present Age (1919), W. H. Tanner (A)

Children of the Sun (M, 1919), S. T. Whitney (B) and J. H. Tutt (B)

They That Sit in Darkness (1919), M. BURRILL

The Voice on the Wire (1919), A. Randle (A)

Screen Works:

The Homesteader and *Within Our Gates* (1918), O. MICHEAUX

1920–1929

Stage Works:

Brothers and Sisters of the Church Council (1920), E. SPENCE

The Deacon's Awakening (1920), W. RICHARDSON

On the Fields of France (1920), J. S. COTTER, JR.

The Racial Tangle (1920), H. F. DOWNING

The Return (1920), E. J. Morgan (A)

Within the Shadow (1920), M. MILLER

Sugar Cain // Sugar Cane (1920–26), F. WILSON

Bamboula (M, 1921), S. T. Whitney (B) and J. H. Tutt (B)

The Gold Piece (1921), L. HUGHES

The Heartbreaker (1921), F. WILSON

The King's Carpenters (1921), O. B. GRAHAM

The Dragon's Tooth and *The King's Dilemma* (1921), W. RICHARDSON

The Niche (1921), D. C. Norman (A)

Put and Take (M, 1921), I. C. Miller (B)

Shuffle Along (1921, 1930, 1933), F. E. Miller (B) and A. Lyles (B)

Strut Miss Lizzie (M, 1921), H. S. Creamer (B)

The Way of the World (1921), R. B. PRATT

Balo (1922), J. TOOMER

The Chip Woman's Fortune (1922), W. RICHARDSON

Christmas Gift (1922), R. EDMONDS

The Eddie Hunter Company (M, 1922), E. Hunter (B)

Genefrede (1922), H. W. HARRIS

Job Hunting (1922), R. EDMONDS

Natalie Mann (1922), J. TOOMER

Shades of Hades (M, 1922/23), T. Owsley (B)

Up and Down (M, 1922), J. Homer Tutt (B) and S. T. Whitney (B)

The Yellow Tree (1922), D. I. BUSEY

The Death Dance (1923), T. M. DUNCAN

Get Set (M, 1923), J. Bright (B) and D. HEYWOOD

Holiday (1923), O. B. GRAHAM

How Come? (M, 1923), E. Hunter (B)

Kabnis (1923), J. TOOMER

A Merchant in Dixie (1923), R. EDMONDS

Milestones of a Race (1923), L. FRENCH-CHRISTIAN

North Ain't South (M, 1923), S. T. Whitney (B), J. H. Tutt (B), J. A. Shipp (B), and D. HEYWOOD

Pa Williams' Gal (1923), F. WILSON

Raisin' Cain (M, 1923), F. Montgomery (B)

Runnin' Wild (M, 1923/24), F. E. Miller (B) and A. Lyles (B)

Select Plays: Jeptha's Daughter, The Prince of Peace, Santa Claus Land, and *Bachelor's Convention* (1923), C.L.M. FIGGS

The Sheik of Harlem (1923), I. C. Miller (B)

A Train North (1923), F. WILSON

Appearances (1924), G. ANDERSON

Because He Lives (1924), W. A. TOWNSEND

The Chocolate Dandies // In Bamville (M, 1924/25), N. Sissle (B) and L. PAYTON

Come Along Mandy (M, 1924), S. T. Whitney (B), J. H. Tutt (B), and D. HEYWOOD

Doom (1924), R. EDMONDS

Ethiopia at the Bar of Justice (1924), E. J. McCOO

Mortgaged (1924), W. RICHARDSON

Negro Nuances (M, 1924), A. Mitchell (B), F. E. Miller (B), and A. Lyles (B)

Out of the Dark (1924), D. C. GUINN

Black Man: A Fantasy (1925), C. BURROUGHS

The Bog Guide (1925), M. MILLER

The Broken Banjo (1925), W. RICHARDSON

The Cabaret Girl (1925), F. JOHNSON

The Church Fight (1925), R. GAINES-SHELTON

Color Struck (1925), Z. N. HURSTON

Compromise (1925), W. RICHARDSON

Fall of the Conjurer (1925), W. RICHARDSON

For Unborn Children(1925), M. S. LIVINGSTON

Frances (1925), G. D. LIPSCOMB

The [Black] Highwayman (1925), R. EDMONDS

Humble Instrument (1925), W. A. McDONALD

Sahdji, an African Ballet (1925), R. B. NUGENT

Spears (1925), Z. N. HURSTON

Sunday Morning in the South (1925), G. D. JOHNSON

Africana // Miss Calico (M, 1926/27), D. HEYWOOD (coauthor)

An' de Walls Came Tumblin' Down (1926), O. HUNTER (coauthor)

Antar of Araby (1926), M. CUNEY-HARE

Black Passion Play (annually 1926/73), W. S. JONES

Blood (1926), W. A. McDONALD

Blue Blood (1926), G. D. JOHNSON

Blue Moon (M, 1926), D. HEYWOOD and I. C. Miller (B)

The Bootblack Lover (1926), W. RICHARDSON

The Chasm (1926), W. RICHARDSON and E. C. WILLIAMS

Color Worship and *Time Flies* (1926), F. WILSON

'Cruiter (1926), J. F. MATHEUS

The Cuss'd Thing (1926), M. MILLER

A Dream of Enchantment (1926), E. A. FOSTER

The First One (1926), Z. N. HURSTON

Foreign Mail (1926), E. SPENCE

4–11–44 // Struttin' Hannah from Savannah (M, 1926/27), E. Hunter (B)

Illicit Love, Peter Stith, and *Rocky Roads* (1926), R. EDMONDS

My Magnolia (M, 1926), A. C. Rogers (B) and E. Hunters (B)

Rooms for Rent (1926), W. RICHARDSON

The Starter (1926), E. SPENCE

Bleeding Hearts (1927), R. EDMONDS

Bottomland (M, 1927), C. Williams (B)

Bring Dat College Home (1927), G. W. Hodges (A)

Broadway Rastus (M, 1927), I. Miller (B)

Brown Sugar (M, 1927), M. Garvey (B) and S. Manning (B)

The Chip Woman's Fortune (3-act version, 1927), W. RICHARDSON

College Life and *In Defense of Him* (pre–1928), C. W. WOOD

Dinah (M, 1927), I. C. Miller (B)

Exit, an Illusion (1927), M. O. BONNER

Flight of the Natives (1927), W. RICHARDSON

(The) Fool's Errand (1927), E. SPENCE

Four Eleven (1927), W. JACKSON

Great Temptations (M, 1927), D. HEYWOOD (coauthor)

Helen Harmon (1927), W. M. ASHBY

Her (1927), E. SPENCE

His Cross (1927), P. Dixon (A)

Hot Stuff (1927), E. SPENCE

The Hunch and *Undertow* (1927), E. SPENCE

Idle Head (1927), W. RICHARDSON

Mandy (1927), W. J. Jefferson (A)

Off Col'uh (1927), A. L. WEBER

Plumes (1927), G. D. JOHNSON

The Purple Flower (1927), M. O. BONNER

Rang Tang (M, 1927), K. Gynt (B)

The Sacred Factory (1927), J. TOOMER

Silas Brown and *The Virginia Politician* (1927), R. EDMONDS

The Wine Seller (1927), W. RICHARDSON

Deep Harlem (M, 1928/29), S. T. Whitney (B) and J. H. Tutt (B)

Episode (1928), E. SPENCE

The Gallonwerps (1928), J. TOOMER

Keep Shufflin' (M, 1928), F. E. Miller (B) and A. Lyles (B)

Meek Mose // *Brother Mose* (1928), F. WILSON

One Side of Harlem (1928), R. EDMONDS

Osceola (1928), F. BUNDY and C. LEDERER

The Peacock's Feather (1928), W. RICHARDSON

Sirlock Bones, Stock Exchange (M), and *Takazee* (1928), R. EDMONDS

Son Boy (1928), J. S. MITCHELL

Toussaint L'Ouverture (1928), L. P. HILL

The Unending War (1928), A. C. Miller (A)

Wine of Life (1928), A. L. WEBER

The Exile and *The Sheriff's Daughter* (pre–1929), E. C. WILLIAMS

Blackbirds of 1930 // *Lew Leslie's Blackbirds of 1930* (M, 1929), F. E. Miller (B)

Black Damp (1929), J. F. MATHEUS

The Black Horseman (1929), W. RICHARDSON

Denmark Vesey (1929), R. EDMONDS

La Divina Pastora (1929), E. SPENCE

Gingersnaps (M, 1929), J. H. Tutt (B), S. T. Whitney (B), and D. HEYWOOD

The Girl from Back Home // *The Girl from Bam* (1929), R. COLEMAN

Harlem (1929), W. THURMAN (coauthor)

Help Wanted (1929), J. S. MITCHELL

Hot Chocolates // Connie's Hot Chocolates (M, 1929), A. Razaf (B)

The House of Sham (1929), W. RICHARDSON

Malinda (M, 1929), D. DONOGHUE

Pierrot at Sea (1929), L. M. ALEXANDER

St. Louis 'Ooman (O, 1929), M. COOK

Stragglers in the Dust (1929), M. MILLER

Summertime (M, 1929), C. MOSS

Tambour (1929), J. F. MATHEUS

The Wall Between (1929), F. WILSON

The Scarlet Shawl (1920s), T. M. DUNCAN

The Slabtown District Convention (1920s), N. H. BURROUGHS

A Song in the Night (1920s), W. A. TOWNSEND

Two Races (1920s), I. M. BURKE

Where Is My Wandering Boy Tonight? (1920s), N. H. BURROUGHS

The Light of the Women (pre–1930), F. GUNNER

And Still They Paused, Midnight and Dawn, A Bill to Be Passed, Blue-Eyed Black Boy, Camel-Legs, Heritage, Miss Bliss, Money Wagon, Safe, Jungle Love, Little Blue Pigeon, The New Day, One Cross Enough, Red Shoes, Well-Diggers, Scapegoat, The Starting Point, and *Sue Bailey* (pre–1930s), G. D. JOHNSON

Screen Works:

The Brute and *Symbol of the Unconquered // The Wilderness Trail* (1920), O. MICHEAUX

Toussaint L'Ouverture (1920), C. MUSE

Deceit, The Gunsaulus Mystery, The Hypocrite, and *The Shadow* (1921), O. MICHEAUX

The Sport of Gods (1921), C. MUSE (adapt. from P. L. DUNBAR)

The Dungeon, The Ghost of Tolson's Manor, Uncle Jasper's Will // Jasper Landry's Will, and *The Virgin of the Seminole* (1922), O. MICHEAUX

By Right of Birth (1923), G. P. JOHNSON

The House Behind the Cedars (1923), O. MICHEAUX

Birthright, Body and Soul, and *A Son of Satan* (1924), O. MICHEAUX

Marcus Garland (1925), O. MICHEAUX

The Conjure Woman and *The Spider's Web* (1926), O. MICHEAUX

The Broken Violin (1927), O. MICHEAUX

Dark Princess (adapt.?), *A Fool's Errand* (adapt.?), *The Racial Tangle* (adapt. from H. F. DOWNING), *Thirty Years Later* (adapt. from H. F. DOWNING) (1928), O. MICHEAUX.

Tenderfeet (1928), S. WILLIAMS

Brown Gravy, Hot Biscuits, The Melancholy Dame, and *Music Hath Charms* (1929), S. WILLIAMS (coauthor)

The Wages of Sin and *When Men Betray* (1929), O. MICHEAUX

1930–1939

Stage Works:

Drama Enters the Curriculum (1930), R. EDMONDS

The Elopement (1930), J. S. MITCHELL

The Faith Cure, Reachin' for the Sun, and *She Dyed for a Prince* (1930), A. C. LAMB

Graven Images (1930), M. MILLER

Hot Rhythm (M, 1930), D. HEYWOOD (coauthor)

Jeremiah the Magnificent (1930), W. THURMAN

Mulatto (1930), L. HUGHES

Paradox (1930), R. COLEMAN

Riding the Goat (1930), M. MILLER

Runnin' de Town (1930), L. Whipper (B)

Sacrifice (1930), T. M. DUNCAN

Shades and Shadows (collection, 1930), R. EDMONDS [Includes: *The Devil's Price, Hewers of Wood, Shades and Shadows, Everyman's Land, The Tribal Chief,* and *The Phantom Treasure*]

Ti Yette, (1930), J. F. MATHEUS

You Must Be Bo'n Again (1930), A. M. BURRIS

Alabama Bound (M, 1931), I. C. Miller (B)

Black Magic (1931), T. M. DUNCAN

Burning the Mortgage (1931), W. JACKSON

Climbing Jacob's Ladder (1931), R. M. ANDREWS

Cock o' de World (M, 1931), L. HUGHES (adapt. from K. Gynt [B])

College Blunders and *The Diamond Necklace* (1931), H. S. FELTON

Environment (1931), M. GILBERT

The Exodus (1931), L. M. Turner (A)

Fast and Furious (M, 1931), Z. N. HURSTON et al. (sketches)

Jethro (1931), L. P. HILL

Job Hunters (1931), H.F.V. EDWARD

The Man of God (1931), R. EDMONDS

Pitfalls of Appearances (1931), G. A. Woods (A)

Sacrifice (1931), C. MOSS and R. Huey (A)

Scottsboro Limited (1931), L. HUGHES

Sermon in the Valley (1931), Z. N. HURSTON

Shade of Cottonlips (1931), A. C. LAMB

Sugar Hill // Meet Miss Jones (M, 1931, 1947, 1950), F. E. Miller (B) and A. Lyles (B)

Sunrise (1931), H. DREER

Taxi Fare (1931), R. McCLENDON and R. B. NUGENT

Bad Man (1932), R. EDMONDS

Blackberries of 1932 (M, 1932), E. Green (B)

Black Souls (1932), A. N. Meyer (A)

The Bright Medallion, The Eyes of the Old, and *Two Gods: A Minaret* (1932), D. PRICE

George Washington and the Black Folk (1932), W.E.B. DuBOIS

Get Thee Behind Me, Satan (1932), R. Dorsey (A)

Great Day // From Sun to Sun // Singing Steel (1932/34), Z. N. HURSTON

Ham's Daughter (M, 1932), D. DONOGHUE

Hoo-dooed (1932), E. H. Huffman (A)

Little Stone House (1932), G. Cogman (A)

Ol' Man Satan (1932), D. HEYWOOD

The Opener of Doors (1932), A. C. Miller (A)

The Prodigal Son (1932), H. Camp (A)

Tom-Tom (O, 1932), S. G. DuBOIS

Underground (1932), R. M. ANDREWS

The Watchword Is Forward (1932), D. Campbell (A)

Backstage and *Drifting Souls* (1933), H. S. FELTON

Louisiana (1933), J. A. SMITH

Nails and Thorns (1933), M. MILLER

Run, Little Chillun! (M, 1933), H. JOHNSON

St. Louis Woman (M, 1933), A. BONTEMPS and C. CULLEN

Africana (O, 1934), D. HEYWOOD

The Call of Jubah, The High Court of Historia, and *For Fatherland* (1934), R. ED-MONDS

Color-Blind (1934), P. Sinclair (A)

Legal Murder and *Beale Street* (1934), D. DONOGHUE

Mimi La Croix (1934), E. Coles (A)

New Courage and *A Sign* (1934), G. STREATOR

Richard Allen: From a Slave to the First Bishop of African Methodist Episcopal Church, 1716–1816 (1934), D. M. BAXTER

Six Plays for a Negro Theatre: Bad Man, Old Man Pete, Nat Turner, Breeders, Bleeding Hearts, and *New Window* (1934), R. EDMONDS

Antonio Maceo, Attucks, the Martyr, The Elder Dumas, In Menelik's Court, and *Near Calvary* (1935), W. RICHARDSON

Blood on the Fields and *Little Ham* (1935), L. HUGHES

Christophe's Daughters, Harriet Tubman, Samory, and *Sojourner Truth* (1935), M. MILLER

Cinda (1935), H. J. BATES

Crack of the Whip (1935), R. T. HAMILTON

Doc's Place and *Rho Kappa Epsilon* (1935), J. M. ROSS

A Drama of the Southwest (1935), J. TOOMER

Drums of the Bayou (1935), R. Ingram (A)

The Emperor of Haiti // Troubled Island and *Drums of Haiti* (1935), L. HUGHES

The Fiery Chariot (1935), Z. N. HURSTON

The Medea // By-Word for Evil (adapt., 1935), C. CULLEN

The Royal Road to Damascus (1935), W. M. ASHBY

Sweet Land (1935), C. SEILER

The Two Gifts (1935), A. C. LAMB

William and Ellen Craft (1935), G. D. JOHNSON

Yellow Death (1935), R. EDMONDS

Angelo Herndon Jones, No Left Turn, and *St. Louis Woman* (revision of A. BONTEMPS and C. CULLEN's script) (1936), L. HUGHES

Black Rhythm (M, 1936), D. HEYWOOD

(The) Conjur Man Dies (adapt., 1936), A. BONTEMPS and C. CULLEN (from R. FISHER)

De Gospel Train // Jim Crow (1936, 1940), J. H. Tutt (B) [and S. T. Whitney (B)]

Heaven Bound (1936), L. L. EDWARDS

Jane (adapt.) and *Including Laughter* (1936), O. DODSON

John Henry (1936), F. B. WELLS

Lysistrata (adapt.) and *Natural Man // This Ole Hammer* (1936), T. BROWNE

The Man of God (1936), H. DREER

One Clear Call (1936), J. M. ROSS

One Way to Heaven (1936), C. CULLEN

Turpentine (1936), J. A. SMITH (coauthor)

Walk Together Chillun (1936), F. WILSON

When the Jack Hollars, or Careless Love (1936), A. BONTEMPS and L. HUGHES

The Case of Philip Lawrence (1937), G. MacENTEE

Did Adam Sin? and Other Stories of Negro Life in Comedy, Drama and Sketches (collection, 1937), L. PAYTON [Includes *Did Adam Sin?, A Bitter Pill, A Flyin' Fool, A Bitter Pill, A Flying' Fool, Some Sweet Day, Two Sons of Ham,* and *Who Is de Boss?*]

Don't You Want to Be Free, *Soul Gone Home*, and *Joy to My Soul* (1937), L. HUGHES

Go Down Moses (1937), R. E. HAYDEN

How Come, Lawd? (1937), D. HEYWOOD

John Henry (1937), I. DeA. REID

Just Ten Days (1937), J. A. SMITH

The Seer (1937), J. W. BUTCHER

The Shining Town (1937), O. DODSON

Sick and Tiahd (1937), T. WARD

So Shall You Reap and *Stealing Lightning* (1937), A. HILL

Strivin' (1937), J. M. ROSS

Swing, Gates, Swing (M) and *A Black Woman Called Moses // Go Down Moses* (1937), T. BROWNE

Swing Song (1937), R. COLEMAN

The Trial of Dr. Beck (1937), H. ALLISON

Big White Fog, *Falcon of Adowa*, and *Even the Dead Arise* (1938), T. WARD

Crossroads, Shattered Dreams, Blood in the Night, and *Cocktails* (1938), L. Mitchell (A)

Darker Brother (1938), C. SEILER

De Organizer (O, 1938), L. HUGHES

Divine Comedy (1938), O. DODSON

Dust to Earth // Coal Dust (1938), S. G. DuBOIS

Hell's Alley (1938), ALVIN CHILDRESS

Hell's Half Acre (1938), A. HILL

In Greener Pastures and *Ma Johnson's Harlem Boardinghouse* (series of sketches, 1938), M. GILBERT

Jedgement Day and *Smokey* (1938), T. D. PAWLEY III

Liberty Deferred (1938), A. HILL and J. SILVERA

Little Eva's End, *Like a Flame* (adapt. from Hughes), *Em-Fuehrer Jones*, *Front Porch*, and *Limitations of Life* (1938), L. HUGHES

Panyared (1938), H. ALLISON

Unto the Least (adapt. 1938), F. SILVERA

Wives and Blues and *The Land of Cotton // Sharecroppers* (1938), R. EDMONDS

Young Man of Harlem (1938), P. LINDSAY

The Amistad and *Garden of Time // With This Darkness* (1939), O. DODSON

The Black Messiah // The Demi-God (1939), D. DONOGHUE (coauthor)

Booker T. Washington // Let Me Die in the South (1939), W. M. ASHBY

Family Affair (1939), F. W. BOND

Freedom in My Soul (1939), T. D. PAWLEY III

Gangsters over Harlem (1939), R. EDMONDS

Joy Exceeding Glory // Head of the Family (1939), G. E. NORFORD

Place: America (1939), T. RICHARDSON

Prelude in Swing (M, 1939), C. MOSS

A Right Angle Triangle (1939), F. VOTEUR

Scufflin' (1939), L. Hicks (A)

Skin Deep (1939), T. WARD

(On) Striver's Row and *Latin, Greek or Grits* (1939), A. HILL

Festus De Fus (1930s), E. Coles (A)

Juba (1930s), W. Coleman (A)

Milk and Honey (1930s), J. W. BUTCHER, JR.

Mule Bone (1930s), Z. N. HURSTON and L. HUGHES

The Sharecroppers (1930s), G. A. TOWNS

Trouble with the Angels (1930s), adapt. from L. HUGHES

Wanting (1930s), E. ROXBOROUGH

Screen Works:

Darktown Review // Darktown Scandals Review (1930), O. MICHEAUX

A Daughter of the Congo (adapt., 1930), O. MICHEAUX (from H. F. DOWNING)

Easy Street (1930), O. MICHEAUX

The Exile (1931), O. MICHEAUX

The Black King (1932), D. HEYWOOD

Black Magic, Ten Minutes to Live, The Girl from Chicago, Veiled Aristocrats, and *The Phantom of Kenwood* (1932), O. MICHEAUX

Ten Minutes to Kill (1933), O. MICHEAUX

Harlem After Midnight (1934), O. MICHEAUX

High School Girl and *Tomorrow's Children* (1934), W. THURMAN

The Whipping // Ready for Love (1934), E. SPENCE

Lem Hawkins' Confession (1935), O. MICHEAUX

Temptation and *Underworld* (1936), O. MICHEAUX

Spirit of Youth (1937), C. MUSE (coauthor)

God's Stepchildren and *Swing* (1938), O. MICHEAUX

Birthright, Lying Lips, and *The Notorious Elinor Lee* (1939), O. MICHEAUX

Harlem Rides the Range (1939), S. WILLIAMS and F. E. Miller (B)

Paradise in Harlem (1939), F. WILSON

Way Down South (1939), L. HUGHES and C. MUSE

Lifeboat 13 (1930s), S. EASTON

Works for Radio Broadcasting:

"Careless Love" (series, 1931), C. MOSS

Noah and *Folks from Dixie* (1932/33), C. MOSS

1940–1950

Stage Works:

Black Woman in White // Beebee (1940), A. C. LAMB

Cavalcade of the Negro Theatre (1940), L. HUGHES and A. BONTEMPS

The Gravy Train (1940), T. BROWNE

I Gotta Home (1940), S. G. DuBOIS

Jungle Justice (1940), L. J. LOVETTE

No Majesty (1940), F. Yerby (A)

Tropics After Dark (M, 1940), L. HUGHES and A. BONTEMPS

Dead Men Don't Dance and Protest // Protest (post–1940), T. RICHARDSON

Christmas Gifts, Christmas Morning, Jacob and Esau, A Leap in the Dark, The Prodigal Son, Samuel, Tell Mother I'll Be There (pre–1941), H. DREER

The Moses of Beale Street (pre–1941), M. B. TOLSON (coauthor)

Deliver the Goods, Our Lan', and *Shoot Hallelujah!* (1941), T. WARD

Doomsday Tale (1941/42), O. DODSON

Elijah's Ravens and *Track Thirteen* (1941), S. G. DuBOIS

Frederick Douglass (1941), H. W. HARRIS

House of Darkness (1941), H. S. FELTON

It's Midnight over Newark (1941), H. ALLISON

Miss or Mrs. (1941), W. RICHARDSON

Native Son (1941), R. WRIGHT (coauthor)

Ouanga (O, 1941), J. F. MATHEUS

(The) Sun Do Move // Sold Away (M, 1941), L. HUGHES

Tropicana (M, 1941), D. HEYWOOD

Forty Years of Progress (1942), B. V. Kelly (A)

The Land of Cotton and Other Plays (collection, 1942, R. EDMONDS [Contains *The Land of Cotton, Gangsters over Harlem, Yellow Death, Silas Brown*, and *The High Court of Historia*]

That Eagle (1942), L. HUGHES

Someday We're Gonna Tear Them Pillars Down (1942), O. DODSON

Heroes on Parade (series of 16 plays, 1942/43), O. DODSON

Freedom's Children on the March (1943), M. MILLER

G. I. Rhapsody, The Shadow Across the Path, The Shape of Wars to Come, and *Simon in Cyrene* (1943), R. EDMONDS

Hotel Black Majesty (1943), L. HUGHES

Anna Lucasta (adapt., 1944), A. HILL

Famous Women in Haitian History (1944), M. COOK (Trans.)

Goldbrickers of 1944 (M, 1944), O. Davis (A)

Haiti Our Neighbor (1944), H. Ch. ROSEMOND

New World A-Coming (1944), O. DODSON (adapt. from R. OTTLEY)

Polk County (1944), Z. N. HURSTON

Blood Doesn't Tell (1945), E. AUSTIN

Swing Wedding (1945), M. Glanville (A)

The Trial and Banishment of Uncle Tom (1945), R. EDMONDS

Wanga Doll (1945/46), J. M. ROSS

The Choreography of Love (O, 1946), T. Brewster (A)

Earth and Stars (1946), R. EDMONDS

Millsboro Memorial (1946), A. C. LAMB

The Third Fourth of July (1946), C. CULLEN and O. DODSON

Alexis Is Fallen (1947), O. Davis (A)

The Bancroft Dynasty and *The Cellar* (1947), L. Mitchell (A)

Crispus Attucks // Son of Liberty (1947), T. D. PAWLEY III

The Purple Lily (1947/48), J. M. ROSS

Rare Cut Glass (1947), G. D. MADDOX

Street Scene (O, 1947), L. HUGHES (coauthor)

Whatever the Battle Be (1947/50), R. EDMONDS

All over Nothin' (1948), F. L. Lights (A)

Bayou Legend (adapt., 1948), O. DODSON

Cow in the Apartment (1948), H. Holifield (A)

The History of Punchinello (1948), R. E. HAYDEN

Letter and Lottery (1948), T. Brewster (A)

The Power of Darkness (adapt., 1948), A. HILL

Prometheus and the Atom (1948/50), R. EDMONDS

The Sword (1948), J. M. ROSS

A Temporary Island (1948), L. Fuller (A)

This Way Forward (1948), G. Jeannette (A)

The Witch Hunt (1948), G. S. SCHUYLER

Andromeda (M) and *Look Eastward* (M) (1949), T. Brewster (A)

Bought with Cookies (1949), G. P. McBrown (A)

Florence (1949), Alice Childress (A)

The Mayor of Harlem and *Point Blank* (1949), O. Davis (A)

My Mother Came Crying Most Pitifully (1949), C. Seebree (A)

Of Human Grandeur // John Brown (1949), T. WARD

The Pit (1949), J. B. Black (A)

Troubled Island (O, 1949), L. HUGHES

Black Monday's Children (1940s), G. D. MADDOX

Hope of the Lonely (1940s), W. RICHARDSON

Adam and Eve and the Apple (O), *At the Jazz Ball* (O), *Outshines the Sun*, and *Tell It to Telstar* (M) and *Wide River* (O) (pre–1950), L. HUGHES

Christmas Bells (pre–1950), A. J. Cooper (A)

The Fire in the Flint, Black No More, and *Black Boy* (pre–1950), M. B. TOLSON (adapt. from W. White, G. S. SCHUYLER, and R. WRIGHT)

The Hand of Fate; or, Fifty Years After (pre–1950), B. Gale (A)

The Prince of Mandalore (pre–1950), J. MURRAY

The Barrier (O, 1950), L. HUGHES

Constellation of Women (1950), O. DODSON

Country Gentleman (1950), J. Carter (A)

Crosswise and *Frederick Douglass: A Testament of Freedom* (1950), L. C. ARCHER

J. Toth (1950/51), H. Holifield (A)

The Jackal (1950), S. HOWARD

Just a Little Simple (1950), Alice Childress (A)

The Last Dance for Sybil (1950), O. Davis (A)

Legion, the Demoniac (1950), E. M. Huntley (A)

Let the Day Perish (1950s), W. E. TURPIN

Screen Works:

Broken Strings (1940), C. MUSE (coauthor)

Son of Ingagi (1940), S. WILLIAMS

The Blood of Jesus (1941), S. WILLIAMS

Sunday Sinners and *Murder on Lenox Avenue* (1941), F. WILSON and D. HEYWOOD

The Negro Soldier (1943), C. MOSS

Go Down Death (1944), S. WILLIAMS

Team Work (1944), C. MOSS

Marching On and *Of One Blood* (1945), S. WILLIAMS

They Seek a City // Migration, Journey to Paradise // Where You From? (drafts of screenplays, 1945), O. DODSON

Juke Joint (1947), S. WILLIAMS
The Betrayal (1948), O. MICHEAUX

Works for Radio Broadcasting:

Booker T. Washington in Atlanta (1940), L. HUGHES
George Washington Carver, the Wizard of Tuskegee (1940), M. W. BROWN
Fire and Cloud (1941), adapt. from R. WRIGHT
Jubilee: A Cavalcade of the Negro Theatre (1941), L. HUGHES and A. BONTEMPS
Brothers (1942), L. HUGHES
For This We Fight (1942/44), L. HUGHES
Freedom's Plow and *John Henry Hammers It Out* (1943), L. HUGHES
The Midwest Mobilizes (1943), O. DODSON
In the Service of My Country and *The Man Who Went to War* (1944), L. HUGHES
The Negro Domestic ("New World A'Coming" series, 1944), R. OTTLEY
"New World A'Coming" (series, 1944/46), R. OTTLEY (concept and scripts)
St. Louis Woman ("New World A'Coming" series, 1944), adapt. by O. DODSON from
    C. CULLEN and A. BONTEMPS
"New World A'Coming" (series, 1945), O. DODSON (scripts)
Pvt. Jim Crow (1945), L. HUGHES
Portrait of a Pioneer (1949), A. C. LAMB
Swing Time at the Savoy (1949), L. HUGHES (coauthor)

INFORMATION SOURCES

LIBRARIES AND REPOSITORIES

The following libraries and repositories have strong collections in early black American drama and theatre, and may be useful in locating further information on the playwrights included in this Directory:

AMERICAN ACADEMY OF ARTS AND LETTERS LIBRARY
633 W. 155th St.
New York, NY 10032
  (Langston Hughes Papers)

AMISTAD RESEARCH CENTER
(Dillard University)
400 Esplanade Ave.
New Orleans, LA 70116
  (Countee Cullen Papers; Manuscript Collection)

BOSTON PUBLIC LIBRARY
666 Boylston St.
Boston, MA 02117
  (Drama and Theatre Collections)

CHICAGO PUBLIC LIBRARY CULTURAL CENTER
75 E. Washington St.
Chicago, IL 60602
  (Chicago Theatre Collection)

CLARK ATLANTA UNIVERSITY RESEARCH CENTER
Robert W. Woodruff Library
111 James P. Brawley Drive, S.W.
Atlanta, GA 30314
   (Countee Cullen/Harold Jackman Collection; Hoyt Fuller Collection; Papers of Maud Cuney-Hare)

DETROIT PUBLIC LIBRARY
Music and Performing Arts Dept.
5201 Woodward Ave.
Detroit, MI 48202
   (E. Azalia Hackley Memorial Collection)

DuSABLE MUSEUM OF AFRICAN-AMERICAN HISTORY
3806 S. Michigan Ave.
Chicago, IL 60653
   (Library Collection)

FISK UNIVERSITY LIBRARY AND MEDIA CENTER
17th Ave. N.
Nashville, TN 37203
   (Papers of Countee Cullen, Pauline Hopkins, Langston Hughes, Jean Toomer, and others)

HATCH-BILLOPS COLLECTION
491 Broadway
New York, NY 10012
   (Published Play Collection; Oral History Collection; Owen and Edith Dodson Memorial Collection)

HOWARD UNIVERSITY LIBRARIES
Moorland-Spingarn Research Center Library
2400 Sixth St., N.W.
Washington, DC 20059
   (Moorland Collection; Spingarn Collection)

LIBRARY OF CONGRESS
10 First St., S.E.
Washington, DC 20540
   (Manuscript Division; Rare Book Collection; Film Collection)

LOUISVILLE FREE PUBLIC LIBRARY
Fourth and York Sts.
Louisville, KY 40203
  (Papers of Joseph S. Cotter, Sr.)

NATIONAL ARCHIVES
Pennsylvania Ave. and Eighth St., N.W.
Washington, DC 20408
  (Federal Theatre Project Records—Record Group Number 69)

NEW YORK PUBLIC LIBRARY
Performing Arts Research Center
111 Amsterdam Ave.
New York, NY 10023
  (Theatre Collection/New York Public Library, also known as the Billy Rose Theatre Collection)

NEW YORK PUBLIC LIBRARY
Schomburg Center for Research in Black Culture
515 Lenox Ave.
New York, NY 10037
  (Schomburg Collection)

OHIO HISTORICAL SOCIETY
Interstate 71 and 17th Ave.
Columbus, OH 43211
  ([Paul Laurence] Dunbar Collection)

RESEARCH CENTER FOR THE FEDERAL THEATRE PROJECT
(Also called the Institute on the Federal Theatre Project and New Deal Culture)
George Mason University
4400 University Dr.
Fairfax, VA 22030
  (Federal Theatre Project Collection)

STATE HISTORICAL SOCIETY OF WISCONSIN
Archives and Manuscript Division
816 State St.
Madison, WI 52706
  (Langston Hughes Papers)

SYRACUSE UNIVERSITY
Carnegie Library
Syracuse, NY 13210
  (Arna Bontemps Papers)

UNIVERSITY OF MICHIGAN
Dept. of Rare Books and Special Collections
Ann Arbor, MI 48104
  (Special Collections)

UNIVERSITY MICROFILMS INTERNATIONAL
300 N. Zeeb Road
Ann Arbor, MI 48106
  (Dissertations, Theses, Out-of-Print Books, Black Newspapers in Microform)

UNIVERSITY OF WASHINGTON LIBRARIES
Suzallo Library
Seattle, WA 98195
  (Archives of the Seattle Repertory Playhouse)

YALE UNIVERSITY
Beinecke Library
New Haven, CT 06520
  (James Weldon Johnson Memorial Collection)

ANALYTICAL TITLE LIST OF PLAY ANTHOLOGIES THAT INCLUDE ONE OR MORE PLAYS BY BLACK AMERICAN PLAYWRIGHTS

For individually published plays and collections of plays by a single playwright, consult the playwright's entry in the main directory. For the most frequently cited anthologies, bibliographical abbreviations are given in brackets.

American Literature by Negro Authors, ed. by Herman Dreer. New York: Macmillan, 1950. Contains: **The House of Sham,** by WILLIS RICHARDSON. **Legion, the Demoniac,** by Elizabeth Maddox Huntley. [*AmLitNA*]
American Scenes: A Volume of Short Plays, ed. by William Kozlenko. New York: John Day, 1941. Contains: **Fire and Cloud,** adapt. by °Charles K. O'Neill from a short story by RICHARD WRIGHT.
Anthology of American Negro Literature, ed. by V. F. Calverton. New York: Modern Lib., 1944. Contains: **Plumes,** by GEORGIA DOUGLAS JOHNSON.
Anthology of the American Negro in the Theatre, ed. by Lindsay Patterson. New York:

Publishers Co., 1967. Contains: **The Chip Woman's Fortune,** by WILLIS RICH-
ARDSON. [*AnthANT*]

Black American Literature, 1760–Present, ed. by Ruth Miller. New York: Glencoe Press,
1971. Contains: **'Cruiter,** by JOHN MATHEUS.

Black Drama: An Anthology, ed. by William Brasmer and Dominick Consolo. Columbus,
OH: Charles E. Merrill, 1970. Contains: **Mulatto,** by LANGSTON HUGHES.
Native Son, a revised dramatization by [RICHARD WRIGHT and] °Paul Green.

Black Drama in America: An Anthology, ed. by Darwin T. Turner. Greenwich, CT:
Fawcett Publications, 1971. Contains: **The Chip Woman's Fortune,** by WILLIS
RICHARDSON. **The Emperor of Haiti,** by LANGSTON HUGHES. **Our Lan',**
by THEODORE WARD. **Earth and Stars,** by RANDOLPH EDMONDS. **Bayou
Legend,** by OWEN DODSON.

Black Scenes, ed. by Alice Childress. Garden City, NY: Zenith Books, 1971. Contains:
Excerpt from **The Daubers,** by THEODORE WARD. Excerpt from **Natural
Man,** by THEODORE WARD.

Black Theater: A Twentieth Century Collection of the Work of Its Best Playwrights, comp.
by Lindsay Patterson. New York: Dodd, Mead, 1971. Contains: **St. Louis
Woman,** by ARNA BONTEMPS and COUNTEE CULLEN. **Simply Heavenly,**
by LANGSTON HUGHES.

Black Theater, U.S.A.: Forty-Five Plays by Black Americans, 1847–1974, ed. by James
V. Hatch and Ted Shine, consultant. New York: The Free Press, 1974. Contains:
The Black Doctor, by IRA ALDRIDGE. **The Brown Overcoat,** by VICTOR
SÉJOUR. **The Escape; or, A Leap for Freedom,** by WILLIAM WELLS
BROWN. **Caleb the Degenerate,** by JOSEPH S. COTTER, SR. **Appearances,**
by GARLAND ANDERSON. **Rachel,** by ANGELINA GRIMKÉ. **Mine Eyes
Have Seen,** by ALICE DUNBAR-NELSON. **They That Sit in Darkness,** by
MARY BURRILL. **For Unborn Children,** by MYRTLE SMITH LIVINGSTON.
The Church Fight, by RUTH GAINES-SHELTON. **Undertow,** by EULALIE
SPENCE. **The Purple Flower,** by MARITA BONNER. **A Sunday Morning in
the South,** by GEORGIA DOUGLAS JOHNSON. **Balo,** by JEAN TOOMER.
'Cruiter, by JOHN MATHEUS. **The Idle Head** and **The Flight of the Natives,**
by WILLIS RICHARDSON. **Bad Man,** by RANDOLPH EDMONDS. **Big White
Fog,** by THEODORE WARD. **Divine Comedy,** by OWEN DODSON. **Graven
Images,** by MAY MILLER. **Natural Man,** by THEODORE WARD. **Native
Son,** by RICHARD WRIGHT and °Paul Green. **Walk Hard,** by ABRAM HILL.
The Tumult and the Shouting, by THOMAS PAWLEY. **Limitations of Life**
and **Little Ham,** by LANGSTON HUGHES. [*BlkThUSA*]

Black Writers of America: A Comprehensive Anthology, ed. by Richard Barksdale and
Kenneth Kinnamon. New York: Macmillan, 1972. Contains: **The Broken Banjo,**
by WILLIS RICHARDSON.

Cavalcade: Negro American Writing from 1760 to the Present, ed. by Arthur D. Davis
and J. Saunders Redding. Boston: Houghton Mifflin, 1971. Contains: **Everybody
Join Hands,** by OWEN DODSON.

Ebony and Topaz: A Collectanea, ed. by Charles S. Johnson. New York: Opportunity
Press, 1927. Contains: **The First One,** by ZORA NEALE HURSTON.

Fifty More Contemporary One-Act Plays, ed. by Frank Shay and Pierre Loving. New
York: Appleton-Century, 1928. Contains: **Blue Blood,** by GEORGIA DOUGLAS
JOHNSON. **The Chip Woman's Fortune,** by WILLIS RICHARDSON.

Grinnell Plays. Chicago: Dramatic Publishing Co., 1934. Contains: **The Two Gifts,** by ARTHUR CLIFTON LAMB.

Humanities through the Black Experience, ed. by Phyllis Rauch Klotman et al. Dubuque, IA: Kendall Hunt, 1977. Contains: **Jedgement Day** by THOMAS D. PAWLEY.

The Negro Caravan, ed. by Sterling A. Brown, Arthur P. Davis, and Ulysses Lee. New York: Dryden Press, 1941; reprinted by Arno Press, 1970; distributed by Random House. Contains: **The Seer,** by JAMES BUTCHER. Excerpt from **Divine Comedy,** by OWEN DODSON. **Bad Man,** by RANDOLPH EDMONDS. **Jedgement Day,** by THOMAS D. PAWLEY, JR. Excerpt from **Big White Fog,** by THEODORE WARD. [*NegCarav*]

Negro History in Thirteen Plays, ed. by WILLIS RICHARDSON and May Miller. Washington, DC: Associated Publishers, 1935. Contains: **Genefrede,** by HELEN WEBB HARRIS. **Nat Turner,** by RANDOLPH EDMONDS. **Frederick Douglass** and **William and Ellen Craft,** by GEORGIA DOUGLAS JOHNSON. **Christophe's Daughters, Harriet Tubman, Samory,** and **Sojourner Truth,** by MAY MILLER. **Antonio Maceo, Attucks the Martyr, The Elder Dumas, In Menelik's Court** and **Near Calvary,** by WILLIS RICHARDSON. [*NegHistl3*]

The New Negro: An Interpretation, ed. by Alain Locke. New York: Albert and Charles Boni, 1925; reprinted by Arno Press and Atheneum. Contains: **Compromise,** by WILLIS RICHARDSON.

The New Negro Renaissance, ed. by Arthur P. Davis and Michael W. Peplow. New York: Holt, Rinehart and Winston, 1975. Contains: **Mortgaged,** by WILLIS RICHARDSON. **Plumes,** by GEORGIA DOUGLAS JOHNSON. **Nat Turner,** by RANDOLPH EDMONDS. **Don't You Want to Be Free,** by LANGSTON HUGHES.

One Act Plays for Our Times, ed. by Francis Griffith, Joseph Mersand, and Joseph B. Maggio. New York: Popular Lib., 1973. Contains: **Frederick Douglass,** by GEORGIA DOUGLAS JOHNSON.

Plays and Pageants from the Life of the Negro, ed. by Willis Richardson. Washington, DC: Associated Publishers, 1930. Contains: **Two Races,** by INEZ BURKE. **Antar of Araby,** by MAUD CUNEY-HARE. **Sacrifice,** by THELMA DUNCAN. **Ti Yette,** by JOHN MATHEUS. **Ethiopia at the Bar of Justice,** by EDWARD McCOO. **Graven Images** and **Riding the Goat,** by MAY MILLER [SULLIVAN]. **Out of the Dark,** by DOROTHY GUINN. **The Black Horseman, The House of Sham,** and **The King's Dilemma,** by WILLIS RICHARDSON. **Light of the Women,** by FRANCES GUNNER. [*Plays&Pags*]

Plays by American Women, 1900–1930, ed. by Judith E. Barlow. New York: Applause, 1985. Contains: **Plumes,** by GEORGIA DOUGLAS JOHNSON.

Plays of Negro Life: A Source-Book of Native American Drama, ed. by Alain Locke and Montgomery Gregory. New York: Harper, 1927; reprinted by Greenwood Press; xerographic copies available from University Microfilms. Contains: **The Flight of the Natives,** by WILLIS RICHARDSON. **'Cruiter,** by JOHN MATHEUS. **The Starter,** by EULALIE SPENCE. **Balo,** by JEAN TOOMER. **Plumes,** by GEORGIA DOUGLAS JOHNSON. **The Broken Banjo,** by WILLIS RICHARDSON. **The Death Dance,** by THELMA DUNCAN. **Sahdji, an African Ballet,** by RICHARD BRUCE [NUGENT]. [*PlaysNegL*]

Radio Drama in Action, ed. by Erik Barnouw. New York: Farrar and Rinehart, 1945.

Contains: **Booker T. Washington in Atlanta,** by LANGSTON HUGHES. **The Negro Domestic,** by ROI OTTLEY.

Readings from Negro Authors for Schools and Colleges, ed. by Otelia Cromwell, Lorenzo Dow Turner, and Eva B. Dykes. New York: Harcourt, Brace, 1931; xerographic copies available from University Microfilms. Contains: **The Broken Banjo,** by WILLIS RICHARDSON. **'Cruiter,** by JOHN MATHEUS. [*ReadingsNA*]

Representative One-Act Plays, Fourth Series, ed. by Frank Shay. New York: Appleton-Century, 1927. Contains: **Blue Blood,** by GEORGIA DOUGLAS JOHNSON.

Roots of Black Drama, ed. by James V. Hatch and Leo Hamalian. Detroit: Wayne State Univ. Press, 1989. Contains: **On Striver's Row,** by ABRAM HILL. (Other contents not analyzed.)

Skits and Sketches: A Collection of Plays. New York: New Theatre League, 1939. Contains: **Limitations of Life,** by LANGSTON HUGHES.

A Theatre in Your Head, ed. by Kenneth Thorpe Rowe. New York: Funk and Wagnalls, 1960. Contains: **Our Lan',** by THEODORE WARD.

Three Negro Plays, ed. by C.W.E. Bigsby. Harmondsworth: Penguin, 1964. Contains: **Mulatto,** by LANGSTON HUGHES.

To Be a Black Woman: Portraits in Fact and Fiction, ed. by Mel Watkins and Jay David. New York: Morrow, 1976. Contains: Excerpt from **Mulatto,** by LANGSTON HUGHES.

University of Michigan Plays, vol. 3, ed. by Kenneth T. Rowe. Ann Arbor: George Wahr, 1932. Contains: **The Bright Medallion** and **The Eyes of the Old,** by DORIS PRICE.

Wines in the Wilderness: Plays by African-American Women from the Harlem Renaissance to the Present, ed. by Elizabeth Brown-Guillory. Westport, CT: Greenwood Press, 1990. Contains: **The Pot Maker,** by MARITA BONNER. **Blue Blood, Safe,** and **Blue-Eyed Black Boy,** by GEORGIA DOUGLAS JOHNSON. **Hot Stuff** and **Episode,** by EULALIE SPENCE. **The Bog Guide, Riding the Goat,** and **Scratches,** by MAY MILLER. **It's Morning,** by SHIRLEY GRAHAM DuBOIS. **Florence,** by ALICE CHILDRESS.

Yale Radio Plays: The Listeners' Theatre, ed. by Constance Welch. Boston: Expression Co., 1940. Contains: **Track Thirteen,** by SHIRLEY GRAHAM DUBOIS.

Yearbook of Short Plays. New York: Row, Peterson, 1930. Contains: **Black Magic,** by THELMA MYRTLE DUNCAN.

REFERENCE BOOKS AND CRITICAL STUDIES

Includes specific studies of early black American playwrights and dramatic writers as well as more general resource materials pertinent to the subject.

Abramson, Doris E. *Negro Playwrights in the American Theatre, 1925–1959*. New York: Columbia Univ. Press, 1969. [*NegPlaywrs*]

Adams, Russell L. *Great Negroes Past and Present*. Chicago: Afro-American Publishing Co., 1964.

The Afro-American Encyclopedia. 10 vols. North Miami, FL: Educational Book Publishers, 1974.

The American Theatre: A Sum of Its Parts. [Collection of the Distinguished Addresses

Prepared Expressly for the Symposium "The American Theatre—A Cultural Process," at the first American College Theatre Festival, Washington, DC, 1969.] New York: Samuel French, 1971.

Anderson, Doris Garland. *Nigger Lover*. London: N. Fowler, 1938.

Arata, Esther Spring. *More Black American Playwrights: A Bibliography*. Metuchen, NJ: Scarecrow Press, 1978.

Arata, Esther Spring, and Nicholas John Rotoli. *Black American Playwrights, 1800 to the Present: A Bibliography*. Metuchen, NJ: Scarecrow Press, 1976.

Archer, Leonard C. *Black Images in the American Theatre*. Brooklyn: Pageant-Poseidon, 1973.

ASCAP Biographical Dictionary [of Composers, Authors and Publishers]. 4th ed. New York: R. R. Bowker, 1980. Also earlier eds.

Atkinson, Brooks. *Broadway*. Rev. 3rd ed. New York: Macmillan, 1974.

Atkinson, Brooks, and Albert Hirschfeld. *The Lively Years*. New York: Association Press, 1973.

Baker, Blanch M. *Theatre and Allied Arts: A Guide to Books Dealing with the History, Criticism, and Technic of the Drama and Theatre and Related Arts and Crafts*. New York: Benjamin Blom, 1952; reprinted 1967.

Baker, Houston A., Jr. *Modernism and the Harlem Renaissance*. Chicago: Univ. of Chicago Press, 1987.

Baker's Biographical Dictionary of Musicians. 6th ed. New York: Schirmer Books, 1978.

Bardolph, Richard. *The Negro Vanguard*. New York: Rinehart, 1959; Vintage/Random House, 1961; now distributed by Greenwood Press.

Baskin, Wade, and Richard N. Runes. *Dictionary of Black Culture*. New York: Philosophical Library, 1973.

Beckerman, Bernard, and Howard Siegman. *On Stage: Selected Theatre Reviews from the New York Times, 1920–1970*. New York: Arno Press, 1973.

Bergman, Peter N., and Mort N. Bergman. *The Chronological History of the Negro in America*. New York: Bergman Publishers, 1969; distributed by Harper and Row; and by Mentor/New American Library, 1969.

The Best Plays of 1894–99/1949–50. [The Burns Mantle Best Plays Series] Ed. by Burns Mantle, succeeded by John Chapman. Boston: Small, 1920/25; New York: Dodd, 1926/50. [*BesPls* (followed by inclusive years of specific vol. cited)]

Bigsby, C.W.E., ed. *The Black American Writers*. 2 vols. Deland, FL: Everett/Edwards, 1969; Baltimore: Penguin, 1969.

Block, Anita. *The Changing World in Plays and Theatre*. Boston: Little, Brown, 1939?

Blum, Daniel, and John Willis, eds. *A Pictorial History of the American Theatre: 1860–1976*. 4th ed. New York: Crown, 1977.

Bogle, Donald. *Blacks in American Films and Television: An Illustrated Encyclopedia*. New York: Garland, 1988.

———. *Toms, Coons, Mulattoes, Mammies, and Bucks*. New York: Viking Press, 1973. [*TomsCoons*]

Bond, Frederick W. *The Negro and the Drama: The Direct and Indirect Contribution Which the American Negro Has Made to Drama and the Legitimate Stage, with the Underlying Conditions Responsible*. Washington, DC: Associated Publishers, 1940; reprinted by McGrath, 1969; graphic reprints also available from Univ. Microfilms International. [*Neg&Dr*]

Bone, Robert A. *The Negro Novel in America*. New Haven: Yale Univ. Press, 1965.

Bontemps, Arna. *The Harlem Renaissance Remembered*. New York: Dodd, Mead, 1972.

Bontemps, Arna, and Jack Conroy. *Anyplace but Here*. [A revised and enlarged version of Bontemps' *They Seek a City*, 1945.] New York: Hill and Wang, 1966.

Bordman, Gerald. *American Musical Theatre: A Chronicle*. Expanded ed. New York: Oxford Univ. Press, 1986.

———. *The Oxford Companion to American Theatre*. New York: Oxford Univ. Press, 1984.

Boyle, Kay, ed. *365 Days: A Book of Short Stories*. New York: Harcourt, Brace, 1936.

Brawley, Benjamin. *Negro Builders and Heroes*. Chapel Hill: Univ. of North Carolina Press, 1937.

———. *The Negro Genius*. New York: Dodd, Mead, 1937. [*NegGen*]

———. *The Negro in Literature and Art*. New York: Duffield, 1918; reprinted by AMS Press and Reprint International.

———. *Paul Laurence Dunbar: Poet of His People*. Chapel Hill: Univ. of North Carolina Press, 1935.

Brown, Sterling. *Negro Poetry and Drama* and *The Negro in American Fiction*. [A combined printing of two of Brown's earlier books.] Originally pub. by Associates in Negro Folk Education, Washington, DC, 1937; reprinted by Atheneum, 1968, and by Arno Press.

Brown, Warren, comp. *Check List of Negro Newspapers in the United States, 1827–1946*. Jefferson City, MO: Lincoln Univ. Press, 1946.

Brown-Guillory, Elizabeth. *Their Place on the Stage: Black Woman Playwrights in America*. Westport, CT: Greenwood Press, 1988.

Butcher, Margaret Just. *The Negro in American Culture*. [Based on materials left by Alain Locke.] Rev. and updated ed. New York: Mentor/New American Library, 1971.

Byars, J. C., Jr., ed. *Black and White: An Anthology of Washington Verse*. Washington, DC: Crane, 1927.

Campbell, Georgetta Merritt. *Extant Collections of Early Black Newspapers*. Troy, NY: Whitson, 1981.

Carr, Chrystal. *Ebony Jewels: A Selected Bibliography of Books by and About Black Women*. Inglewood, CA: Crenshaw-Imperial Branch Library, 1975.

Chapman, Abraham, ed. *Black Voices: An Anthology of Afro-American Literature*. New York: New American Library, 1968.

Chicorel, Marietta, ed. Chicorel Index Series: Vol. 3, *Chicorel Theatre Index to Plays in Anthologies*. Vol. 3A, *Chicorel Bibliography to the Performing Arts*. Vol. 8, *Chicorel Theatre Index to Plays in Periodicals.* New York: Chicorel Library Publishing Corp., 1972/73.

Charters, Ann. *Nobody: The Story of Bert Williams*. New York: Macmillan, 1970.

Chujoy, Anatole, and P. W. Manchester. *The Dance Encyclopedia*. New York: Simon and Schuster, 1967; rev. and enlarged ed., 1978.

Clarke, John H. *Harlem: A Community in Transition*. Syracuse, NY: Citadel Press, 1964.

———.*Harlem, U.S.A.* Berlin: Seven Sea Books, 1964; rev. ed., Collier Books, Macmillan, 1971.

Conference of Negro Writers. *The American Writer and His Roots*. New York: American Society of African Culture, 1960.

Craig, E. Quita. *Black Drama of the Federal Theatre Era: Beyond the Formal Horizons*. Boston: Univ. of Massachusetts Press, 1980.

Cripps, Thomas R. *Slow Fade to Black*. New York: Oxford Univ. Press, 1977.

Cruse, Harold. *The Crisis of the Negro Intellectual*. New York: Morrow, 1967.

Cuban, Larry, ed. *The Negro in America*. Chicago: Scott-Foresman, 1964.

Cullen, Countee, ed. *Caroling Dusk: An Anthology of Verse by Negro Poets*. New York: Harper & Row, 1927.

Cunard, Nancy, ed. *Negro Anthology [1931–1933]*. London: Wishart, 1934; reprinted in an unabridged facsimile ed. by Negro Universities Press; abridged by Frederick Ungar Publishing Co., 1970.

Cuney-Hare, Maud. *Negro Musicians and Their Music*. Washington, DC: Associated Press, 1936. [*NegMus&M*]

Cunningham, Virginia. *Paul Laurence Dunbar and His Song*. New York: Dodd, Mead, 1948.

Dannett, Sylvia G. Liebovitz. *Profiles of Negro Womanhood*. 2 vols. Yonkers, NY: Educational Heritage, 1964.

Davis, Arthur P. *From the Dark Tower: Afro-American Writers, 1900 to 1960*. Washington, DC: Howard Univ. Press, 1974.

Davis, John, P. *The American Negro Reference Book*. Yonkers, NY: Educational Heritage, 1966.

Detweiler, Frederick G. *The Negro Press in the United States*. College Park, MD: McGrath, 1968.

Dickinson, Donald C. *A Bio-Bibliography of Langston Hughes, 1902–1967*. 2nd ed. Hamden, CT: Archon, 1972.

Dictionary of American Biography, ed. by American Council of Learned Societies. New York: Scribner's, 1928/1937. [*DAB*]

Dictionary of American Negro Biography, ed. by Rayford W. Logan and Michael R. Winston. New York: W. W. Norton, 1982. [*DANB*]

Diggs, Ellen Irene. *Black Chronology*. Boston: G. K. Hall, 1983.

Directory of American Scholars. 5th ed. 2 vols. New York: Jacques Cattell Press, 1969; distributed by R. R. Bowker. [*DirAmSchol*]

Dorman, James H., Jr. *Theater in the Ante-Bellum South, 1815–1861*. Chapel Hill: Univ. of North Carolina Press, 1967.

Downer, Alan S., ed. *The American Theatre Today*. New York: Basic Books, 1967.

Dramatic Index [1909–1949]. 39 vols. Boston: F. W. Faxon Co., 1910/50.

Dreer, Herman, ed. *American Literature by Negro Authors*. New York: Macmillan, 1950. [*AmLitNA*]

DuBois, W.E.B. *An ABC of Color: Selections from over a Half Century of the Writings of W.E.B. DuBois*. Berlin: Seven Seas, 1963; Bell Press, 1964.

DuBois, W.E.B, and Guy Johnson. *Encyclopedia of the Negro: Preparatory Volume with Reference Lists and Reports*. Rev. and enlarged ed. New York: Phelps-Stokes Fund, 1946.

Ebony Magazine, editors of. *The Ebony Handbook*. Chicago: Johnson Publishing Co., 1974.

———. *The Negro Handbook*. Chicago: Johnson Publishing Co., 1966.

Emanuel, James A. *Langston Hughes*. New York: Twayne, 1967.

Emanuel, James A., and Theodore Gross. *Dark Symphony: Negro Literature in America*. New York: The Free Press, 1968.

Embree, Edwin R. *Brown America: The Story of a New Race*. New York: Viking Press, 1940.

————. *Thirteen Against the Odds*. New York: Viking Press, 1944.

Emery, Lynne F. *Black Dance in the United States from 1619 to 1970*. Palo Alto, CA: National Press Books, 1972.

Engel, Lehman. *The American Musical Theatre: A Consideration*. CBS Legacy Collection Book; distributed by Macmillan, New York, 1967.

Ewen, David. *All the Years of American Popular Music*. Englewood Cliffs, NJ: Prentice-Hall, 1977.

————, ed. *Complete Book of the American Musical Theatre*. Rev. ed. New York: Holt, 1959.

Fabre, Geneviève, et al. *Afro-American Poetry and Drama, 1760–1975: A Guide to Information Sources*. Detroit: Gale Research, 1979.

Falb, Lewis W. *American Drama in Paris: 1945–1970*. Chapel Hill: Univ. of North Carolina Press, 1973.

Farrison, William Edward. *William Wells Brown: Author and Reformer*. Chicago: Univ. of Chicago Press, 1969.

Feather, Leonard. *The Encyclopedia of Jazz*. New York: Horizon Press, 1955; rev. 1960, 1970, and 1976 (coauthored with Ira Gitler).

The Federal Theatre Project: A Catalog-Calendar of Productions, comp. by the Staff of the Fenwick Library, George Mason Univ. Westport, CT: Greenwood Press, 1986.

Ferguson, Blanche E. *Countee Cullen and the Negro Renaissance*. New York: Dodd, Mead, 1966.

Flanagan, Hallie (Hallie Ferguson Flanagan Davis). *Arena: The History of the Federal Theatre*. New York: Duell, Sloan, and Pearce, 1940; republished by Benjamin Blom, 1965.

Fleming, Beatrice K., and Marion J. Pryde. *Distinguished Negroes Abroad*. Washington, DC: Associated Publishers, 1946.

Fletcher, Tom. *100 Years of the Negro in Show Business*. New York: Burdge, 1954.

Flexner, Eleanor. *American Playwrights, 1918–1938*. New York: Simon and Schuster, 1938.

Ford, Nick Aaron, and H. L. Faggett, eds. *Best Short Stories by Afro-American Writers, 1924–1950*. Boston: Meador, 1950.

Franklin, John Hope. *From Slavery to Freedom: A History of American Negroes*. New York: Alfred A. Knopf, 1947.

Freedman, Morris. *American Drama in Social Context*. Carbondale: Southern Illinois Univ. Press, 1971.

French, Warren, ed. *The Thirties: Fiction, Poetry, Drama*. Deland, FL: Everett/Edwards, 1967.

Gagey, Edmond McAdoo. *Revolution in American Drama*. New York: Columbia Univ. Press, 1947.

Gale Research Company, editors of. *Biography and Genealogy Master Index*. 2nd ed. Detroit: Gale Research, 1980.

Gassner, John. *Human Relations in the Theatre*. (A Freedom Pamphlet) New York: Anti-Defamation League of B'nai B'rith, 1949.

Gates, Henry Louis, Jr., ed. *Black Literature and Literary Theory*. New York: Methuen, 1984.

Gautier, Théophile. *Histoire de l'art dramatique en France depuis vingt-cinq ans*. 6 vols. Paris: Magnin, Blanchard, 1853/59.

Gayle, Addison, ed. *Black Expression: Essays by and About Black Americans in the Creative Arts*. New York: Weybright and Talley, 1969.

Gibson, Donald B., ed. *Five Black Writers: Essays on Wright, Ellison, Baldwin, Hughes and Jones*. New York: New York Univ. Press, 1970.

Gilder, Rosamond, et al. *Theatre Arts Anthology*. New York: Theatre Arts Books, 1934.

Green, Elizabeth Lay. *The Negro in Contemporary Literature: An Outline for Individual and Group Study*. Chapel Hill: Univ. of North Carolina Press, 1928; reprinted by McGrath, 1968.

Green, Stanley. *Encyclopedia of the Musical Theatre*. New York: Dodd, Mead, 1976; reprinted by Da Capo Press, New York, 1980.

———. *The World of Musical Comedy*. New York: A. S. Barnes, 1974.

Greene, Harry W. *Two Decades of Research and Creative Writing at West Virginia State College*. Institute, WV: West Virginia State Coll., 1939. (Bulletin series 26, no. 4, Aug.-Nov. 1939)

Grinstead, S. E. *A Select, Classified, and Briefly Annotated List of Two Hundred Fifty Books by or About the Negro Published During the Past Ten Years*. Nashville, TN: Fisk Univ. Library, 1939. (Mimeographed)

Gross, Seymour L., and John Edward Hardy, eds. *Images of the Negro in American Literature*. Chicago: Univ. of Chicago Press, 1966.

Guernsey, Otis L. *Directory of the American Theatre, 1894–1971*. [Indexed to the complete series of *Best Plays* Theatre Yearbooks.] New York: Dodd, Mead, 1971.

Halstead, William P., and Clara Behringer. *History of Speech Education in America: Background Studies*. New York: Appleton-Century-Crofts, 1954.

Hampton Institute, Collis P. Huntington Memorial Library. *Dictionary Catalog of the George Foster Peabody Collection of Negro Literature and History*. Westport, CT: Greenwood Press, 1972. [An update of *A Classified Catalog of the Negro Collection in the Collis P. Huntington Library, Hampton Institute, 1940*. (Mimeographed)]

Harris, M. A. *A Negro History Tour of Manhattan*. New York: Greenwood Press, 1968.

Hartnoll, Phyllis, ed. *The Oxford Companion to the Theatre*. 3rd ed. New York: Oxford Univ. Press, 1970.

Haskins, James. *Black Theater in America*. New York: Crowell, 1982.

Hatch, James V. *Black Image on the American Stage: A Bibliography of Plays and Musicals, 1770–1970*. New York: DBS Publications, 1970.

Hatch, James V., and Omanii Abdullah. *Black Playwrights, 1823–1977: An Annotated Bibliography of Plays*. New York: R. R. Bowker, 1977.

Hicks, Granville, et al., eds. *Proletarian Literature in the United States*. New York: International Publishers, 1935.

Hill, Errol. *The Theater of Black Americans: A Collection of Critical Essays*. 2 vols. Englewood Cliffs, NJ: Prentice-Hall, 1980; also in 1-vol. edition.

Himelstein, Morgan Y. *Drama Was a Weapon: The Left-Wing Theatre in New York, 1929–1941*. New Brunswick, NJ: Rutgers Univ. Press, 1963.

Howard University Library, Washington, DC. *Dictionary Catalog of the Arthur B. Spingarn Collection of Negro Authors*. 2 vols. Boston: G. K. Hall, 1970.

———. *Dictionary Catalog of the Jesse E. Moorland Collection of Negro Life and History*. 9 vols. Boston: G. K. Hall, 1970.

Huggins, Nathan. *Harlem Renaissance*. New York: Oxford Univ. Press, 1971.

Hugh, Carl M. *The Negro Novelist, 1940–1950*. New York: Citadel Press, 1952.

Hughes, Langston. *The Big Sea: An Autobiography*. New York: Knopf, 1940.

———.*Famous Negro Music Makers*. New York: Dodd, Mead, 1955.

Hughes, Langston, and Milton Meltzer. *Black Magic: A Pictorial History of the Negro in American Entertainment*. Englewood Cliffs, NJ: Prentice-Hall, 1967; rev. 1971. [*BlkMagic*]

———. *A Pictorial History of the Negro in America*. New York: Crown, 1956. Rev. and retitled *A Pictorial History of Black Americans,* ed. by Hughes, Meltzer, and C. Eric Lincoln. New York: Crown, 1973.

Hull, Gloria T. *Color, Sex and Poetry: Three Women Writers of the Harlem Renaissance*. [A biographical study of Angelina Weld Grimké, Alice Dunbar-Nelson, and Georgia Douglas Johnson.] Bloomington: Indiana Univ. Press, 1987.

Hurston, Zora Neale. *Dust Tracks on the Road*. Philadelphia: Lippincott, 1942; reprinted by Arno Press, 1970.

Hutton, Laurence. *Curiosities of the American Stage*. New York: Harper, 1891.

Hyatt, Marshall, ed. and comp. *The Afro-American Cinematic Experience: An Annotated Bibliography & Filmography*. Wilmington, DE: Scholarly Resources, 1983.

Index to Full Length Plays, 1895 to 1925; 1926 to 1944, ed. by Ruth Gibbons Thompson; *1944 to 1964,* ed. by Norma Olin Ireland. Boston: Faxon, 1946/65.

An Index to One-Act Plays, 1900–1925; with Supplements through 1948, comp. by Hannah Logasa and Winifred Ver Nooy. Boston: Faxon, 1924/48.

An Index to Skits and Stunts, ed. by Norma Olin Ireland. Boston: Faxon, 1958.

Isaacs, Edith J. R. *The Negro in the American Theatre*. New York: Theatre Arts, 1947; reprinted by McGrath. [*NegAmTh*]

———. *Theatre: Essays on the Arts of the Theatre*. Boston: Little, Brown; reprinted by Books for Libraries, Freeport, NY, 1968.

Jahn, Janheinz. *Neo-African Literature: A History of Black Writing*. Originally pub. as *Geschichte der neoafrikanischen Literatur*. Trans. from the German by Oliver Coburn and Ursula Lehrburger. London: Faber and Faber, 1958; New York: Grove, 1968.

Johnson, James Weldon. *Along This Way*. New York: Viking Press, 1935.

———. *Black Manhattan*. New York: Alfred A. Knopf, 1930; reprinted by Arno Press and Atheneum.

Kallenbach, Jessamine S., et al., comps. *Index to Black American Literary Anthologies*. Boston: G. K. Hall, 1979.

Katz, William Loren. *Eyewitnesses: The Negro in American History*. New York: Pitman Publishing, 1969.

Keller, Dean H. *Index to Plays in Periodicals—Revised and Expanded Edition*. Metuchen, NJ: Scarecrow Press, 1979. Also earlier volumes: *Index to Plays in Periodicals* (1971) and its *Supplement* (1973).

Kellner, Bruce. *The Harlem Renaissance: A Historical Dictionary for the Era*. Westport, CT: Greenwood Press, 1984. [*HarlRenD*]

Kirby, I. E., and C. I. Martin. *The Rise and Fall of the Black Caribs of St. Vincent*. St. Vincent, Aug. 1972. (Mimeographed)

Kramer, Victor. *The Harlem Renaissance Re-examined*. New York: AMS Press, 1986.

Laurintzen, Einar, and Gunnar Lundquist. *American Film Index, 1908–15* and *1916–20*. Stockholm: Film-Index, 1976/1988.

Leab, Daniel J. *From Sambo to Superspade: The Black Experience in Motion Pictures*. Boston: Houghton Mifflin, 1975.

Leiter, Samuel, ed. *The Encyclopedia of the New York Stage, 1920–1930*. 2 vols. Westport, CT: Greenwood Press, 1986.

Lewis, Allan. *American Plays and Playwright of the Contemporary Theatre*. New York: Crown, 1965.

Lewis, David Levering. *When Harlem Was in Vogue*. New York: Oxford Univ. Press, 1989.

Malone, Mary. *Actor in Exile: The Life of Ira Aldridge*. New York: Crowell-Collier, 1969.

Malvel, Fritz J., comp. *A Guide to the Archives of Hampton Institute*. Westport, CT: Greenwood Press, 1985.

Mantle, Burns. *Contemporary American Playwrights*. New York: Dodd, Mead, 1940.

Mapp, Edward. *Blacks in American Films: Today and Yesterday*. Metuchen, NJ: Scarecrow Press, 1972.

———. *Directory of Blacks in the Performing Arts*. Metuchen, NJ: Scarecrow Press, 1978. [*DirBlksPA*]

Marshall, Herbert, and Mildred Stock. *Ira Aldridge—The Negro Tragedian*. New York: Macmillan, 1958.

Mathews, Jane DeHart. *The Federal Theatre, 1935–1939*. Princeton, NJ: Princeton Univ. Press, 1967.

Matthews, Geraldine O., et al., comps. *Black American Writers, 1773–1949: A Bibliography and Union List*. Boston: G. K. Hall, 1970.

Mikolyzk, Thomas A. *Langston Hughes: A Bio-Bibliography*. Westport, CT: Greenwood Press, 1990.

Miller, Elizabeth W. *The Negro in America: A Bibliography*. Cambridge, MA: Harvard Univ. Press, 1966.

Miller, Ruth. *Backgrounds to Blackamerican Literature*. Scranton, PA: Chandler Publishing, 1971; distributed by Intext Educational Publishers, Scranton, PA.

———, ed. *Blackamerican Literature: 1760–Present*. Beverly Hills, CA: Glencoe Press, 1971.

Mitchell, Loften. *Black Drama: The Story of the American Negro in the Theatre*. New York: Hawthorn, 1967. [*BlkDr*]

———. *Voices of the Black Theatre*. Clifton, NJ: James T. White, 1975. [*VoicesBTh*]

Moses, Montrose, and John Brown, eds. *The American Theatre as Seen by Its Critics*. New York: W.W. Norton, 1934.

Munden, Kenneth. *The American Film Institute Catalog of Motion Pictures Produced in the United States, 1921–1930*. 2 vols. New York: Bowker, 1971.

Murray, James P. *To Find an Image: Black Films from Uncle Tom to Superfly*. Indianapolis: Bobbs-Merrill, 1974.

Nathan, George Jean. *Passing Judgment*. New York: Alfred A. Knopf, 1933.

———. *Testament of a Critic*. New York: Alfred A. Knopf, 1931.

———. *The Theatre Book of the Year, 1943–1944*; also *1947–1948*. New York: Alfred A. Knopf, 1944, 1948.

National Conference on Black American Protest Drama and Theatre (April 18–19, 1985). *Final Report*. Baltimore: Morgan State Univ., Feb. 1, 1986. (Mimeographed)

National Council of Teachers of English. *Guide to Play Selection*. New York: Appleton-Century-Crofts, 1958.

National Urban League, Department of Research. *Selected Bibliography on the Negro*. 4th ed. New York: National Urban League, 1951.

The Negro Handbook [1942]; *1944, 1946–47; 1949,* ed. by Florence Murray. Various New York publishers: Wendell Malliet, 1942; Current Reference Publications, 1944; Current Books, 1947; Macmillan, 1949.

Negro Yearbook: An Annual Encyclopedia of the Negro, 1912/1937–38, ed. by Monroe N. Work. Tuskegee, AL: Negro Year Book Co., 1912/38. Continued as *Negro Year Book: A Review of Events Affecting Negro Life, 1941–46,* and *1952,* ed. by Jessie P. Guzman. Tuskegee, AL: Dept. of Records and Research, Tuskegee Institute, 1947, 1952.

Newman, Richard, comp. *Black Access: A Bibliography of Afro-American Bibliographies.* Westport, CT: Greenwood Press, 1984.

New York Public Library. *Dictionary Catalog of the Schomburg Collection of Negro Literature and History,* 9 vols., 1962. *1st Supplement,* 2 vols., 1967. *2nd Supplement,* 4 vols., 1972. *Supplement 1974,* 1976. Boston: G. K. Hall, dates as indicated.

New York Times [Reference Services]. *The New York Times Directory of the Theatre.* [A separate issue of the index of *The New York Times Theatre Reviews,* cited below, covering the period 1920–70.] New York: Arno Press, 1973.

———. *The New York Times Film Reviews:* Vol. 1, 1913–31; Vol. 2, 1932–38; Vol. 3, 1939–48; Vol. 4, 1949–58; Vol. 6, Index, 1913–68. New York: New York Times Books, 1970–; distributed by Garland. [*NYTFR*]

———. *The New York Times Obituaries Index, 1858–1968.* New York: New York Times, 1970.

———. *The New York Times Theatre Reviews:* Vol. 1, 1870–85; Vol. 2, 1886–95; Vol. 3, 1896–1903; Vol. 4, 1904–11; Vol. 5, 1912–19; Vol. 6, Index, 1870–1919; Vol. 7, 1920–26; Vol. 8, 1927–29; Vol. 9, 1930–34; Vol. 10, 1935–41; Vol. 11, 1942–51; Vols. 15 & 16, Index, 1920–70. New York: New York Times Books, 1971–; distributed by Garland. [*NYTTR*]

Noble, Peter. *The Negro in Films.* London: Skelton Robinson, 1948; reprinted by Arno, New York, 1970.

Notable Names in the American Theatre, ed. by Raymond D. McGill. [A revision of *The Biographical Encyclopedia & Who's Who of the American Theatre,* ed. by Walter Rigdon, 1966.] Clifton, NJ: James T. White, 1976; distributed by Gale Research.

O'Connor, John, and Lorraine Brown, eds. *Free, Adult, Uncensored: The Living History of the Federal Theatre Project.* Washington, DC: New Republic Books, 1978.

Odell, George C. D. *Annals of the New York Stage.* 15 vols. New York: Columbia Univ. Press, 1927/39.

Oliver, Clinton F., and Stephanie Sills, eds. *Contemporary Black Drama.* [Useful for its historical introduction.] New York: Scribner's, 1971.

Ottemiller, J. H. *Index to Plays in Collections.* New York: H. W. Wilson, 1943; also later eds.

Ottley, Roi. *Black Odyssey: The Story of the Negro in America.* New York: Scribner's, 1948.

Ottley, Roi, and William J. Weatherby, eds. *The Negro in New York: An Informal Social History.* New York: New York Public Library, Oceana Publications, 1967; reprinted by Praeger, 1969.

Ovington, Mary White. *Portraits in Color.* New York: Viking Press, 1927.

Page, James A. *Selected Black American, African, and Caribbean Authors: A Biobib-*

liography. [*Orig*. pub. by G. K. Hall in 1977 as *Selected Black American Authors: An Illustrated Bio-Bibliography*.] Littleton, CO: Libraries Unlimited, 1985.

Patterson, Charlotte A., comp. *Plays in Periodicals: An Index to English Language Scripts in Twentieth Century Journals*. Boston: G. K. Hall, 1970.

Patterson, Lindsay, ed. *Anthology of the American Negro in the Theatre: A Critical Approach*. New York: Publishers Co., under the auspices of the Association for the Study of Negro Life and History, 1967. [*AnthANT*]

————. *Black Films and Film-Makers: A Comprehensive Anthology from Stereotype to Superhero*. New York: Dodd, Mead, 1975.

————. *An Introduction to Black Literature*. New York: Publishers Co., under the auspices of the Association for the Study of Negro Life and History, 1969.

————. *The Negro in Music and Art*. New York: Publishers Co., under the auspices of the Association for the Study of Negro Life and History, 1968.

————. *A Rock Against the Wind: Black Love Poems*. New York: Dodd, Mead, 1973.

Performing Arts Biographies Master Index, ed. by Barbara McNeil and Miranda Herbert. Detroit: Gale Research, 1979.

Perry, Margaret. *A Bio-Bibliography of Countee P. Cullen, 1903–1946*. Westport, CT: Greenwood Press, 1971.

Plosky, Harry A., et al. *Afro USA: A Reference Book on the Black American Experience*. Also published simultaneously as *Reference Library of Black Americans*. 4 vols. [A revision of *The Negro Almanac*, originally pub. in 1967, which was also apparently updated and republished in 1976 and 1980, concurrently with the above two books.] New York: Bellwether Publishing, 1971; distributed by Afro-American Press.

Porter, Dorothy B. *A Working Bibliography on the Negro in the United States*. Published as *A Catalog of Out-of-Print Titles from the Negro in the United States* by Univ. Microfilms International, Ann Arbor, MI, 1969, 1972. [All titles in the bibliography available from UMI.]

Powers, Ann, ed. *Blacks in American Movies: A Selected Bibliography*. Metuchen, NJ: Scarecrow Press, 1974.

Rabkin, Gerald. *Drama and Commitment: Politics in the American Theatre of the Thirties*. Bloomington: Indiana Univ. Press, 1966.

Rampersad, Arnold. *The Art and Imagination of W.E.B. DuBois*. Cambridge, MA: Harvard Univ. Press, 1977.

————. *Life of Langston Hughes*. 2 vols. Cambridge, MA: Harvard Univ. Press, 1986/ 88.

Ray, David, and Robert M. Farnsworth, eds. *Richard Wright: Impressions and Perspectives*. Ann Arbor: Univ. of Michigan Press, 1974.

Reardon, William R., and Thomas D. Pawley, eds. *The Black Teacher and the Dramatic Arts: A Dialogue, Bibliography, and Anthology*. Westport, CT: Greenwood Press for Negro Universities Press, 1970.

Rigdon, Walter, ed. *The Biographical Encyclopedia & Who's Who of the American Theatre*. [Revised as *Notable Names in the American Theatre,* ed. by Raymond D. McGill, 1976.] New York: James H. Heineman, 1966.

Robinson, Wilhelmena A. *Historical Negro Biographies*. 2nd ed. New York: Publishers Co., 1968.

Rollins, Charlemae Hill. *Famous Negro Entertainers of Stage, Screen and TV*. New York: Dodd, Mead, 1967.

————. *They Showed the Way: Forty American Negro Leaders*. New York: Thomas Y. Crowell, 1964.

Rowland, Mabel, ed. *Bert Williams: Son of Laughter—A Symposium of Tribute to the Man and His Work*. New York: English Crafters, 1923; xerographic reprints available from Univ. Microfilms International.

Rush, Theresa Gunnels, et al. *Black American Writers Past and Present: A Biographical and Bibliographical Dictionary*. 2 vols. Metuchen, NJ: Scarecrow Press, 1975.

Ryan, Pat M., comp. *Black Writing in the U.S.A.: A Bibliographic Guide*. Brockport, NY: Drake Memorial Library, 1969.

Sader, Marion. *Comprehensive Index to English-Language Little Magazines, 1890–1970*. 2 vols. New York: Kraus-Thompson, 1976.

Salem, James. *A Guide to Critical Reviews, Parts I, II, and IV. Part I: American Drama, 1909–1982*, 3rd ed., 1984. *Part II: The Musical, 1909–1974*, 2nd ed., 1976. *Part IV: The Screenplay from "The Jazz Singer" to "Dr. Strangelove,"* 2 vols., 1971. Metuchen, NJ: Scarecrow Press, dates as indicated.

Samples, Gordon. *The Drama Scholars' Index to Plays and Film-scripts: A Guide to Plays and Filmscripts in Selected Anthologies and Periodicals*. 2 vols. Metuchen, NJ: Scarecrow Press; orig. vol., 1974; vol. 2, 1980.

Sampson, Henry T. *Blacks in Black and White: A Source Book on Black Films*. Metuchen, NJ: Scarecrow Press, 1977. [*BlksB&W*]

————. *Blacks in Blackface: A Source Book on Early Black Musical Shows*. Metuchen, NJ: Scarecrow Press, 1980. [*BlksBF*]

Sanders, Leslie Catherine. *The Development of Black Theater in America: From Shadows to Selves*. Baton Rouge: Louisiana State Univ. Press, 1988.

Schatz, Walter, ed. *Directory of Afro-American Resources*. New York: R. R. Bowker, 1970.

Seller, Maxine Schwartz, ed. *Ethnic Theatre in the United States*. Westport, CT: Greenwood Press, 1983.

Shockley, Ann Allen. *Afro-American Women Writers, 1746–1933: An Anthology and Critical Guide*. Boston: G. K. Hall, 1988. [*AfrAmWW*]

Shockley, Ann Allen, and Sue P. Chandler. *Living Black American Authors: A Biographical Directory*. New York: R. R. Bowker, 1973.

Simmons, William J. *Men of Mark*. Cleveland: George M. Rewell, 1887; reprinted by Arno Press and the New York Times, 1968.

Slide, Anthony, ed. *Selected Theatre Criticism*. 3 vols. Vol. 1: 1900–1919. Vol. 2: 1920–30. Vol. 3: 1931–50. Metuchen, NJ: Scarecrow Press, 1985.

Slide, Anthony, et al., comps. *Sourcebook for the Performing Arts: A Directory of Collections, Resources, Scholars, and Critics in Theatre, Film, and Television*. Westport, CT: Greenwood Press, 1988.

Sloan, Irving J. *The American Negro: A Chronology and Fact Book*. Dobbs Ferry, NY: Oceana Publications, 1965.

Smith, Jessie Carney, ed. *Images of Blacks in American Culture: A Reference Guide to Information Sources*. Westport, CT: Greenwood Press, 1988.

Smythe, Mabel, ed. *The Black American Reference Book*. [A revision of *The American Negro Reference Book*, ed. by J. P. Davis, 1966.] Englewood Cliffs, NJ: Prentice-Hall, 1976.

Sobel, Bernard. *Theatre Handbook and Digest of Plays*. New York: Crown, 1953.

Southern, Eileen. *Biographical Dictionary of Afro-American and African Musicians*. Westport, CT: Greenwood Press, 1982. [*BioDAfMus*]

————. *The Music of Black Americans: A History*. New York: W. W. Norton, 1971; rev. 1983. [*MusBlkAms*]

Southgate, Robert L. *Black Plots and Black Characters: A Handbook for Afro-American Literature*. Syracuse, NY: Gaylord Professional Publications, 1979. [*BlkPlots*]

Spradling, Mary Mace, ed. *In Black and White: A Guide to Magazine Articles, Newspaper Articles, and Books Concerning More than 15,000 Individuals and Groups*. 3rd ed., 2 vols. and Supplement. Detroit: Gale Research, 1980, 1985.

Sprecher, Daniel. *Guide to Films About Negroes, 16mm*. Alexandria, VA: Serina, 1970.

Starke, Catherine J. *The Negro in American Literature: Black Stock and Archetypal Characters, 1820–1970*. New York: Harper and Row, 1971.

Taylor, Karen M. *People's Theatre in Amerika*. New York: Drama Book Specialists, 1972.

Tennessee Department of Education, Division of School Libraries. *The Negro: A Selected List for School Libraries of Books by or About the Negro in Africa and America*. Rev. ed. Nashville: State Dept. of Education, 1935.

Thonssen, Lester, et al., comps. *Bibliography of Speech Education*, and *Supplement: 1939–1948*. New York: H. W. Wilson, 1939, 1950.

Tinker, Ed. *Les écrits de langue française en Louisiana au XIXe siècle*. Paris: H. Campion, 1932.

Toll, Robert C. *Blacking Up: The Minstrel Show in Nineteenth Century America*. New York: Oxford Univ. Press, 1974.

Turner, Darwin T. *Afro-American Writers*. [Goldentree Bibliographies in Language and Literature.] New York: Appleton-Century-Crofts, Meredith Corp., 1970.

University Microfilms International. Various catalogs and updates, including: *The Arts: A Catalog of Current Doctoral Dissertation Research*, 1983. *The Arts: A Catalog of Selected Doctoral Dissertation Research*, 1985. *Black Studies: A Dissertation Bibliography*, 1977. *Black Studies II: A Dissertation Bibliography*, 1980. *A Catalog of Out-of-Print Titles from the Negro in the United States*. Ann Arbor, MI, dates as indicated.

Variety Film Reviews: Alphabetical Title Index: Vol. 1, 1907–20; Vol. 2, 1921–25; Vol. 3, 1926–29; Vol. 4, 1930–33; Vol. 5, 1934–37; Vol. 6, 1938–42; Vol. 7, 1943–48; Vol. 8, 1949–53. Hollywood, CA: Hollywood Film Archive, 1982.

Waldeau, Roy S. *Vintage Years of the Theatre Guild: 1928–1939*. Cleveland: Case Western Reserve Univ., 1972.

Weaver, John T., comp. *Forty Years of Screen Credits, 1929–1969*. 2 vols. Metuchen, NJ: Scarecrow Press, 1970.

————. *Twenty Years of Silents, 1908–1928*. Metuchen, NJ: Scarecrow Press, 1971.

Welsch, Erwin K. *The Negro in the United States: A Research Guide*. Bloomington: Indiana Univ. Press, 1965.

Whitlow, Roger. *Black American Literature: A Critical History, with a 1,520-Title Bibliography of Works Written by and About Black Americans*. Chicago: Nelson-Hall, 1973.

Who's Who in America. Various editions, 1930/50. New York: Who's Who, Inc., dates as indicated.

Who's Who in Colored America: A Biographical Dictionary of Notable Living Persons of African Descent Living in America. 7 eds.: first ed., 1927, ed. by Joseph Boris;

second, third, fourth, fifth, and sixth eds., 1928–29, 1930–32, 1933–37, 1938–40, 1941–44, ed. by Thomas Yenser; seventh ed., 1950, ed. by G. James Fleming and Christian E. Burckel. New York: Who's Who in Colored America, dates as indicated. Xerographic reprints of first five editions available from Univ. Microfilms International.

Who's Who of the Colored Race: A General Biographical Dictionary of Men and Women of African Descent. Ed. by Frank Lincoln Mather. Chicago: Memento Edition Half-Century of Negro Freedom in the U.S., 1915. Xerographic reprints available from Univ. Microfilms International.

Wilson, Garff B. *Three Hundred Years of American Drama and Theatre.* Second ed. Englewood Cliffs, NJ: Prentice-Hall, 1982.

Wittke, Carl. *Tambo and Bones: A History of the American Minstrel Stage.* Durham, NC: Duke Univ. Press, 1938, 1968.

Woll, Allen. *Black Musical Theatre: From "Coontown" to "Dreamgirls."* Baton Rouge: Louisiana State Univ. Press, 1989.

————. *Dictionary of the Black Theatre: Broadway, Off-Broadway, and Selected Harlem Theatre.* Westport, CT: Greenwood Press, 1983. [*DBlkTh*]

Work, Monroe. *A Bibliography of the Negro in Africa and America.* New York: H. W. Wilson, 1928; reprinted by Octagon Books, 1965, and Argosy-Antiquarian Ltd., 1965.

WPA [Works Progress Administration], Federal Theatre Project. *A List of Negro Plays.* New York: National Service Bureau, Publication No. 24-L, 1938. Xerographic prints available from Univ. Microfilms International.

————, Illinois Writers' Project. *Cavalcade of the American Negro.* Chicago: Diamond Jubilee Exposition Authority, 1940.

————, New York Writers' Program. "Negroes of New York: An Informal Social History," ed. by Roi Ottley. Unpub. study in Schomburg [c. 1940].

————, Virginia Writers' Project. *The Negro in Virginia.* New York: Hastings House, 1940.

Young, James. *Black Writers of the Thirties.* Baton Rouge: Louisiana State Univ. Press, 1973.

DISSERTATIONS AND THESES

Where order numbers are given in parentheses, dissertations and theses are available in paper or microform copies from University Microfilms International, P. O. Box 1764, Ann Arbor, MI 48106. For current pricing information, call the Dissertation Hot Line 1–800–521–3042, toll free.

In the main body of the directory, dissertations are abbreviated by the author's last name, followed by the type of dissertation or thesis and the date, e.g.: Abramson, Ph.D. diss. (1969). A further abbreviation is used in the References at the end of an entry, e.g.: Abramson diss.

Abookire, Noerena. "Children's Theatre Activities at Karamu House in Cleveland, Ohio, 1915–1975." Ph.D. diss., New York Univ., 1982. (GAX82–14861)

Abramson, Doris Elizabeth. "A Study of Plays by Negro Playwrights, from 'Appearances' to 'A Raisin in the Sun' (1925–1959)." Ph.D. diss., Columbia Univ., 1969.

(BEJ67–14016) [Published as *Negro Playwrights in the American Theatre, 1925–1959*. See Reference Books and Critical Studies, above.]

Adubato, Robert A. "A History of the WPA's Negro Theatre Project in New York City, 1935–1939." Ph.D. diss., New York Univ., 1978. (BWK78–18122)

Alkire, Stephen Robert. "The Development and Treatment of the Negro Character as Presented in American Musical Theatre, 1927–1968." Ph.D. diss., Michigan State Univ., 1972. (BEJ73–05314)

Archer, Leonard Courtney. "The National Association for the Advancement of Colored People and the American Theatre: A Study of Relationships and Influences." (Vols. 1 and 2). Ph.D. diss., Ohio State Univ., 1959. (BEJ59–02728) [Published as *Black Images in the American Theatre*. See Reference Books and Critical Studies, above.]

Austin, Adell Patricia. "Pioneering Black Authored Dramas: 1924–27." Ph.D. diss., Michigan State Univ., 1986. (GAX86–25006)

Belcher, Fannin Saffore, Jr. "The Place of the Negro in the Evolution of the American Theatre, 1762–1940." Ph.D. diss. Yale Univ., 1945. (BEJ69–17658)

Bisbane, Eva Mae. "Théâtre de Victor Séjour." Master's thesis, Hunter College, 1942.

Bond, Fredrick W. "The Direct and Indirect Contributions Which the American Negro Has Made to the Drama and the Legitimate Stage, with the Underlying Conditions Responsible." Ph.D. diss., New York Univ., 1938. (BWK78–13518) [Published as *The Negro and the Drama*. See Reference Books and Critical Studies, above.]

Brown, Elizabeth [now Elizabeth Brown-Guillory]. "Six Female Black Playwrights: Images of Blacks in Plays by Lorraine Hansberry, Alice Childress, Sonia Sanchez, Barbara Molette, Martie Charles, and Ntozake Shange." Ph.D. diss., Florida State Univ., 1980. (KWN81–00634) [Published as *Their Place on Stage: Black Woman Playwrights in America*, by Elizabeth Brown-Guillory. See Reference Books and Critical Studies, above.]

Buchanan, Singer Alfred. "A Study of the Attitudes of the Writers of the Negro Press Towards the Depiction of the Negro in Plays and Films: 1930–1965." Ph.D. diss., Univ. of Michigan, 1968. (BEJ68–13288)

Caldwell, Hansonia Laverne. "Black Idioms in Opera as Reflected in the Works of Six Afro-American Composers." Ph.D. diss., Univ. of Southern California, 1974. (GAX75–06403)

Campbell, Georgetta Merritt. "Extant Collections of Black Newspapers 1880–1915 in the Libraries of the United States: The Need for a Scholarly Index." Ed.D. diss., Fairleigh Dickinson Univ., 1978. (BWK78–16881)[Published as *Extant Collections of Early Black Newspapers*. See Reference Books and Critical Studies, above.]

Cochran, James P. "The Producer-Director on the New York Stage, 1890–1915." Ph.D. diss., State Univ. of Iowa, 1968.

Coleman, Edwin Leon, Jr. "Langston Hughes: As American Dramatist." Ph.D. diss., Univ. of Oregon, 1971. (BWK72–08518)

Collins, John D. "American Drama in Anti-Slavery Agitation." Ph.D. diss., State Univ. of Iowa, 1963. (63–4727)

Cowan, Mary Frances. "The Negro in the American Drama, 1877–1900." M.A. thesis, Howard Univ., 1950. [Abstract pub. as "Some Unknown Plays About the Negro," *Neg. Hist. Bull.*, June 1951, pp. 200–204.]

Davidson, Frank C. "The Rise, Development, Decline and Influence of the American Minstrel Show." Ph.D. diss., New York Univ., 1952.

Dewberry, Jonathan. "Black Actors Unite: The Negro Actors Guild of America, 1937–1982." Ph.D. diss., New York Univ., 1988. (GAX88–12625)

Ellington, Mary Davis. "Plays by Negro Authors with Special Emphasis upon the Period from 1916–1934." Master's thesis, Fisk Univ., 1934.

Guillaume, Bernice F. "The Life and Work of Olivia Ward Bush [Banks], 1869–1944." Ph.D. diss., Tulane Univ., 1983.

Hicklin, Fannie Ella Frazier. "The American Negro Playwright, 1920–1964." Ph.D. diss., Univ. of Wisconsin, 1965. (BWK65–6217)

Johnson, Evamarii Alexandria. "A Production History of the Seattle Federal Theatre Project Negro Repertory Company, 1935–1939." Ph.D. diss., Univ. of Washington, 1981. (SAB82–12558)

Lawson, Hilda Josephine. "The Negro in American Drama." Ph.D. diss., Univ. of Illinois, 1939. [Abstract pub. in *Bull. of Bibliog.*, in two installments: Part I, Jan./April 1940; Part II, May/Aug. 1940.]

Lewis, Ellistine Perkins. "The E. Azalia Hackley Memorial Collection of Negro Music, Dance and Drama: A Catalog of Selected Afro-American Materials." Ph.D. diss., Univ. of Michigan, 1978. (BWK79–07122)

McLaren, Joseph. "Edward Kennedy (Duke) Ellington and Langston Hughes: Perspectives on Their Contributions to American Culture, 1920–1966." Ph.D. diss., Brown Univ., 1980. (GAX81–11144)

Miller, Jeanne-Marie Anderson. "Dramas by Black American Playwrights Produced on the New York Professional Stage (from 'The Chip Woman's Fortune' to 'Five on the Black Hand Side')." Ph.D. diss., Howard Univ., 1976. (BWK78–05440)

Monroe, John Gilbert. "A Record of the Black Theatre in New York City: 1920–29." Ph.D. diss., Univ. of Texas/Austin, 1980. (SAB81–09212)

Pawley, Thomas D., Jr. "Experimental Productions of a Group of Original Plays." Ph.D. diss., Univ. of Iowa, 1949.

Pembrook, Carrie Davis. "Negro Drama Through the Ages—An Anthology." Ph.D. diss., New York Univ., 1946.

Pettit, Paul B. "The Important American Dramatic Types to 1900: A Study of the Yankee, Negro, Indian and Frontiersman." Ph.D. diss., Cornell Univ., 1949.

Pitts, Ethel Louise. "The American Negro Theatre: 1940–1949." Ph.D. diss., Univ. of Missouri/Columbia, 1975. (BEJ76–07538) [Abstract pub. as "The American Negro Theatre," in *The Theatre of Black Americans,* vol. 2, ed. by Errol Hill. Englewood Cliffs, NJ: Prentice-Hall, 1980.]

Poag, Thomas E. "The Negro in Drama and the Theatre." Ph.D. diss., Cornell Univ., 1943.

Richards, Sandra. "Bert Williams: His Stage Career and Influence on American Theatre." Ph.D. diss., Stanford Univ., 1973.

Riis, Thomas Laurence. "Black Musical Theatre in New York, 1890–1915." Ph.D. diss., Univ. of Michigan, 1981. (GAX82–04745)

Ross, Ronald Patrick. "Black Drama in the Federal Theatre, 1935–1939." Ph.D. diss., Univ. of Southern California, 1972. (BEJ72–27693) [Abstract pub. as "The Role of Blacks in the Federal Theatre, 1935–1939," in *The Theatre of Black Americans,* vol. 2, ed. by Errol Hill. Englewood Cliffs, NJ: Prentice-Hall, 1980.]

Sandle, Floyd Leslie. "A History of the Development of the Educational Theatre in

Negro Colleges and Universities from 1911 to 1959." Ph.D. diss., Louisiana State Univ. and A. & M. Coll., 1959. (GAX59–05527)

Seward, Adrienne Lanier. "Early Black Film and Folk Tradition: An Interpretive Analysis of the Use of Folklore in Selected All-Black Feature Films (Hallelujah, The Green Pastures, The Blood of Jesus)." Ph.D. diss., Indiana Univ., 1985. (MBS75–22529)

Shakong, Samuel. "A Study of Black Theatre from the 1930's Through the 1960's." M.A. thesis, Adelphi Univ., 1975. (BWK13–07610)

Sherman, Alphonso. "The Diversity of Treatment of the Negro Character in American Drama Prior to 1860." Ph.D. diss., Univ. of Indiana, 1964. (GAX65–03518)

Silver, Reuben. "A History of the Karamu Theatre of Karamu House, 1915–1960." Ph.D. diss., Ohio State Univ., 1961. (GAX62–00811)

Speisman, Barbara Waddell. " 'Zora,' 'Color Struck and Weary Blues,' and 'Tea with Zora and Marjorie.' " (Three original plays about the life of Zora Neale Hurston) Ph.D. diss., Florida State Univ., 1988. (GAX88–14435)

Stevenson, Robert Louis. "The Image of the White Man as Projected in the Published Plays of Black Americans, 1847–1973." Ph.D. diss., Indiana Univ., 1976. (GAX76–21607)

Thomas, Marjorie Ann. "An Overview of Miss Anne: White Women as Seen by Black Playwrights." Ph.D. diss., Florida State Univ., 1973. (GAX73–30297)

Thompson, Sister Francesca. "The Lafayette Players, 1915–1932: America's First Dramatic Stock Co." Ph.D. diss., Univ. of Michigan, 1972. [Abstract pub. as "The Lafayette Players, 1917–1932," in *The Theatre of Black Americans,* vol. 2, ed. by Errol Hill. Englewood Cliffs, NJ: Prentice-Hall, 1980.]

Washington, J. Charles. "Course Design for Teaching Black Drama." Ph.D. diss., Catholic Univ. of America, 1981. (GAX81–16719)

Williams, Allen. "Sheppard Randolph Edmonds: His Contributions to Black Educational Theatre." Ph.D. diss., Georgia State Univ.—School of Education, 1975. (BEJ73–12357)

Williams, Eddie Ray. "The Rise of the Negro Actor in the American Theatre from 1900–1950." M.A. thesis, Univ. of Tennessee, 1951.

Woods, Porter S. "The Negro on Broadway: The Transition Years, 1920–1930." D.F.A. diss., Yale Univ., 1965 (BEJ70–24050)

Young, Artee Felicita. "Lester Walton: Black Theatre Critic." Ph.D. diss., Univ. of Michigan, 1980. (GAX81–06254)

Young, Era Brisbane. "An Examination of Selected Dramas from the Theater of Victor Séjour Including Works of Social Protest." Ph.D. diss., New York Univ., 1979. (KWN79–18874)

Young, Patricia Alzatia. "Female Pioneers in Afro-American Drama: Angelina Weld Grimké, Georgia Douglas Johnson, Alice Dunbar-Nelson, and Mary Powell Burrill." Ph.D. diss., Bowling Green State Univ., 1986. (GAX86–28856)

Zieton, Edward Robert. "Wright to Hansberry: The Evolution of Outlook in Four Negro Writers." Ph.D. diss., Univ. of Washington, 1967.

PERIODICALS

The following list includes journals, magazines, and newspapers that regularly or intermittently featured articles, reviews, and/or bibliographical materials on black activity and participation in the theatre, on the radio, and in motion pictures from the 1800s to 1950. No attempt has been made to list individual articles in these or other periodicals. For bibliographies of articles in periodicals, consult the pertinent reference books, dissertations, and theses listed in the two preceding sections. Especially useful are the following studies: *Black American Playwrights, 1800 to the Present: A Bibliography* (Arata & Rotoli, 1976); *More Black American Playwrights: A Bibliography* (Arata, 1978); *Afro-American Poetry and Drama, 1760–1975: A Guide to Information Sources* (Fabre et al., 1979); *Black Playwrights, 1823–1977: An Annotated Bibliography of Plays* (Hatch & Abdullah, 1977); *Dictionary of the Black Theatre: Broadway, Off-Broadway, and Selected Harlem Theatres* (Woll, 1983); and *Negro Playwrights in the American Theatre, 1925–1959* (Abramson, 1969). Black periodicals are marked with an asterisk (*). The abbreviation *esp.* (especially) is frequently used in the following citations.

*Abbott's Monthly (1930–33)

American Mercury (esp. 1925–48)

*Atlanta World (1931–50)

*Baltimore Afro-American (national edition) (1898–1950)

Billboard (esp. black critic James A. Jackson's page of theatrical news, 1921–25)

*Birmingham World (1945–50)

*Black American Literature Forum (formerly *Negro American Literature Forum* (1967–present)

Black Stars (1970s)

Bulletin of Bibliography (esp. 1940–present)

Bulletin of the New York Public Library (esp. Spring 1975)

*Call and Post (Cleveland) (esp. 1930s)

Carolina Magazine (esp. issues of April 1927 and April 1929)

Carolina Play-Book (esp. Dec. 1933 and June 1940)

Catholic World (esp. Aug. 1945)

*Chicago Defender (esp. 1920s)

*CLA Journal (College Language Association) (1957–present)

Cleveland Plain Dealer (esp. 1930s)

*The Competitor (1920–21)

*Crisis (1910–present)

Current History (esp. 1920s)

Daily Worker (esp. 1930s)

Drama Magazine (esp. Dec. 1921 and Jan. 1931)

*Ebony (1945–present)

Educational Theatre Journal (esp. 1960s–present)

Etude (esp. 1930s)

*Fire!! (1926)

*First World (1977)

The Forum (esp. 1920s)

*Freeman (Indianapolis) (1884–1926)

Harper's Magazine (esp. 1920s and 1930s)

*Inter-State Tattler (1925–32)

*Jet (1951–present)

*Journal and Guide (Norfolk) (1899–1950)

*Journal of Negro Education (1932–present)

*Journal of Negro History (1916–present)

Life (1940s)

*Messenger(1917–38)

*Michigan Chronicle (1943–50)

Modern Music (1940s)

Nation (esp. 1920s)

*Negro College Quarterly (esp. March 1945–Dec. 1946)

*Negro Digest (1942–70). Superseded by *Black World* (1970–c. 1977)

*Negro History Bulletin (1937–present)

New Masses (1930s and 1940s)

New Republic (esp. 1920s)

*Newsletter (Negro Actors Guild of America) (1940–46)

Newsweek (1940s)

New Theatre (esp. July 1935 issue)

*New York Age (1881–1960)

*New York Amsterdam News (1909–present)

New York Times (1920–present)

New York World (1920s)

*Norfolk Journal and Guide (1901–present)

*Opportunity (1923–49)

*Philadelphia Tribune (1912–50)

*Phylon (1940–present)

*Pittsburgh Courier (1910–50)

PM (1940s)

Saturday Review of Literature (esp. 1940s)

Southern Workman (esp. 1930s)

Survey Graphic (1925)

Theatre Arts (Monthly) (1920s–1952)

Theatre Magazine (esp. 1920s and 1930s)

Variety (esp. 1940s)

TITLE INDEX

This is an alphabetical index of all plays and dramatic works written or coauthored by the early black American playwrights and dramatic writers included in the main Directory and the three Appendixes of this volume. The following abbreviations are occasionally used in this index, primarily to differentiate among identical or similar titles: (M) for musicals, (O) for operatic works, (R) for radio broadcast scripts, and (S) for screenworks. Double virgules (//) are used to separate current titles from original or earlier titles of the same work.

Index of Early Black American Theatre Organizations and Producing Groups

Following is an alphabetical list of predominantly black theatre organizations and groups that have produced at least one of the plays in this Directory. This list, though relatively short, is considered an essential part of the Directory and should be of great value to many users of this book. Since several groups are identified by more than one title, or slight variations in title, virgules (/) are often used to separate the various appellations by which a group may have been known. Cross references are also liberally used to assist the reader in locating a given group. Cities (and states, where necessary) are given for those groups which had a permanent location.

GENERAL INDEX

This is a selective, general index of important theatrical subjects, themes, genres, persons, awards, special collections, titles, and organizations not included in the preceding two indexes. Because of space limitations, many names—especially of persons appearing in only one play or dramatic work—have been excluded. A name in all capitals (e. g., CULLEN, COUNTEE) indicates that the person is one of the playwrights included in the main Directory. A name followed by either (A) or (B) indicates that the entry is also included in Appendix A or B. Writers in the main directory and the two appendixes are indexed only if they are also referred to in other entries or sections of the book.

About the Author

BERNARD L. PETERSON, JR., is Professor Emeritus of English and Drama at Elizabeth City State University, North Carolina. He is the author of *Contemporary Black American Playwrights and Their Plays* (Greenwood Press, 1988) and is currently completing an *Encyclopedia of the Black American Musical Stage* (forthcoming from Greenwood Press).